Abstracts of Lancaster County Pennsylvania Wills

1786-1820

Willow Bend Books
Westminster, Maryland
2001

WILLOW BEND BOOKS
AN IMPRINT OF HERITAGE BOOKS, INC.

Books, CDs, and more – Worldwide

For our listing of thousands of titles see our website
at
www.HeritageBooks.com

Published 2003 by
HERITAGE BOOKS, INC.
Publishing Division
1540 Pointer Ridge Place #E
Bowie, Maryland 20716

International Standard Book Number: 1-58549-320-1

INTRODUCTION

These wills were abstracted under the auspices of the Historical
Society of Pennsylvania in the early 1900s. Copies of these
abstracts were made available to various libraries in Pennsylvania and microfilm copies were made by the Genealogical Society
of Utah (LDS). Recently bound photostat copies of the abstracts
were offered for sale by the Genealogical Society of Pennsylvania.

We extend our appreciation to the staffs of the Historical
Society of Pennsylvania (1300 Locust Street, Philadelphia, PA
19107) and encourage use and support of its facilities and to the
Genealogical Society of Pennsylvania whose collections are housed
in the Historical Society Library. We also encourage membership
in the Genealogical Society of Pennsylvania (address same as
HSP).

F. Edward Wright
Westminster, Maryland
1995

5 May 1789   7 May 1790
ANKRUM, SAMUEL
    Wife. Mary Ankrum. Bro. and Sister: Archibald and Sarah
Ankrum.
    Ex. Mary Ankrum. Drumore Twp.

6 April 1790   1 June 1790
ANDERSON, JAMES
    Wife. Margaret Anderson. Children: James and Susanna wife of
William Kelly. Grandchildren: Eliza, John and Ruth Kelly; James,
Margaret, Joseph, Ruth, Thomas, Jane, John, Mary and William
Anderson.
    Ex. Richard Keys, Margaret and James Anderson. Dounegal
[Donegal] Twp.

1 June 1790   13 July 1790
AMWEG, JACOB
    Wife. Catharine. Children: Henry, Jacob, Sophia, Catharine,
Magdalena, William, Mary and Samuel.
    Ex. Catharine Amweg and Christopher Henry. Cocalico Twp.

23 Feb. 1790   7 May 1790
ARTZB, PHILIP
    Wife. Anna Barbara Artzb. Children: Henry, Christian, Peter,
Christiana, Sophia and Cornelius.
    Ex. Anna Artzb and Jacob Kumler. Cocalico Twp.

28 Dec. 1789   2 Nov. 1793
ACKER, PETER
    Wife. Ann Acker. Children: Peter, Esther, Jacob, Casper,
Henry, Barbara, Magdalena and Elizabeth.
    Ex. John Longenecker. Hempfield Twp.

21 Jan. 1793   23 Feb. 1795
ACHENBACH, MATHIAS
    Wife. Ann Margaret Achenbach. Children: Anthony, Margaret,
Eve, Anna, Mary, George and Henry.
    Ex. Anthony Achenbach. Cocalico Twp.

6 Nov. 1795   21 May 1796
ALTZ, MICHAEL
    Wife. Barbara Altz. Children: Philip, Michael, Barbara wife
of George Everhart, Mary and Sally.
    Ex. Philip and Michael Altz. Salsbury Twp.

21 March 1787   16 Aug, 1797
AXER, MARY BARBARA
    Children: Christopher, Anna, Elizabeth, Michael.
    Ex. Christopher Axer. Lancaster Borough.

14 May, 1798   2 June 1798
AMEND, JOHN
    Wife. Mary Amend. Children: Philip, Catharine and Jacob.
    Ex. Adam Amend and John Rohrer. Lampeter Twp.

2

5 April 1798   7 May 1798
ADAMS, SAMUEL
     Wife. Esther Adams. Child: Kezia.
     Ex. John Bechdol and William Adams. Cocalico Twp.

21 Aug. 1798   20 Sept. 1798
ANTRICAN, SAMUEL
     (Note: This should be ENTRICAN). Wife. Mary Entrican.
Children: William, James, Elizabeth and Mary.
     Ex. William Ewing and William Entrican. Little Britton Twp.

23 Feb 1795   31 Jan 1799
ANDREW, CHRISTIAN
     Wife. Not named. Children: Elizabeth and Magdalen.
     Ex. John Becktoll and Jacob Vonida. Cocalico Twp.

3 Feb. 1795   11 Nov. 1799
ANDREWS, ARTHUR
     Wife. Phebe Andrews. Children: Jennet wife of James
Anderson, Robert, Arthur, Joseph and Alexander. Grandchildren:
Isabella and Phebe (children of Robert); Sarah, Phebe and Arthur
(children of Joseph); and James (child of Alexander).
     Ex. Arthur and Joseph Andrews. Cowlrain [sic] Twp.

--- ---[ca 1799]
ALTER, JOHN
(This will is not to be found. Letters of Administration with
will annexed granted in 1799.)

26 May 1796   16 Dec. 1800
ACKER, ANN
     (Note: This should be OCKER.) Children: Peter, Jacob,
Casper, Henry, Esther, Barbara, Ann and Martha.
     Ex. Henry Ocker and Christian Metz. Hempfield Twp.

10 June 1809   29 Feb. 1810
ANCRIM, MARY
     Husband. Samuel Ancrim. Nephews: Samuel and Alexander
Snodgrass.
     Ex. Samuel Snodgrass and Hugh McCullough. Dromore [sic] Twp.

15 Dec. 1800   7 March 1801
ACKER, ESTHER
     Bros.: Casper Acker (and others, names not stated).
     Ex. Henry Acker and Jacob Legrist. Hempfield Twp.

19 Aug. 1799   8 Feb. 1802
ANDERSON, MARGARET
     Husband. James Anderson. Children: Adam Tate, John Tate,
Benjamin Tate and James Anderson. Grandchildren: James Anderson,
Margaret Weekley, Ruth Williamson and Jane Bayley.
     Ex. Benjamin Tate. Donegall Twp.
N.B. There was a bequest made to Rev. John Ewing (the Provost of
the University of Philadelphia).

29 March 1800   8 May 1802
ALBRECHT, ANDREW
    Wife. Elizabeth Albrecht. Children: Andrew, Henry, Jacob,
Godfried and Susanna.
    Ex. Elizabeth Albrecht and Mathew Tsudy. Warwick Twp.

27 Jan. 1802   20 March 1802
ALEXANDER, JAMES
    (Sergeant of arms for Senate of Penna.)
    Wife. Sarah Alexander.
    Ex. Sarah Alexander. Lancaster Borough.

2 Oct. 1802   11 Nov. 1802
ACHEY, GEORGE
    Wife. Elizabeth Achey.
    Ex. Elizabeth Achey. Cocalico Twp.

7 Sept. 1798   9 Aug. 1803
ATKINSON, MARGARET
    Widow of Mathew Atkinson. Children: Ann, Margaret and
Hannah.
    Ex. Ann Davis. Lancaster Borough.

26 June 1806   2 Aug. 1806
ALBRIGHT, JOHN
    Wife. name not given. Children: Anthony, George, Peter,
John, Jacob, William, Frederick, Elizabeth and Daniel.
    Ex. George Albright and Matthew Zahn. Lancaster Borough.

11 Aug. 1800   13 Jan. 1807
ALEXANDER, JAMES
    Wife. Hannah Alexander. Children: John, Samuel, Elizabeth,
Ann and Jean wife of William Taylor. Son-in-law: John McConel
(wife's name not given).
    Ex. Samuel Alexander. Martic Twp.

16 Sept. 1808   21 Nov. 1808
ARMSTRONG, REUBEN
    Wife. Mary Armstrong. Children: Hannah, Samuel, Thomas,
William, David, Westly, Mary and James.
    Ex. David Cooke and John Hess. Donegal Twp.

12 Feb. 1808   16 Feb. 1808
AUX, JOHN
    Wife. Susanna Aux. Child: John.
    Ex. Susanna Aux. Lampeter Twp.

15 Oct. 1810   16 Feb. 1811
ARMSTRONG, WILLIAM
    Sisters: Isabella wife of Frederick Shoff and Margaret wife
of Charles Oneal and Jane wife of John Lavid. Bros.: Hugh and
John Armstrong.
    Ex. Frederick Shoff. Conestoga Twp.

10 Nov. 1811   7 April 1812
ABT, JOHN HENRY
    Wife. Anna Abt. Children: Elizabeth, Ann wife of ---
Bodensled, Barbara, Daniel, Verona, Magdalen and Henry.
    Ex. Anna Abt. Warwick Twp.

28 July 1812   13 Sept. 1813
ALBRIGHT, ELIAS
    Wife. Catharine Albright. Children: Henry, George, Jacob and
Elizabeth wife of John Weaver.
    Ex. John Weaver, Catharine and George Albright. Lancaster
Borough.

14 Nov. 1815   14 Dec. 1815
ANDREWS, JANE
    Bros.: John and James Andrews. Aunts: Margaret Andrews and
Mary Clendenan.
    Ex. James Patterson. Dromore Twp.

23 June 1816   7 Sept. 1816
ALBERT, ELIZABETH
    Children: Susanna, Fanny, Mary and Catherine.
    Ex. Jacob Grabil Miller. Donegal Twp.

11 Feb. 1813   18 Feb. 1816
ADAMS, RICHARD
    Wife. Susanna Adams. Children: Mary, Anna, Margaret,
Susanna, Magdalena, William, Catherine, Elizabeth and Samuel.
Grandchild: Casie Adams (child of Samuel). Son-in-law: Henry
Flickinger (wife's name not stated).
    Ex. Williams Adams and Henry Flickinger. Cocalico Twp.

13 Oct. 1817   12 Dec. 1817
AXER, MICHAEL JR.
    Wife. Catharine Axer. Children: Amelia, Philip, William and
Adam.
    Ex. Catharine Axer and Philip Albert. Mt. Joy Twp.

22 Aug. 1718   30 Oct. 1818
ANDERSON, JOHN
    Wife. name omitted. Children: Francis wife of Christopher
Griffith, Isabella wife of --- Sterrett, Hannah wife of John
Rutter, Sarah wife of Henry Rutter and Juliana wife of --- Davis.
Grandchildren: John and Clarkson Griffith and Grabill Davis.
    Ex. Joel Lightner and Nathaniel Rutter. Sadsbury Twp.

--- --- 1818
ALLISON, REBECCA
(This will is recorded as unfinished business and there appears
no further record concerning it.)

30 Oct. 1819   23 Dec. 1819
ALBRIGHT, HERMAN

Wife. Dorrothy Albright. Children: Fane, Francess. (There may have been others, as records are very indefinite as to number and names. The above are the only names that appear.)
Ex. George Ellemaker and William Lightner. Twp. omitted.

28 Feb. 1786   11 March 1786
BRENEISEN, VALENTINE
Wife. Salome Breneisen. Children: Christian, Valentine, Jacob, Simon, Benjamin, Joseph, John, George and Emanuel.
Ex. George Hoof and Jacob Krug. Lancaster Borough.

5 Sept. 1784   24 May 1786
BOLLINGER, MARIA ESTHER
Children: Maria and Peter. Grandchildren: Peter and Elizabeth Bollinger (children of Peter).
Ex. Maria E. Kuntz. Lancaster Borough.

25 Dec. 1781   5 June 1786
BROWN, JOHN
Children: John, Agness, Elizabeth wife of William Patterson, Mary, Margaret wife of William Dunlap, William and James.
Grandchild: John Brown (son of James).
Ex. William McCleary. Bart Twp.

7 Jan. 1786   20 July 1786
BUSH, WILLIAM
Wife. Barbara Bush. Children: Elizabeth wife of Casper Fordine.
Ex. Barbara Bush and Casper Fordine. Lancaster Borough.

5 Dec. 1786   24 March 1787
BRUBAKER, ANN
(Widow of John Brubaker.) Bros.: John, Jacob and Abraham Hostetter. Sisters: Elizabeth Bomberger and Margaret Kreeter.
Ex. Christian Boumberger. Manheim Twp.

15 Sept. 1787   6 Nov. 1787
BUCHER, BENEDICT
Wife. Mary Bucher. Children: John, Benedict, Ann, Elizabeth wife of John Yunt, Jacob and Mary.
Ex. Benedict Bucher and John Mohler. Cocalico Twp.

26 July 1787   30 Nov. 1787
BUCHANNAN, WALTER
Wife. Jean Buchannan. Children: Sarah, Margaret, Agness, John, James and Gilbert. Son-in-law: James Glen (wife's name not stated). Grandchild: Walter Buchannan (son of Gilbert).
Ex. Gilbert Buchannan and James Glen. Little Britton Twp.

30 May 1785   21 April 1787
BREIDENHART, CHRISTOPHER
Wife. Magdalena Breidenhart. Children: Dorothea, Barbara, Molly, Christopher, John, Peggy, Elizabeth, Sally, George and Maria.

Ex. Magdalena Breidenhart, John Leopold and John Hubley.
Lancaster Borough.

5 Dec. 1787   16 April 1788
BRUNNER, GEORGE MICHAEL
    Wife. Barbara Brunner. Children: John, George, Peter,
Margaret, Sophia, Anna, Barbara and Catharine.
    Ex. John Brunner and John Kuntz. Cocalico Twp.

14 Nov. 1782   26 May 1788
BEGHTHOLT, PHILIP
    Wife. Margaret Beightholt. Children: John and Elizabeth wife
of Nicholas Lutz.
    Ex. John Beightholt. Cocalico Twp.

29 July 1783   28 Aug. 1788
BRENNER, PHILIP
    Wife. Ann Brenner. Children: Catharine wife of Jacob Young,
Ann wife of Jacob Hoffman, Susanna, Philip and Elizabeth wife of
John Gorner. Grandchild: Elizabeth Forner.
    Ex. Ann and Philip Brenner. Donegal Twp.

1 April 1788   8 Dec. 1788
BIERLY, ANNA MARIA
    Legatees: Luthern Church, Lancaster, and others.
    Ex. Jacob Stahl. Lancaster Borough.

29 Jan. 1789   5 Feb. 1789
BRINTON, MOSES
    Children: Joseph, William, Moses, Mary wife of Robert Moore
and Abigail wife of Ellis Pusy. Grandchildren: Susanna, Eleanor,
Abigail and Phebe Pusy and Moses Moore. N.B. There was a bequest
to the Friends' Meeting House, Lampeter.
    Ex. Joseph and William Brinton. Leacock Twp.

2 Dec. 1788   6 May 1789
BUCH, CHRISTIAN
    Wife. Susanna Buch.
    Ex. Susanna Buch. Lancaster Borough.

28 July 1786   6 March 1789
BOAL, THOMAS
    Wife. Elizabeth Boal. Children: Agness, Robert, Mary and
William. Grandchildren: Grace, Francis and Thomas Boal (children
of Robert); Elizabeth, Moses, Grizel, Thomas, Agness, John and
Robert McClure (parents' names not stated).
    Ex. William Boal, Robert Robinson and Thomas McCallan. Mt.
Joy Twp.

21 Nov. 1788   4 Nov. 1789
BRAND, JACOB
    Legatee: John Lesher.
    Ex. John Lesher. Strasburg Twp.

15 Nov. 1785   20 Dec. 17--
BICKHAM, JAMES
    Wife. Mary Bickham. Children: George, Jo---, Ann wife of
James Quinley, James and Elizabeth.
    Ex. Joseph Hubley. Lancaster Borough.

3 Dec. 1782   18 Jan. 17--
BLANK, JOHN F.
    Wife. Magdalena Blank. Children: John, M--- wife of
Christian Zug, Barbara, Catharine, Anna and Christina wife of
Jacob Yoder.
    Ex. Christian Zug and Jacob Yoder. Salisbury Twp.

13 May 1789   15 May 1790
BOYD, THOMAS
    Bros.: John, James and George. Sister: Isabella Boyd.
    Ex. John and James Boyd. Salisbury Twp.

27 May 1785   16 Oct. 1790
BOGGS, ANN
    Child: Alexander Boggs.
    Ex. Alexander Boggs. Donnegal Twp.

20 Aug. 1790   12 March 1791
BARTAGES, MICHAEL
    Wife. Catharine Bartages. Children: Margaret, Catharine,
Mathias and Magdalena.
    Ex. Catharine Bartages. Lancaster Borough.

28 March 1791 28 March 1791
BITZMAN, JOHN MICHAEL
    Sister: Catharine Bitzman. N.B. There was a bequest to Mary
Beck living at Sisters House, Litiz.
    Ex. John G. Stewart. Litiz [Lititz] Twp.

15 Dec. 1788   25 July 1791
BUSH, BARBARA
    Children: Margaret wife of Michael Krebs, Jacob, Casper and
Francis Fortiney (children by former husband). Grandchildren:
William Krebs and William Foriney [sic] (son of Jacob).
    Ex. Michael Krebs. Lancaster Borough.

21 Nov. 1791   20 Dec. 1791
BOILSTONE, JACOB
    Wife. Sophia Boilstone. Bro.: Adam.
    Ex. William Cunkle and Jacob Stoutsberger. Bart Twp.

3 Feb. 1789   15 Nov. 1791
BAISHER, BALTZER
    Wife. Anna Baisher. Children: Balsor, Elizabeth wife of
Peter Stemer [Steiner], Mary wife of Peter Smith, Margaret wife
of Jospeh Rutter, Peter, John and Charlotte wife of (name not
given). N.B. It appears that both Elizabeth and Mary were married
twice, and that there were children by the first husbands -

Elizabeth had been married to Christian Stoutzberger and Mary to Jacob Pachart. The names and numbers of the children not given.
Ex. Baltzer and Daniel Baisher. Leacock Twp.

(Omitted) 2 March 1792
BRABSON, THOMAS
Children: Thomas, John, Precilla and Mary.
Ex. John Brabson and Thomas Brabson. Little Britton Twp.

5 March 1792   19 April 1792
BRUNKHART, MARTIN
Children: George, Christiana wife of John Swenck, Barbara wife of Jacob Diller, Elizabeth wife of John Sively, Eve wife of John Ween, Peter and Adam.
Ex. John Ween and George Brunkhart. Lancaster Borough.

22 April 1793   29 Oct. 1792 [sic]
BLUMENSHEIM, HENRY
Wife. Catharine Blumensheim. Step-son: Jacob Bickel.
Ex. David Meiner. Cocalico Twp.

14 May 1792   14 Nov. 1792
BUCKSRITTER, ISREAL
Children: Anna wife of Jacob Stofft. Grandchildren: George Rhode, Jacob, Elizabeth and Catharine Gross (parents' names not given).
Ex. Jacob Stofft. Lancaster Borough.

18 Nov. 1792   13 March 1793
BEAR, MARTIN
Wife. Freany Bear. Children: David, Hannah, Andrew, Mary wife of John Beashore, Magdalena wife of Bastian Bower, Anna wife of John Cling and Elizabeth.
Ex. David Bear and Bastian Bower. Earl Twp.

14 Oct. 1793   16 Nov. 1793
BAUM, PHILIP
Wife. Barbara Baum. Children: Philip and Adam.
Ex. Barbara Baum and Philip Baum. Rapho Twp.

1 Oct. 1793   2 Oct. 1793
BAYLY, JAMES
Wife. Mary Bayly. Children: Thomas and John. Step-daughter: Margaret Cook. Son-in-law: Richard Keys (wife's name not given).
Ex. Mary and John Bayly and Richard Keys. Donegal Twp.

- April 1792   28 Nov. 1794
BAYLY, JOHN
Wife. Hannah Bayly. Children: James, Thomas, John, Margaret, Mary, Ruth and Hannah. Son-in-law: John Greer (wife's name not given).
Ex. Hannah, Thomas and James Bayly. Donegal Twp.

9 Oct. 1791   28 March 1794
BLATTENBERGER, GEORGE

Wife. Margaret Blattenberger. Children: John, Christian,
Daniel, Frederick, Peter, Ann wife of John Berstler, Rosina wife
of George Hauenstein and Margaret wife of John Eby.
Ex. Margaret Blattenberger and George Hauenstein. Rapho Twp.

20 Aug. 1792   5 Sept. 1793
BUCHER, JOHN
John, Jacob, Benedict Bucher and Anna Grebill. N.B. The
relationship of the above to writer of the will is not stated,
but supposed to be his children.
Ex. Jacob Moler and Benedict Bucher. Cocalico Twp.

26 June 1793   --- 1793
BARD, GEORGE PHILIP
Wife. Margaret Bard. Children: Michael, Elizabeth wife of
Henry Gerber, John, Margaret, George, Mary and Jacob.
Ex. Margaret and Michael Bard. Leacock Twp.

27 March 1783   17 Feb. 1794
BAMBERGER, MARTIN
Wife. Mary Dorothea Bamberger. Child: John. Step-children:
George, Jacob and Peter Messersmith and Eve wife of Francis Bieg.
Ex. George Messersmith and George Reitzel. Lancaster
Borough.

6 Feb. 1794   25 March 1794
BARGE, BOLTZER
Wife. Barbara Barge. Children: Elizabeth, Catharine and
Barbara.
Ex. Barbara Barge and John Miller. Strasburg Twp.

1 April 1794   9 April 1794
BERG, FREDERICK
Wife. Magdalena Berg. Children: Barbara and David. Step-
children: Jacob and John Beidler.
Ex. Michael Kauffman, Jacob and David Berg. Hempfield Twp.

2 June 1791   17 May 1794
BEEMERSDOERFER, JOHN
Wife. Elizabeth Beemersdoerfer. Children: Mary Elizabeth,
John, Barbara, Salome and George.
Ex. Elizabeth Beemersdoerfer and Ludwig Wolfarth. Elizabeth
Twp.

9 Nov. 1793   23 May 1794
BEAR, HENRY
Wife. Margaret Bear. Children: Martin, Barbara, Ann,
Elizabeth and John. Grandchild: Elizabeth (child of John).
Ex. Rudy Herr, Benjamin and Martin Bear. Hempfield Twp.

1 July 1794   21 Oct. 1794
BRANDT, FREDERICK
Wife. Anna Brandt. Children: Jacob and Anna wife of John
Bender.
Ex. John Hiller and John Killheffer. Manor Twp.

11 Aug. 1794   28 Oct. 1794
BALLANCE, ROBERT
        Wife. Ann Ballance. Legatees: Bro. John and others.
        Ex. Hugh Peaydon and Richard Keys. Donegal Twp.

21 March 1786   13 Sept. 1794
BRENNEMAN, MELCHOIR
        Wife. Ann Brenneman. Children: Peter, Melchoir, Isaac,
David, Jacob, John, Henry, Margaret wife of Peter Stouffer, Ann
wife of John Horst, Elizabeth wife of Henry Road and Eve wife of
John Bowman. Grandchildren: Melchoir, John and Barbara (children
of Peter).
        Ex. Jacob Brenneman and Peter Stouffer. Conestoga Twp.

22 Aug. 1794   26 Aug. 1794
BLANK, JOHN
        Wife. Mary Blank. Children: Jacob & Catharine wife of John
Konig (there were other children, names and number not stated).
        Ex. Peter and Jacob Blank. Cocalico Twp.

25 May 1795   12 Nov. 1795
BOWMAN, JOHN
        Children: Christian and John (there were others, names and
number not given).
        Ex. John Bowman. Brecknock Twp.

10 Jan. 1795   22 March 1796
BAILSTONE, SOPHIA
        Widow of Jacob Bailstone. Sisters-in-law: Margaret Evans and
others.
        Ex. William Crunkle and Peter Sides. Bart Twp.

27 May 1792   15 April 1795
BARKLY, MARTHA
        Bro. Daniel McConnels. Niece: Martha McConnels.
        Ex. Daniel McConnels. Colerain Twp.

4 July 1792   27 April 1795
BRADRAUFF, ANDREW
        Wife. Elizabeth Bradrauff. Children: Andrew, Margaret,
Christiana, Susan and John.
        Ex. Philip Brehm and Samuel Ensminger. Manheim Twp.

11 May 1795   8 Aug. 1795
BRENNER, GEORGE
        Wife. Anna Brenner. Children: Gerhart, Catharine, Polly and
Margaret.
        Ex. Jacob Carly and Andrew Bausman. Manor Twp.

7 Dec. 1795   19 Dec. 1795
BEAR, ANN
        Wife of Jacob Bear. Legatees: Rachel Krokery and others.
        Ex. Jacob Bear. Bart Twp.

1 Oct. 1794   27 March 1796
BOGGS, MARGART
    Children: Mary wife of --- Boggs, Sarah, Nancy, Sables wife
of --- Craige, [?] Elizabeth and Rebecca.
    Ex. Hugh Pedin. Rapho Twp.

9 Aug. 1796   29 Aug. 1796
BORY, LUDWIG
    Wife. Ann Bory. Children: Peter, Magdalena wife of Martin
Geistweid, Barbara wife of Christian Shlichty, Elizabeth wife of
John Gentzemer, Mary wife of Peter Gear and Christiana wife of
Conrad Vanalmer.
    Ex. Peter Bory and Christian Shlichty. Cocalico Twp.

20 April 1789   28 April 1789
BOTTER, GEORGE
    Wife. Elizabeth Botter (this was the third wife). Children:
Adam and Anna (these are the children of the first wife, whose
name was Maria); John, Abraham, Catharine and Elizabeth (children
of third wife, there were no children by second wife).
    Ex. Henry Brenneman and Christian Stouffer. Manor Twp.

29 April 1795   4 May 1796
BELL, WALTER
    Wife. Catharine Bell. Child: John.
    Ex. John Whitehill and Zachariah Moore. Donegal Twp.

19 Dec. 1783   19 July 1796
BERG, ANDREW
    Wife. Maria Berg. Children: Jacob, Frederick, Fronica wife
of Michael Kauffman, David and Barbara wife of Jacob
Shallenberger.
    Ex. Jacob Berg and Michael Kauffman. Hempfield Twp.

25 June 1795   24 Oct. 1795
BRUBACHER, PETER
    Wife. Ann Brubacher. Children: Mary wife of Henry Landis,
Elizabeth wife of Christian Brubacher, Ann wife of --- Eby and
Benjamin. Grandchildren: Peter, Magdalena and Elizabeth Brubacher
(children of Benjamin).
    Ex. Jacob Brubacher and Jacob Frantz. Hempfield Twp.

30 Jan. 1796   29 July 1796
BOLLINGER, CHRISTIAN
    Bros.: Daniel, Rudolph and Abraham Bollinger. N. B. There
was a bequest to the Seven Day Baptists in Ephrata.
    Ex. Rudolph and Abraham Bollinger. Cocalico Twp.

29 Dec. 1792   17 Feb. 1797
BOLLINGER, CATHARINE
    Children: Abraham, Christiana wife of --- Meader, Daniel and
John.
    Ex. Abraham Bollinger. Cocalico Twp.

8 Aug. 1797   3 Sept. 1797
BINKLEY, JOHN

Wife. Susanna Binkley. Children: John, Felix, Christian, Rudolph, Henry, Elizabeth, Fronica and Anna.
Ex. Johnston Binkley and Martin Mellinger. Lampeter Twp.

21 April 1797   7 Aug. 1797
BUNTING, WILLIAM
Wife. Rachel Bunting. Children: Robert, Mary, Peggy, Eleanor, Elizabeth, John, Walter, Samuel and David.
Ex. John, Walter and William Bunting. Colerain Twp.

19 July 1797   27 Aug. 1797
BROWN, WILLIAM
Wife. Mary Brown.
Ex. Mary Brown. Leacock Twp.

2 Nov. 1796   15 Aug. 1797
BRAND, ANDREW
Child: Christiana wife of Isaac Ellmaker.
Ex. Jacob Keller Jr. Earl Twp.

13 May 1797   9 Jan. 1798
BUCHANAN, JAMES
Wife. Mary Buchanan. Children: James and Arthur. Grandchild: James Luckey (parents' names not given).
Ex. James and Arthur Buchanan. Drumore Twp.

8 Jan. 1798   26 Feb. 1798
BARE, ELIZABETH
Children: Barbara wife of --- Berkhouse (there were three other children, names not stated).
Ex. Michael and George Bare. Earl Twp.

19 Oct. 1797   17 June 1798
BAILEY, ROBERT
Wife. Margaret Bailey. Children: Francis, Jacob, Lydia wife of James Tompson, Elizabeth wife of William Steele, Abigail wife of John Steele and Jennet wife of James Sterrett. Grandchildren: Margaret, Rachel, Almira, Elizabeth and Harriet (children of Jacob).
Ex. Francis Bailey and James Tompson. Sadsbury Twp.

5 April 1797   30 April 1798
BAKER, JOHN
Wife. Christiana Baker. Children: Philip, Catharine wife of John Meck and Mary wife of John Amend.
Ex. Philip Brussel and George Messersmith. Conestoga Twp.

1 Sept. 1796   5 May 1798
BRANNON, JOHN
Wife. Margaret Brannon. Children: Sarah wife of James Regan, Martha wife of John Macky, Alexander and John.
Ex. Patrick Campbell and Robert Long. Martic Twp.

15 Jan. 1795   7 Nov. 1798
BOSS, JACOB

Wife. Elizabeth Boss. Children: Henry and Reginia wife of Philip Steiger.
Ex. Henry Oates. Lancaster Borough.

19 March 1799   2 April 1799
BAHM, PETER
Children: Barbara wife of Casper Migenfelder and Magdalena wife of Philip Stocksleger.
Ex. Martin Griner and John Herr Sr. Rapho Twp.

7 Dec. 1797   31 Aug. 1799
BEAR, BENJAMIN
Wife. Mary Bear. Children: Martin, Henry, Christian, Ann wife of John Landis, Mary wife of John Neidy and Barbara wife of Jacob Steman.
Ex. Martin Bear, John Leman and Jacob Frantz. Hempfield Twp.

12 June 1794   10 June 1799
BROWN, JOSHUA
Wife. Fillah Brown. Children: Elisha, Patience, Jeremiah, Isaak, Mary, Samuel and Lydy.
Ex. Fillah Brown. Little Britton Twp.

19 Oct. 1799   2 Dec. 1799
BROWN, JEREMIAH
Wife. Anna Brown. Children: Abner, Ezra, William, Anna and Rachel.
Ex. Anna and Abner Brown. Little Brittain Twp.

1 May 1798   16 Nov. 1799
BOUMBARGER, ELIZABETH
Children: John, Christian, Jacob, Joseph, Abraham, Ann wife of Christian Erb, Elizabeth wife of John Brubacher, Barbara wife of Christian Huber and Mary wife of Joseph Shank.
Ex. John and Jacob Boumbarger. Warwick Twp.

4 Jan. 1799   26 Nov. 1799
BOYD, JOHN
Wife. Agness Boyd. Children: Stephen, Nicholas, John, Cooper, Thomas and Alice.
Ex. Stephen and Nicholas Boyd. Drumore Twp.

17 Sept. 1799 22 Dec. 1799
BRINTZEL, GEORGE
(The will is signed PRITZEL) Wife. Margaret Printzel. Nephews: George Kantz and George Hebzell.
Ex. Peter Brunner and Godlieb Mauman. Lancaster Borough.

5 March 1800   16 April 1800
BRUA, JACOB
Children: John, Jacob, Elizabeth wife of Henry Kinser, Catharine, Sally wife of Daniel Ferree, Susanna wife of Christian Shirts and Mary wife of George Rockey.
Ex. Jacob Brua. Strasburg Twp.

25 Oct. 1798   8 April 1800
BEAR, MARTIN
    Wife. Elizabeth Bear. Sisters: Anna, Elizabeth and Barbara.
Ex. John Leman and Martin Bear. Hempfield Twp.

4 March 1799   1 Aug. 1800
BLICKENSDERFER, CHRISTIAN
    Wife. Catharine Blickensderfer. Children: Christian,
Matthew, Jacob and Catharine wife of --- Muckeys.
    Ex. George Kapp and Christian Blickensderfer. Warwick Twp.

17 Aug. 1799   11 Aug. 1800
BOLLINGER, ELIZABETH
    Children: Peter, Ann wife of John Mohler, Isaac and Jacob.
Grandchildren: Samuel (son of Isaac) and Elizabeth (parents'
names not given).
    Ex. Peter Bollinger. Cocalico Twp.

28 May 1798   22 Nov. 1800
BLASER, MATHIAS
    Children: Barbara wife of Joseph Shenk, Magdalena wife of
John Weiland, Esther wife of Leonard Negley and Elizabeth wife of
John Ebersole.
    Ex. John Hoist and Daniel Smith. Donegal Twp.

8 April 1799   4 Nov. 1800
BOYD, GEORGE
    Sisters: Isabella and Mary Boyd and Margaret wife of James
Hamilton. Bros.: James and John Boyd.
    Ex. John Boyd. Salsbury Twp.

20 July 1801   20 July 1801
BUYERS, ROBERT
    Wife. Jean Buyers. Children: John, Robert, James, Margaret
and Letitia.
    Ex. Andrew Caldwell, John and Robert Buyers. Salisbury Twp.

21 Oct. 1796   2 Feb. 1801
BURKHOLDER, JOHN
    Wife. Ann Burkholder. Children: John, Jacob, Ann, Esther
wife of Jacob Harnish, Barbara wife of Benj. Landis, Elizabeth
[wife of] John Landis, Susanna and Magdalena. Grandchildren: Ann
and Fornica Harnish.
    Ex. Benjamin Landis, John and Jacob Burkholder. Conestoga
Twp.

18 Feb. 1801   25 March 1801
BROWN, WILLIAM
    Wife. Anna Brown. Children: James, Mary and William.
    Ex. William Brown and John Crawford. Colerain Twp.

1 Dec. 1798   19 Aug. 1801
BEER, PETER
    Wife. Elizabeth Beer. Children: Peter and Elizabeth wife of
William Bausman.

Ex. William Bausman, Elizabeth and Peter Beer. Lancaster Borough.

6 May 1802   23 June 1802
BROWN, ARCHIBALD
        Ex. The creditors of his estate. Rapho Twp. (The legatees of this will were his creditors — eight in number — for stock of merchandise in his store.)

12 July 1802   2 Aug. 1802
BLETZ, ANDREW
        Legatee: George Huber.
        Ex. George Huber. Lancaster Borough.

19 Jan. 1790   18 Sept. 1802
BRUBACHER, JOHN JACOB
        Children: John, Jacob, Barbara, Elizabeth, Feronica and Ann.
        Ex. Christian Gouchenauer and Isaac Herr. Martic Twp.

10 Jan. 1792   30 Oct. 1802
BRECKER, PETER
        Children: Martin, Justina, Veronica, Christian, Jacob, Peter, Valentine and Henry.
        Ex. John Wenger, Christian Becker and Peter Eby. Cocalico Twp.

19 Jan. 1802   1 March 1802
BEAR, BENJAMIN
        Children: Polly and Katharine.
        Ex. Stephen Hornberger and Martin Bair. Hempfield Twp.

27 Sept. 1802   22 Feb. 1803
BERRINGER, MICHAEL
        Wife. Elizabeth Berringer. Children: Jacob and Elizabeth.
        Ex. Martin Gross and John Putimer. Elizabeth Twp.

8 March 1802   5 March 1803
BOWMAN, ANN
        Children: Mary wife of Christian Herr, Esther wife of John Miller, Susanna wife of Abraham Leaman and Wendel.
        Ex. Christian Herr. Strasburg Twp.

12 Feb. 1800   12 March 1803
BARR, JACOB
        Children: Barbara and Eve.
        Ex. Abraham Hoober. Drumore Twp.

21 Dec. 1802   7 June 1803
BRUBAKER, JACOB
        Wife. Christina Brubaker. Children: (the names and number not given).
        Ex. Jacob Brubaker. Lancaster Borough.

5 May 1803   15 June 1803
BRUBAKER, JOHN

Children: Philip, Margaret, Anna, Elizabeth, Catharine, John, George, Abraham and Michael.
Ex. David Diffinderfer and David Witmer. Earl Twp.

15 March 1803   1 Nov. 1803
BARR, JACOB
Wife. Anna Barr. Children: (of first wife) Martin, Jacob, Christian, Abraham, Elizabeth wife of Daniel Keehnports and Barbara wife of Christian Forry; (of second wife) Veronica wife of James Citch, Susanna wife of Jacob Graff, Anna wife of John Shenk and John. Grandcildren: Jacob and Maria Barr (children of John).
Ex. Jacob and Christian Barr. Bart Twp.

17 Dec. 1803   10 Jan. 1804
BRUBACHER, JACOB
Wife. Ann Brubacker. Children: (the names and number not given).
Ex. Abraham Brubaker and Henry Kauffman. Hempfield Twp.

9 March 1798   30 April 1804
BRUBACHER, JOHN
Wife. Maria Brubacher. Children: John, Magdalena wife of John Breckard and Jacob, (there were five other daughters, names not given).
Ex. John Bear and John Mier. Warwick Twp.

--- 1801   9 March 1804
BRIGAM, JAMES
Wife. Margaret Brigam. Child: Judith wife of Henry McCrabb. Grandchild: David McCrabb.
Ex. John Reed and Henry McCrabb. Drumore Twp.

5 March 1804   22 March 1804
BEAIRD, DAVID
Wife. Agness Beaird. Children: John, Robert, Margaret and Elizabeth.
Ex. James Johnson. Little Britton Twp.

1 Aug. 1804   19 Dec. 1804
BECKER, JOHN
Child: John. Grandchild: Mary (child of John).
Ex. Samuel Grosch and Daniel Christ. Warwick Twp.

10 Oct. 1804   12 Nov. 1804
BECKER, PETER
Wife. Elizabeth Becker. Children: Peter, Henry, Jacob, Elizabeth wife of Balser Hofman, Barbara wife of Conrad Leninger and Regina wife of John Frye.
Ex. Henry Becker and John Frye. Brecknock Twp.

10 Sept. 1804   17 Sept. 1804
BURKHOLDER, ULRICH
Wife. Ann Burkholder. Children: John, Christian and Maria.
Ex. John Bauman and Abraham Guth. Brecknock Twp.

29 April 1797   9 Oct. 1804
BERG, MARIA
    Children: Frederick, Jacob and David. Son-in-law: Michael Kauffman (wife's name not stated).
    Ex. David Berg.   Hempfield Twp.

8 April 1804   4 Aug. 1804
BERG, FREDERICK
    Bros. and sister: David, Barbara wife of Christian Ober, Benj., Andrew, Mary and Veronica. Step-bro. and sister: John Beitler and Ann wife of Henry Musser.
    Ex. George Kneisely.   Hempfield Twp.

10 July 1804   26 Sept. 1804
BRENNEMAN, ISAAC
    Wife. Feronica Brenneman. Children: Christian, Mary, Feronica, Martin and Ann. Grandchild: Esther (child of Ann - last name not stated).
    Ex. Jacob Brenneman and Jacob Stoner. Conestoga Twp.

8 July 1797   27 Oct. 1804
BOWMAN, MARY
    Children: Jacob, Maria wife of John Kraliss and Catharine Shelly (children by former husband — Peter Bowman being the second).
    Ex. David Longenecker. Hempfield Twp.

1 Sept. 1790   16 March 1805
BACHERT, GEORGE
    Wife. Ann Margaret Bachert. Children: Eve, Catharine and Margaret.
    Ex. Ann Margaret Bachert. Warwick Twp.

4 Oct. 1803   5 May 1804
BOWMAN, GEORGE
    Wife. (name not given). Children: Rosana, John, Elizabeth and George.
    Ex. Jacob Riser and Jacob Stauffer. Mt. Joy Twp.

30 Oct. 1804   27 Dec. 1804
BEILER, CHISTIAN
    Wife. Anna Beiler. Child: Jacob. N.B. There were four other children, names not given.
    Ex. Christian Fisher and Christian Koenick. Lampeter Twp.

20 Jan. 1805   5 March 1805
BRENNEMAN, FERONICA
    Children: Christian, Martin, Mary Feronica wife of Isaac Heeney and Ann.
    Ex. Martin Brenneman. Conestoga Twp.

4 March 1803   20 Feb. 1805
BRUBACHER, MARIA
    Child: Maria wife of Abraham Brubacher.
    Ex. John Leaman. Hempfield Twp.

20 Feb. 1804   30 July 1805
BINKLEY, HENRY
     Children: John, Jacob, Peter and Henry (there were four
daughters, names not given). Son-in-law: Nicholas Sasher.
     Ex. Henry Binkley and Nicholas Sasher. Cocalico Twp.

9 July 1796   11 Nov. 1805
BARD, GEORGE
     Wife. Christiana Bard.
     Ex. Christiana Bard and Samuel Ensminger. Rapho Twp.

20 April 1792   28 May 1805
BACHMAN, MARY
     Children: Michael, Peter, Mary wife of Jacob Hostetter,
Catharine wife of Isaac Kaufman, Eve wife of Andrew Kaufman,
Christian, John, Andrew and Ann wife of Benjamin Bear.
     Ex. Jacob Hostetter.   Manheim Twp.

3 Nov. 1804   15 Jan. 1805
BRENNEMAN, JOHN
     Children: Christian and Michael.
     Ex. Christian and Michael Brenneman. Donegal Twp.

3 Nov. 1804   2 Feb. 1805
BULLA, WILLIAM
     Wife. Temperance Bulla. Child: Mary
     Ex. Joseph Dickinson and Asahil Walker. Salsbury Twp.

27 March 1805 9 Dec. 1805
BUCKWALTER, HENRY
     Wife. Elizabeth Buckwalter. Children: Abraham, Henry, John,
Christian and Esther.
     Ex. Martin Mellinger and John Buckwalter. Lampeter Twp

19 March 1804 14 Feb. 1805
BOYD, JAMES
     Wife. Siley Boyd. Child: John
     Ex. Siley and John Boyd. Colerain Twp.

23 Jan. 1799   8 June 1805
BOWMAN, PETER
     Wife. Mary Bowman. Children: Peter, Ann wife of Bernard
Lutz, Henry, Christian, Jacob and Michael.
     Ex. Christian Bowman and Benjamin Hershey. Hempfield Twp.

3 March 1806   12 May 1806
BLANCK, JOHN
     Wife. Freany Blanck. Children: John, Nicholas, Martha, Jane,
Catharine and Barbara.
     Ex. John Blanck and Christian Ornby. [Omby?] Salsbury Twp.

30 Oct. 1803   29 April 1806
BOWERS, ANN
     Widow of Michael Bowers. Children: Jacob, David, Samuel,
Ann, Mary wife of Isaac Leman, Joseph and Benjamin.
     Ex. Joseph and Ben Bowers. Strasburg Twp.

23 Feb. 1806   8 March 1806
BRENNEMAN, JOHN
     Wife. Anna Brenneman. Children: Samuel (and others, names
and numbers not stated).
     Ex. Christian Kilhafer and Jacob Brenneman. Twp. omitted.

15 Jan. 1806   11 Feb. 1806
BUCHANAN, ARTHUR
     Wife. Mary Buchanan. Child: James (there were other
children, names and number not stated).
     Ex. Mary and John Buchanan. Drumore Twp.

24 Feb. 1806   8 March 1806
BROSEY, JOHN
     Wife. Barbara Brosey. Children: Henry, John, Jacob,
Catharine, Elizabeth, Maria wife of Jacob Judy and Barbara wife
of Henry Witson.
     Ex. Barbara Brosey and Henry Witson. Rapho Twp.

4 July 1806   19 July 1806
BORREL, JOHN
     Children: Barbara, Jacob, Catharine, Elizabeth, Jane,
Margaret and Mary.
     Ex. John Marstelber and Michael Eby. Salsbury Twp.

4 July 1806   16 Oct. 1806
BRESSLER, GEORGE
     Wife. Veronica Bressler. Children: Mary, Catharine,
Elizabeth, Rebecca, Fanny, Charlotte, Harriet and George. Son-in-
law: Jacob Hartman (wife's name not given).
     Ex. Veronica Bressler and Peter Bressler. Strasburg Twp.

23 Aug. 1805   7 Feb. 1806
BLACK, JAMES
     Wife. Jane Black. Children: Mary, Thomas, James, David,
Margaret, John and Hugh.
     Ex. James and Thomas Black. Martic Twp.

13 July 1805   9 Aug. 1806
BUFFEMYER, MATHIAS
     Wife. Rosina Buffemyer. Children: Henry, David, John, Jacob,
Margaret wife of --- Krall, Elizabeth, Maria and Catharine.
     Ex. John Erbb and Joseph Kratzer. Elizabeth Twp.

7 June 1805   24 July 1807
BACKENSTOSS, JACOB
     Wife. Susanna Backenstoss. Children: Jacob and Susanna wife
of Valentine Hoffman.
     Ex. Susanna and Jacob Backenstoss. Lancaster Borough.

12 March 1805   10 Nov. 1807
BOYD, JOHN
     Wife. Mary Boyd. Children: Thomas, David and Sarah wife of
James Clark. Grandchildren: John Clark and John (son of David).
     Ex. Thomas and David Boyd. Martic Twp.

11 May 1803   18 Feb. 1807
BENNET, HENRY
     Wife. Elizabeth Bennet. Child: Sarah.
     Ex. Michael Gundacker and Leoy [sic] Philips. Lancaster
Borough.

8 March 1806   7 March 1807
BECKER, HENRY
     Wife. Salome Becker. Children: Magdalena wife of John
Martzall, Henry, Ludwig, Jacob, Salome wife of Christian
Martzall, Catharine, John and Peter.
     Ex. Jacob Becker and Martin Gross. Hempfield Twp.

20 Dec. 1806   21 Jan. 1807
BENDER, LEONARD
     Children: Leonard, Michael,Jacob, John and Susanna wife of -
-- Habecker. Grandchildren: David and Daniel Habecker.
     Ex. John Bender and John Bender (a nephew). Lancaster
Borough.

11 March 1807   5 May 1807
BRICKER, JOHN
     Wife. Anna Bricker. Children: Benjamin, Samuel, Joshua (and
three other children, two daughters and a son, names not given).
     Ex. Benjamin and Samuel Bricker. Cocalico Twp.

29 June 1807   15 Aug. 1807
BLONTZ, GEORGE
     (Will is signed PLONTZ.) Wife. Barbara Ploutz.
     Ex. John Hoyle. Warwick Twp.

14 May 1808   30 July 1808
BRENNEMAN, JACOB
     Wife. Catharine Brenneman. Children: (names and numbers not
given).
     Ex. Frederick Gramm and Jacob Brunnenman. Donegal Twp.

9 May 1808   9 June 1808
BRENNEMAN, HENRY
     Wife. Mary Brenneman. Children: (names and numbers not
given).
     Ex. Melchoir Brenneman and Jacob Berg. Twp. omitted.

6 April 1807   9 May 1807
BERG, FERONICA
     Widow of Jacob Berg. Children: Jacob, Christian and Barbara
wife of John Sherich.
     Ex. Jacob Berg. Manor Twp.

22 Sept. 1808   21 Nov. 1808
BASSLER, JOSEPH
     Wife. Esther Bassler. Children: Joseph, Catharine, Mary,
Elizabeth wife of John Lesher and Magdalena wife of Peter
Andrews. Son-in-law: Martin Mellinger (wife's name not stated).
     Ex. Joseph Bassler and Martin Mellinger. Stasburg Twp.

9 April 1808   21 May 1808
BOTT, JOHN
      Wife. Catharine Bott. Children: Catharine wife of David
Eichholtz, Susanna, Margaret, Anna, Elizabeth, Barbara, John and
Jacob.
      Ex. John Sensenick and Michael Bender. Manor Twp.

23 Dec. 1797   14 Nov. 1808
BUCKWALTER, JOHN
      Wife. Catharine Buckwalter. Children: David, Barbara, Henry,
Joseph, Samuel, Elizabeth and Daniel.
      Ex. Henry Buckwalter and Martin Mellinger. Lampeter Twp.

24 Dec. 1807   20 Feb. 1808
BROWN, DAVID
      Wife. Christiana Brown. Children: Ann wife of Jacob Landis.
Grandchildren: Mary, Abraham and Jacob Landis. Lampeter Twp.
      Ex. Christian Houser, Christian Rohrer.

17 Nov. 1807   22 Feb. 1809
BLANCK, NICHOLAS
      Wife. Barbara Blanck. Children: Jacob, Samuel, John and
David.
      Ex. John Blanck, Frederick Reinhold and Peter Burkholder.
Cocalico Twp.

18 April 1809   6 May 1809
BLICKENSDERFER, MATHIAS
      Wife. Catharine Blickensderfer. Children: Jacob, Benjamin,
William, Joshua, Henry, Rosina and Matilda.
      Ex. Christian Blickensderfer and Mathias Tshudy. Lititz Twp.

27 April 1809   26 May 1809
BURKHOLDER, CHRISTIAN
      Children: Abraham, David, Ann and Elizabeth.
      Ex. Abraham and Daniel Burkholder. Earl Twp.

13 April 1809   10 Aug. 1809
BASSLER, ESTHER
      Widow of Joseph Bassler. Children: Veronica wife of John
Longanacker, Esther wife of John Shleiffer (these were children
by first husband); Catharine, Mary wife of Martin Mellinger,
Elizabeth wife of John Lesher and Joseph (children by second
husband).
      Ex. John Longanacker. Strasburg Twp.

30 Aug. 1808   7 Sept. 1809
BOWER, FREDERICK
      Wife. Maria Bower. Children: Magdalena, Susanna, Christiana,
Elizabeth, Frederick, Catharine, Mary, Nancy and John.
      Ex. Frederick Bower and Anthony Hains. Donegal Twp.

8 July 1809   30 Sept. 1809
BRYAN, CHRISTOPHER
      Legatees: Jacob Musser and (bro.) James Bryan.

Ex. Jacob Musser. Manor Twp.

11 June 1805   20 Dec. 1809
BENDER, JOHN
    Wife. Catharine Bender. Children: Mary, David, Susanna,
Sarah, Isaac, Joseph and Catharine.
    Ex. Adam Miller Jr. Leacock Twp.

---   10 Jan. 1810
BRODHEAD, DANIEL
    N.B. This will is recorded in Wayne Co., PA. The record of
which appears on the Lancaster Co. Records, where a certificate
to that effect (by the recorder of Wayne Co.) is filed.

20 Aug. 1808   18 Nov. 1809
BRUBAKER, JOHN
    Wife. Mary Brubaker. Children: Henry, Juliana, Mary and
John.
    Ex. Henry Moeler, Philip Brubaker and Frederick Seiger. Earl
Twp.

9 Sept. 1808   20 Jan. 1809
BRUBAKER, ABRAHAM
    Children: Elizabeth and Anna.
    Ex. John Leaman and John Swar.[?] Hempfield Twp.

11 July 1809   7 March 1810
BITZER, JOHN
    Wife. Eve Bitzer. Children: John, Ann wife of Abraham
Swagart, Catharine wife of Martin Werntz, Sybilla wife of John
Swagart, Barbara, Solomon and Andrew. Grandchildren: George and
William Werntz.
    Ex. John Bitzer. Earl Twp.

4 Nov. 1808   9 Jan. 1810
BRENNEMAN, MELCHOIR
    Wife. Ann Brenneman. Children: Catharine, Henry, Susanna,
John, Elizabeth, Christian, Mary, Ann, Barbara and Susanna.
    Ex. Not given. Donegal Twp.

2 June 1810   22 Aug. 1810
BIRNEY, WILLIAM
    Bros. and sisters: John, Mary, Margaret and Rebecca Birney.
    Ex. Neal McCloy and George McKenny. Strasburg Twp.

26 Feb. 1808   13 April 1810
BARTLETT, SARAH
    Children: John, Mary, Edward and Thomas.
    Ex. Thomas Bartlett. Columbia Twp.

4 May 1809   19 May 1810
BRADHURST, HENRY
    Wife. Sarah Bradhurst. Children: Mary, Rebecca, Elinor,
Elizabeth, John, Else and Anne.
    Ex. Sarah and John Bradhurst. Drumore Twp.

21 Feb. 1810   10 May 1810
BECHTOLT, JOHN
     Wife. Mary Bechtolt. Children: Magdalena wife of Frederick
Fisher, John, William, Susanna wife of Philip Vonieda, Philip,
Polly and Samuel.
     Ex. Jacob Vonieda and Adam Grill. Cocalico Twp.

12 June 1809   8 Oct. 1810
BUCKANON, DORCAS
     Children: William, James and Thomas.
     Ex. James and Thomas Buckanon. Maytown Twp.

8 April 1806   1 Feb. 1811
BERG, JACOB
     Wife. Catharine Berg. Children: Andrew, Maria, Susanna wife
of Daniel Heisy, Frederick, Henry, Fornica and Jacob.
     Ex. Andrew and David Berg. Douegal Twp.

--- 27 March 1811
BRUBACKER, ABRAHAM
     Children: John, Jacob, Daniel, Abraham and Christian. Sons-
in-law: Michael Eberly, Henry Kendig and Henry Eberly. (Names of
their wives not given.)
     Ex. Michael Eberly and Abraham Brubacker. Cocalico Twp.

12 April 1806   30 March 1811
BACKMAN, CHRISTIAN
     Wife. Elizabeth Bachman. Bros. and sisters: Peter, Ann
Witmer, Barbara Sigrist, Elizabeth Gilbert, Elizabeth Hershey,
Catharine Bear, John and Michael.
     Ex. Peter Bachman and Henry Neff. Lancaster Borough.

20 Dec. 1809   7 April 1811
BUCK, HENRY
     Wife. Anna Maria Buck. Children: Henry, Peter and Ephraim.
     Ex. Henry and Ames M. Buck. Manheim Twp.

20 Oct. 1805   18 April 1811
BOYER, PETER
     Wife. Anne Maria Boyer.
     Ex. Anna Maria Boyer. Lancaster Borough.

19 Feb. 1802   27 April 1811
BARE, GEORGE
     Children: Barbara wife of Michael Wearly, John, George and
Samuel.
     Ex. George Bare. Earl Twp.

10 June 1810   22 July 1811
BRADLEY, PATRICK
     Wife. Margaret Bradley. Child Barney (now living in
Ireland).
     Ex. Samuel Rex. Elizabeth Twp.

22 June 1805   30 Oct. 1811
BOMBERGER, JACOB
    Bros. and sisters: Elizabeth, Barbara, John and Christian.
    Ex. Christian Bomberger. Warwick Twp.

8 May 1811   24 July 1811
BOWMAN, JOSEPH
    Wife. Feronica Bowman. Children: Joseph, Esther wife of John
Witmer and Barbara wife of Benjamin Miller.
    Ex. John Witmer and Benjamin Miller. Lampeter Twp.

3 Aug. 1807   6 Aug. 1811
BERGMAN, BALTZER
    Wife. Mary Bergman. Children: John, Sally and Mary.
Grandchildren: Jacob Ludwick, Mary wife of Christian Wolf and
Magdalena wife of Peter Rockey (parents' names not stated).
    Ex. John Bergman and George Eckert. Strasburg Twp.

21 Jan. 1806   8 Aug. 1811
BECK, PETER
    Wife. Margaret Beck. Children: John, Peter, George, Henry,
Adam, David, Daniel, Susanna, Catharine and Elizabeth.
    Ex. John and Adam Beck. Earl Twp.

7 March 1810   19 Aug. 1811
BRANNON, MARGARET
    Widow of John Brannon. Legatte: Sarah Pegan.
    Ex. Andrew Pegan. Martic Twp.

14 Dec. 1803   26 Oct. 1811
BUHRMAN, BILLY
    Wife. (name not stated). Bro.: Henry Buhrman.
    Ex. Peter Bishop and John Albert. Mt. Joy Twp.

15 July 1811   30 Oct. 1811
BORKHOLDER, MARTIN
    Children: Eve, George, Peter, Sophia wife of Samuel Bodiger
and Michael.
    Ex. George and Peter Borkholder. Cocalico Twp.

18 May 1811   22 Nov. 1811
BRISBEN, WILLIAM
    Wife. (name not given). Children: John, Elizabeth, William,
David, Mary and Henry. Grandchildren: James Brisben and Elizabeth
Fullerton (parents' names not given).
    Ex. John, David and Henry Brisben. Salsbury Twp.

30 Aug. 1803   12 Sept. 1812
BEILER, CHRISTIAN
    Wife. Barbara Beiler. Children: Christian, Magdalena, John,
Lizzy, Maria, Ann, Jacob, Henry, Joseph and Frenie.
    Ex. Christian Hertzler and John Lapp. Caernarvon Twp.

13 Dec. 1807   14 Oct. 1812
BEAR, BARBARA

Children: Magdalena wife of Michael Bard, David, Henry, Martin, Feronica wife of John Eby and Salome wife of Benjamin Eby.
    Ex. David Bear. Leacock Twp.

6 Nov. 1811   25 Jan. 1812
BROWN, CHRISTIANA
    Grandchildren: Mary, Abraham and Jacob Landie.
    Ex. Christian Howser. Lampeter Twp.

6 Dec. 1805   7 April 1812
BEAM, MARTIN
    Wife. Eve Beam. Children: John, Jacob, Henry and Barbara wife of Abraham Keagy.
    Ex. Henry Beam and Abraham Keagy. Conestoga Twp.

19 Jan. 1804   19 May 1812
BEAR, JOHN
    Wife. (name not given). Children: Andrew, Elizabeth wife of John Longenecker, Barbara wife of David Bear, Catharina wife of Andrew Rudy, Mary wife of Jacob Meyer and Feronica wife of Rudolph Stodlartheir.
    Ex. David and John Bear. Leacock Twp.

2 April 1812   22 May 1812
BLACK, GEORGE
    Wife. (name not given). There were two sons, names not stated.
    Ex. James Kelton. Colerain Twp.

1 Jan. 1809   6 Feb. 1813
BOSSLER, JOHN
    Wife. Anna Bossler. Children: Elizabeth wife of John Harnish, Ann, John, Jacob, Christian, Barbara wife of Christian Brubacher, Magdalena and Maria wife of Andrew Shenk.
    Ex. John Bossler and Andrew Shenk. Manheim Twp.

5 Jan. 1813   20 Feb. 1813
BRENNER, JOHN ADAM
    Wife. Elizabeth Brenner. Children: John, Jacob, Polly, Peggy, Catharine, George, Betsey and Christopher.
    Ex. Christopher Brenner and Michael Bender. Manor Twp.

22 Jan. 1809   10 March 1813
BAUER, ELIZABETH
    Widow of Nicholas Bauer. Children: Susanna, Muma, Catharine, Jacob, Elizabeth, Christian and John.
    Ex. Andrew Gerber. Hempfield Twp.

26 Feb. 1813   11 March 1813
BRENNEMAN, HENRY
    Wife. Mary Brenneman. Children: Abraham, Mary and John.
    Ex. Mary Brenneman and George Snyder. Marietta Borough.

13 Sept. 1811   3 April 1813
BARR, JOHN
    Wife. Elizabeth Barr. Children: John and Martin.
    Ex. John Hubley, John and Martin Barr. Strasburg Twp.

18 March 1813   13 April 1813
BOWMAN, JOHN
    Children: David, Barbara and Elizabeth.
    Ex. Martin Nisle. Donegal Twp.

4 April 1813   8 Sept. 1813
BRACKBILL, JOHN
    Legatees: Bro. Benjamin Brackbill and (sisters) Feronica
wife of George Weaver and Ann wife of Jacob Neff (and numerous
special bequests to others).
    Ex. Jacob Neff, Jr., John and Henry Brackbill. Twp omitted.

13 Sept. 1813   8 Nov. 1813
BAILEY, JAMES
    Wife. Jane Bailey. Children: William, Thomas, Margaret,
Jane, Eleanor and Mary.
    Ex. Jane and Alexander Bailey. Colerain Twp.

12 June 1811   24 Jan. 1814
BIGLEY, MORRIS
    Legatees: (uncle) Michael Bigley and (sister) Mary Kirk.
    Ex. Christopher Nagle. Twp. omitted.

3 Feb. 1814   23 March 1814
BARR, GEORGE
    Children: Owen, John, Margaret wife of John Stoner,
Elizabeth wife of Richard Ferree, George, Jacob, Nancy wife of
John Spangler and Fanny wife of John Snyder.
    Ex. Owen Barr and John Spangler. Donegal Twp.

23 May 1813   12 April 1814
BEAR, MARTIN
    Wife. Magdalena Bear. Children: Martin, Benjamin, Henry and
Anne wife of John Blank.
    Ex. John Hibsham and Peter Elser. Elizabeth Twp.

6 April 1814   7 June 1814
BENTZ, PETER
    Wife. Barbara Bentz.
    Ex. George Leed and Charles Montelins. Cocalico Twp.

8 Sept. 1814   22 Sept. 1814
BAUSMAN, ANDREW
    Wife. Elizabeth Bausman. Bros.: Peter and Henry. Sisters:
Margaret Dick and Anna Maria Frick.
    Ex. John Bausman and John Reitzel. Lancaster Twp.

10 July 1814   6 Aug. 1814
BURGARD, WILLIAM

Wife. Catharine Burgard. Children: (the names and number not given).
Ex. Jacob Frantz and John Leib. Warwick Twp.

17 Dec. 1813   15 Oct. 1814
BEAR, MARGARET
Children: John and Samuel.
Ex. Samuel and John Bear. Manor Twp.

17 Feb. 1806   3 Jan. 1815
BAMBARGER, CHRISTIAN
Wife. Catharine Bambarger. Children: Elizabeth, Catharine, Eve, Mary, Joseph, Moses, Samuel, Peter, Christian, Esther, Susanna, John and David. Grandchildren: Isaac, Christian and Elizabeth Bambarger (children of David).
Ex. John Erb and John Bambarger. Warwick Twp.

19 Feb. 1815   6 April 1815
BISHOP, PETER
Wife. Margaret Bishop. Children: Jacob, Elizabeth, Catharine, Margaret and Peter.
Ex. Peter Bishop and Leonard Negley. Mt. Joy Twp.

11 July 1814   9 June 1815
BAKER, FREDERICK
Wife. Margaret Baker. Children: Elias, Diller, Elizabeth, Mary wife of David Ferree, Catharine and Margaret. Child by former wife — Susanna Smith.
Ex. Margaret and Frederick D. Baker. Salisbury Twp.

1 July 1815   24 July 1815
BARNETZ, MICHAEL
Wife. Mary Barnetz. Children: John, Anna and Augusta.
Ex. Mary Barnetz and Samuel White. Lancaster Borough.

23 June 1815   31 July 1815
BECHTOLT, WILLIAM
Wife. Catharine Bechtolt.
Ex. Catharine Bechtolt and Philip Moneida. Brecknock Twp.

8 Aug. 1815   13 Sept. 1815
BITTING, ANN MARIA
Child: Susanna wife of --- Krider.
Ex. Susanna Krider. Lancaster Borough.

10 Sept. 1815   11 Oct. 1815
BRENNEMAN, ABRAHAM
Wife. Margaret Brennerman. Children: Jacob, Jonathan, Henry, Abraham, Nancy, Sally, Benjamin and Solomon.
Ex. Margaret Brenneman and Henry Frankhouser. Brecknock Twp.

10 June 1815   15 Oct. 1815
BAUMAN, CHRISTIAN
Wife. Maria Bauman. Children: Benjamin, Joseph, Peter, Daniel, John, Samuel, Henry, Sarah and Adam.

Ex. Benjamin Bauman and Henry Hibshman. Cocalico Twp.

4 Feb. 1801   27 Oct. 1815
BRENNEMAN, HENRY
    Wife. Margaret Brenneman. Children: John, Henry, Adam, Ann wife of Jacob Mosser, Elizabeth wife of Jacob Wisler and Mary.
    Ex. John and Henry Brenneman. Manor Twp.

30 April 1815   24 Nov. 1815
BALMER, MICHAEL
    Wife. Charlotte Balmer. Children: John, Henry and Catharine.
    Ex. Frederick Byrod. Mountgomery Twp.

10 March 1809   9 Dec. 1815
BRETZ, PHILIP
    Wife. Elizabeth Bretz. Children: Jacob, Catharine, Barbara, William, Magdalena, Ann, Maria and John; (children by first wife) -Margaret, Catharine, John, Elizabeth, Hannah, Maria, Barbara, Andrew and Jacob.
    Ex. William Bretz and David Kuentzel. Manheim Twp.

1 Sept. 1805   15 Dec. 1815
BEAR, ANDREW
    Children: Andrew, Elizabeth wife of Christian Newcomer and John.
    Ex. John and David Bear. Leacock Twp.

20 March 1808   2 Feb. 1816
BRAUN, JOHN
    Wife. Ernstina Braun. Children: Maria wife of Jacob Koenig, John and William.
    Ex. Christian Strenge and Michael Gross. Lancaster Borough.

13 March 1814   18 March 1816
BOWMAN, DANIEL
    Children: Jacob and Daniel. Son-in-law: Peter Bollinger (wife's name not given).
    Ex. Jacob and Daniel Bowman. Cocalico Twp.

20 March 1816   26 March 1816
BUCKWALTER, FRANCIS
    Wife. Mary Buckwalter. Children: Henry, John, Anna wife of --- Seigrist (and five others, names not given).
    Ex. John Buckwalter and Christian Myer. Leacock Twp.

14 April 1815   6 April 1816
BAKER, HENRY
    Wife. Christiana Baker. Child: Elizabeth.
    Ex. Christiana Baker and Jacob Bowman. Cocalico Twp.

13 Jan. 1816   13 July 1816
BRIEN, EDWARD
    Wife. Dorothea Brien. Children: Edward, Sarah and Henry.
Sister-in-law: Mary Hand.
    Ex. John Brien, Samuel Bethel and James Wright. Martic Twp.

10 Feb. 1816   9 July 1816
BINKLEY, HENRY
    Wife. Elizabeth Binkley. Children: Henry, John, Samuel,
William and Benjamin.
    Ex. Elizabeth Binkley and Jacob Hibshman. Cocalico Twp.

11 May 1816   23 June 1816
BARKLEY, WILLIAM
    Wife. Elizabeth Barkley. Children: Ann, Elizabeth, Nancy,
Matilda and Mary wife of --- Loomise. Grandchildren: William,
Henrietta and another not yet named (children of Mary).
    Ex. Elizabeth Barkley and Robert Anderson. Colerain Twp.

13 Feb. 1810   16 Aug. 1816
BENDER, MICHAEL
    Wife. Margaret Bender. Children: John, Michael, George, Eve
wife of Michael Haberstick and Ann wife of John Gall.
    Ex. John and Michael Bender. Lancaster Borough.

--- 1811   19 Oct. 1816
BREHM, PHILIP
    Children: Philip, George, John, Henry and Margaret.
    Ex. Christopher Shower and George Rudisil. Manheim Twp.

24 Oct. 1816   28 Oct. 1816
BUBACH, GERHART
    Wife. Anna Mary Bubach. Child: John. Son-in-law: David
Ryneer (wife's name not stated).
    Ex. David Ryneer and George Reckel. Manheim Twp.

7 March 1814   5 Dec. 1816
BRANDT, YOST
    Wife. Feronica Brandt. Children: David, Ann, Maria,
Christian, Henry, Feronica, Catharine and Elizabeth.
    Ex. Christian Metz and Christian Brandt. Rapho Twp.

13 Nov. 1816   26 Dec. 1816
BARR, CHRISTIAN
    Wife. Susanna Barr. Children: Michael, Christian, Jacob,
Amos, Benjamin, Susanna, Mary, Hannah, Elizabeth and Judith.
    Ex. Michael and Christian Barr. Twp. omitted.

29 Nov. 1813   14 Jan. 1817
BALMER, MICHAEL
    Wife. Mary Balmer. Children: Christian, Samuel, Mary wife of
Daniel Kinzy, Juliana wife of David Whipler, Benjamin and Daniel.
    Ex. John Eby and Daniel Erb. Warwick Twp.

26 Feb. 1815   21 April 1817
BEAR, ABRAHAM
    Wife. Julian Bear. Children: Henry, Abraham, Susanna wife of
David Eberly, Elizabeth wife of Jacob Bowman and Catharine wife
of Samuel Eberly.
    Abraham and Henry Bear. Cocalico Twp.

29 Jan. 1817   2 May 1817
BEAR, JOHN
    Wife. Mary Bear. Children: Adam, Maria wife of Henry Bear,
Juliana and Lydia wife of Henry Good.
    Ex. Adam and Henry Bear. Leacock Twp.

23 March 1817   5 May 1817
BORGER, GEORGE
    Wife. (name not stated). There was one daughter, name not
given.
    Ex. Mathias Musser and Peter Bowman. Earl Twp.

30 April 1817   30 July 1817
BARD, MARTIN
    Wife. Susanna Bard. Children: Casper, Susanna, Margaret wife
of Philip Broug [Brong?], Daniel, Martin, Catharine, Elizabeth
and Mary.
    Ex. Susanna and Daniel Bard. Lancaster Borough.

2 Feb. 1807   26 Oct. 1817
BOFFENMEYER, ROSINA
    Widow of Mathias Boffenmeyer. Children: Adam, Baltzer,
Peter, Jacob, Michael, Catharine, Eichor, Juliana and Rosina.
    Ex. Baltzer Boffenmeyer. Elizabeth Twp.

23 Nov. 1817   23 Dec. 1817
BASSLER, JACOB
    Wife. Barbara Bassler. Children: Elizabeth wife of Jacob
Doner, Magdalena wife of Benjamin Musser, John, Jacob, Catharine
wife of Christian Nisle, Barbara wife of Benjamin Ebersol, Joseph
and Ann wife of Henry Lichty.
    Ex. Jacob Gish and Christian Nisle. Donegal Twp.

3 Dec. 1816   23 Dec. 1817
BRENNEMAN, MELCHOIR
    Wife. Jenny Brenneman. Children: John, Adam, Rebecca and
Joseph.
    Ex. George Whislar and Jacob Gish. Donegal Twp.

2 Dec. 1815   19 June 1818
BOYSS, ELIZABETH
    Sister: Margaret McLewee. Bro.: William Barton.
    Ex. Joseph Vance and John Clark. Donegal Twp.

22 Oct. 1816   1 Sept. 1818
BAMBERGER, JOHN
    Wife. Maria Bamberger. Children: Christian, John, Jacob,
Abraham, Joseph and Peter.
    Ex. John Bamberger (a friend) and John Bamberger (son).
Warwick Twp.

16 Nov. 1816   29 Sept. 1818
BRENNEMAN, JOHN
    Wife. Maria Brenneman. Child: George.
    Ex. Maria and George Brenneman. Donegal Twp.

6 Nov. 1818   23 Nov. 1818
BROWN, WILLIAM
     Children: Mary wife of William Barkley, Juliana wife of ---
Kennedy, John, Andrew, James, Margaret wife of James Graham and
William.
     Ex. William Brown. Bart Twp.

27 Dec. 1818   1 Jan. 1819
BROWN, ABRAHAM
     Children: Joseph, John, Abraham, Elizabeth, Maria and
Catharine.
     Ex. Philip Snyder and John Mann. Manor Twp.

9 July 1819   19 Jan. 1819
BERG, DAVID
     Wife. Anna Berg.
     Ex. Joseph Gochnauer and David Kauffman. Hempfield Twp.

5 Dec. 1818   26 Jan. 1819
BRUBACHER, JACOB
     Wife. Catharine Brubacher.
     Ex. Jacob and Christian Haldeman. Rapho Twp.

16 Jan. 1802   Feb. 4, 1819
BUCKWALTER, ABRAHAM
     Wife. Barbara Buckwalter. Children: John, David, Elizabeth
wife of Jacob Ruth, Magdalena and Ann.
     Ex. John and Henry Buckwalter. Lampeter Twp.

22 June 1818   17 March 1819
BRITZIUS, ISAAC
     Wife. Elizabeth Britzius. Sisters: Catharine wife of John
Light, Magdalena and Elizabeth.
     Ex. Isaac Heiny. Lancaster Twp.

10 Jan. 1818   23 March 1819
BECKER, JOHN
     Wife. Christiana Becker. Children: Samuel, Catharine,
Barbara, Daniel and William.
     Ex. Christiana Becker and George Readle. Earl Twp.

28 Oct. 1816   6 April 1819
BIXLER, ABRAHAM
     Wife. Ann Bixler. Children: Barbara wife of D. Gauckley and
Margaret.
     Ex. Henry Mohler and Jacob Hagey. Cocalico Twp.

21 Dec. 1818   7 May 1819
BEAR, DAVID
     Wife. Barbara Bear. Children: Henry, David, Daniel, Susanna
wife of John Kessby, Catharine wife of Martin Heller, Mary wife
of Frederick Swobe, Feronica wife of Martin Myer and Elizabeth.
     Ex. Henry Bear and John Hershey. Leacock Twp.

20 Aug. 1819   21 Sept. 1819
BOLLINGER, DAVID
      Wife. Hannah Bollinger. Children: John, Emanuel and Samuel.
      Ex. Gungel and Benjamin Ober. Cocalico Twp.

6 Feb. 1819   6 Nov. 1819
BEAM, RUDOLPH
      Wife. Anna Beam. Children: Jacob, Christian, Magdalena,
Elizabeth and Catharine wife of --- Beam. Grandchildren:
Christian and Nancy Beam (children of Catharine).
      Ex. Jacob Beam (son) and Jacob Beam (nephew). Londonderry
Twp.

9 Oct. 1819   25 Nov. 1819
BIRGELBAUGH, CATHARINE
      Children: Martin and Barbara wife of John Erb.
      Ex. John Erb. Elizabeth Twp.

28 Oct. 1818   13 May 1819
BRUBAKER, JACOB
      Children: Andrew, Christian, Jacob, Maria and Susan.
      Ex. Benjamin Hershey and Daniel Brubaker.

2 Sept. 1818   2 Dec. 1819
BOETTNER, ADAM
      Wife. Fanny Boettner. Children: Adam, David, Daniel, Jacob,
Christiana, Elizabeth, Anamaria and Fanny. (These are children by
second wife). (Children by first wife) Christiana, George, John
and Catharine wife of Jacob Lindeman. Grandchildren: Jacob, Henry
and Mary Lindeman.
      Ex. Benjamin Mussler. Manor Twp.

9 Jan. 1786   22 Feb. 1786
CARPENTER, JOHN
      Children: Henry, Barbara wife of Henry Martin, Ann wife of
Mathias Springer, Elizabeth wife of Peter Lance, Mary wife of
John Tulce and Esther.
      Ex. Henry Martin and Peter Carpenter. Earl Twp.

19 Nov. 1778   10 May 1786
COWAN, DAVID
      Wife. Hannah Cowan. Children: Jarred, David, Margaret,
Elizabeth, Hannah, Janet and Sarah.
      Ex. William Briesin and John Fleming. Salsbury Twp.

8 Sept. 1787   3 Oct. 1787
COLEMAN, WILLIAM
      Bro.: Robert. Sisters: Mary, Susanna, Faith and Elizabeth.
      Ex. Robert Coleman. Warwick Twp.

20 April 1787 13 May 1788
COOK, DAVID
      Wife. Martha Cook. Children: John, Samuel, David, Gracel,
Pedian and James. Grandchild: David Cook (son of Pedian).

Ex. Martha and Samuel Cook. Donegal Twp.

7 Oct. 1788   28 Nov. 1788
CLINGAN, THOMAS
    Wife. Margaret Clingan. Children: Jenny, George, Mary and
William.
    Ex. William and George Clingan. Donegal Twp.

15 Nov. 1788   6 May 1789
CARBAUGH, SIMON
    Children: Magdalena wife of Jacob King, Susanna wife of
Ulrick Tanner, Sarah wife of Isaac Grober, Peter, Jacob and Anna
wife of Christian Etter.
    Ex. Jacob King and Ulrich Tanner. Mt. Joy Twp.

17 Jan. 1786   6 Nov. 1789
COPPOCK, JOHN
    Children: John, Joseph, Ann, Thomas and Samuel.
    Ex. Thomas Coppock and Joseph McCreary. Twp. omitted

14 May 1789   18 May 1789
CHAMBERS, STEPHEN
    Wife. Lydia Chamers. Legatees: William McCurdy and Mary his
wife, John Joseph Henry and Jane his wife, and Charles and Henry
Morris (minor children, now under the care of Patrick Duffy, a
broker of Philadelphia).
    Ex. Jasper Yeates and Robert Coleman. Lancaster Borough.

7 Dec. 1786   10 May 1790
CHRISTEY, JOHN
    Wife. Anna Maria Christey. Children: Henry, John, Barbara,
Elizabeth (and another daughter, name not given).
    Ex. Henry and John Christey. Lancaster Borough.

1 April 1789   27 Aug. 1790
CUMMINS, JOHN
    Father: James Cummins. Bros.: William and Andrew Cummins.
Sisters: Margaret, Betsey and Anne.
    Ex. James Cummins. Drumore Twp.

10 Nov. 1790   13 Nov. 1790
CREIGHTON, WILLIAM
    Wife. Barbara Creighton. Children: Mary, Martha, Margaret
and Ann. Grandchildren: Isaac Lightner, William, Samuel and
Margaret Erven (parents' names not given).
    Ex. Robert McCurdy and William Brisbin. Leacock Twp.

3 Aug. 1790   24 Nov. 1790
CUCKERLY, JACOB
    (This name should be GUCKERLE.) Wife. Magdalena. Children:
David, John, Sebastian, Catharine wife of Christian Weist,
Dietrich and Christina.
    Ex. John and Dietrich Guckerle. Rapho Twp.

20 March 1792   5 July 1792
CLEMSON, JAMES
        Wife. Margaret Clemson. Children: Rachel wife of David
Whitehill, Elizabeth wife of Herman Spiles, Sarah wife of John
McCally, Mary wife of Isaac Aetty, Rebecca, James and John.
        Ex. James and John Clemson. Salsbury Twp.

14 June 1792   17 Aug. 1792
CARPENTER, GEORGE
        Mother: Mary Carpenter. Sisters: Elizabeth wife of Jacob
Weidman and Polly. Bros.: Gabriel and Jacob.
        Ex. Mary Carpenter and David Lene. Earl Twp.

30 March 1792 15 May 1793
CUNNINGHAM, JAMES
        Wife. Janet Cunningham. Children: John, Samuel, David,
Robert and Margaret.
        Ex. Janet and John Cunningham. Lancaster Borough.

13 Aug. 1791   14 Aug. 1793
CHRISTIE, ANNA MARIA
        Bros.: Frederick and Henry Gass. Name of first husband was
Andrew Berfinger (no mention of children by either marriage).
        Ex. Christian Lang. Lancaster Borough.

30 Oct. 1793   17 Dec. 1793
CLARK, DANIEL
        Wife. Anna Maria Clark. Child: Catharine.
        Ex. Christian Krall. Elizabeth Twp.

25 Sept. 1793 2 Oct. 1793
COWAN, WILLIAM
        Bros.: Robert, Thomas and Walter.
        Ex. James Old and John Huston. Caernarvon Twp.

11 Feb. 1789   15 Jan. 1794
CLEMSON, JOHN
        Child: Hannah wife of John Buckley. Grandchildren: Daniel
Buckley (child of Hannah), Beulah Pyle, Ann Grubb and Mary Hannum
(parents' names not stated).
        Ex. Daniel Buckley. Salsbury Twp.

15 Nov. 1793   4 March 1794
CREAIG, JOHN
        Wife. Agness Creaig. Sisters: Jane Buck, Elizabeth Boyle
and Ann Moore.
        Ex. Agness Creaig and Samuel Boyd. Lampeter Twp.

1 Aug. 1794   25 Oct. 1794
COCHRAN, JOSEPH
        Wife. Elizabeth Cochran. Bro.: James.
        Ex. Hugh Long. Drumore Twp.

17 Aug. 1793   5 April 1794
CULP, HENRY

(This should be KULP.) Wife. Susanna Kulp. Children:
Jacob, Henry,Catharine, Christian, Nancy, Susanna, Barbara, David
and Samuel. Son-in-law: Michael Horst (wife's name not stated).
Ex. John Stoffer and Michael Horst. Mt. Joy Twp.

2 Sept. 1794   22 Oct. 1795
CRAWFORD, JOHN
Wife. Nancy Crawford. Children: Ann, Samuel, Polly, Jenny,
Moses, Arthur, Elizabeth, James, Daniel, Sarah, Jane, Thomas and
John.
Ex. Thomas and John Crawford. Twp. omitted

19 Jan. 1789   3 Feb. 1795
CUNNINGHAM, MATTHEW
Child: John
Ex. John Cunningham. Martic Twp.

11 Dec. 1793   7 March 1795
CHRISTY, MARY BARBARA
Legatee: Frederick Frick (a friend).
Ex. Frederick Frick. Lancaster Borough.

10 Dec. 1785   28 March 1796
COFFROTH, GERHART
Children: Elizabeth, Barbara, Catharine, Dorothea,
Christiana, Henry and Jacob.
Ex. Henry and Jacob Coffroth. Cocalico Twp.

3 Aug. 1792   9 April 1796
COCKLEY, JOHN
Wife. Magdalena Cockley. Children: Sebastian, Catharine
wife of Christian Weist, David, John, Dietrick and Christiana
wife of Joseph Dornback.
Ex. John and Dietrick Cockley. Cocalico Twp.

24 July 1797   22 Sept. 1797
CARPENTER, HENRY
Wife. Elizabeth Carpenter. Children: Esther, Henry, Mary,
Sarah, Anna, Barbara, Magdalena and Susanna. Sons-in-law: George
Weaver and Henry Sousman (wives' names not given).
Grandchildren: Henry Weaver and Henry Sousman.
Ex. George Weaver and Henry Sousman. Earl Twp.

20 Dec. 1794   1 Nov. 1797
CARPENTER, JACOB
Wife. Anna Maria Carpenter. Children: Jacob, Emanuel,
Susanna wife of Peter Ellemaker and Catharine.
Ex. Peter Ellemaker and Christian Carpenter. Earl Twp.

20 Sept. 1794   7 Aug. 1797
CAMBELL, ANDREW
Legatees: Daniel McNeil, Archibald McNeil, John McNeil and
others.
Ex. Archibald and John McNeil. Salsbury Twp.

15 April 1797   27 March 1798
CARPENTER, JOHN
     Wife. Susanna Carpenter.   Children: Abraham, Susanna wife of
Frederick Yeiser, Mary wife of John Smith and Salome wife of
Joseph Lefever.   Grandchildren: Susanna, John and Joseph Lefever.
     Ex. Abraham Carpenter, John Smith and Christian Hartman.
Strasburg Twp.

28 April 1798   30 May 1798
CULLEY, THOMAS
     Wife. Isabella Culley.   Children: Margaret, George, Rutha,
Ann, Thomas, William, Jean, Mary and Elizabeth.
     Ex. John Reed and John Robinson.   Strasburg Twp.

26 June 1798   5 Oct. 1798
CONRAD, PETER
     Wife. Magdalena Conrad.   Child: Magdalena.
     Ex. Magdalena Conrad.   Earl Twp.

18 Sept. 1787   29 May 1799
CAMPBELL, JOHN
     Sisters: Mary and Jean Campbell.   Bro.: Robert Campbell.
     Ex. James Baxton.   Bart Twp.

25 Oct. 1799   27 Nov. 1799
CHRISTY, HENRY
     Children: Susanna wife of Frederick Hersh, Henry and Daniel
     Ex. Frederick Hersh.   Lancaster Twp.

30 Aug. 1799   30 Aug. 1799
CONNOR, CATHARINE
     Sister: Elizabeth Connor.
     Ex. Elizabeth Connor.   Lancaster Borough.

5 March 1798   16 Oct. 1790 [1799]
CENNEDY, JAMES
     (This should be KENNEDY.)
     Wife. Jane Kennedy.   Children: Ann, Thomas, William, John,
Maxwell, Jane, Elizabeth, Robert, Mary and James.
     Ex. James and Robert Kennedy.   Salsbury Twp.

7 Sept. 1799   26 Feb. 1800
CALDWELL, MARY
     Children: John, William, Agness, James, Oliver and Mary.
     Ex. Oliver Caldwell.   Little Britton Twp.

2 Feb. 1795   19 Nov. 1800
CARPENTER, CHRISTIAN
     Wife. Susanna Carpenter.   Children: Catharine wife of Henry
Carpenter, Mary wife of Michael Cover, Susanna wife of Jacob
Forney, John and Salome.
     Ex. Jacob and Daniel Carpenter.   Earl Twp.

2 Nov. 1800   27 Feb. 1801
CHAMBERLIN, JOSHUA

Wife. (name omitted). Children: Joseph, Gershon, Joshua, Jonas, William, John, Hannah, Elizabeth and Alice.
Ex. His wife and Joshua Chamberlin. Sadsbury Twp.

5 March 1796   11 Jan. 1802
CHAMBERS, LYDIA
Sister-in-law: Mary McCurdy. Legatees: Margaret Coleman, Stephen, Henry and David Chambers, and others.
Ex. Jasper Yeates and Robert Coleman. Lancaster Borough.

7 May 1794   11 Dec. 1802
CARAGAN, MICHAEL
(This should be KARAGAN.) Children: Jacob, Susanna and Mary.
Ex. Christian Shanck. Conestoga Twp.

27 Jan. 1803   1 March 1803
CARPENTER, JACOB
Wife. Catharine Carpenter. Child: Catharine.
Ex. Catharine and Martin Carpenter. Lancaster Borough.

5 May 1801   12 April 1803
CLARK, THOMAS
Wife. Margaret Clark. Children: Thomas, Gabriel, Violet, Jean, Eliza and Robert. Sons-in-law: Robert Huchinson and David Scott (wives' names not stated).
Ex. Robert Clark and James Morrison. Drumore Twp.

28 Dec. 1802   9 Aug. 1803
CLARK, THOMAS
Wife. (name omitted). Children: David, William, Peggy, John, James, Rebecca, Polly, Sally and Ann. Sons-in-law: James Collins and William Clark (wives' names not stated).
Ex. John Reed and John Clark. Martic Twp.

1 April 1800   5 April 1803
CRISTE, EDWARD
(This should be GRISTE.) Wife. Mary Griste. Children: Job and Mary.
Ex. Job Griste and Emanuel Reynolds. Little Britton Twp.

8 Dec. 1803   1 Feb. 1804
CARPENTER, MAGDALEN
Children: Martin, Esther, Catherine and John.
Ex. Martin Carpenter. Lampeter Twp.

3 April 1804   24 Dec. 1804
COOPER, JAMES
Wife. Jane Cooper. Children: John, William, James and Mary.
Ex. John and James Cooper. Leacock Twp.

4 March 1804   11 April 1804
COOKE, SAMUEL
Wife. (name omitted). Bros.: James, John and David.

N.B. A bequest was made to the heirs of James Fulton (of Donegal Twp.).
  Ex. His wife and David Cooke. Donegal Twp.

4 March 1805   14 May 1805
CARSON, JAMES
  Wife. Mary Carson. Child: Elizabeth.
  Ex. Robert Maxwell and Edward Porter. Drumore Twp.

27 May 1805   1 June 1805
CUMMINS, ELIZABETH
  Nephew: William Cummins.
  Ex. Joseph Walker. Sadsbury Twp.

25 Feb. 1802   4 Oct. 1806
CLOUSE, MICHAEL
  Children: Adam, Elizabeth and Jacob.
  Ex. Adam Clouse and Anthony Hains. Donegal Twp.

8 Nov. 1804   10 Jan. 1805
CURRAN, JAMES
  Wife. Sarah Curran. Children: Eleanor, Mary, Margaret,
Rebecca and Brice.
  Ex. Brice Clark and James Patterson. Rapho Twp.

19 April 1805   13 May 1805
COOK, EDWARD
  Wife. Elizabeth. Children: Francis and Philip.
  Ex. Abraham Hoover. Twp. omitted.

4 Oct. 1803   15 March 1806
CLOPPER, LEONARD
  (This should be KLOPPER.) Wife. (name omitted). Children:
Susanna, Magdalena and Eva.
  Ex. Peter Good. Earl Twp.

8 Aug. 1800   27 March 1805
CRAWFORD, WILLIAM
  Wife. Margaret Crawford. Children: John, Alexander,
Elizabeth wife of Robert Rea and Mary wife of James Donaldson.
Sons-in-law: Nathaniel Lightner and Jacob Linton (wives' names
not stated). Grandchild: Crawford W. Linton.
  Ex. Thomas Lyon and John Crawford. Leacock Twp.

25 Aug. 1806   27 Sept. 1806
CULBERT, MOSES
  Bros.: John, Samuel and James Culbert. Sister: Rebecca
Culbert.
  Ex. William Wright. Conestoga Twp.

8 June 1804   28 Nov. 1806
COULTER, HUGH
  Children: Nathaniel, Isabella, Agness, Mary and John.
  Ex. John Coulter and Robert McCalmont. Bart Twp.

14 Jan. 1805   16 April 1806
CLINGAN, JAMES
     Wife. Nancy Clingan. Child: Thomas. N.B. There was a
former wife and children, names and number of children not
stated.
     Ex. Henry Brineman. Donegal Twp.

15 Jan. 1798   25 April 1826
CELLEN, CLAUS
     (This should be KELLEN.) Wife. Elizabeth Kellen. Children:
John, Christian and Henry.
     Ex. Elizabeth Kellen and William Lahnius. Warwick Twp.

27 Dec. 1793   26 Sept. 1807
CAROLUS, JOHN
     Wife. Elizabeth Carolus. Children: Mary, Francis, George
and John.
     Ex. Elizabeth Carolus. Lancaster Borough.

25 Feb. 1806   2 April 1808
COHN, JOHN
     (This should be KOHN.) Wife. Anna Kohn. Children: the
names and number not given.
     Ex. Christian Sherrer and Abraham Longenecker. Rapho Twp.

29 Oct. 1807   23 May 1808
CLEMSON, JOHN
     Wife. (name omitted). Children: Thomas, James, Joseph,
Hannah, Elizabeth, Mary, Sarah, Rachel, Sophia and Susanna wife
of Samuel Mickle.
     Ex. Thomas and James Clemson. Salsbury Twp.

23 Feb. 1809   25 March 1809
CAMPBELL, DANIEL
     Children: Mary, Richard, Daniel and John.
     Ex. James Crawford and William Daniel. Lampeter Twp.

10 Aug. 1805   31 March 1810
CRAIG, AGNESS
     Legatees: (nephew) Richard Crain, (niece) Agness and
(nephew) James Humes. N.B. There was a bequest to the English
Presbyterian Church of Lancaster.
     Ex. Richard Crain and James Humes. Lancaster Borough.

27 March 1810   2 May 1810
COLLINS, CORNELIUS
     Wife. Ann Collins. Children: Anna and Mary. Bros.: James
and David. Sister: Esther.
     Ex. Ann Collins and Joseph Hutchinson. Bart Twp.

17 Oct. 1810   24 Nov. 1810
CAMPBELL, ROBERT
     Legatees: Isaac Funston (of Colebrook Furnace) and John
Reigart.
     Ex. David McMackin and Robert Coleman. Mt. Joy Twp.

11 July 1807   12 Oct. 1811
CHESNUT, HENRY
    (This should be CHESNEY.) Wife. Hannah Chesney.
    Ex. Hannah Chesney. Leacock Twp.

23 Dec. 1801   19 Nov. 1811
CAHEY, FRANCIS
    Wife. Jean Cahey. Children: John, Eley, Jean and Elizabeth.
    Ex. John Cahey. Bart Twp.

5 Oct. 1811   26 Nov. 1811
CARPENTER, JACOB
    Bros.: Henry and Daniel.
    Ex. Henry and Daniel Carpenter. Lancaster Borough.

7 Sept. 1811   2 Nov. 1811
CROH, CHRISTIAN
    (This should be GROH.) Wife. Barbara Groh. Children: Anna
wife of Andrew Kauffman, John Christian, Barbara wife of
Christian Gute and Mary.
    Ex. Benjamin Miller and John Groh. Donegal Twp.

19 Aug. 1807   19 May 1812
CONRAD, DANIEL
    Wife. Barbara Conrad. Children: Jacob, Catharine, George,
Michael, John, Daniel, Frederick, Peter, Henry and Theobold.
    Ex. Henry Gileford. Mt. Joy Twp.

14 Aug. 1809   4 Jan. 1812
CUNKLE, CHRISTIAN
    (This should be KUNKLE.) Children: Henry, Barbara,
Christina, Elizabeth wife of Daniel Eckman, George, Peter and
Jacob.
    Ex. Peter Sides. Bart Twp.

15 March 1810 8 April 1812
CANN, JOHN
    (This should be KANN.) Children: Anna, Catharine wife of
Conrad Stormfels and Peter. Grandchildren: John, Elizabeth and
Philip (last names not given).
    Ex. Henry Kann and Conrad Stormfels. Lancaster Borough.

4 April 1812   24 Feb. 1813
CRIDER, HENRY
    Wife. Magdalena Crider. Child: Susanna wife of David
Burkholder.
    Ex. Magdalena and Tobias Crider. Lampeter Twp.

9 Oct. 1812   26 March 1813
COOPER, REBECCA
    Children: James, John, William, Jeremiah, Ann and Rebecca.
Grandchild: Hannah Cooper (parents' names not given).
    Ex. John Moore and John Cooper. Sadsbury Twp.

22 March 1813   3 May 1813
CALDWELL, OLIVER
    Child: James.
    Ex. Stephen Boyd and Timothy Hains. Little Britton Twp.

1 Dec. 1812   27 Aug. 1813
CAMPBELL, ROBERT
    Children: Martha, Elizabeth, Ann and Mary. Son-in-law:
Alexander Ewing (wife's name not stated). Grandchildren:
Sinclear Ewing, Andrew, William and Margaret Ferguson (parents'
names not given).
    Ex. Alexander Ewing and Martha Campbell. Little Britton
Twp.

28 Sept. 1813 22 Aug. 1814
CROW, ALEXANDER
    Sisters: Mary, Anna and Jean. Bros.: Daniel, William and
James.
    Ex. Jacob Miller. Twp. omitted.

10 April 1814   16 April 1814
CASTER, BENJAMIN
    Legatees: Daniel, Samuel and Dietrich.
    Ex. Henry Dietrich. Manheim Twp.

26 Feb. 1815   11 March 1815
CARPENTER, ABRAHAM
    Wife. Salome Carpenter. Children: Henry, John, Mary,
Harriet, Matilda and Susanna wife of William C. Frazer.
    Ex. John and Henry Carpenter. Strasburg Twp.

2 Dec. 1815   23 Jan. 1816
CROSS, GEORGE
    Wife. Sarah Cross. Children: George and Elizabeth.
    Ex. Martin R. Nailor and John Reis. Manheim Twp.

--- 1816   3 March 1817
CAMPBILL, PATRICK
    Nieces: Isabella Knox and Eleanor Wallace (children of
Robert Wallace). Legatee: Samuel Stevenson and others.
    Ex. Samuel Stevenson. Martic Twp.

17 Sept. 1817 30 Oct. 1817
CLEPPER, JOSEPH
    Wife. Anne Clepper. Children: John and Joseph.
    Ex. Christian Peck and Henry Haines. Donegal Twp.

6 Oct. 1815   3 Nov. 1817
CLEMENS, GEORGE
    Wife. Elizabeth Clemens. Children: Abraham, Christian,
George, Catharine wife of George Sheaffer and Mary wife of Peter
Emmery.
    Ex. George Schaeffer and Peter Emmery. Salsbury Twp.

22 Jan. 1817   5 July 1817
CREAMER, SOLOMON
    Wife. Mary Creamer. Children: Matilda, Harriet and Salome.
N.B. This will is not entered on Records, but is on file in
office.
    Ex. Mary Creamer. Martic Twp.

17 April 1809   18 March 1818
CANN, ADAM
    Wife. Sabina Cann.
    Ex. Sabina Cann. Lancaster Borough.

13 March 1814   6 April 1818
CLARK, WILLIAM
    Bros.: John and Brice Clark.
    Ex. John Clark. Donegal Twp.

4 May 1816   27 April 1818
COBLE, JOHN
    Wife. Barbara Coble.
    Ex. Christian Longnecker, Jacob Root and Thomas Eagan.
Donegal Twp.

17 Aug. 1819   23 Nov. 1819
CRALL, CATHARINE
    Children: Jacob, John, Joseph, Magdalena, Elizabeth and
Catharine.
    Ex. John Sybert. Manheim Twp.

7 March 1785   7 March 1786
DAVIS, WILLIAM
    Legatees: John McCay, James Beaty, (his wife) Jean Beaty and
others.
    Ex. John McCay. Little Britton Twp.

--- 7 Nov. 1786
DANNER, ABRAHAM
    N.B. This is a German will, and not copied on records. The
origial records are lost.
    Ex. ---. Lampeter Twp.

17 Dec. 1781   18 Aug. 1787
DENLINGER, JACOB
    Wife. Anna Derlinger. Children: John, Abraham, Christian and
Jacob.
    Ex. John and Christian Denlinger. Lampeter Twp.

31 Jan. 1788   7 May 1789
DOWNING, WILLIAM
    Wife. Margaret Downing. Children: Samuel, William, Thomas,
Hannah wife of Andrew Daniel, Jean wife of Andrew Moore and Ruth
wife of Jesse Falkner.
    Ex. Samuel and William Downing. Bart Twp.

12 Aug. 1786   9 April 1788
DAVIS, ZACCHEUS
        Children: Zaccheus, Jenkin, Dinah, Sarah, Ann wife of Willis
Davis, Elizabeth and Hannah.
        Ex. Zaccheus and Willis Davis and Thomas Carter. Earl Twp.

30 Oct. 1780   26 April 1788
DISE, JOHN
        Wife. Elizabeth Dise. Child: Peter. Step-son: John Ressler.
        Ex. Elizabeth Dise and John Ressler. Breaknock Twp.

3 Sept. 1788   15 April 1789
DANTZ, SIMON
        Wife. Sarah Dantz. Children: Elizabeth and Mary.
        Ex. Jacob Kickaegger. Warwick Twp.

7 Aug. 1788   8 Sept. 1789
DIEFENDERFER, MICHAEL
        Wife. Christina Diefenderfer. Children: Michael, Daniel,
Margaret wife of Jacob Fortince, David, Peter, Philip, George and
Ludwick.
        Ex. Christina Diefenderfer and Mathias Young. Lancaster
Borough.

30 March 1787 7 Aug. 1790
DEHUFF, CATHARINE
        Children: John, Susanna wife of --- Stone, Abraham, Henry
and Mathias. Grandchildren: Susanna Dehuff (child of John) and
Susanna Weiss (parents' names not given).
        Ex. Abraham and Henry Dehuff. Lancaster Borough.

8 Nov. 1788   23 Feb. 1791
DOYLE, THOMAS
        Wife. Elizabeth Doyle. Children: Prudence, Nancy and
Elizabeth. Sons-in-law: Thomas Cullon and Robert Gray (wifes'
names not stated). Grandchildren: Elizabeth and Nancy Cullon and
Thomas and John Doyle (parents' names not given).
        Ex. John Carrot, Prudence and Elizabeth Doyle. Lancaster
Borough.

3 June 1790   3 May 1791
DAVIS, WILLIAM
        Wife. Sarah Davis. Children: Willis, Hannah wife of John
Willis, Samuel, Thomas, Sarah wife of Joshua Kittera, William,
James and Elizabeth wife of David McClure.
        Ex. William Davis and William Smith. Earl Twp.

1 Nov. 1791   18 Jan. 1792
DILLER, ADAM
        Wife. Elizabeth Diller. Children: Margaret, Catharine,
Susanna and Elizabeth.
        Ex. Elizabeth Diller and Adam Brown. Earl Twp.

25 Sept. 1792 2 Feb. 1793
DAVIS, MARY

Child: Sarah. Grandchildren: James Douglass; Mary Weaver; Mary Jones; Edward and John Davis; John, James, William and Robert Good (parents' names not given).
Ex. John Zell and David Jenkins. Caernarvon Twp.

4 Jan. 1793   9 April 1793
DUCK, NICHOLAS
Wife. (name omitted). Children: Jacob (there were others, names and number not given).
Ex. George Duck. Earl Twp.

25 April 1793   2 June 1793
DAVIS, ZACHAUS
Bro.: Jenkins. Sisters: Anne wife of Willis Davis, Dinah wife of Thomas Kannaday, Mary wife of --- Park, Sarah wife of --- Ferree, Elizabeth wife of Thomas Carter and Hannah wife of John Gordon.
Ex. Gabriel Davis and William Smith. Earl Twp.

17 Feb. 1794   26 Feb. 1794
DERSTLER, ADAM
Children: Adam, Michael, Barbara and Elizabeth. N.B. There was a bequest to Evangelic Lutheran Church, Lancaster.
Ex. Michael Derstler and John Shock. Manor Twp.

10 Sept. 1793   28 June 1794
DOUGLASS, THOMAS
Sister: Jane Davis. N.B. There was a bequest of £50 to St. Johns Episcopal Church, Pequea, Lancaster Co.
Ex. Gabriel Davis and John Wilson. Salsbury Twp.

28 April 1795   1 May 1795
DECKER, HANNETTA
Legatte: Edward Powel.
Ex. Edward Powel [Porvel?]. Lancaster Borough.

20 June 1795   24 Aug. 1795
DIFFENDEFER, CHRISTIAN
Children: Peter, Ludwick and Philip. Grandson: William (son of Peter).
Ex. Philip Diffenderfer. Lancaster Borough.

24 April 1792   25 Feb. 1797
DAVIS, ELIZABETH
Children: Sarah, Richard and Isaac. Grandchild: William Wallace (parents' names not given).
Ex. Isaac Davis. Earl Twp.

2 May 1797   18 July 1797
DARWARD, MARTIN
Wife. Mary Darward. Children: Martin, Jonas, John, Adam, George, Henry, Jacob, Philip and Michael.
Ex. Mary Darward. Lancaster Borough.

--- (omitted) --- 1797
DAVIS, MARY BARBARA
     Legatees: Her parents and sister, names not given.
     Ex. (omitted). Twp. omitted

21 Jan. 1797   14 Oct. 1800
DICKINSON, GAUIS
     Wife. Mary Dickinson. Children: Nathaniel, Joseph, Daniel,
Isaac, James, Esther, Elizabeth, Rebecca, Mary and Deborah.
     Ex. Nathaniel and James Dickinson. Salsbury Twp.

21 April 1800   15 Dec. 1800
DOSH, GEORGE
     Step-daughters: Eve wife of --- Groe and Magdalena wife of
John Miller. Step-son: Peter Klein. Catharine (child of Eve) wife
of Jacob Witmer.
     Ex. Jacob Witmer. Lancaster Borough.

24 Nov. 1800   8 Dec. 1800
DEHUFF, HENRY
     Children: Henry, Elizabeth wife of Daniel Oesterlein,
Catharine wife of --- Ehrenzeller, Mary wife of Thomas Lyons,
Sarah and Rebecca.
     Ex. Henry Dehuff. Lancaster Borough.

8 Sept. 1801   30 Dec. 1801
DIERDORF, ABRAHAM
     Children: Henry, John, Jacob, Abraham and Elizabeth wife of
Jacob Wolf.
     Ex. George Weidman and John Dierdorf. Warwick Twp.

11 April 1802   5 May 1802
DAWSON, ROBERT
     Wife. Lydia Harriet Dawson. Sisters: Elizabeth wife of
Thomas Kennedy and Ann. Bro.: John. Half-bro.: Thomas Dawson.
     Ex. William Kirkpatrick, William Pool and John Moore. Late
of the Parish Lisburn, Antrim Co., north of Ireland, but now of
the Borough of Lancaster.

1 March 1802   21 May 1802
DANIEL, ANDREW
     Wife. Hannah Daniel. Children: Margaret, William, Jane,
Hannah and Robert.
     Ex. Hannah and William Daniel. Bart Twp.

--- 1801   3 Dec. 1803
DAMBACH, ADAM
     Wife. Susanna Dambach. Children: Barbara, Susanna and Adam.
     Ex. John Miller and Philip Shissler. Manor Twp.

9 Oct. 1796   25 June 1800
DANNENBERY, DAVID
     (This should be TANNENBERY.) Children: David, Anna, Rosina
and Maria wife of John Bachman. Sons-in-law: William Cassler and
John Shropp (wives' names not stated).

46

        Ex. John Shropp and William Cassler. Warwick Twp.

8 May 1804   11 June 1804
DITZ, CHRISTIAN
        Wife. Juliana Ditz. Children: Christian, Dorothea and
Catharine.
        Ex. Christian Ditz and John Lapp. Caernaroon Twp.

11 Aug. 1801   6 Feb. 1806
DIFFENDERFER, EVE
        Widow of Philip Diffenderfer. Sisters: Elizabeth wife of
Christopher Reidel and Catharine.
        Ex. (omitted). Twp. omitted.

31 Dec. 1805   26 Feb. 1806
DIFFENDERFER, PHILIP
        Wife. Eve Diffenderfer. Bros.: George, Michael, Peter and
David. Sister: Margaret wife of Jacob Fordney.
        Ex. Mathias Yound, Philip Gleninger and John Landis.
Lancaster Borough.

12 Sept. 1806   18 Oct. 1806
DRUCKENMILLER, JACOB
        Wife. Elizabeth Druckenmiller. Children: Jacob, John, Lewis,
Emanuel, Catharine and George.
        Ex. Elizabeth and Jacob Druckenmiller. Manheim Twp.

16 April 1802   8 Sept. 1807
DOWNING, MARGARET
        Sister: Rachel wife of Andrew Moore. N.B. There were
numerous legatees, their relationship not stated.
        Ex. John Moore. Bart Twp.

2 May 1808   18 July 1808
DEHUFF, HENRY
        Wife. Elizabeth Dehuff. Children: Henry and Rebecca.
Sisters: Elizabeth wife of Daniel Oesterlein, Catharine wife of
Sebastian Salade, Mary, Salome wife of Joseph Cassaline and
Rebecca. Bro.-in-law: Isaac Wampoole of Philadelphia.
        Ex. John Eberman and Sebastian Salade. Lancaster Borough.

26 Oct. 1808   11 Sept. 1809
DAVIS, ANNA
        Child: Sarah wife of Thomas Foster. Grandchild: Ann Foster.
        Ex. Joseph Thombury. Lancaster Borough.

16 Nov. 1808   10 Jan. 1809
DURNBACK, JOHN
        Wife. Mary Durnback. Children: John, Jacob (and three
others, names not given).
        Ex. Mary Durnback, Samuel Mellinger and George Buckholder.
Cocalico Twp.

16 Feb. 1810   24 April 1810
DEALING, JACOB

Uncle: Andrew Graff.
Ex. John Graff. Lancaster Borough.

10 Jan. 1810   5 May 1810
DANAR, CHRISTIAN
    Wife. Catharina Danar. Children: Adam and Anna wife of John
Wagoner.
    Ex. Jacob Hochstatter and Dietrich Buhler. Rapho Twp.

28 Nov. 1810   15 Jan. 1811
DRITCH, CHARLES
    (This should be FRITCH.) Wife. Justina Fritch. Children:
Magdalena, Catharine, William, John, Philip and Eve.
    Ex. William Fritch and John Frymeyer. Cocalico Twp.

6 Jan. 1811   4 Feb. 1811
DICKINSON, JOSEPH
    Wife. Elizabeth Dickinson. Children: Elizabeth, Hannah,
Margaret, Phebe, Mary, Joseph and Henry.
    Ex. Joseph and Henry Dickinson. Sadsbury Twp.

15 April 1811   9 May 1811
DAMPMAN, JOHN
    Wife. Catharine Dampman. Children: Margaret, Peter and John.
    Ex. Catharine and Peter Dampman. Cocalico Twp.

19 Jan. 1810   7 Jan. 1812
DOOM, JACOB
    Child: Peter.
    Ex. Jonas Witwer. Earl Twp.

1 May 1804   16 Feb. 1813
DAVIS, GABRIEL
    Children: Juliana, Archibald, Jean, George and John. Son-in-
law: Joseph Jones (wife's name omitted).
    Ex. John Davis and Joseph Jones. Twp. omitted

--- --- [ca. 1814]
DIETRICH, PHILIP
    This will was vaccated, therefore not recorded.

23 Oct. 1814   25 March 1815
DICK, ANNA MARGARET
    Children: Philipina wife of John Becker, Lenhart, Jacob and
William.
    Ex. William Dick. Lancaster Twp.

14 Nov. 1804   8 Dec. 1817
DITERICH, LORENZ
    Wife. Magdalena Diterich. Children: John, Michael, Lorentz,
Catharine and Maria.
    Ex. Magdalena Diterich. Lancaster Borough.

17 Nov. 1815   13 Dec. 1815
DAVIS, WALTER

Wife. Elizabeth Davis. Children: Jane, Nancy and Joseph.
Son-in-law: John Davis (wife's name not given).
Ex. John and Jane Davis. Bart Twp.

10 April 1811   3 May 1816
DRAGER, JACOB
(This should be TRAGER.) Wife. Maria Trager. Children:
Elizabeth, Maria wife of John Gochenower, Anna and Catharine wife
of John Barr.
Ex. John Gochenower and John Barr. Martic Twp.

28 May 1815   7 Jan. 1817
DANNER, GODLIEB
Wife. Agness Danner. The names and number of children not
given.
Ex. Michael Danner and John Sensenig. Earl Twp.

16 Oct. 1816   14 Jan. 1817
DILLER, PETER
Wife. Elizabeth Diller. Children: Samuel, Roland, Solomon,
Levi, Elizabeth wife of John Luther, Maria wife of Henry Shirk,
Catharine and Lydia wife of Peter Filbert.
Ex. Henry Roland, Elizabeth and Samuel Diller. Newholland
Twp.

10 Aug. 1816   8 April 1818
DENLINGER, JACOB
Children: Joseph, Jacob and John. Grandchildren: Magdalena,
Barbara and Elizabeth Shaub (parents' names not stated).
Ex. Jacob Denlinger and Jacob Denlinger Jr. Lampeter Twp.

4 Nov. 1816   29 May 1818
DICKENSON, MARY
Children: Nathaniel, Joseph, Daniel, Isaac, James, Esther,
Rebecca, Mary, Deberah and Elizabeth wife of --- Turman. Son-in-
law: Thomas Pasmore (wife's name not stated). Grandchildren:
Sarah wife of Warrick Miller, Rachel wife of Jesse Moor, Rebecca
and Elizabeth (all children of Elizabeth).
Ex. Thomas Pasmore and James Turman. Salsbury Twp.

9 April 1817   12 Sept. 1818
DEMUTH, CHRISTOPHER
Wife. Elizabeth Demuth. Children: Mary wife of John Eberman,
John and Jacob.
Ex. William Eberman and Benjamin D. Gill. Lancaster Borough.

5 April 1808   16 Oct. 1818
DIFFENDERFER, JOHN
Wife. Eve Diffenderfer. Children: Benjamin, Samuel, John,
Eve wife of Jacob Holl, Margaret wife of Joel Carpenter, Mary
wife of Martin Brown, Salome wife of Henry Holl, Sophia wife of
Henry Road and Judith wife of John Ruddy. Grandchildren: Samuel
and Emanuel Ruddy.
Ex. Benjamin Diffenderfer and Mathias Sherck. Earl Twp.

8 April 1819   15 May 1819
DENLINGER, ABRAHAM
    Children: Elizabeth, Barbara, Nancy, Christian, Henry,
Abraham, John, Esther, Susanna and Martin.
    Ex. Jacob Denlinger and Christian Neff. Lampeter Twp.

4 Aug. 1818   6 Dec. 1819
DREISH, ADAM
    (This should be TREISH.) Wife. Magdalena Treish. Children:
(there were six, names not given).
    Ex. Adam Treish and Henry Treish. Elizabeth Twp.

30 July 1781   27 Feb. 1786
ELSER, PETER
    Children: Adam, George, Peter, John, Margaret and Christina.
    Ex. George Eichelberger and Christian Eby. Warwick Twp.

31 Dec. 1785   1 March 1786
EWING, PATRICK
    Wife. Elizabeth Ewing. Child: Alexander.
    Ex. Thomas Whiteside, John and Robert Johnson. Little
Britton Twp.

15 Jan. 1785   21 Oct. 1786
ENSMENGER, NICHOLAS
    Wife. Margaret Ensmenger. Children: Nicholas, Christian,
Ludwick, Elizabeth, Catharine, Mary and Margaret. Son-in-law:
Adam Oberlin (wife's name not given). Grandchildren: Catharine,
Mary and Margaret (last name not given).
    Ex. Adam Oberlin. Cocalico Twp.

14 Feb. 1786   26 March 1787
ESHLEMAN, ANNA
    Children: Benjamin, David, John, Ann wife of Peter Resh,
Frena wife of John Muley, Elizabeth wife of George Kendrick,
Barbara wife of Abraham Herr and Mary wife of Richard Burk.
Grandchild: Ann Resh.
    Ex. Michael Shenck and John Musser. Conestoga Twp.

18 Jan. 1787   20 Feb. 1787
ENCK, JACOB
    Wife. Catharine Enck. Children: John, Mary, Margaret, Jacob,
Catharine, Barbara and Elizabeth.
    Ex. Catharine and John Enck. Warwick Twp.

11 July 1787   31 July 1787
ECKSTEIN, CHRISTIAN
    Sisters: Magdalena wife of --- Weaver, Elizabeth and Barbara
Eckstein. Nephew & nieces: John, Barbara, Catharine and Betsey
Weaver. N.B. There was a bequest made to the "Society of Bathania
and Saron" in Cocalico Twp., followers of "Conrad Beisel, Seventh
Day Sabbath".
    Ex. Benjamin Bowman and Peter Fahnstick. Cocalico Twp.

50

28 Jan. 1783   7 Sept. 1788
ERFORT, ANTHONY
    Wife. Anna M. Erfort. Children: Anna, Dewalt, Catharine,
John, Barbara, Jacob, Henry and Frederick.
    Ex. Anna Maria Erfort and John Erfort. Hempfield Twp.

27 May 1788   11 Feb. 1789
EICHELBERGER, GEORGE MICHAEL
    Wife. Christina Eichelberger. Children: George, Barbara,
Margaret and Catharine. Son-in-law: Michael Zartman (wife's name
not stated).
    Ex. Christina Eichelberger and Michael Zartman. Twp.
omitted.

20 April 1787   4 Aug. 1789
EUTENEYER, JACOB
    Wife. Anna Maria Euteneyer. Children: Christiana, Betsey,
Catharine, Sally, Jacob, Polly and Susy.
    Ex. Anna M. Euteneyer and Christian App. Lancaster Borough.

12 July 1787   18 Sept. 1789
ERNST, HERMAN
    Wife. Catharine Ernst.
    Ex. Catharine Ernst and Peter Eby. Warwick Twp.

1 March 1790   28 Aug. 1790
ECKMAN, HENRY
    Children: Peter, Henry, Catharine and Elizabeth.
    Ex. Peter and Henry Eckman. Lampeter Twp.

8 Nov. 1788   9 Sept. 1790
EDWARDS, JOHN
    Wife. Sarah Edwards. Child: Dinah wife of William Smith.
Grandchildren: William & Edward Smith (children of Dinah) and
John Edwards Long (parents' names not given).
    Ex. Sarah Edwards and Joshua Evans. Earl Twp.

16 June 1792   16 Nov. 1792
ERISMAN, JACOB
    Wife. Elizabeth Erisman. Children: Christian, Jacob,
Abraham, John, Ottilia wife of Henry Strickler, Esther and Mary
wife of Abraham Brubacher.
    Ex. Christian and Jacob Erisman. Rapho Twp.

7 Jan. 1793   27 Nov. 1793
ERHARD, CHRISTIAN
    Children: Jacob, Christian, Mary wife of John Huber,
Elizabeth and Catharine. Son-in-law: Jacob Judy (wife's name not
stated).
    Ex. Jacob Erhard and Samuel Ensminger. Rapho Twp.

1 May 1790   14 Dec. 1793
EVERSOHL, JACOB
    Wife. Catharine Eversohl. Children: Jacob, John, Magdalena,
Benjamin, Susanna, Maria, Elizabeth and Ann.

Ex. Jacob Eversohl and John Lonegnecker. Donegal Twp.

5 Jan. 1794   25 Jan. 1794
ESHLEMAN, JACOB
    Wife. Elizabeth Eshleman. Children: Jacob (there were
others, names and number not given).
    Ex. Christian Stouffer and Joseph Musser. Manor Twp.

1 Feb. 1794   19 Feb. 1794
EDWARDS, THOMAS
    Wife. Susanna Edwards.
    Ex. Susanna Edwards, John Smith and Jacob Grael[Grall?].
Lancaster borough.

21 March 1793   13 June 1794
EBY, JACOB
    Wife. Hannah Eby. Children: Peter, Joseph, Benjamin, Jacob,
Elizabeth, Magdalena, Barbara, Anna and Christian.
    Ex. Anna, Christian, Joseph and Daniel Eby. Leacock Twp.

9 July 1790   21 July 1794
EVERSOLE, SALOME
    Children: Yost, Christian, Jacob, Abraham, Peter, Feronica,
Elizabeth and Salome wife of Frederick Sauser. Son-in-law:
Christian Brand (wife's name not given).
    Ex. Christian Brand. Rapho Twp.

26 June 1793   6 Sept. 1794
EBY, PETER
    Children: Peter, Samuel, Henry, Andrew, John, David,
Christian and Anna wife of Abraham Wenger.
    Ex. Peter and Samuel Eby. Leacock Twp.

4 May 1794   9 Jan. 1795
ELLIOT, JOSEPH
    Wife. (name omitted). Children: Ruth wife of Robert Watson,
John, Elizabeth wife of John Murry, Ann wife of Isaac Griffith
and Eleanor wife of George Gibson.
    Ex. Isaac Taylor and Asahel Walker. Sadsbury Twp.

28 Nov. 1792   20 April 1795
ESHLEMAN, BENEDICT
    Wife. Elizabeth Eshleman. Children: Benedict, John, Ann wife
of Christian Nolb, Henry, Martin, Barbara, Jacob and David.
    Ex. Christian Shenck and Abraham Miller. Conestoga Twp.

22 July 1795   29 Aug. 1795
ECKMAN, HENRY
    Wife. Catharine Eckman. Children: Elizabeth and Catharine.
    Ex. Catharine Eckman and Henry Diffenbach. Lampeter Twp.

25 May 1793   23 March 1796
EVANS, AMOS
    Wife. Christiana Evans. Children: Ruth, Susanna and Joshua.
Grandchild: Philip Evans (parents' name not given).

Ex. Joshua Evans. Salsbury Twp.

27 April 1796   30 June 1796
ECKMAN, ELIZABETH
     Bros.: Henry and Peter Eckman.
     Ex. Peter Eckman. Lancaster Borough.

2 Nov. 1789   --- 1796
ECKMAN, BARBARA
     Widow of Hieronimus Eckman. Children: John, Barbara wife of
Jacob Stoutseberg, Eve wife of John Bushum, Heironimus, Esther
wife of George Cunkle, Martin, Jacob and Magdalena.
     Ex. John Eckman. Bart Twp.

22 April 1795   12 May 1796
ECKSTEIN, ELIZABETH
     Sisters: Barbara Eckstein and Magdalena wife of --- Weaver.
N.B. There was a bequest to the Sisterhood at Ephrata.
     Ex. Peter Fahnstock, Zenobia Stettler and Sophia Funk.
Ephrata Twp.

2 Aug. 1797   --- 1797
ECKSTEIN, BARBARA
     Sister: Magdalena Weaver. Nephews and nieces: John,
Elizabeth, Conrad, Catharine and Barbara Weaver (children of
Magdalena).
     Ex. John Weaver and Daniel Lester. Cocalico Twp.

20 Jan. 1798   28 Feb. 1798
ERVINS, JOHN
     Children: James, John and David.
     Ex. James and David Ervins. Drumore Twp.

11 May 1789   17 Sept. 1798
EVANS, NATHAN
     Bros.: David and John.
     Ex. John and David Evans. Caernarvon Twp.

21 Aug. 1798   20 Sept. 1798
ENTRICAN (ANTRICAN), SAMUEL
     Wife. Mary Entrican. Children: James, William, Elizabeth
wife of Michael Humes and Mary wife of James Whiteside.
Grandchildren: Samuel Entrican (son of William), Samuel Humes
(son of Elizabeth) and Samuel Entrican (son of James).
     Ex. William Antrican. Little Britton Twp.

1 May 1794   --- 1799
EVANS, MARY
     Widow of Nathan Evans, Children: Nathan and Jacob.
     Ex. Jacob Fox and William Smith. Earl Twp.

10 Dec. 1795   22 June 1799
ELLENBERGER, FERONICA
     Children: Eve, Anne and Ulrick. Sons-in-law: Christian
Ellenberger and Christian Kaufman (wives' names not stated).

Ex. Christian Ellenberger and Christian Kaufman. Manor Twp.

25 July 1799   10 Sept. 1799
ECKMAN, PETER
    Wife. Elizabeth Eckman. Children: Esther and Henry.
    Ex. John Eckman and Henry Lefever. Lampeter Twp.

18 Oct. 1796   21 Oct. 1799
ENGLE, ULRICH
    Wife. Magdalena Engle. Children: Ann wife of Christian
Shelly, Barbara wife of Henry Forrey, Christiana wife of John
Wisler, Magdalena, Mary and Susanna. Grandchildren: Jacob,
Magdalena, Elizabeth, Mary and Christiana Shelly.
    Ex. Henry Forrey and John Wisler. Donegal Twp.

4 March 1801   2 May 1801
EBERMAN, GODLIEB
    Wife. Elizabeth Eberman. Children: May, Jacob and Abraham.
    Ex. Elizabeth Eberman and Peter Walter. Lancaster Borough.

18 March 1800   23 Oct. 1801
EVANS, JAMES
    Wife. Elizabeth Evans. Children: William, James, John,
Nathan and Caleb.
    Ex. Elizabeth and William Evans. Caernarvon Twp.

6 Jan. 1801   12 Dec. 1801
EVANS, JOHN
    Wife. Mary Evans. Children: Nathan, John, David, Mary and
Elizabeth. Grandchild: John Evans (son of David).
    Ex. John Evans. Caernarvon Twp.

25 Oct. 1800   12 May 1802
ESHLEMAN, ULRICH
    Wife. Catharine Eshleman. Children: Anna, Barbara, Abraham,
Elizabeth, John, Catharine, Jacob and Peter.
    Ex. Christian Hershey. Warwick Twp.

9 March 1802   2 Oct. 1802
ENGLE, JOHN
    Wife. Catharine Engle. Children: Peter, Catharine, Marchia,
Elizabeth and Susanna.
    Ex. Catharine Engle and Martin Obernoltzer. Earl Twp.

5 Oct. 1790   11 Nov. 1802
EDWARDS, SARAH
    Children: Dinah (names of other children not given).
Grandchildren: Mary Henderson; Sarah, Margaret, Lydia and Rebecca
Smith.
    Ex. Grabriel Davis. Earl Twp.

8 Jan. 1803   30 March 1803
ESHLEMAN, CHRISTIAN

Wife. Elizabeth Eshleman. Children: Abraham, Christian, Elizabeth, Catharine wife of George Kapps, Rosina wife of George Slabach and Maria wife of Nicholas Mosser.
Ex. Wendel Threaemer and John Bear. Brecknock Twp.

--- 21 Nov. 1803
ELLENBERGER, BARBARA
N.B. This is a German will, and the translation is lost.
Ex. Christian Hershey and Benjamin Hershey.

19 April 1802   31 July 1804
ETTER, MARGARET
Child: Catety wife of Jacob Musselman.
Ex. Jacob Musselman. Mt. Joy Twp.

26 June 1804   31 July 1804
EHRHART, JACOB
Wife. Susanna Ehrhart. Children: (the names and number not given).
Ex. Alexander Zartman. Twp. not given.

13 March 1804   3 March 1804
ERB, JOSEPH
Wife. Barbara Erb. Child: Maria.
Ex. John Erb. Warwick Twp.

30 Dec. 1800   16 May 1804
EPPLER, MARIA
Brother: David Eppler. Sister: Ann Eppler.
Ex. Peter Becker and Christian Becker. Warwick Twp.

31 May 1804   24 July 1804
EDWARDS, SUSANNA
Children: Henry, Susanna, Elizabeth and John.
Ex. Henry Edwards and Jacob Graeff. Lancaster Borough.

22 Nov. 1804   12 March 1805
EBY, CHRISTIAN
Wife. Christiana Eby. Children: Isaac, Mary wife of George Bear and John. Grandchildren: John, Susanna wife of John Hart, Elizabeth, Theodorus and Mary Eby (parents' names not given).
Ex. Isaac Eby and George Bear. Leacock Twp.

5 Oct. 1805   25 Nov. 1805
ERNST, JOHN F.
Wife. Elizabeth Ernst. Children: Elizabeth, Margaret, John, William, Christiana and Maria.
Ex. Elizabeth Ernst and Elizabeth Ernst Jr. Manheim Twp.

11 March 1806   31 March 1806
ECKMAN, JACOB
Children: Daniel, Jacob, Mary, Elizabeth, Magdalena, John and Susan wife of George Sides.
Ex. Peter and Daniel Eckman. Strasburg Twp.

20 Jan. 1806   24 Feb. 1806
ECKMAN, HENRY
     Wife. Elizabeth Eckman. Children: Magdalena, Christian,
Henry, Juliana, Simon and Susey.
     Ex. John Lingh and John Albert. Mt. Joy Twp.

18 Oct. 1805   3 Jan. 1806
EBERMAN, JOHN
     Wife. Mary Eberman. Children: Dorothea, John, Philip, Mary
wife of John Todd, Hannah wife of Ernst Theodore Benoit,
Elizabeth wife of Peter Sugar, Philipina wife of Henry Dehuff and
Godlieb. Grandchildren: Mary and Jacob Eberman (children of
Godlieb).
     Ex. Peter Sugar, Philip and John Eberman. Lancaster Borough.

8 Dec. 1805   15 March 1806
ESHLEMAN, ELIZABETH
     Bro. Christian Eshleman. Sisters: Maria Masser, Rosina
Sleback and Catharine Copbles.
     Ex. Abraham Eshleman. Brecknock Twp.

5 Jan. 1805   20 June 1806
ENK, CATHARINE
     Children: Elizabeth (and two others, names not stated).
     Ex. Nicholas Lutz and Elizabeth Enk. Manheim Twp.

5 Feb. 1804   27 Aug. 1806
ELLIOTT, ANNE
     Children: Ruth, Elizabeth and Ellinger.
     Ex. Robert Moore. Sadsbury Twp.

9 Sept. 1807   2 Dec. 1807
EBY, CHRISTIAN
     Wife. Catharine Eby. Children: John, Christian, Mary wife of
Jacob Brubacher, Andrew and Benjamin. Son-in-law: Jacob Wissler
(wife's name not given.)
     Ex. Christian and John Eby. Warwick Twp.

3 Jan. 1807   25 Feb. 1807
EBERLY, JACOB
     Wife. Anna Eberly. Children: Elizabeth, Anna, Susanna,
Samuel, Joseph, Jacob, John and David.
     Ex. David Eberly and Peter Martin. Cocalico Twp.

7 May 1807   9 June 1807
ESHLEMAN, ISAAC
     Wife. Christiana Eshleman. Children: John, Ann wife of John
Baker, Christiana wife of Christian Wohlgemuth, Elizabeth wife of
Dorst Shneeberger, David, Mary wife of Noah Flory and Henry.
Grandchild: John Eshleman (son of Henry).
     Ex. David Eshleman and Christian Wohlgemuth. Rapho Twp.

27 Jan. 1807   14 Feb. 1807
ELLIOT, MARY

Legatees: Elizabeth Jenkins wife of John Jenkins, George Douglass of Berks Co., Mary, George, Sarah and Thomas (children of Bridget May of Reading).
Ex. George Douglass. Caernarvon Twp.

6 June 1808   20 June 1808
ESHLEMAN, MARTIN
Children: John, Martin, Samuel, Anna wife of Adam Thomas, Elizabeth wife of John Herr, Feronica wife of Andrew Reese, Susanna wife of David Martin, David, Mary wife of Martin Hoober, Catharine, Jacob, Barbara and Abraham.
Ex. Samuel Eshleman and David Martin. Martic Twp.

4 March 1808   19 March 1808
ESHLEMAN, JOHN
Wife. Margaret Eshleman. Children: John, Jacob, Anna, Nancy, Elizabeth and Henry.
Ex. John Brenneman and Margaret Eshleman. Manor Twp.

1 Oct. 1807   18 Jan. 1808
EVANS, WILLIAM
Wife. (name omitted). Children: Abner (there were others, names and number not given).
Ex. John Zell and Edward Davis. Caernarvon Twp.

29 July 1808   14 Feb. 1809
ERHARD, CHRISTIAN
Wife. Barbara Erkard. Children: Christian, Jacob, John, Mary and Ann.
Ex. Jacob Holdeman and John Miskey. Rapho Twp.

4 June 1807   11 Oct. 1809
ECKMAN, MARTIN
Wife. Elizabeth Eckman. Children: Henry, Martin, Daniel, Mary, Susanna, Elizabeth and Sarah.
Ex. Elizabeth and Henry Eckman. Bart Twp.

3 Nov. 1803   6 Nov. 1809
EBERLY, ULRICH
Children: Barbara, Michael, Veronica, Henry, Anna, Maria, Abraham and John.
Ex. Michael Eberly and Martin Barr. Martic Twp.

13 Feb. 1807   17 Jan. 1810
EWING, ELIZABETH
Children: Alexander, Mary, John and Margaret.
Ex. Alexander Ewing. Little Britton Twp.

23 March 1810   3 April 1810
ESBEN, DAVID
Wife. Lydia Easen.
Ex. Elisha Grizel and William Steele. Drumore Twp.

19 Sept. 1804   5 May 1810
ESHLEMAN, CATHARINE

Widow of Ulrich Eshleman. Children: Jacob and Catharine wife of Abraham Westheffer.
Ex. Jacob Eshleman. Warwick Twp.

6 July 1810   27 July 1810
EAKN, DAVID
Wife. Hannah Eakn. Children: Kitty, William, Elizabeth, Susanna and John.
Ex. Hannah Eakn and Abraham King. Salsbury Twp.

4 Aug. 1808   30 Nov. 1810
ERHARD, DANIEL
Children: Elizabeth wife of Abraham Gerber and Jacob.
Ex. Jacob Erhard. Rapho Twp.

1 Dec. 1810   17 Dec. 1810
ERB, JOHN
Wife. Judith Erb. Children: Jacob, John, Samuel, Isaac, Magdalena wife of Abraham Erb, Elizabeth wife of Michael Shapler, Ann wife of Abraham Bear, David, Catharine and Joseph.
Ex. Jacob and John Erb. Cocalico Twp.

13 Feb. 1809   19 Dec. 1810
ERB, JACOB
Children: Ann wife of --- Bucher, Maria wife of Henry Landis, Magdalena wife of David Bricker, Elizabeth wife of Henry Eberly, John, Christian and Barbara wife of David Sherck.
Ex. John and Christian Erb. Cocalico Twp.

9 July 1811   17 July 1811
ETTER, GEORGE
Wife. Christiana Etter. Children: George, Magdalena wife of Adam Schrose, Hannah wife of Jacob Miller, Elizabeth wife of Jacob Fortney, Sebella wife of John Leamon, Catharine wife of Michael Bundel and Mary wife of Jacob Bundel.
Ex. Christiana Etter and Peter Holl. Strasburg Twp.

30 April 1812   19 Aug. 1812
ERB, CHRISTIAN
Wife. Ann Erb. Children: Christian, Jacob and Mary wife of Henry Hostetter.
Ex. John and Peter Erb. Warwick Twp.

8 Feb. 1813   5 April 1813
ENGLE, JACOB
Wife. Anna Maria Engle. Children: Jacob, Peter and Mary.
Ex. Frederick Byrode. Mt. Joy Twp.

17 Jan. 1812   20 April 1813
ENGLE, PETER
Wife. Catharine Engle. Children: John, Christian, Jacob, Philip, Peter and Magdalena wife of Abraham Rickert.
Ex. Jacob Engle and Abraham Rickert. Mt. Joy Twp.

58

7 Jan. 1813   27 April 1813
EVANS, JOSHUA
    Legatees: (Brother and sister) Elizabeth Hodskins and Amos
Evans, and (nephew) Philip (son of Amos). N.B. There was a
bequest of £10 to Bangor Church, also £10 to Rev. Joseph
Clarkson.
    Ex. Cyrus Jacobs, Esq. and John Huston. Caernavon Twp.

13 July 1813   7 Sept. 1813
EVANS, JOHN
    Wife. Margaret Evans. Children: (the names and number not
given).
    Ex. Margaret Evans, John Jones and John Welsh. Caernarvon
Twp.

17 Oct. 1812   6 Jan. 1813
ELWES, WILLIAM
    Wife. Anna Elwes. Children: Alfred and Henry.
    Ex. Anna Elwes. Columbia [borough].

22 April 1809   3 March 1814
EHRMAN, PETER
    Wife. Elizabeth Enrman. Children: Elizabeth, Barbara, Ann,
John, Peter, Christian, Michael, Andrew and Margaret wife of ---
Huber. Grandchildren: George Ehrman (son of Andrew) and Jacob
Huber.
    Ex. Peter Huber and Peter Ehrman. Warwick Twp.

11 Feb. 1806   March 1814
EALEY, GEORGE
    Children: Michael and John. N.B. There is a bequest to the
German Lutheran Church of New Holland.
    Ex. Michael and John Ealey. Earl Twp.

19 Aug. 1813   10 May 1814
ETTER, ABRAHAM
    Wife. Susanna Etta [sic]. Children: Henry, Elizabeth wife of
Jacob Kepler, Mary wife of Andrew Betman, Jacob, George, Daniel
and Philip.
    Ex. Jacob and George Etter. Donegal Twp.

18 July 1814   4 Feb. 1815
EBY, ABRAHAM
    Wife. Barbara Eby. Children: John, Abraham, Moses, Elizabeth
wife of Samuel Eby, Esther, Ann, Maria and Magdalena. Sons-in-
law: Samuel Weaver, Christian Martin and John Buckwalter (wives'
names not stated).
    Ex. Abraham Eby and John Buckwalter. Leacock Twp.

2 Aug. 1814   13 Feb. 1815
ERB, JOHN
    Wife. Salome Erb. Children: Joshua (and four daughters,
names not given).
    Ex. Salome and Samuel Erb. Warwick Twp.

10 April 1815   28 June 1815.
EBY, MARTIN
    Brother: John Eby.
    Ex. Jacob Groff and Peter Erb. Warwick Twp.

20 Feb. 1815   18 June 1816
ELLMAKER, JACOB
    Wife. Juliana Ellmaker. Children: Susanna and Peter.
    Ex. Henry Roland and Samuel Houston. Salsbury Twp.

30 May 1815   13 May 1816
ERWIN, JOHN
    Wife. (name omitted). Children: Elizabeth, John, George,
Joseph (and three others, names not given).
    Ex. George and Joseph Erwin. Cocalico Twp.

16 Oct. 1816   24 Oct. 1816
EVANS, CHARLES
    Wife. Christiana Evans.
    Ex. John Mathid and Robert Barber. Columbia Borough.

24 Nov. 1816   7 Jan. 1817
ERHARD, SUSANNA
    Child: Elizabeth.
    Ex. Jacob Zartman. Twp. omitted.

30 Jan. 1813   3 May 1817
ELLMAKER, ANTHONY
    Children: Isaac, Leonard, Anthony, George, Mary wife of John
Roberts, Elizabeth and Lydia.
    Ex. Isaac and Anthony Ellmaker. Earl Twp.

20 June 1816   20 July 1818
EBY, JACOB
    Wife. Anna Eby. Children: Christian, Jacob, Elizabeth and
Esther.
    Ex. Martin Funck and Christian Martin. Manor Twp.

2 Feb. 1818   6 April 1819
ERB, JACOB
    Children: David, John, Emanuel, Samuel and Nancy wife of
Jacob Gerber.
    Ex. Peter Reist and Jacob Kurtz. Warwick Twp.

20 Nov. 1815   24 Dec. 1819
EBY, PETER
    Wife. Elizabeth Eby. Children: Joseph, Peter, Abraham and
Elizabeth wife of Christian Long.
    Ex. Joseph and John Eby. Warwick Twp.

2 May 1813   19 May 1819
EBY, DANIEL
    Children: Jacob, Ann and Elizabeth wife of Christian Resh.
Grandchildren: Abraham, Ann and Daniel Resh.
    Ex. Jacob Eby and Christian Resh. Leacock Twp.

19 Feb. 1819   26 April 1819
EBY, ROSINA
     (Should be Rosina Shauer.) Children: John, Elizabeth,
George, Jacob, Henry and Susanna wife of Peter Blattenberger.
     Ex. Peter Blattenberger. Rapho Twp.

18 May 1819   3 July 1819
ERB, SAMUEL
     Wife. Salome Erb. Children: Jacob, Catharine, Louisa and
Salome.
     Ex. Michael Shapler and Peter Martin. Elizabeth Twp.

2 Feb. 1786   23 Feb. 1786
FORRER, CHRISTIAN
     Wife. Maria. Children: Veronica wife of --- Brenneman and
Anna wife of --- Graff.
     Ex. Henry Good and --- Burkholder. Conestoga Twp.

13 Jan. 1787   20 Feb. 1787
FAAS, ADAM
     Wife. Veronica Faas. Children: Jacob, Peter, Elizabeth and
David.
     Ex. Samuel Bowman and Peter Rayer. Cocalico Twp.

20 Jan. 1787   16 March 1787
FLICKINGER, JOHN
     Wife. (name not given). Children: John, Joseph, Jacob,
Christian, Henry, Barbara and Catharine.
     Ex. John Newman and George Brunner. Cocalico Twp.

3 March 1786   10 Feb. 1787
FRANTZ, JOHN
     Children: John, Christian, Jacob, Michael and Elizabeth.
     Ex. Jacob Brubacher and Jacob Frantz. Manor Twp.

10 June 1778   7 April 1787
FRANK, JACOB
     Wife. Maria Frank. Children: Jacob, Daniel, Margaret wife of
Frederick Lutes and Elizabeth wife of John Eberman.
     Ex. Maria and Jacob Frank. Lancaster Borough.

10 June 1787   8 Aug. 1787
FUNDERSMITH, LUDWIG
     Wife. Isabella Fundersmith. Children: John, Valentine and
Margaret wife of Daniel Eler.
     Ex. John and Valentine Fundersmith. Strasburg Twp.

24 June 1775   12 Nov. 1787
FUCHS, JACOB
     Wife. Barbara Fuchs. Children: Mary, Barbara wife of Peter
Leaman, Magdalena, Fritz, Catharine, Abraham, Esther and Samuel.
     Ex. Peter Leaman and John Fritz. Rapho Twp.

13 Jan. 1787   5 Nov. 1788
FREDERICK, ABRAHAM

Wife. Elizabeth Frederick. Children: Abraham, Elizabeth wife of Jacob Reckseker, John, Philip, Peter and Rachel wife of John Reckseker.
Ex. Philip Frederick and John Reckseker. Warwick Twp.

14 Aug. 1787   18 Nov. 1788
FUNK, HENRY
Children: Samuel, Abraham, Elizabeth wife of Abraham Strickler, Anna wife of Jacob Hershberger, Magdalena wife of Peter Steigelman and Barbara wife of Jacob Hochstetter.
Ex. Abraham Funk and Christian Whisler. Manor Twp.

20 March 1784   3 March 1790
FREDERICK, ANNA MARIA
Children: Christopher, Barbara and Anna. Step-son and daughters: Noah, Eva and Maria.
Ex. Sebastian Hower. Earl Twp.

7 Sept. 1780   3 Feb. 1790
FUNK, MARTIN
Wife. (name not given). Children: Samuel, John, Michael, Feronica, Martin, Jacob and Henry.
Ex. Jacob Carly and Henry Brenneman. Manor Twp.

25 Jan. 1791   2 Feb. 1791
FREE, RICHARD
Wife. Barbara Free. Children: Elizabeth, Peter, Agness, Christiana, Mary and Margaret.
Ex. Joseph Miller and John Patterson. Colerain Twp.

13 Jan. 1791   16 Dec. 1791
FIESER, PETER
Wife. Catharine Fieser. Children: Elizabeth, Anna and Susanna. Sons-in-law: Rudolph Bear, Peter Smith, Jacob Leib and George Rup (wives' names not given).
Ex. Rudolph Bear, Peter Smith and Jacob Leid. Cocalico Twp.

27 Nov. 1790   20 Aug. 1791
FRANKHOUSER, CHRISTIAN
Wife. Margaret Frankhouser. Children: (the names and number not given).
Ex. Martin Fry and John Becktol. Twp. omitted.

5 Jan. 1792   31 March 1792
FRY, JACOB
Wife. Catharine Fry. Children: Jacob, Catharine wife of Andrew Zerrerrer, Peter, Margaret wife of Jacob White, John, Dorothea, Juliana wife of --- Mumma, and Elizabeth.
Grandchildren: John and Juliana Mumma and Elizabeth and Catharine (children of Elizabeth — last name not given).
Ex. Jacob Voneada and Adam Grill. Brecknock Twp.

4 Feb. 1793   6 March 1793
FORRY, DANIEL
Wife. Ann Elizabeth Forry. Child: John.

Ex. John Hertzler, Ann E. and John Forry.

25 Sept. 1790   22 Oct. 1793
FEGLEY, JOHN
    Wife. Ann Fegley. Nieces: Elizabeth, Mary and Barbara Fegley
(children of brother Paul Fegley).
    Ex. Conrad Dull and Isaac Latcha. Rapho Twp.

17 Sept. 1793   25 Nov. 1793
FUCKS, CHRISTIAN
    Wife. Christina Fucks.
    Ex. Mathias Buffeunyer. Elizabeth Twp.

27 March 1794   7 April 1794
FASSNACHT, PHILIP
    Wife. Margaret Fassnacht. There were six children — names
not given.
    Ex. Jacob Sherick and Michael Hildebrand. Earl Twp.

22 Dec. 1792   19 July 1794
FEATHER, GRETRAUT
    Child: Elizabeth wife of John Frymyer.
    Ex. John Frymyer. Warwick Twp.

10 Aug. 1794   14 Oct. 1794
FUNK, SAMUEL
    Wife. Magdalena Funk. Children: Martin (there were others,
names not given).
    Ex. Jacob Carle and Christian Habecker. Manor Twp.

29 Sept. 1794   6 Oct. 1794
FANNON, JAMES
    Sisters: Nancy and Catharine Fannon. Legatees: Cornelius
Harkins, Hugh McGrann and John Dillan.
    Ex. (omitted). Twp. omitted.

1 Oct. 1793   23 Feb. 1795
FLORI, DAVID
    Wife. Eve Flori. Children: John, Christoffel, David and
Henry.
    Ex. John and Daniel Flori. Rapho Twp.

16 Dec. 1794   21 March 1795
FOEHL, ANDREW
    Wife. Anna Foehl. Children: George, Jacob and Frederick.
    Ex. Anna Foehl and Henry Deitrich. Conestoga Twp.

15 March 1795   6 May 1795
FASS, DAVID
    Wife. Elizabeth Fass. Children: Jacob (there were others,
names and number not given).
    Ex. Elizabeth Fass and Valentine Greiner. Warwick Twp.

4 Feb. 1794   15 Nov. 1794
FRANCK, HENRY

Wife. Christiana Franck. Children: Elizabeth, John,
Christiana, Catharine, Susanna, Ann and George.
    Ex. Charles Rudy and John Franck. Warwick Twp.

13 Jan. 1795   19 Nov. 1795
FERREE, PETER
    Children: John, Peter, Samuel, Jacob, Hannah wife of Henry
Hoke, Mary wife of Andrew Ferree, Rachel and Elizabeth wife of
Joel Ferree.
    Ex. Jacob Shirts. Lampeter Twp.

9 Sept. 1796   29 Nov. 1796
FREY, RUDY
    Wife. Barbara Frey. Children: John, Eve wife of John
Detwiler, Veronica wife of Peter Ressler, Barbara wife of Jacob
Marckle, Christiana wife of Conrad Orth, Anna wife of Dewald
Powman, Magdalena wife of Philip Stober and Mathias.
    Ex. Philip Stober and John Lesher. Brecknock Twp.

24 Feb. 1796   12 April 1796
FISSEL, JOHN
    Wife. Catharine Fissel. Children: Frederick, Catharine,
Elizabeth, Mary, Margaret, Susanna, Eve, Gertrude, Ann and
Feronica.
    Ex. John Nissly and John Kuntz. Mt. Joy Twp.

20 April 1796   2 April 1805
FERREE, PHILIP
    Wife. Ann Ferree. Children: William, Mary wife of ---
Williams, Elizabeth wife of --- Foster, Tamer wife of Marsh,
Philip, Rachel wife of --- Trout, Joel, Richard, Abraham and
James.
    Ex. Adam Lightner and Philip Ferree. Strasburg Twp.

6 Jan. 1797   2 March 1797
FAUSSET, CHARLES
    Wife. Eleanor Fausset. Children: William, Francis, Ann,
Elizabeth, Anna, John and Margaret.
    Ex. John Zell and Eleanor Fausset. Elizabeth Twp.

16 April 1799   1 June 1799
FRANTZ, JACOB
    Wife. Maria Frantz. Children: John, Jacob, Christian and
Anna.
    Ex. John and Christian Frantz. Lampeter Twp.

9 Jan. 1797   7 July 1798
FUNK, JACOB
    Legatees: (Sisters) Efigenia and Sophia Funk. "Brethern of
Moses" - Ash Lebrecht, John Frederick and John Georgas.
    Ex. Daniel Neagley and John Senseman. Ephrata Twp.

22 March 1800   22 May 1800
FUNCK, HENRY

Wife. Magdalena Funk. Children: John, Abraham, Henry, Jacob, Daniel, Barbara wife of John Eberly, Christian, Mary wife of Peter Gander and Elizabeth wife of James Philip.
Ex. Michael Bender and Joseph Carley. Lancaster Borough.

2 Nov. 1799   4 May 1800
FRANK, VALENTINE
Wife. Catharine Frank. Children: Jacob, John, Valentine, Susanna, Catharine and Elizabeth.
Ex. Catharine Frank and Henry Kinser. Strasburg Twp.

21 June 1791   6 Dec. 1800
FOUTS, JACOB
Children: Jacob, Michael, Martin, Elizabeth wife of William Cunkle and Catharine wife of John Eckman.
Ex. Martin Fouts and John Eckman. Strasburg Twp.

3 Nov. 1797   13 July 1801
FERREE, JOEL
Wife. Sarah Ferree. Children: Isaac, Leah wife of Adam Lightner and Rachel wife of Jacob Ferree. Grandchildren: Joel, Isaac, Elijah, Uriah and Reuben (children of Isaac), Joel, Rebecca, Jane and Elizabeth (children of Jacob).
Ex. Isaac Ferree. Leacock Twp.

18 May 1801   21 Aug. 1801
FIRESTONE, JOHN
Wife. Justina Firestone. Children: Jacob and George. N.B. There may have been other children as the expression in the will is "All my children." The two above mentioned are the only names given.
Ex. Jacob and George Firestone. Cocalico Twp.

4 Nov. 1797   15 April 1802
FRANCISCUS, STOPHEL
Children: Elizabeth wife of Henry Pinkerton, Magdalena wife of --- Cooper, George, Catharine wife of Bantz and Margaret wife of Ludwick Shell. Grandchildren: Charles (son of Magdalena), John, George, William and Charles (sons of George), Margaret (child of Catharine) and Elizabeth (child of Margaret).
Ex. Henry Pinkerton and Henry Musser. Lancaster Borough.

14 Feb. 1801   25 June 1802
FULK, MARY M.
Children: Catharine (there were others, names not given).
Ex. (omitted). Conestoga Twp.

13 Oct. 1804   13 Nov. 1804
FREYMEYER, JOHN
Wife. Elizabeth Freymeyer. Children: John, Elizabeth, Henry, Jacob and Catharine.
Ex. Elizabeth Freymeyer. Warwick Twp.

23 Dec. 1802   17 Dec. 1804
FRANKS, MARY

Children: Jacob, Daniel and Elizabeth wife of John Eberman.
Grandchildren: Catharine wife of --- Deeler (parents' names not
stated), Jacob, John, Elizabeth, Jasper, William and Mathias
Eberman (children of Elizabeth).
Ex. Jacob Frank and John Eberman. Lancaster Borough.

27 July 1805   20 Sept. 1805
FAHNSTOCK, PETER
Children: Conrad, Obed, Hannah wife of John Landis,
Margaret, Elizabeth, Sarah, Samuel and Andrew. Grandchildren:
Peter and Ann (children of Conrad), Benjamin, Elizabeth and
Joseph (children of Sarah).
Ex. Samuel and Obed Fahnstock. Cocalico Twp.

9 Oct. 1805   12 Nov. 1805
FRANCISCUS, ROSINA
Child: Catharine wife of John Patterson.
Ex. John Patterson. Lancaster Borough.

29 Dec. 1804   11 March 1805
FUNCK, RUDOLPH
Wife. Catharine Funck. Children: Henry, Maria wife of
Abraham Herr, Magdalena wife of Ulrich Ellenberger and Elizabeth.
Ex. Abraham Horr and Henry Neff. Manor Twp.

22 Aug. 1805   18 April 1806
FIGHT, ARNOLD
Wife. Margaret Fight. Children: Jacob, Elizabeth, Eve wife
of Henry Eberly, Hannah wife of Andrew Miller, Susanna wife of
Michael Shenk, Benjamin and Mary.
Ex. Benjamin Fight. Bart Twp.

4 Dec. 1802   22 March 1806
FREY, MARTIN
Wife. Elizabeth Frey. Children: Henry, Mary wife of ---
Ferntzler, Martin, Peter, Jacob, John, Susanna wife of Conrad
Holtzinger, Margaret wife of Christian Frankhouser, Eve wife of
Ludwig Roth, Elizabeth wife of George Redle, Catharine wife of
Adam Hoh, Regina wife of Michael Kegerise and Dorothea wife of --
- Heft. Grandchildren: George and Jacob (children of Dorothea),
Susanna wife of Michael Young (daughter of Dorothea) and
Catharine wife of Jacob Breitenstine (parents' names not stated).
Ex. Martin Frey and Adam Grill. Cocalico Twp.

7 Aug. 1802   6 Jan. 1807
FREY, JOHN
Wife. Magdalena Frey. Children: John, Jacob, Peter, George,
Frederick, Joseph, Adam, Catharine wife of Adam Brenner,
Magdalena wife of Philip Fenstemacher, Margaret and Conrad.
Ex. Jacob and John Frey. Manor Twp.

--- 1806   --- 1808
FERREE, EPHRAIM
Wife. Elizabeth Ferree.
Ex. Elizabeth Ferree. Strasburg Twp.

1 Jan. 1807   13 Feb. 1809
FRANKHOUSER, MARGARET
      Children: Peter, Henry, Jacob, Catharine, Christian and
Susanna.
      Ex. Henry Frankhouser. Brecknock Twp.

16 Feb. 1809   4 March 1809
FRANK, GEORGE
      Wife. Molly Frank. Children: Martin and David. Sisters:
Elizabeth, Catharine and Margaret Frank.
      Ex. Christian Carpenter and Henry Finfrock. Earl Twp.

23 Feb. 1809   17 March 1809
FLOWER, JOHN
      Wife. Catharine Flower. Children: John, Jacob, Elizabeth,
George, Valentine, Henry, Mary, Catharine, William and Christian.
      Ex. John Bardrauff and George Dutt. Warwick Twp.

15 July 1808   1 Sept. 1809
FORRER, CHRISTIAN
      Wife. Barbara Forrer. Children: Christian, Ann wife of
Christian Herr, Mary wife of Joseph Herr, Magdalena and Barbara.
      Ex. Christian Herr. Conestoga Twp.

20 Nov. 1809   3 Jan. 1810
FUNCK, JACOB
      Wife. Barbara Funck. Children: John, Susanna wife of John
Sauder [Sander], Ann wife of Michael Kauffman, Barbara wife of
Peter Witmer, Jacob, Martin and Henry.
      Ex. John Herr and Michael Kauffman. Manor Twp.

15 Jan. 1811   8 April 1811
FEATHER, HENRY
      Wife. Salome Feather. Children: George, Hannah (and four
others, names not given).
      Ex. George Feather. Cocalico Twp.

25 Aug. 1811   24 Sept. 1811
FURNIS, GARDNER
      Bros.: Thomas and Gardner Furnis. Nieces: Phebe and Hannah
Furris (parents' names not given).
      Ex. Gardner Furnis. Drumore Twp.

23 May 1807   29 July 1811
FORREER, JOHN
      Wife. Elizabeth Forrer. Children: Martin, Chrisly, Ann wife
of Daniel Kendig, John, Mary wife of Chrisly Roser, Elizabeth
wife of George Knisely, Barbara wife of Henry Myer and Christiana
wife of Daniel Knisely. Grandchildren: John, Henry and Daniel
Forrer (children of John).
      Ex. Chrisly Roser. Lampeter Twp.

2 July 1811   29 March 1812
FORDNEY, CASPER

Wife. Elizabeth Fordney. Children: Casper, George, Samuel and Mary.
Ex. Elizabeth Fordney. Lancaster Borough.

18 Oct. 1811   30 May 1812
FAHNSTICK, JOHN
Wife. Catharine Fahnstick. Children: Henry, Rebecca, Hannah and Jacob. Granddaughter [?]: Clement Hutenbeecher (parents' names not stated).
Ex. Jacob Fahnstick and Jacob Korrigmacher. Cocalico Twp.

6 July 1812   10 July 1812
FOUTS, MICHAEL
Bros. and sisters: Martin, Jacob, Catharine wife of --- Eckman and Elizabeth wife of William Cunele.
Ex. Daniel Eckman and John Cunkle. Strasburg Twp.

24 Feb. 1813   9 March 1813
FREY, JOHN
Bros. and Sisters: Jacob, Peter, George, Frederick, Joseph and Peggy wife of Jacob Mek.
Ex. Jacob Frey and Jacob Wittmer. Manor Twp.

--- 1811 1 May 1813
FRICK, JOHN
Children: Maria, Elizabeth wife of Christian Bowman, John, Christian, Anna wife of Peter Brubaker and Barbara wife of John Workman. Grandchildren: Elizabeth wife of Henry Herr (parents' names not stated), Maria, Christian, Elizabeth, Anna, John, Catharine, Peter, Susanna and Abraham Bowman (all children of Elizabeth).
Ex. Abraham Frick and John Blocher. Manheim Twp.

13 May 1812   15 Sept. 1813
FOUST, GEORGE
Wife. Barbara Foust.
Ex. Barbara Foust. Lancaster Borough.

26 Dec. 1811   18 May 1813
FOGHT, CHRISTIAN
(This should be VOGHT.)
Legatee: Michael Dietrich.
Ex. Jacob Strein. Lancaster Borough.

11 Nov. 1813   21 Feb. 1814
FRANCISCUS, JOHN
Wife. Anna Franciscus. Children: Christopher, Catharine wife of Jacob Miller, Margaret wife of John Engle, John and Jacob.
Ex. Anna Franciscus and Jacob Leman. Lancaster Borough.

2 Feb. 1814   24 June 1815
FLEMING, WILLIAM
Wife. Elizabeth Fleming. Children: Isaac, Margaret, John and James.
Ex. Isaac Fleming. Caernavon Twp.

5 Dec. 1815   29 Dec. 1815
FEHL, GEORGE
    Wife. Elizabeth Fehl. Children: Jacob, George, Catharine,
John, Mary wife of Melchoir Brenneman and Elizabeth. Grandchild:
Elizabeth Brenneman.
    Ex. Jacob and Frederick Fehl. Conestoga Twp.

31 Oct. 1816   2 Nov. 1816
FREY, GEORGE
    Brother and sister: Jacob and Margaret Frey.
    Ex. Nathaniel Lightner and Dr. John Fisher. Lancaster
Borough.

22 Nov. 1815   16 Feb. 1816
FUNK, HENRY
    Wife. Barbara Funk. Children: (the names and number not
given).
    Ex. Andrew Kauffman and Christian Martin. Manor Twp.

27 Aug. 1814   4 April 1816
FINDLEY, JAMES
    Legatee: Henry Brenneman Jr.
    Ex. Henry Brenneman. Strasburg Twp.

13 March 1816   7 June 1816
FEATHER, BERNHARD
    Wife. Juliana Feather. Brother: Peter Feather. Nieces:
Susanna wife of --- Brubacker, Christiana, Elizabeth wife of
Henry Slabach, Mary wife of Michael Klingman (children of brother
Henry).
    Ex. Peter Martin. Cocalico Twp.

11 March 1816   30 July 1816
FORDNEY, JOHN
    Wife. Sophia Fordney.
    Ex. Sophia Fordney. Lancaster Borough.

22 Jan. 1817   8 March 1817
FRANCK, ELIZABETH
    Child: Catharine.
    Ex. John and George Franck. Warwick Twp.

10 Dec. 1813   17 March 1817
FAHNESTOCK, DIETRICK
    Children: Mary wife of George Bealer and wife of John
Rudisill [?], Samuel, Margaret wife of John Bowman [John written
in later], Peter, John, Susanna, Esther wife of Kemmel and
Josepha wife of --- Hay. Grandchildren: Michael, Juliana, Hay,
Susanna and Mary Kemmel and Samuel and George Bealer.
    Ex. Samuel and Daniel Fahnestock. Cocalico Twp.

--- 1803   7 Jan. 1818
FAINOT, FREDERICK

Wife. Frances Fainot. Child: Catharine wife of --- Fetter. Grandchildren: Catharine, Rebecca, Frederick, Jacob, Sophia and Mary Fetter.
Ex. Frances Fainot, Catharine Fetter and William Riechenbach. Lancaster Borough.

7 Jan. 1818   23 March 1818
FOSTER, JOHN
Children: Philip, John, James, Joel, Elizabeth, Rachel and Margaret.
Ex. Philip and James Foster, Strasburg Twp.

25 Dec. 1807   5 April 1818
FREY, ELIZABETH
Children: Peter, Eve wife of Ludwig Road, Elizabeth wife of George Readle, Catharine wife of Adam Howe, Henry, John, Jacob and Rechena [or Rachel] wife of Michael Keger.
Ex. Jacob and John Frey. Cocalico Twp.

2 Jan. 1719   14 June 1819
FORDNEY, JACOB
Wife. Margaret Fordney. Children: William, Jacob, Melchoir, Daniel, Philip, Margaret wife of Frederick Glasser, Elizabeth wife of Abraham Schveitzer and Mary wife of John Upperman.
Ex. Margaret and Jacob Fordney. Lancaster City.

6 April 1819   3 July 1819
FORDNEY, SAMUEL
Sister: Mary Burg.
Ex. Mary Burg. Lancaster City.

5 Aug. 1817   1 Oct. 1819
FRANTZ, GEORGE ADAM
Children: Adam, Baltzer, Elizabeth, Eve wife of Henry Landis, Barbara wife of John Stiesse and David.
Ex. David Frantz. Elizabeth Twp.

8 Nov. 1819   17 Dec. 1819
FECHTLY, HENRY
Brother: Jacob Fechtly. Sister: Barbara Fechtly. N.B. There were no executors named in will, and letters of administration were granted to Jacob Fachtly.
Adm. Jacob Fechtly. Lampeter Twp.

4 April 1817   6 Dec. 1819
FREDERICK, JOHN
Legatees: Magdalena Hoffman and the "Society of Ephrata." N.B. There were directions left that there should be a "Love feast" held at his death — agreeable to the custom of the "Society of Ephrata."
Ex. Jacob Koeigmacher. Ephrata Twp.

17 March 1785   8 May 1786
GEBLE, WILLIAM

70

Wife. Eva Elizabeth Geble. Children: Anna, Henry, Martin,
Elizabeth wife of Christian Gettich and Jacob.
Ex. Eva Geble. Lancaster Borough.

16 Dec. 1784   2 June 1786
GRAYBILL, SHEM
Wife. Susanna Graybill. Children: Isaac, Samuel and Salome.
Ex. Susanna and Michael Graybill. Earl Twp.

16 Jan. 1786   31 July 1786
GINGRICH, PETER
(The will is signed "GINGERY".) Children: Michael, Catharine
wife of Nicholas Hoober, Jacob, Mary wife of Andreas Andrew,
Magdalena wife of Abraham Hoober, Peter, Susanna wife of Peter
Hoober, Tobias, Christian and Barbara. Grandchildren: Tobias,
Jacob, Peter, Abraham and Elizabeth Gingery (children of
Christian).
Ex. Joseph Boumberger and Martin Thomas. Lebanon Twp.

5 Dec. 1786   27 April 1787
GERNER, MATHIAS
Wife. Maria. Children: Michael, Catharine, Susan, Eve, Anna
and Margaret. Son-in-law: Bernard Geiger (wife's name not
stated).
Ex. Benj. Leesle and Bernard Geiger. Earl Twp.

29 May 1787   11 June 1787
GATTINGER, ANDREW
Wife. Barbara Gattinger. Child: Catharine wife of Gabriel
Shop.
Ex. Henry Gross. Lancaster Borough.

21 June 1785   12 Dec. 1787
GLESS, CHRISTINA
Children: Peter, Elizabeth, Ann, Mary and Barbara.
Ex. Christian Myer and Abraham Rife. Cocalico Twp.

4 April 1787   2 Feb. 1788
GREIDER, MICHAEL
Wife. Elizabeth Greider. Children: Christian, Michael, John,
Jacob, Martin, Elizabeth and Susanna.
Ex. Elizabeth and Michael Greider. Lancaster Borugh.

31 March 1788 17 April 1788
GREYBILL, SUSANNA
The wife of Shem Greybill. Children: George, Sally, Isaac
and Shem.
Ex. Jacob Hole. Earl Twp.

12 April 1788 29 July 1788
GRUBB, HENRY
Children: Andrew, Jacob, Michael, Catharine, Christiana,
Henry, Melichoer, Elizabeth, Nancy and Barbara.
Ex. (omitted). Strasburg Twp.

9 Aug. 1788   20 Sept. 1788
GODSHALL, PETER
    Wife. Catharine Godshell. Children: Ludwig, Peter, Michael,
Godlieb, John, Elizabeth wife of John Hahn and Catharine wife of
George Folk.
    Ex. Jacob Kauffman and Martin Pfeiffer. Hempfield Twp.

17 Jan. 1789   26 Feb. 1789
GAY, WILLIAM
    Children: William and Ann wife of John Johnson.
    Ex. John Johnson. Sadsbury Twp.

5 Dec. 1786   25 May 1789
GRUBB, ANN MARGARET
    Children: Michael and Jacob.
    Ex. Jacob Grubb. Manheim Twp.

30 July 1781   13 June 1789
GLICK, PHILIP
    Wife. Elizabeth Glick. There were children, the names and
number not given.
    Ex. Elizabeth Glick. Warwick Twp.

7 Dec. 1789   15 Dec. 1789
GLOTZ, ALBRECHT
    Children: Daniel, Anna, Catharine and Benigna.
    Ex. David Tanneberger and George Cap. Warwick Twp.

10 Sept. 1789   13 Dec. 1789
GISH, ABRAHAM
    Wife. Susanna. Children: Jacob, Abraham and John. (there
were daughters, — names omitted).
    Ex. Jacob Gish, John Haldeman and Martin Nissly. Donegal
Twp.

19 Aug. 1789   1 Jan. 1790
GILLCREEST, ROBERT
    Sister: Margaret wife of Charles Harro.
    Ex. Robert Campbell. Little Brittian Twp.

16 Sept. 1788   19 March 1790
GRAFF, ELIZABETH
    Husband: Michael Graff. Children: Fronica wife of John
Miller, Christian, Elizabeth wife of John Lyon and (three other
children - names not given).
    Ex. John Miller. Martic Twp.

6 Feb. 1790   24 Feb. 1790
GRUBB, CURTIS
    Sister: Elizabeth Grubb.
    Ex. John W. Kittera. Lebanon Twp.

20 April 1790   22 May 1790
GERBER, FELIX

Wife. Mary Gerber. Children: Abraham, John, Felix, Christian, Jacob, Mary, Elizabeth and Barbara.
Ex. Mary and Abraham Gerber. Rapho Twp.

16 April 1790   9 June 1790
GRUBB, JOHN
Children: Jacob, Catharine wife of John Creemer and Elizabeth.
Ex. John Creemer and John Brackbill. Strasburg Twp.

12 Sept. 1789   23 Sept. 1790
GERBER, MICHAEL
Children: John, Michael, Ann, Elizabeth, Barbara and Catharine.
Ex. John Johnston and Jacob Kurtz. Manheim Twp.

4 July 1790   19 Oct. 1790
GUT, CHRISTIAN
Wife. Anna. Children: Jacob, John and Barbara. Son-in-law: Jacob Ebersol (wife's name not stated).
Ex. Jacob Gut and Jacob Ebersol. Donegal Twp.

22 Nov. 1784   24 Nov. 1790
GUCKERLE, JACOB
Wife. Susanna Guckerle. Children: John, Jacob and Peter.
Ex. Adam Minick and Peter Guckerle. Rapho Twp.

10 Nov. 1790   20 Nov. 1790
GREIGHTON, WILLIAM
(This should be CRIGHTON.) Wife. Barbara Creighton.
Children: Mary, Martha, Margaret and Ann. Grandchildren: William, Samuel and Margaret Erven and Isaac Litner (parents' names not stated).
Ex. Robert McCurdy and William Brisben. Leacock Twp.

4 Dec. 1790   1 March 1791
GREEN, THOMAS
Children: Hannah wife of Joshua Way and Susanna wife of John Clemson. Grandchildren: Mary, Joshua, Matilda, Elizabeth, Susan, Phebe, Faithful and Sidney Way and Thomas, James, Joseph, Hannah, Elizabeth and Susanna Clemson.
Ex. Samuel Downing and John Feree. Salsbury Twp.

29 Aug. 1789   24 March 1791
GRYDER, TOBIAS
Wife. Anna. Children: John, Tobias, Ann, Barbara, Mary, Susanna and Jacob. Grandchildren: John, Ann, Elizabeth, Tobias, Henry, David and Daniel (children of Jacob).
Ex. John Stauffer and Jacob Hartman. Lampeter Twp.

1 July 1791   3 Sept. 1791
GRAFF, SEBASTIAN
Wife. Catharine Graff. Children: George, Sebastian, Andrew, Sarah, Mary and Catharine.
Ex. Paul Zantzinger and Adam Reigar. Manheim Twp.

6 Dec. 1784   2 Nov. 1791
GROF, MARK
    Wife. Anna Grof. Children: Mark, Susanna wife of David
Martin, Feronica wife of Abraham Huntsperger, Barbara wife of
Michael Martin, Margaret wife of Jacob Sumy, Magdalena wife of
Christian Meyer, Elizabeth wife of George Hildebrand, Christiana
wife of Abraham Metzler and Mary wife of Michael Wenger.
    Ex. David Martin and Jacob Sumy. Earl Twp.

3 July 1792   4 Aug. 1792
GOOD, JOHN
    Wife. Barbara Good. Children: John, Samuel, Anna, Christian
and Elizabeth.
    Ex. Christian Bowman and Peter Mosser. Brecknock Twp.

28 July 1789   2 Nov. 1792
GLICK, ELIZABETH
    Children: John, Mary wife of John Bower and Elizabeth.
    Ex. John Glick. Warwick Twp.

7 Aug. 1792   28 April 1793
GRAYBILL, MARY
    Child: Mary wife of Christian Hole.
    Ex. Michael Bare. Earl Twp.

21 April 1793 28 Aug. 1793
GRIDER, MICHAEL
    (This should be KRIDER.) Wife. Anne Krider. Children: John
and Jonas.
    Ex. John Krider and Christian Over. Donegal Twp.

12 Sept. 1793 25 Oct. 1793
GALLAUGHER, GEORGE
    Bro. and sister: Mary and John Gallaugher.
    Ex. Patrick Green. Lancaster Twp.

6 Oct. 1792   1 March 1794
GERBER, MICHAEL
    Wife. Christiana Gerber. Sisters: Anne, Catharine, Eve and
Elizabeth.
    Ex. John Johnson and Christian Frantz. Manheim Twp.

15 Nov. 1793   4 March 1794
GRAIG, JOHN
    (This should be CRAIG) Wife. Agness Craig. Sisters: Jane
wife of --- Buck, Elizabeth wife of --- Boyle and Ann wife of ---
Moore.
    Ex. Agness Craig and Samuel Boyd. Lampeter Twp.

6 June 1794   4 July 1794
GALT, WILLIAM
    Wife. Margaret Galt. Legatees: James Galt and Alexander
Galt, (these two are not named as children — nor is their
relation to the writer of the will given). There is also a
bequest made to the Presbyterian Church, Salsbury.

Ex. James and Alexander Galt. Salsbury Twp.

31 Dec. 1792   19 July 1794
GREIDER, MICHAEL
    Wife. Elizabeth Greider. Children: Michael, Anne, Elizabeth,
Catharine, Barbara and George.
    Ex. John Snebly and John Myley. Conestoga Twp.

12 Aug. 1794   24 Oct. 1794
GREINER, VALENTINE
    Wife. Barbara Greiner. Children: Philip, Martin, Valentine
and Barbara.
    Ex. Martin Greiner and Valentine Greiner. Warwick Twp.

26 Nov. 1794   18 Feb. 1795
GRUBB, ANN
    Wife of Curtis Grubb. Children: Martha, Juliana and Samuel.
Mother: Hannah Grubb. Uncle: Nathaniel Grubb.
    Ex. Nathaniel Grubb. Lancaster Borough.

8 Oct. 1793   25 Feb. 1795
GILMORE, WILLIAM
    Wife. Agness Gilmore. Children: Isabella wife of --- Carson,
James, Elizabeth wife of --- Berry, Agness wife of ---Galbraith
and Ann wife of --- Boyle.
    Ex. William Carson and John Berry. Colerain Twp.

13 July 1794   10 April 1795
GREINER, COLEMAN
    Wife. Barbara Greiner. Children: John, Rosina, Catharine,
Elizabeth and Mary.
    Ex. Barbara Greiner and Peter Bram. Rapho Twp.

5 March 1795   7 April 1795
GILCHRIST, WILLIAM
    Children: Sarah wife of James Cummings and Samuel.
    Ex. James and Sarah Cummings. Twp. omitted.

12 Oct. 1795   24 Oct. 1795
GLEN, JOHN
    Wife. Helen Glen. There was a post-humous child.
    Ex. Henry Landis. Hempfield Twp.

21 Dec. 1793   25 April 1795
GIBSON, WILLIAM
    Children: John, Mary, Margaret, Elizabeth, Agness, Susana
and William. Grandchildren: Margaret and Hugh Allison (parents'
names not stated).
    Ex. John and William Gibson. Little Brittain Twp.

10 May 1791   31 March 1796
GERMAN, GEORGE
    Wife. Dorothea German. Children: John and George.
    Ex. Dorothea and John German. Rapho Twp.

3 Aug. 1792   29 April 1796
GOCKLEY, JOHN
    (This should be COCKLEY.) Wife. Magdalena Cockley. Children:
Sebastian, Catharine wife of Christian Weist, David, John,
Dietrich and Christiana wife of Joseph Dornbach.
    Ex. John and Dietrick Cockley. Cocalico Twp.

29 June 1796   16 July 1796
GORNER, JOHN
    Wife. Elizabeth Gorner. Children: Philip and Catharine.
    Ex. Philip Gorner. Donegal Twp.

5 July 1796   11 Aug. 1796
GERINGER, JACOB
    Wife. Elizabeth Geringer.
    Ex. Elizabeth Geringer and John Good. Conestoga Twp.

3 March 1796   13 May 1796
GETZ, JOHN
    Wife. Mary Getz. Children: John, Catharine wife of Charles
Reisinger, Peter, Jacob, George, Daniel and Frederick.
    Ex. Peter Getz. Lancaster Borough.

3 Nov. 1792   29 July 1796
GERBER, ADAM
    Legatee: Daniel Gebel.
    Ex. Benjamin Long. Warwick Twp.

25 May 1796   17 June 1796
GROVE, JOHN
    Wife. Anna Grove. Children: Abraham, Christian, Anna wife of
John Royer, Magdalena, John and David.
    Ex. John Myer and Benjamin Landis. Earl Twp.

12 May 1795   1 June 1796
GRUBB, HANNAH
    Child: Hannah Elizabeth Grubb.
    Ex. Samuel Jones. Elizabeth Twp.

8 April 1797   17 April 1797
GALBOUGH, JOHN
    Wife. Mary Galbough. Bro.: Frederick Galbough. Sister:
Barbara wife of --- Garnon.
    Ex. Anthony Haines and Christian Rountz. May Town Twp.

18 Oct. 1796   28 Jan. 1797
GUNDACKER, MARGARET
    Children: Michael, George, Justina, Mary wife of Michael
Kline, Magdalena wife of Philip Kline and Barbara wife of Ludwig
Denigh.
    Ex. Michael Gundacker. Lancaster Borough.

10 Sept. 1797   20 Oct. 1797
GREBILL, JOHN

Wife. Sarah Grebill. Children: John, Isaac, Jacob, Elizabeth wife of Daniel Swobe, Salome wife of Adam Swobe and Catharine wife of George Weider.

Ex. John Grebill and Daniel Wobe [Swobe]. Earl Twp.

16 Dec. 1796   14 March 1797
GELBACK, FREDERICK

Wife. Anna Gelback. Children: Frederick, Catharine, Barbara and John. Son-in-law: James Mackey (wife's name not stated).

Ex. Frederick Gelback and James Mackey. May Town Twp.

13 Dec. 1788   29 Jan. 1798
GRAFF, CATHARINE

Widow of George Graff. Children: Eve wife of Valentine Krug and Catharine wife of William VonPhul. Grandchildren: Sarah Krug (child of Eve), George and William Graff (parents' names not stated). Nephew: Jacob Krug.

Ex. Sebastian Graff and Jacob Krug. Lancaster Borough.

9 Jan. 1798   6 Feb. 1798
GLATZ, JACOB

Children: Catharine wife of John Gundacker, Elizabeth wife of Christopher Brenner, William and George.

Ex. John Gundacker and Christopher Brenner. Lancaster Borough.

19 Sept. 1797   9 Nov. 1798
GIBBONS, ABRAHAM

Children: William, Abraham, Lydia, Hannah, Mary and Elizabeth. N.B. There was a bequest of £20 made to The Yearly Meeting of Friends (commonly called Quakers) of Pennsylvania and New Jersey - for schools in religious education of the youth in one or more boarding schools.

Ex. Samuel Camby and William Gibbons. Leacock Twp.

7 March 1798   22 Sept. 1798
GROSS, HENRY

Wife. Mary Gross. Children: Susanna wife of Stephen Hornberger. Grandchild: Catharine Hornberger.

Ex. Andrew Keiss and Conrad Shwartz. Lancaster Borough.

20 Aug. 1798   1 Oct. 1798
GERBER, JOHN

Wife. (name not given). Children: There were three daughters - names not given.

Ex. John Kortz and Peter Gerber. Cocalico Twp.

21 Feb. 1798   3 May 1798
GACKLIN, MARGARET

Widow of Dietrick Gacklin. Children: Joseph and Samuel Zimmerman and Salome wife of John Hucky.

Ex. John Hucky. Elizabeth Twp.

1 Sept. 1799   9 Nov. 1799
GYER, GEORGE

Wife. Anna Margaret Gyer. Children: George, John, Jacob, Andrew, David, Elizabeth, Barbara, Catharine, Gertrude and Henry. Son-in-law: Mathias Young (wife's name not stated).
Ex. George and John Gyer. Warwick Twp.

16 Jan. 1799   29 March 1799
GODSHALL, LUDWICK
Wife. Barbara Godshall. Children: Catharine, Daniel, David and Elizabeth.
Ex. George Folck. Hempfield Twp.

8 May 1799   12 Feb. 1800
GINDER, HENRY
Wife. Barbara. Children: Jacob, Ann wife of Christian Hammacher, Mary wife of John Stauffer, Barbara wife of David Meissenhelder, Susanna wife of Francis Graff and Fornica wife of Abraham Brubacker.
Ex. Jacob Ginder and Francis Graff. Mt. Joy Twp.

9 Aug. 1798   24 April 1800
GROFF, JOHN
Child: Magdalena wife of Andrew Wissler.
Ex. Andrew Wissler. Warwick Twp.

7 July 1794   30 Aug. 1800
GRYDER, ELIZABETH
Widow of Michael Gryder. Children: Martin, Michael, Susanna and Christian.
Ex. Michael and Christian Gryder. Lancaster Twp.

17 Aug. 1798   27 Oct. 1800
GALL, ADAM
Wife. Elizabeth Gall. Step-children: John and Christian Long.
Ex. John Long and Jacob Jonas. Lancaster Borough.

30 Nov. 1800   27 Dec. 1800
GARMAN, JACOB
Wife. Eleanor Garman. Children: (The names and number not given).
Ex. Leonard Garman and Christian Snider. Earl Twp.

6 March 1800   20 Jan. 1801
GERBER, JACOB
Children: Catharine, Andrew, Mary, Adi, John, Ann, Christian and Jacob.
Ex. Andrew and John Gerber. Donegal Twp.

23 Feb. 1798   27 April 1801
GRILL, ADAM
Wife. Charlotte Grill. Children: John, Adam, Elizabeth wife of Peter Wincholt, Catharine wife of John Ream and Philip.
Ex. Charlotte, Philip and Adam Grill. Cocalico Twp.

6 Aug. 1801   20 Oct. 1801
GUMPF, JOHN DIETRICH
    Wife. Margaret Gumpf. Children: Christopher, Michael and
Margaret wife of John Lightner.
    Ex. Christopher and Michael Gumpf. Lancaster Borough.

6 Nov. 1801   19 Nov. 1802
GALT, MARGARET
    Sister: Elizabeth McCool. Bros.: John, Robert and James
Hanna.
    Ex. James Hanna and William Galt. Salsbury Twp.

21 Dec. 1801   5 May 1802
GRUBB, MARTHA
    Bros. and sister: Juliana, Peter and Samuel Grubb. Legatee:
Elizabeth Fulton (wife of John Fulton).
    Ex. William Kirkpatrick and William Crabb. Lancaster
Borough.

31 May 1802   19 June 1802
GENRICH, JACOB
    Bros. and sisters: David, Abraham, Annie and Freny wife of
John Shenk.
    Ex. John Erb. Warwick Twp.

24 Feb. 1798   1 Oct. 1802
GRIDER, MICHAEL
    Wife. Anna Grider. Children: Martin, John and Michael.
    Ex. Martin Grider and Samuel Nisly. Rapho Twp.

16 Oct. 1794   23 Jan. 1802
GODDETTLE, MICHAEL
    Wife. Margaret Goddettle.
    Ex. Henry Rassman and Jacob Schrit. Rapho Twp.

21 May 1774   --- 1802
GREYBILL, CHRISTIAN
    Wife. Frenna Greybill. Children: Nancy, John, Christley and
Jacob.
    Ex. Jacob Byers and Jacob Harness. Drumore Twp.

12 March 1794   14 March 1803
GREIDER, MARTIN
    Wife. Elizabeth Greider. Children: Christian, Martin, Ann
and Henry.
    Ex. Jacob and Henry Greider. Little Brittain Twp.

1 April 1800   5 April 1803
GRISTE, EDWARD
    Wife. Mary Griste. Children: Job, Mary and Margaret.
    Ex. Job Griste and Emanuel Reynolds. Little Brittain Twp.

3 July 1801   10 June 1803
GUTH, HENRY

Sister: Ann wife of --- Huber. Nieces and nephews: Martin, Jacob, Ann wife of Martin Houser, Christian, Abraham, Magdalena wife of Henry Rohrer and Feronica wife of George Huber (all children of (sister) Ann Huber).
Ex. Abraham and Henry Huber. Conestoga Twp.

6 Jan. 1792   1 July 1803
GLASSER, JACOB
Wife. Catharine Glasser. Children: Dorothea wife of Balsar Bitzer, Christiana and Jacob. Grandchildren: Catharine and Jacob Bitzer.
Ex. Jacob Glasser. Earl Twp.

17 Aug. 1803   3 Sept. 1803
GILLIS, DANIEL
Legatte: John Hentzelman. N.B. It is stated in the will that Daniel Gillis was a Scotchman and had no relatives in America.
Ex. (there were no executors, but letters of Administration were granted). Rapho Twp.

10 Sept. 1803   26 Sept. 1803
GRUBB, JULIANA
Bro.: Samuel Grubb. Step-Bro.: Peter Grubb. Legatees: Elizabeth Fulton and The Presbyterian Church, Lancaster.
Ex. William Kirkpatrick. Lancaster Borough.

19 May 1798   1 March 1804
GREINER, ADAM
Children: Martin and John. Son-in-law: Michael Steckbeck (wife's name not given).
Ex. Martin Greiner. Warwick Twp.

10 May 1800   6 Nov. 1804
GREYBILL, PETER
Wife. Susanna Greybill. Children: Peter and Susanna.
Ex. Susanna Greybill and Christian Huber. Manheim Twp.

20 Nov. 1803   4 Feb. 1804
GETZ, JACOB
Children: Juliana wife of --- Speer, John, Catharine wife of Henry Wolf, Magdaline, Elizabeth wife of --- Eshbach, Peter and Barbara. Son-in-law: Jacob Brand. Grandchildren: Catharine, Elizabeth, George, Maria, Anna and Margaret Speer, John, Elizabeth and Mary Brand.
Ex. John and Jacob Getz. Humpfield Twp.

9 Dec. 1803   1 Oct. 1804
GOOD, ELIZABETH
Children: Peter, John, Margaret wife of Jacob Gochenauer, Ann wife of John Harwick, Elizabeth wife of Jacob Eshleman and Feronica wife of Christian Good.
Ex. John Good. Martic Twp.

17 Jan. 1804   12 Oct. 1805
GRAFF, ELIZABETH

Children: Eve wife of George Graeff and George. Grandchild: Rosana (child of George).
Ex. George Graff and Adam Reigart. Lancaster Borough.

10 June 1795   25 May 1805
GRAFF, HENRY
Wife. Ann Graff. Children: Christian, John, Henry and Ann wife of Abraham Shock.
Ex. Ann and John Graff. Donegal Twp.

10 Jan. 1803   19 Oct. 1805
GROVE, JACOB
Children: Jacob, Martin, Henry, Peter, Feronica wife of Casper Shrick and Margaret.
Ex. Jacob and Henry Grove. Earl Twp.

15 March 1805   21 May 1805
GRUBB, SAMUEL
Step-Bro.: Peter Grubb. Curtis, George, Martha and Mary Grubb (children of Peter).
Ex. William Kirkpatrick. Middletown Twp.

25 March 1805   5 Nov. 1805
GOEPFERT, JOHN
Wife. Elizabeth Goepfert. Children: Catharine wife of --- Small, John, Elizabeth wife of --- Menig, Christiana wife of --- Frederick and Magdalena wife of --- Rickert.
Ex. Peter Lehnert and George Menig. Warwick Twp.

25 Feb. 1802   4 Oct. 1805
GLOUSE, MICHAEL
(This should be CLOUSE.) Children: Adam, Elizabeth and Jacob.
Ex. Adam Clouse and Anthony Hains. Donegal Twp.

10 Sept. 1805   10 Oct. 1805
GLEE, JACOB
(This should be KLEE.) Wife. Barbara Klee. N.B. The names and number of cildren - not given.
Ex. Barbara Klee and John Wumnver. Brecknock Twp.

31 Dec. 1803   25 Nov. 1806
GERBER, CHRISTIAN
Wife. Catharine Gerber. Children: Christian, Anna wife of Michael Segrist, Catharine wife of John Stouffer and Andrew.
Ex. Andrew and Christian Gerber. Hempfield Twp.

6 Feb. 1806   19 July 1806
GRAY, JOSEPH
Wife. Ann Gray. Children: Elizabeth, Jacob, Ann, Margaret, Joseph and Hannah wife of --- Richardson. Grandchildren: Elizabeth and Vincent Richardson.
Ex. Jacob Gray. Little Brittain Twp.

29 Aug. 1806   11 Oct. 1806
GILMORE, ISAAC
      Wife. (name not given). The names and number of children not given.
      Ex. Jack Gilmore. Lancaster Borough.

24 Aug. 1803   25 Aug. 1806
GARMAN, ADAM
      Wife. Barbara Garman. Children: George, Leonard, John, Lewis, Adam, Jacob, Peter, Eve and Susanna.
      Ex. George and Leonard Garman. Earl Twp.

--- 1800   21 Nov. 1807
GROFFEN, MARGARET
      Children: George, Susanna wife of Frederick Brown, Barbara wife of Christian Gognauer and Margaret wife of David Hoober.
      Ex. Jacob Raub and Mathias Miller. Strasburg Twp.

18 Jan. 1807   2 Feb. 1807
GALT, JOHN
      Bros.: James and William Galt. N.B. There was a bequest to the Presbyterian Church of Salsbury.
      Ex. James and William Galt. Salsbury Twp.

1 April 1807   29 May 1807
GIESY, HENRY
      Wife. Magdalena Giesy. Children: John, Elizabeth wife of John Senzel, Susanna wife of Christian Musselman and Magdalena.
      Ex. John and Magdalena Giesy. Hempfield Twp.

8 Aug. 1805   17 Sept. 1808
GOOD, CHRISTIAN
      Wife. Christiana Good. Children: David, Samuel, Mary, Susanna and Christiana.
      Ex. Christiana and David Good. Earl Twp.

25 July 1798   8 Jan. 1808
GRUB, CASPER
      Wife. Elizabeth Grub. Children: Christian, George, Casper, Peter, Jacob, Susanna wife of Martin Bard and Elizabeth wife of Frederick Kissel. Grandchild: Daniel Bard.
      Ex. Christian Grub and Charles Rudy. Warwick Twp.

20 March 1808   --- 1808
GETTINGER, BARBARA
      Wife of Abraham Gettinger who was the second husband - Joel Witmer being the first. There were three children by the second husband and one with the first - their names are not given.
      Ex. (omitted). Earl Twp.

1 Sept. 1806   20 July 1808
GROSH, JOHN
      Wife. Mary Magdalena Grosh. Children: Magdalena wife of --- Kreiter, Daniel, Jacob and Elizabeth. N.B. There was a bequest made to the resident and director of "The Society for the

Propagating of the Gospel among the Heathen" established at
Bethlehem.
Ex. Daniel and Mathias Grosh. Warwick Twp.

17 Oct. 1806   14 March 1809
GRAFF, WILLIAM
Mother: Susanna Reichenbach. Step-father: William
Reichenbach. Half-Bro.: Edward Reichenbach.
Ex. Susanna Reichenbach and William Reichenbach. Lancaster
Borough.

5 Jan. 1808   9 Feb. 1810
GEHMAN, DANIEL
Children: Daniel, Maria and Veronica. Son-in-law: John
Oberholtzer (wife's name not stated).
Ex. Daniel Gehman and John Oberholtzer.

10 Aug. 1805   31 March 1810
GRAIG, AGNESS
(This should be CRAIG.) Nephew: Richard Crain. N.B. There
was a bequest to the Presbyterian Church of Lancaster.
Ex. Richard Crain, James Humes. Lancaster Borough.

22 May 1810   5 June 1810
GEBEL, WILLIAM
Children: Henry, Johannes, Valentine, Daniel, John, Martin,
Abraham, Catharine wife of John Johnson, Elizabeth wife of John
Michael, Mary Esther wife of Francis Furman, Susanna wife of
Samuel Linton and Barbara wife of John Frankfaster.
Ex. Johannes Gebel and Christian Frantz. Manheim Twp.

15 Feb. 1810   10 May 1810
GERHARD, JOHN
Wife. Susanna Gerhard. Children: John, Frederick, Catharine
wife of Jacob Bixler, Susanna wife of Joseph Yochy, Jacob,
Elizabeth, Barbara wife of Henry Harnish, Christian, William and
Peter.
Ex. John and Frederick Gerhard. Cocalico Twp.

21 Jan. 1810   18 Aug. 1810
GIBBONS, JAMES
Wife. Deborah Gibbons. Children: Daniel, Samuel, Mary wife
of John Kendall and Rachel wife of William Daniel. Grandson:
James Gibbons Bonsall (parents' names not stated).
Ex. Samuel and Daniel Gibbons. Lampeter Twp.

27 March 1810   3 May 1810
GERBER, HENRY
Wife. Elizabeth Gerber.
Ex. Christian Gerber and George Bard. Cocalico Twp.

29 April 1810   28 July 1810
GREBILL, JACOB
(This should be KREBILL.) Children: Henry, John, Catharine
and Ann.

Ex. John Forrer and Henry Krebill. Manor Twp.

29 Sept. 1793 27 Aug. 1810
GOCHET, ISAAC
    (This should be COCHET.) Wife. Elizabeth Cocket. Children:
Sophia, Elizabeth, Isaac, Dietrich, Mathias, Bernard and Juliana
wife of Ludwig Dietrick.
    Ex. Henry Grim. Earl Twp.

1 Oct. 1810   18 Oct. 1810
GROSMAN, MICHAEL
    Wife. Mary Grosman. Children: John and George.
    Ex. John and George Grosman. Warwick Twp.

19 Feb. 1811   7 March 1811
GRAY, GEORGE
    Children: Isabella and George. Bro.: James Gray.
    Ex. Dietrich Deshong. Earl Twp.

15 May 18097   20 Aug. 1807
GEHR, GEORGE
    Wife. Elizabeth Gehr. Children - (The names and number not
given).
    Ex. Elizabeth Gehr. Cocalico Twp.

26 May 1810   3 Dec. 1811
GEESY, PHILIP
    Wife. Anna Geesy. Children: Joseph, Christian, Barbara wife
of John Funk, Elizabeth wife of Thomas Marlen and John.
Grandchild: Susanna Marlen.
    Ex. Joseph and Christian Geesy. Town of New Hannn (?)
(Lancaster Co).

18 Oct. 1810   23 Jan. 1811
GERTEL, MARGARET
    Children: Barbara, Elizabeth wife of Christian Smith and
Anna wife of Joseph Hogentobler. Bro.: John Waller.
    Ex. Philip Schnyder. Hempfield Twp.

7 Sept. 1811   2 Nov. 1811
GROH, CHRISTIAN
    Wife. Barbara Groh. Children: Anna wife of Andrew Kauffman,
John, Christian, Mary and Barbara wife of Christian Gute.
    Ex. Benjamin Miller and John Groh. Donegal Twp.

2 June 1805   19 Dec. 1811
GALT, JAMES
    Children: James, Alice, Letitia, Ann, Jane wife of Robert
Right, John, Thomas and William.
    Ex. William and James Galt. Salsbury Twp.

10 Nov. 1810   11 Feb. 1811
GREBILL, JACOB

84

(This should be KREBILL.) Wife. Elizabeth Krebill. Children:
Jacob, Peter, Christian, Anna, Elizabeth and Maria wife of
Christian Nissley.
    Ex. Jacob Krebill and Christian Nissely. Donegal Twp.

1 May 1806   24 Jan. 1812
GAUL, MATHIAS
    Wife. Ann Margaret Gaul. Children: Catharine wife of
Christian Richert and Philipina wife of John Paul.
    Ex. Christian Richert and Jacob Mainzer. Earl Twp.

9 Oct. 1815   2 March 1812
GRAFF, BENJAMIN
    Wife. Catharine Graff. Stepson: Abraham Graff. Bro.: John
Graff. Sisters: Mary wife of --- Herr, Barbara wife of Jacob
Eshleman and Veronica wife of --- Herr.
    Ex. Jacob Neff Jr., Jacob Graff and Jacob Eshleman.
Strasburg Twp.

10 Feb. 1812   19 May 1812
GROSS, CONRAD
    Wife. Julina Gross. Children: Mary, Catharine, John, Samuel,
Lawrence, Henry and Elizabeth. [Book K, p. 233]
    Ex. Simon Eckenroth and Thomas Masterson. Elizabethtown.

10 Oct. 1807   6 Aug. 1812
GUTH, CHRISTIAN
    Wife. Barbara Guth. Children: Christian, Magdalena, Mary,
Barbara, Elizabeth, Esther and Catharine.
    Ex. Christian Guth and John Burkert. Brecknock Twp.

13 May 1806   18 March 1812
GROSH, PHILIP
    Wife. Anna Grosh. Children: Peter, Mathias, John, Samuel,
Christian, Rosana wife of John Shreiner and George.
    Ex. Mathias Grosh and Christian Huber. Hempfield Twp.

16 March 1812   15 April 1812
GOURLY, MARTHA
    Children: Eliza and Catharine.
    Ex. John Henderson and Samuel Muller. Lampeter Twp.

7 Nov. 1811   25 April 1812
GUTH, JACOB
    Wife. Veronica Guth. Children: John, Christian, Jacob and
Samuel.
    Ex. John Brockert and Peter Guth. Brecknock Twp.

5 March 1819   15 June 1812
GENSEMER, GEORGE
    Wife. Margaret Gensemer. Children: Daniel, Christiana,
Sophia, Henry (and six others, names not given).
    Ex. Henry and Daniel Gensmer. Cocalico Twp.

25 May 1812   15 June 1812
GRUB, ISREAL
    Wife. Elizabeth Grub. Children: John, Elizabeth, Ann,
Daniel, Susanna and Christian.
    Ex. John Gisch and John Albert. Mt. Joy Twp.

27 May 1812   8 Aug. 1812
GREBILL, JOHN
    (This should be KREBILL.) Mother: Magdalena Krebill.
    Ex. Magdalena Krebill. Conestoga Twp.

30 July 1810   2 Oct. 1812
GUMPF, MARGARET
    Children: Elizabeth wife of --- Wright, Mary wife of John
Yenser, Margaret wife of Michael Gumpf, Christiana wife of Isreal
Nestlebroad, Peter, Henry, Susanna wife of Daniel Wenditz and
Catharine wife of John Sowerbeer.
    Ex. Michael Gumpf and Philip Messencope. Lancaster Borough.

14 Aug. 1809   4 Jan. 1812
GUNKLE, CHRISTIAN
    (This should be KUNKLE.) Children: George, Peter, Jacob,
Henry, Barbara, Christiana and Elizabeth.
    Ex. Peter Sider and Daniel Eckman. Bart Twp.

3 June 1797   16 Aug. 1813
GUETY, MARTIN
    Wife. Barbara Guety. Children: Catharine, Elizabeth and
Mary.
    Ex. Barbara Guety. Lancaster Borough.

6 Oct. 1809   15 Oct. 1813
GARMAN, LEONARD
    Wife. Catharine Garman. Children: Adam, Catharine, Elizabeth
wife of Henry Leppert, Anna wife of John Seitze, John, Eve wife
of John Gill, Leonard, Mary wife of Henry Roth, Susanna wife of
John Myers, Jacob, George and Christiana wife of Leonard Glais.

4 April 1812   24 Feb. 1813
GRIDER, HENRY
    (This should be CRYDER.) Wife. Magdalena Cryder. Child:
Susanna wife of David Burkholder.
    Ex. Magdalena and Tobias Cryder. Lampeter Twp.

3 Aug. 1813   21 March 1814
GRAFF, CATHARINE
    Bros. and sisters: George, Andrew, Sebastian, Mary Magdalena
wife of Conrad Doll and Margaret wife of (name omitted).
    Ex. John Graff and Adam Reigart. Bethlehem, Northampton Co.

29 March 1814   25 April 1814
GOOD, ABRAHAM
    Wife. Barbara Good. Children: Jonas. (there were others,
name and number not given).
    Ex. Jonas and John Good. Brecknock Twp.

4 Dec. 1813   28 May 1814
GEYER, BARBARA
    Bros. and sisters: Andrew, David, George, Elizabeth wife
of --- Shimp, Catharine wife of --- Berkenbein and Gertrude wife
of --- Young.
    Ex. Georg Geyer. Warwick Twp.

2 Oct. 1813   25 Jan. 1814
GRYDER, JACOB
    Children: Eliza and Nancy.
    Ex. Christian Gryder and John Buchanan. Drumore Twp.

20 March 1814   22 March 1814
GRISELL, ELISHA
    Wife. Edith Grissell. Children: Morris, Lydia wife of David
Herron, Abby, Thomas, Elisha, Susan, Jesse, Edith and Christiana.
    Ex. Edith Grisell and Morris Grisell. Colerain Twp.

22 April 1814   17 May 1814
GRAEBILL, ABRAHAM
    Wife. Catharine Graebill. Children: Christian, John,
Abraham, Catharine wife of Felix Binkley, Nancy wife of Abraham
Grove, Peggy wife of George Meyer and Maria wife of Isaac Diller
(her second husband - John Ditto being the first).
    Ex. George Meyers, John and Abraham Graebill.

9 Aug. 1811   12 Feb. 1813
GRBHARD, JACOB
    Wife. Mary Grbhard. Children: Gotlieb, Jacob, Joseph,
Benjamin and Frena.
    Ex. Mary Grbhard and Frederick Byroad. Donegal Twp.

20 Oct. 1814   16 Nov. 1814
GUNDACKER, JOHN
    Children: Catharine and Elizabeth.
    Ex. Samuel Carpenter and Nathaniel Lightner. Lancaster
Borough.

10 De.c 1814   26 Jan. 1815
GOOD, CATHARINE
    Bros.: Jacob, Samuel, Christian and Peter.
    Ex. Peter Good. Earl Twp.

12 Jan. 1815   11 Feb. 1815
GREENLAND, FLOWER
    Wife. Mary Greenland. Children: Abner, Anna wife of Richard
Fisher, John, Jacob, Thomas and Mary.
    Ex. John Beam. Conestoga Twp.

16 Oct. 1808   8 April 1815
GREINEWALD, ABRAHAM
    Wife. Susanna Greinewald. Children: Abraham, Jacob,
Elizabeth wife of George Albert, Christopher, Susanna wife of
Henry Shoff, Christian, Michael, Henry and Peter.
    Ex. Abraham Greinewald. Manor Twp.

9 April 1812   27 April 1815
GEST, JOSEPH
    Wife. (name omitted). Children: Joseph, Deborah, Elizabeth, Hannah wife of Isaac Hains, Margaret wife of John Williams, John and Benjamin.
    Ex. Joseph, John and Benjamin Gest. Sadsbury Twp.

3 Feb. 1815   29 May 1815
GERBER, CHRISTIAN
    Wife. Anna Gerber. Children: Jacob and John.
    Ex. Anna Gerber and Christian Frantz. Earl Twp.

16 Aug. 1814   14 June 1815
GIBSON, JAMES (Colonel)
    Wife. Matilda Henrietta Gibson. N.B. Colonel Gibson was "Colonel of the Fourth Rifle Regiment of the United States."
    Ex. Matilda Henrietta Gibson. Twp. omitted.

29 Oct. 1814   5 Dec. 1815
GOOD, CHRISTIANA
    Child: Barbara wife of John Herr.
    Ex. John Herr. Warwick Twp.

6 Jan. 1816   6 May 1816
GISCH, ABRAHAM
    Wife. (name omitted). Children: Elizabeth, Nancy, Abraham, John, Jacob, Christian, Polly, Catharine, David and Michael
    Ex. Jacob Hoarst, Samuel and Jacob Gisch. Donegal Twp.

12 Jan. 1816   20 Jan. 1816
GRAFF, ANDREW
    Wife. Catharine Graff. Children: John, Margaret, Catharine, Mary wife of Conrad Doll, Elizabeth wife of William Moore, George, Henry and Michael. Grandchildren: Catharine and Elizabeth Doll and John Stoy (who was a son of Catharine who was the wife of Gustavus Stoy).
    Ex. John Graff and Adam Reigart. Lancaster Borough.

7 Jan. 1816   20 Feb. 1816
GRUBB, HENRY
    Wife. Barbara Grubb. The names and number of children not given. There is mention made in will of three daughters.
    Ex. Barbara Grubb and Martin Carpenter. Lampeter Twp.

13 Feb. 1816   14 March 1816
GUTJAHR, CHRISTIAN
    Wife. (name omitted). Children: Christian, Elizabeth, Mathias, John, Susan, Regina and Samuel.
    Ex. Benjamin Krider and Mathias Gutjahr. Warwick Twp.

19 May 1813   26 March 1816
GOOD, HENRY
    Wife. Wallindine Good. Children: Peter, Barbara, Elizabeth, Joseph and Henry.
    Ex. Peter and Joseph Good. Brecknock Twp.

2 Dec. 1815   23 Jan. 1816
GROSS, GEORGE
    (This should be CROSS.) Wife. Sarah Gross. Father:
Christopher Gross. (there were children - the names and number
not given).
    Ex. Martin Rudisell and John Reis Jr. Manheim Twp.

7 Feb. 1815   17 March 1817
GETZ, MARY
    Children: Jacob, Catharine wife of Charles Reisinger,
George, Daniel, Frederick and Peter.
    Ex. John Getz and John Getz Jr. Lancaster Borough.

4 Feb. 1818   31 March 1818
GEITNER, JOHN G.
    Wife. Maria Elizabeth Geitner. Children: Jacob, Rosina,
Susan, Maria and Elizabeth.
    Ex. Mathias Tshudy and Jacob Geitner. Lititz Twp.

20 Feb. 1818   21 April 1818
GANTZ, GEORGE
    Children: Magdalena wife of George Blasterer, Frederick,
Catharine wife of John Stoneroad and Peter.
    Ex. Christopher Shower and John Arnd. Rapho Twp.

21 Feb. 1818   8 May 1818
GAULT, LETISHA
    Children: William, Elsie, James and Thomas. Grandchildren:
Letisha (child of Thomas) and Letisha (child of William).
    Ex. William Robinson. Salsbury Twp.

1 March 1815   8 Aug. 1818
GERBER, MAGDALENA
    Bros. and sisters: Peter, Catharine, John, Ann, Barbara and
Elizabeth.
    Ex. Charles Gerber. Lampeter Twp.

11 April 1818   28 Oct. 1818
GLAIS, LEONARD
    Children: George, Sarah and Lydia. N.B. There was a bequest
to Lutheran Church named Berg Stross.
    Ex. Christian Hurst and Leonard Garman. Earl Twp.

17 Feb. 1815   5 Dec. 1818
GIBBEL, JOHN
    Wife. Elizabeth Gibbel. Children: Christian, Elizabeth,
Samuel, Henry, Salome, Daniel, Christiana, Mary, Abraham, Joseph
and John. Grandchild: Susanna (child of John).
    Ex. Christian and Abraham Gibbel. Warwick Twp.

19 Feb. 1813   30 Dec. 1818
GESSLER, JOHN
    Wife. Elizabeth Gissler. Children: Mary wife of Christian
Killheffer, John, Henry and Michael.
    Ex. Philip Schissler. Manor Twp.

19 Aug. 1818   17 Oct. 1818
GOUTER, PETER
    Wife. Susanna Gouter. Children: Elizabeth wife of Jacob
Eberman, Susanna wife of John Weidler and Mary wife of Henry
Smith.
    Ex. Susanna Gouter and John Weidler. Lancaster City.

7 May 1816   13 March 1819
GERNER, FREDERICK
    Children: Jacob, Catharine, Mark, Frederick, Michael and
Christiana.
    Ex. Jacob Gerner. Cocalico Twp.

8 May 1819   26 May 1819
GRAY, WILLIAM
    Wife. Elizabeth Gray. Sister: Nancy.
    Ex. James and Thomas Setrrett. Mt. Joy Twp.

18 Sep 1797   8 Nov. 1797
HAND, SARAH
    Half-sister: Jane Henry.
    Ex. Henry Stewart. Twp. omitted.

3 Oct. 1793   7 Sept. 1797
HERSH, CONRAD
    Wife. Sophia Hersh. Child: John
    Ex. John Hersh. Lampeter Twp.

9 Sept. 1794   18 April 1797
HACKMAN, ULERICH
    Wife. Eve. Children: Barbara wife of Abraham Beydler and
Catharine wife of Jacob Ruff. Bro.: Henry Hackman.
    Ex. Eve and Henry Hackman. Mt. Joy Twp.

22 March 1797   2 Feb. 1798
HOOK, MICHAEL
    Wife. Anna Hook. Children: Michael, Maria, Ferdinand,
Christine, Anthony and Andrew.
    Ex. Anna and Anthony Hook. Lancaster Borough

27 Sept. 1788   12 June 1798
HABECKER, JOSEPH
    Children: Christian, Joseph, Elizabeth wife of John Shenck
and Barbara wife of Abraham Miller.
    Ex. Jacob Carl. Manor Twp.

17 July 1790   10 Nov. 1798
HESS, JOHN
    Wife. (name omitted). Children: David (there were others,
names and number not given).
    Ex. Christian Shenck and David Hess. Conestoga Twp.

1 Nov. 1798   28 Nov. 1798
HEGER, FERONICA

Children: John and Elizabeth. Grandchildren: John, Elizabeth, Catharine, George, Hannah and David (children of Elizabeth - husband's name not stated).
Ex. Henry Westly. Warwick Twp.

3 May 1797   28 Nov. 1798
HAYES, CATHARINE
Children: David and Jean. Grandchildren: Robert, Patrick and Elenor Hayes.
Ex. James Hays. Rapho Twp.

28 March 1789   8 Oct. 1798
HUBER, PETER
Wife. Anna Huber. Children: Joseph, John, Elizabeth, Anna and Johanna.
Ex. Joseph, John, Anna and Johanna Huber. Warwick Twp.

9 Jan. 1793   3 April 1799
HUBER, JOHN
Wife. Anna Huber. Children: Henry, Mary, Jacob, John, Christian, David, Anna and Christina.
Ex. John and Henry Huber. Warwick Twp.

6 April 1799   20 April 1799
HILLER, JACOB
Wife. Magdalena Hiller. Children: Jacob, John and Susanna.
Ex. Adam Minigh Jr. and Magdalena Hiller. Rapho Twp.

4 Oct. 1798   1 July 1800
HUBER, JOSEPH
Wife. Susanna Huber. Children: Joseph, Peter and Michael. Step-son: John Graham. Bro.: Michael Huber.
Ex. Susanna and Michael Huber. Lancaster Borough.

21 Oct. 1800   26 Nov. 1800
HABECKER, JOSEPH
Wife. Maria Habecker. Children: John, Barbara and Maria.
Ex. Jacob Carly and Isaac Kauffman. Manor Twp.

8 Oct. 1783   18 Feb. 1802
HOOLE, MARY
Widow of Wendle Hoole. Children: Christian, Joseph, Jacob, Barbara wife of Isaac Rife, Anna wife of David Landis, Mary wife of Abraham Shefer, Susanna wife of Shem Graybill, Elizabeth wife of John Bookwalter and Judith wife of John Erb.
Ex. Jacob Hoole. Earl Twp.

8 Sept. 1802   23 Oct. 1802
HERSH, JOHN
Wife. Catharine Hersh. Children: John, Catharine, Sophia, Elizabeth and Jacob.
Ex. (Bro.) Frederick Hersh. Lampeter Twp.

30 April 1791   10 Jan. 1803
HARTAFEL, SOPHIA

Children: Elizabeth wife of Christopher Demuth, Mary wife of Henry Gross and Sophia wife of Charles Heinitsh.
Ex. Christopher Demuth. Lancaster Borough.

20 March 1794   22 Jan. 1803
HERR, ABRAHAM
    Wife. Feronica Herr. Children: Christian, Ann wife of John Graff, Magdalena wife of Jacob Smith and Feronica wife of Henry Kauffman.
    Ex. Feronica and Christian Herr. Lancaster Twp.

5 Jan. 1803   21 Feb. 1803
HOFFMAN, MICHAEL
    Wife. Barbara. Children: John, Michael, Ann wife of ---
Brenneman, Elizabeth and Jacob. Grandchildren: Feronica Brenneman.
    Ex. Abraham Hammacher and Michael Hoffman. Hempfield Twp.

7 Feb. 1802   14 March 1803
HENRY, JAMES
    Mother: Ann Henry. Bros.: Dominic, Patrick, John and Francis. Half-sister: Sarah Henry.
    Ex. Dominic and Patrick Henry. Lancaster Borough.

10 Nov. 1802   28 March 1803
HOUGH, BENJAMIN
    Wife. Sarah Hough. Child: Benjamin.
    Ex. Sarah Hough and Joshua Brown. Little Brittain Twp.

7 April 1797   31 May 1809
HOFFER, MATHIAS
    Children: Rudolph, George and Christian (there were other children, names omitted). N.B. The writer of the will was married twice — names of wives not given.
    Ex. John Erb and Joseph Bamberger. Warwick Twp.

23 Dec. 1793   2 July 1803
HUBLEY, BERNARD
    Wife. Mary Hubley. Children: Adam, Magdalena, Frederick, Bernard, Jacob, Elizabeth, Barbara, Michael, Samuel, Isaac and Ann. Grandchildren: Hannah, Mary, Charles, Sophia, Sarah, William and Eliza (children of Adam).
    Ex. Mary Hubley and Rev. Henry Muhlenberg. Lancaster Borough.

26 Aug. 1803   9 Sept. 1803
HEINITCH, CHARLES
    Children: Charlotte, Sophia, Augustus, Henry, Frederick and Henrietta.
    Ex. John Eberman and Philip Diffenderfer. Lancaster Borough.

30 Aug. 1798   17 Sept. 1803
HUBER, JOHN

Wife. Anna Huber. Children: Christian, Elizabeth wife of
Peter Bauchman and Mary wife of Jacob Steman.
Ex. Christian Kauffman and Christian Huber. Hempfield Twp.

15 July 1803   24 Oct. 1803
HOOBER, JACOB
Wife. Susanna Hoober. Child: Jacob. Mother: Mary Hoober
(the wife of Christian Hoober). Sisters: Mary Hoober and
Catharine wife of --- Hershy. Bros.: Henry, Christian and
Abraham.
Ex. John Funk and Martin Mellinger. Strasburg Twp.

20 Oct. 1803   15 Feb. 1804
HATHORN, SAMUEL
Wife. Anna Hathorn. Children: Samuel, Nancy wife of ---
Miller, Elizabeth, Margaret, Mary, Anna, Sarah and Abigail.
Ex. Cornelius Collins and Samuel Hathorn. Twp. omitted.

1 Sept. 1802   30 July 1804
HUBLEY, MICHAEL
Wife. Rosenna Hubley. Children: Adam, Elizabeth, Sabina
and John.
Ex. John Hubley. Lancaster Borough.

28 Feb. 1804   14 April 1804
HOFFMAN, MICHAEL
Bros.: John and Jacob Hoffman. Sister: Elizabeth Hoffman.
Step-mother: Barbara Hoffman. Uncles: Christian Kauffman and
Joseph Charles.
Ex. Christian Kauffman and Joseph Charles. Hempfield Twp.

---   30 Oct. 1804
HURST, JOSEPH
N.B. This is a German will - it was not copied on records
and the translation lost.
Ex. John and Michael Hurst. Earl Twp.

11 Aug. 1804   15 Aug. 1804
HUBER, JACOB
Wife. Barbara Huber.
Ex. Barbara Huber. Strasburg Twp.

28 Aug. 1804   24 Sept. 1804
HOPSON, JOHN
Children: Elizabeth and Rebecca wife of Jacob Krug.
Ex. Jacob Krug and Elizabeth Hopson. Lancaster Borough.

20 Oct. 1804   11 Nov. 1804
HAMAKER, JOHN
Wife. Mary Hamaker. Children: Elizabeth wife of Joseph
Evans, Abraham, John, Christian, Daniel and Joseph.
Ex. Abraham Hamaker and Joseph Evans. Hempfield Twp.

22 Oct. 1805   28 Nov. 1805
HOFFMAN, GEORGE

Wife. Elizabeth Hoffman. Children: Christian, John, Jacob, Henry and Elizabeth.
Ex. Christian Zimmervian and Henry Hoffman. Carnarvon Twp.

23 March 1802   4 March 1805
HERR, BARBARA
Children: Fronica, Esther, Abraham, John, David, Benjamin and Christian.
Ex. Christian and Abraham Herr. Manor Twp.

19 July 1800   12 Feb. 1805
HOUSEHOLDER, LAWRENCE
Wife. Margaret Householder. Children: Jacob, Barbara wife of Frederick Adam, Catharine wife of George Stober, Elizabeth, Susanna and Margaret.
Ex. Jacob Householder and George Weidman. Cocalico Twp.

19 June 1805   31 Oct. 1805
HAGY, JACOB
Wife. Elizabeth Hagy. Children: Samuel, Elizabeth wife of John Stover (and four other children - names not given).
Grandchildren: Elizabeth and Susanna Stover.
Ex. Jacob Hagy. Cocalico Twp.

15 Dec. 1804   28 Dec. 1805
HIESTAND, HENRY
Wife. Elizabeth. Children: John, Henry, Peter, Jacob, Elizabeth and Barbara. Grandchildren: Samuel and Henry (sons of Henry), Jacob, Andrew, Henry, John and Peter (sons of John).
Ex. John Newkomer Jr. Manor Twp.

5 July 1803   13 Dec. 1805
HERR, FERONICA
Children: Christian, Ann, Magdalena wife of Jacob Smith and Feronica wife of Henry Kauffman.
Ex. Christian Herr. Lancaster Twp.

16 Jan. 1806   29 April 1806
HARLACHER, SAMUEL
Wife. Elizabeth Harlacher. Children: Charles and Samuel (there were three daughters - names omitted).
Ex. Ludwig Gross and Peter Martin. Cocalico Twp.

25 July 1806   11 Aug. 1806
HAMBRIGHT, JOHN
Wife. Susanna Hambright. Children: John, George, Elizabeth, Frederick, William and Sarah.
Ex. Susanna and Henry Hambright. Lancaster Borough.

16 Oct. 1805   12 April 1806
HUBER, ELIZABETH
Children: Barbara, Elizabeth, Susanna, Anna and Mary.
Ex. Martin Metzler. Warwick Twp.

28 April 1802   30 May 1806
HENDERSON, MATTHEW
     Wife. Rachel Henderson. Children: James, Barton, Matthew,
John, David, Thomas, Archibald and Clemson.
     Ex. Rachel and James Henderson. Salisbury Twp.

4 Jan. 1801   20 Aug. 1806
HERSHEY, ANDREW
     Wife. Maria Hershey. Children: Catharine, Ann, Jacob,
Maria, Andrew, Henry, Elizabeth and John.
     Ex. Maria and Jacob Hershey. Donegal Twp.

1 Aug. 1806   22 Nov. 1806
HERMAN, CHRISTIAN
     Wife. Elizabeth Herman. Children: Joseph, John, Elizabeth
wife of John Meyer, Mary wife of John Bender, Catharine wife of
Ludwig Gross, Salome wife of John Serts and Peggy wife of John
McCloud.
     Ex. Joseph Herman and Ludwig Grose. Earl Twp.

21 Jan. 1806   25 May 1806
HARKEN, CHARLES
     Wife. Elizabeth Harken. Children: Mary and Anna.
     Ex. George Deett. Manheim Twp.

6 Dec. 1805   17 March 1806
HOLL, BARBARA
     Widow of Peter Holl. Child: Christian. Grandchildren:
Samuel, Christian and Jacob (children of Christian).
     Ex. Christian Herr. Manor Twp.

22 July 1806   15 Aug. 1806
HAYS, ROBERT
     Bros. and sisters: Samuel, John and Margaret Hays.
     Ex. Samuel Hays. Little Brittain Twp.

23 Jan. 1805   3 Jan. 1806
HOLTZINGER, MAGDALENA
     Children: Casper, Peter Kessler, Margaret wife of John
Shreck, John, Mell, Anna wife of Jacob Miller, Rosinah and
Abraham Kessler. N.B. It would appear that the writer of the
will had been formerly married to a Kessler - as her two sons
Peter and Abraham bear that name. No mention of it is made in
the will.
     Ex. John and Abraham Kessler. Brecknock Twp.

15 Oct. 1806   19 Oct. 1806
HERSHY, CHRISTIAN
     Children: Christian, Andrew, Abraham, Joseph and Catharine
wife of --- Bauman. Grandchildren: Christian, Mary and Peter
Bauman.
     Ex. Christian and Abraham Hershy. Manor Twp.

24 June 1805   29 Dec. 1806
HARNISH, MICHAEL

Wife. Barbara Harnish. Children: Michael, Jacob, Abraham, Joseph, Rudolph and Barbara wife of Samuel Meyers.
Ex. Jacob and Abraham Harnish. Conestoga Twp.

13 July 1807   11 Aug. 1807
HERR, ABRAHAM
Children: Christian, Mary wife of Andrew Hershy, Elizabeth wife of Christian Bear, Anna wife of John Hershy and Esther.
Ex. Christian Herr and Andrew Hershy. Manor Twp.

28 June 1806   25 Nov. 1807
HEFFLY, JOSEPH
Wife. Rachel Heffly. Children: John, Jacob, Mary, Hannah, Joseph and Susanna. Grandchild: John Widder (parents' names not stated).
Ex. Joseph Heffly and Peter Martin. Cocalico Twp.

28 Sept. 1804   16 May 1807
HANS, JOHN
Wife. Anna Hans. Children: Henry, Elizabeth, Barbara and Susanna. Son-in-law: Frederick Demay (wife's name not stated).
Ex. Henry Hans and John Erb. Warwick Twp.

7 Aug. 1805   21 April 1807
HOYLE, GEORGE
Wife. Philibina Hoyle. Children: John, George and Barbara wife of --- Fether (there were four other children, names not given). Grandchild: Susanna Fether.
Ex. John and George Hoyle. Elizabeth Twp.

5 May 1805   31 Oct. 1807
HERR, MARY
Children: Mary wife of Andrew Kauffman, Barbara wife of Jacob Bixler, Feronica wife of John Seegrist, Elizabeth wife of George Hyde, Abraham and Anna wife of --- Kendig. Grandchildren: John, Henry, Mary, Jacob, Feronica, Christian, Daniel, Samuel and Martin Kendig.
Ex. George Hyde. Manor Twp.

15 April 1807   8 Nov. 1807
HAMILTON, JAMES
Children: William, James, Jennet wife of --- McIlvain, Margaret, Mary wife of Samuel Humes, Elizabeth, Sarah wife of --- Porter. Grandchildren: Hamilton and Elizabeth Humes (children of Mary) and Mary Stell (parents' names not stated).
Ex. William and James Hamilton. Leacock Twp.

20 March 1798 6 July 1807
HONE, VALENTINE
Wife. Mary Hone. Children: John, Nicholas, George, Mary wife of Henry Bugh, Elizabeth wife of William Beltz and Christina wife of Isaac Barr.
Ex. Christian Frantz and Peter Reist. Manheim Twp.

10 Sept. 1808   18 Oct. 1808
HOPSON, ELIZABETH
      Sisters: Christina Musser (widow of George Musser) and
Rebecca wife of --- Krug. Nephews: George and Frederick Krug.
N.B.   There were bequests made to the "Sisters' House" at
Nazereth and to "The Congregation" at Lititz and Bethlehem.
      Ex. Jacob Krug. Lititz Twp.

17 Jan. 1808   30 Jan. 1808
HIESTAND, JACOB
      Wife. Margaret. Children: John, Peter, Magdalena wife of
Michael Zittel, Jacob, Barbara wife of Peter Erb, Elizabeth wife
of Jacob Harkman, Catharine wife of Jacob Meyer and Christian.
      Ex. Joseph Goohmarier and Abraham Hammaker. Hempfield Twp.

2 Jan. 1808   --- 1808
HOLL, CHRISTIAN
      Wife. Mary Holl. Children: Daniel, Elizabeth, Susanna and
Samuel.
      Ex. Daniel Witwer. Earl Twp.

10 Sept. 1807   1 Aug. 1808
HARRIS, RICHARD
      Children: Samuel, George and Joseph. Grandchildren: Joseph,
Richard, Rebecca and Susanna Harris (children of Joseph).
      Ex. George Harris. Warwick Twp.

12 June 1808   5 Dec. 1808
HOLL, EPHRAIM
      Wife. Magdalena Holl. Child: Daniel. Bro.: Peter Holl
      Ex. John Keller, Magdalena and Peter Holl. Warwick Twp.

3 March 1808   9 April 1808
HOFF, ANDREW
      Wife. Barbara Hoff. Children: Elizabeth wife of Christian
Hershey and Ann wife of Abraham Hostetter. Stepsons: John and
Abraham Hiestand.
      Ex. John Hiestand and John Steman. Manor Twp.

16 Oct. 1803   2 Feb. 1809
HELD, HENRY
      Wife. Juliana Held. Children: Henry, Susan, Anna, Mary,
Elizabeth and Catharine.
      Ex. John Lemon. Rapho Twp.

8 Sept. 1808   21 Feb. 1809
HIMMELBERGER, JACOB JR.
      Wife. Catharine Himmelberger. Father: Jacob.
      Ex. Catharine Himmelberger. Cocalico Twp.

5 Aug. 1708   4 May 1809
HUFFNAGLE, GEORGE
      Wife. Magdalena Huffnagle. Children: Catharine wife of
George Shaeffer, George, Peter, Michael, Elizabeth wife of Martin

Jordan, Mary wife of John Bamberger and Charlotte wife of
Frederick Nagel. Grandchildren: Eliza, Ann and Maria Nagel.
    Ex. John Bomberger and Casper Shaeffer. Lancaster Borough.

23 July 1802   1 Sept. 1809
HUTTENSTEIN, HENRY
    Bros.: Jacob and William Huttenstein. Sisters: Catharine
Kepner and Dorothea Reifehneider.
    Ex. William and Henry Huttenstein. Lancaster Borough.

1 March 1806   19 Sept. 1809
HENLY, MICHAEL
    Wife. Barbara Henly. There were four children - names not
given.
    Ex. Barbara Henly. Cocalico Twp.

24 Sept. 1809   23 Nov. 1809
HAFFLY, JOHN
    Wife. Elizabeth Haffly. Children: Mary, Elizabeth and
Margaret.
    Ex. Frederick Byrode. Donegal Twp.

6 April 1809   6 Feb. 1810
HERR, FRANCIS
    Wife. Feronica Herr. Children: John, Francis, Martin,
Elizabeth, Esther wife of Martin Eshleman, Matty wife of Abraham
Graff, Anna wife of Jacob Weaver and Fanny wife of Benjamin
Eshleman. Grandchildren: Marry Myley (parents' names not
stated).
    Ex. John Herr and Abraham Graff. Lampeter Twp.

2 June 1800   12 May 1810
HUMMER, JOHN
    Wife. Feronica Hummer. Children: John, Michael, Mary,
Elizabeth, Sarah, Jacob, Abraham, Froney, Catharine and Rachel.
    Ex. John Gibble and Michael Hummer. Rapho Twp.

16 Nov. 1808   30 Nov. 1808
HUBER, JACOB
    Wife. Barbara Huber. Children: Martin, Barbara wife of
Henry Hoober, Jacob, Ann wife of Abraham Hoober and Susanna wife
of Abraham Gochnower. Grandchildren: Jacob and Barbara Huber
(children of Jacob).
    Ex. Martin and Abraham Huber. Martic Twp.

11 Feb. 1810   23 March 1810
HERR, JOHN
    Wife. Feronica Herr. Children: Elizabeth, Catharine,
Barbara and Magdalena.
    Ex. Frederick Byrode and John Thome. Mt. Joy Twp.

28 Feb. 1810   20 March 1810
HARTMAN, HENRY
    Wife. Ann Hartman. Children: Frena wife of Henry Hess,
Henry, Esther wife of David Hoover, Ann, Christian and Samuel.

98

Ex. Henry Hartman and Henry Hess.   Lampeter Twp.

-- Oct. 1805   27 April 1810
HERR, MARTIN
     Children: Mary wife of David Longnecker, Daniel, Martha wife
of Martin Frantz, Joel, John and Samuel.
     Ex. Martin and Samuel Herr. Strasburg Twp.

2 Dec. 1807   21 Nov. 1810
HEIDELBAUGH, HENRY
     Wife. Elizabeth Heidelbaugh. Children: Mary, Barbara,
Nancy, Jacob and John.
     Ex. Jacob and John Heidelbaugh. Bart Twp.

1 May 1810   19 Dec. 1810
HUBER, MARTIN
     Wife. Elizabeth Huber. Children: Christian, Joseph,
Martin, Daniel, Mary, Elizabeth, Susanna and Veronica.
     Ex. Christian Huber and Joseph Wenger. Earl Twp.

5 March 1811   28 March 1811
HOAR, JONATHAN
     Children: Robert, Jonathan, Isaac, Susanna, Ruth wife of
Daniel Pehar, Elizabeth wife of --- Wike and Mary.
     Ex. Jonathan and Robert Hoar. Salsbury Twp.

29 Sept. 1810   8 Nov. 1811
HENRY, JOHN JOSEPH
     Wife. Jane Henry. Children: Ann, Caroline, Elizabeth,
Harriet, Amelia, Lydia, Julian and Stephen. N.B. The last named
son (Stephen) is mentioned as the "oldest son" but for reasons
not given was mentioned last and disenherited.
     Ex. Jane Henry and (all the children). Twp. omitted.

9 July 1811   24 Aug. 1811
HERTZOG, NICHOLAS
     Wife. Margaret Hertzog. Children: Nicholas, Peter, Sophia
wife of Joseph Lesser, Mary wife of Christian Bricker, Eve wife
of Samuel Funck, Catharine wife of George Wackerman, Christina
wife of Frederick Shreider, Margaret wife of John Diebler and
Elizabeth wife of Leonard Diebler.
     Ex. Nicholas and Peter Hertzog. Cocalico Twp.

26 May 1810   11 Oct. 1811
HERR, CHRISTIAN
     Wife. Catharine Herr. Bros.: David and Christian Herr.
Sisters: Barbara wife of --- Beam and Mary wife of --- Bachman.
     Ex. John Eahbach and David Herr. Manor Twp.

7 July 1811   9 Oct. 1811
HEGE, JOHN
     Wife. Elizabeth Hege. Children: Mary and Ann.
     Ex. John Lehman and Abraham Reiff. Manheim Twp.

6 March 1811   17 April 1811
HUBER, MICHAEL
    Wife. Hannah Huber. Children: Sarah and Sophia.
    Ex. Henry Swentzel. Lancaster Borough.

14 March 1811   17 April 1811
HOCK, GEORGE
    Wife. Catharine Hock. Children: George, Barbara wife of
Christian Geib, Elizabeth, Catharine wife of Emanuel Dyer, John,
Peter, Jacob, Ann, Mary, Susanna and Hannah.
    Ex. Benjamin Hershey and Abraham Riff. Warwick Twp.

21 Feb. 1810   6 June 1811
HERSHBERGER, BARBARA
    Child: John.
    Ex. John Hershberger. Cocalico Twp.

1 May 1809   1 May 1810
HERSHY, ABRAHAM
    Children: Christian, Abraham (there were six daughters,
names omitted).
    Ex. David Meyet and John Bassler. Manheim Twp.

5 Nov. 1812   3 Dec. 1812
HILLER, JOHN
    Wife. Catharine Hiller. Children: John, Elizabeth wife of
John Bletz, Daniel, Catharine and Jacob.
    Ex. Philip Schissler and Casper Schneider. Manor Twp.

23 Oct. 1797   21 April 1812
HOFFER, JOSEPH
    Wife. Anna Hoffer. Children (of second wife): Magdalena,
Mary and Isaac, (children of first wife) John, Joseph, Barbara,
Abraham, Elizabeth and Anna.
    Ex. John Kenig and John Blank. Leacock Twp.

21 March 1812   6 May 1812
HARDMAN, PHILIP
    Wife. Christina Hardman. Children: John, Peter, Elizabeth,
Barbara and Molly.
    Ex. John Hardman and Philip Vonnida. Cocalico Twp.

9 May 1912   7 Sept. 1812
HUBER, JACOB
    Wife. Elizabeth Huber. Children: Nancy, Jacob, John and
Christian. Son-in-law: Joseph Baughman (wife's name not stated).
    Ex. Joseph Baughman and Henry Hershberger. Cocalico Twp.

22 March 1806   25 Nov. 1812
HUMMER, MICHAEL
    Bro. and sister: Jacob and Rachel Hummer.
    Ex. Jacob Hummer and Abraham Zug. Warwick Twp.

25 Oct. 1812   8 Dec. 1812
HERSHY, BENJAMIN

Children: Mary, Christian, Benjamin, Ann, Magdalena and Barbara wife of John Hiestand.
Ex. Benjamin Hershy. Lancaster Twp.

--- Entered on Index 1812
HUBERT, GERTRAUT
This will was never finished and al the records of it lost.

28 Oct. 1812   8 March 1813
HORST, JOHN
Wife. Ann Horst. Children: Henry, Joseph, John, Christian, Mary, Ann, Elizabeth, Magdalena, Freney, Susanna, Christina and Catharine.
Ex. John Hershy and Joseph Wenger. Leacock Twp.

18 Jan. 1803   23 Feb. 1813
HERSHBERGER, JOHN
Mother: Barbara Hershberger. Sisters: Susanna and Margaret.
Ex. John Mohler. Cocalico Twp.

12 Oct. 1813   12 Nov. 1813
HESTON, MORDICAI
Mother: Mary Heston. Bro.: Charles Heston. Sister: Mary Heston.
Ex. Levi H. Jackson and Charles Heston. LIttle Britton Twp.

27 Oct. 1813   10 Dec. 1813
HARR, JOHN
Wife. Sarah Harr. Children: Mary, Joseph, Susanna, Sarah, Rachel and Levi. Bro.: Samuel Harr.
Ex. Samuel Harr and Henry Miller. Strasburg Twp.

24 June 1812   28 Dec. 1813
HEISTAND, PETER
Wife. Elizabeth Heistand. Children: Jacob, Peter and Elizabeth wife of Abraham Hamacker.
Ex. Jacob and Peter Heistand. Rapho Twp.

22 Jan. 1814   1 March 1814
HARNISH, JACOB
Wife. Magdalen Harnish. Children: Samuel, Jacob, Mary wife of Jacob Palm, Catharine wife of John Burkholder, Magdalena, Sarah, Elizabeth, Eve, Rebecca, Hannah and John.
Ex. Samuel and Jacob Harnish. Cocalico Twp.

13 Dec. 1813   10 March 1814
HIPPLE, FREDERICK
Wife. Magdalena Hipple. Children: Mary, Elizabeth, Magdalena, Catharine, Susanna, Henry, Ann and Frederick.
Ex. Joseph Shank and Jacob Brubecker. Donegal Twp.

1 April 1814   27 June 1814
HOKE, CONRAD
Wife. Elizabeth Hoke. Children: Henry, George, Elizabeth, Jacob, John, Mary wife of John Wicart and Daniel.

Ex. Henry Brenneman and John Brackbill. Strasburg Twp.

24 May 1814   12 July 1814
HALL, DAVID
      His mother was the sole legatee - name not given.
      Ex. (omitted). Twp. omitted.

23 April 1808   8 Nov. 1814
HESS, FERONICA
      Nephews: John and Christian Hess (sons of Bro. Samuel Hess).
      Ex. John and Henry Hess. Conestoga Twp.

8 April 1814   22 Nov. 1814
HAINES, ANTHONY
      Wife. Susanna Haines. Children: Henry, Frederick,
Charlotte and Mary. Bro.: Henry Haines.
      Ex. Henry Haines and Henry Haines [sic]. Donegal Twp.

19 Oct. 1814   2 Dec. 1814
HARTER, ANDREW
      Wife. Anna Barbara Harter. Children: John, Jacob, Wendle,
Anna wife of Jacob Oberlin and Catharine wife of Henry Sower.
      Ex. Jacob Oberlin and John Harter. Earl Twp.

15 Oct. 1812   6 March 1815
HARLACHER, ANN
      Children: Susanna wife of Abraham Landis, Elizabeth,
Catharine, Sarah, Ann, Mary and Samuel. Grandchildren: Sally
wife of Henry Foltz (parents' names not stated). Son-in-law:
Benjamin Royer (wife's name not stated).
      Ex. Benjamin Royer. Cocalico Twp.

12 Jan. 1815   21 March 1815
HIPPLE, ELIZABETH
      Mother: Magdalena Hipple. Bros. and sisters: Mary,
Magdalena, Catharine, Susanna, Henry, Anne and Frederick Hipple.
      Ex. Joseph Shenck. Donegal Twp.

29 April 1814   18 March 1815
HELLER, CATHARINE
      Sisters: Letty, Barbara, Nancy, Elizabeth and Christina.
Bros.: David, Ephriam, John and Samuel.
      Ex. David Hiller. Leacocok Twp.

22 May 1800   20 March 1815
HIFFNER, CHRISTIAN
      Wife. Elizabeth Hiffner.
      Ex. Elizabeth Hiffner. Lampeter Twp.

12 July 1815   1 Aug. 1815
HOAR, JOSEPH
      Wife. Margaret Hoar. Children: Joseph, William, Adam,
Sarah, Mary and Margaret. N.B. There was a bequest to the

102

Friends Meeting House of Sadsbury, for the support of their graveyard.
Ex. William Linvill and Joseph Hoar. Salisbury Twp.

7 June 1811   28 Aug. 1815
HELD, JULIANA
Children: Peter, Philip, Catharine and Elizabeth Kemara and Henry Held. N.B. The writer of the will appears to have been married to a Kemara - as four of her children bear that name - no mention of it is made in the will.
Ex. Peter Kemara and Henry Held. Twp. omitted.

17 Aug. 1815   16 Oct. 1815
HESS, DAVID
Wife. Anna Hess. Children: Nancy, Elizabeth, Fronica, Maria, Susanna, David, John and Michael.
Ex. Samuel Moyel and Anna Hess. Conestoga Twp.

7 Aug. 1815   10 Nov. 1815
HERSHEY, BENJAMIN
Wife. Elizabeth Hershey. Children: Jacob, Nancy, Elizabeth and Benjamin.
Ex. John Leman Jr. and John Swar. Hempfield Twp.

19 July 1815   21 Sept. 1815
HAMILTON, JAMES
Wife. Margaret Hamilton. Children: William, Jane, Catharine, Mary and George.
Ex. George Jenkins and William Hamilton. Salisbury Twp.

13 Nov. 1813   18 Dec. 1815
HERR, CHRISTIAN
Children: Christian, Susanna, Anna wife of John Funk, Elizabeth wife of Daniel Miller, Mary wife of George Diffenbach, Esther wife of Henry Bowman and Magdalena wife of Christian Rohrer. Grandchildren: David and Elias Rohrer.
Ex. Christian Herr and Christian Rohrer. Lampeter Twp.

22 April 1816   30 May 1816
HOUGH, JOSEPH
Wife. Elizabeth Hough. Children: John, (there were two daughters mentioned, names not given). Step-daughter: Julia Ford.
Ex. John Hough and Joseph Shenk. Donegal Twp.

14 March 1816   23 April 1816
HAMILTON, MARGARET
Sister: Jane Hamilton. Bros.: Hugh and James Hamilton.
Ex. James Hamilton. Leacock Twp.

21 May 1816   18 June 1816
HOFFMAN, FREDERICK
Wife. Margaret Hoffman. Children: Jacob, Philip, Elizabeth wife of Henry Kehler, Margaret wife of Martin Kreiner and Polly wife of George Erisman.

Ex. Jacob and Philip Hoffman. Manor Twp.

11 Feb. 1807   21 Aug. 1816
HOFF, GEORGE
    Children: George, John, Catharine wife of Frederick Heissly,
Magdalena wife of John Reiter, Elizabeth wife of John Hippy and
Jacob.
    Ex. John and Valentine Hoff. Lancaster Borough.

25 Aug. 1816   26 Nov. 1816
HEISTAND, JACOB
    Wife. Barbara Heistand. Children: Mary, (there were
others, names and numbers not given).
    Ex. Cornelius Crum, Jacob and Barbara Heistand. Hempfield
Twp.

20 May 1815   26 Dec. 1816
HESS, CHRISTIAN
    Wife. Anna Hess. Children: Jacob, John, Christian, Maria,
Anna, Susanna and Barbara. Grandchildren: Henry, David and
Elizabeth Hess (children of John).
    Ex. John Hess and Henry Metzler. Salsbury Twp.

23 April 1812 28 March 1817
HORA, MATHIAS
    Wife. Christina Hora.
    Ex. Frederick Kuhn. Martic Twp.

8 Aug. 1816   11 April 1817
HARTMAN, JOHN
    Wife. Catharine Hartman. Bros. and sisters: Philip,
Christopher, Michael, William, Barbara, Maria and Catharine.
    Ex. Samuel Mayer. Lampeter Twp.

6 Dec. 1810   27 May 1817
HOYL, PHILIBINA
    Children: Catharine, Elizabeth, Anna, Christina wife of
Conrad Barteline, John and George.
    Ex. George Hoyl. Elizabeth Twp.

7 June 1817   20 Sept. 1817
HEITLER, ANDREAS
    Wife. Susanna Heitler. Children: Israel and Richard.
    Ex. Susanna and Richard Heitler. Cocalico Twp.

10 June 1814   15 Sept. 1817
HAINES, SAMUEL
    Children: Samuel and Elizabeth wife of --- Binkley.
    Ex. Elizabeth Binkley and John Witmer. Lampeter Twp.

11 Nov. 1817   16 Dec. 1817
HOPKINS, CATHARINE
    Bros. and sisters: Michael, George and Ann Withers.
    Ex. Michael and George Withers. Salisbury Twp.

18 Oct. 1813   15 Feb. 1818
HEPPENHIMER, DAVID
     Wife. Margaret Heppenhimer. Children: David, Susanna and
William.
     Ex. Margaret and William Heppenhimer. Cocalico Twp.

8 Dec. 1811   2 June 1818
HOSTETTER, JOHN
     Wife. Magdalena Hostetter. Children: John, Abraham,
Susanna, Barbara, Magdalena, Anna and Maria.
     Ex. Abraham and Christian Hostetter. Manor Twp.

3 Sept. 1816   10 Aug. 1818
HESS, CHRISTIAN
     Wife. Catharine Hess. Children: Christian, John, Esther,
David, Catharine, Adam and Elizabeth wife of --- Shenck.
Grandchildren: Catharine, Ann and Elizabeth Shenck.
     Ex. John and Christian Hess. Conestoga Twp.

6 July 1815   12 Oct. 1818
HOFF, JOHN
     Children: (the names and number not given).
     Ex. Mary Hoff. Lancaster Borough.

21 Jan. 1817   23 Nov. 1818
HOLLADAY, SAMUEL
     Sister: Mary Holladay.
     Ex. Barton Henderson. Salisbury Twp.

3 Sept. 1817   6 Sept. 1718
HARTMAN, FREDERICK
     Children: Jacob, Adam, John, Barbara and Henry.
     Ex. Adam Hartman and William Coldren. Brecknock Twp.

2 Aug. 1817   12 Jan. 1819
HERR, ISAAC
     Wife. Susanna Herr. Children: Elizabeth wife of Frederick
Krug, Barbara wife of Peter Line, Isaac and Henry.
     Ex. Isaac and Martin Herr. Martic Twp.

7 Aug. 1814   10 Feb. 1819
HEISS, DIETRICH
     Children: John, Jacob, William, Catharine and Sally.
     Ex. John, Jacob and William Heiss. Lancaster Borough.

15 Sept. 1815   14 April 1819
HAGER, CHRISTOPHER
     Wife. Catharine Hager. Children: Frank, Christopher, Mary
wife of John Long and wife of --- Miller, Elizabeth wife of
Frederick Shrauler, Margaret wife of George Hoff, Catharine,
Louisa and Susanna. Grandchild: John Long.
     Ex. Catharine Hager. Lancaster Borough.

15 Dec. 1817   24 April 1819
HESSE, MARY

Children: Abraham, Martin and John.
Ex. Martin Hess. Lampeter Twp.

24 Aug. 1816   21 May 1819
HOLL, PETER
    Wife. (name omitted). Children: John, Peter, Catharine
wife of George Hammer and Elizabeth wife of Jacob Varns.
    Ex. Peter and John Holl. Strasburg Borough.

22 Sept. 1812   10 June 1819
HESS, SAMUEL
    Wife. Anna. Children: Christian, Elizabeth wife of Jacob
Gall, Barbara wife of --- Huell, Susanna wife of John Blanck,
Anna, Samuel, Abraham, Catharine and Mary.
    Ex. Christian Hess and John Blanck. Donegal Twp.

25 June 1819   29 July 1819
HOUCK, GEORGE
    Wife. Susanna Houck. Children: (there were fourteen, names
not given).
    Ex. John Franck and Jacob Keller. Cocalico Twp.

4 Aug. 1819   17 Sept. 1819
HARLAN, JAMES
    Wife. Elizabeth Harlan. Children: Elwood, Mary, Benjamin,
Milton, Jonathan and Sarah. Grandchildren: John, Hannah and
Matilda (children of Elwood) and Hannah Reynolds (parents' names
not given).
    Ex. Benjamin Harlan and Richard Reynolds. Little Brittain
Twp.

4 Aug. 1819   1 Oct. 1819
HIBSHMAN, WENDEL
    Wife. Hannah Hibshman. Children: Jacob, Henry, John,
(there were two others, names not given).
    Ex. Jacob, Henry and John Hibshman. Cocalico Twp.

30 May 1818   25 Oct. 1819
HERSH, JACOB
    Wife. Elizabeth. Children: Christian, Ann, Maria,
Magdalena, Susanna, Barbara, Feronica and Esther. Son-in-law:
John Nissly.
    Ex. Christian Hersh and John Nissly. Donegal Twp.

1 Jan. 1819   26 Oct. 1819
HERR, CHRISTIAN
    Wife. Elizabeth Herr. Children: Christian, Elizabeth,
Henry, Ann wife of John Springer, Mary wife of Jacob Gingrich and
John.
    Ex. Jacob Keenor and Christian Brubaker. Mt. Joy Twp.

2 Dec. 1799   15 March 1802
IRWIN, THOMAS
    Wife. Rachel Irwin. Children: William, Samuel, Rachel and
Mary.

Ex. William and Samuel Irwin. Salsbury Twp.

8 March 1802   12 May 1802
IRWIN, WILLIAM
    Bro.: Samuel.
 Ex. Samuel Irwin. Sadsbury Twp.

5 Nov. 1801   9 Aug. 1804
ILLIG, GEORGE
    Children: John, George, Barbara wife of George Weidman,
Catharine, Elizabeth wife of George Gross and Susanna.
Grandchildren: Salome and George Illig (children of John).
    Ex. George Weidman and George Gross. Cocalico Twp.

7 April 1809   30 Oct. 1809
IRWIN, BENJAMIN
    Wife. Mary Irwin. Bros.: Gideon, John and Isaac. Sisters:
Esther wife of --- Holmes and Mary wife of Col. Patterson. N.B.
There was a bequest of £100 to "The Middle Octorara Meeting
House."
    Ex. Amos Slaymaker and William Ramsey. Sadsbury Twp.

9 June 1812   11 Dec. 1812
IRWIN, HANNAH
    Children: Hannah, Gideon, Rachel and Samuel. Grandchildren:
Harriet, Amelia, Sarah and Almirah Rea (parents' names not
given).
    Ex. Samuel Irwin. Sadsbury Twp.

17 Aug. 1812   7 Jan. 1813
IRWIN, RACHEL
    Bros.: Samuel and William Irwin.
    Ex. John Haymaker Jr. Salisbury Twp.

30 May 1815   13 May 1816
IRWIN, JOHN
    [should be Erwin] Wife. (name omitted). Children: Jacob,
Elizabeth, John, George and Joseph. (there were two other
children - names not given).
    Ex. George and Joseph Erwin. Cocalico Twp.

3 April 1818   23 April 1818
IHLING, CHRISTOPHER
    Wife. Magdalena Ihling. Children: Christopher, John,
William, Catharine wife of Stacy Swem, George and Mary.
Grandchildren: William and Mary Ihling (children of George).
    Ex. Magdalena and John Ihling. Lancaster Borough.

27 March 1797 1 July 1797
JENKINS, DAVID
    Wife. Martha Jenkins. Children: Robert, David, Billy,
Rebecca wife of William Wilson, Margaret wife of Lewis Kreider,
Martha and William.
    Ex. Robert and David Jenkins. Caernarvon Twp.

19 Feb. 1798   22 March 1798
JOHNS, CHRISTIAN
    Wife. Feronica Johns. Children: (the names and number not
given). Bro.: Peter Johns.
    Ex. Peter Johns and John Heller. Lampeter Twp.

23 July 1794   20 July 1799
JOHNTZ, JOHN
    Wife. Catharine Johntz. Children: Jacob, John, Abraham,
Catharine wife of Michael Garber and Anna wife of Christian
Garber.
    Ex. Jacob and John Johntz. Leacock Twp.

14 Dec. 1799   6 March 1800
JONES, JOHN
    Wife. Anna Jones. Children: Joel, John, Cyrus and Lydia.
N.B. There is a codicil to will making provision for the
publicaton of his book "The Power of Deception Unvailed and Man
of Sin Revealed."
    Ex. Jeremiah Brown, Joseph Harlan and Thomas Richards.
Little Brittain Twp.

14 Jan. 1802   34 April 1802
JENKINS, MARTHA
    Children: William, David, Robert and Martha. Grandchild:
Martha Krider (parents' names not given).
    Ex. William Jenkins. Caernarvon Twp.

9 Jan. 1802   25 Sept. 1802
JACKS, JAMES
    Sisters: Ann wife of --- Bachman and Mary wife of --- Boyle.
    Ex. William Montgomery. Lancaster Borough.

12 March 1802   22 March 1804
JOHNSON, JOHN
    Children: Catharine wife of John Young, Alexander, Mary wife
of James Carswell, Jean wife of Thomas Hakins, Margaret wife of
John Creg, Hugh, Joseph, John and James.
    Ex. James Johnson and John Steele. Little Brittain Twp.

23 March 1804   30 April 1804
JETTER, MARTIN
    Wife. Margaret Jetter. Children: Susanna wife of Abraham
Andrew, John, Barbara, Magdalene and Elizabeth. Grandchild:
Susanna wife of --- Moyer.
    Ex. Margaret Jetter and Michael Kauffman. Manheim Twp.

6 July 1806   --- Oct. 1806
JONES, JONATHAN
    Wife. Mary Jones. Children: Elizabeth, Christian, Susanna,
Barbara, Mary, Sarah and Anna. Son-in-law: Joseph Steiner
(wife's name not given).
    Ex. Mary Jones and Joseph Steiner. Rapho Twp.

--- 10 May 1807
JOHN, HANS
    N.B. This is a German will - not copied on the records -
and translation lost.
    Warwick Twp.

11 July 1807   16 March 1808
JAMES, PHILIP
    Wife. Fanny James. Children: Samuel, Jane, Betsey and
Polly.
    Ex. Robert Maxwell Jr. Little Brittain Twp.

5 Dec. 1804   30 May 1808
JORDAN, OWEN
    Wife. Elizabeth Jordan. Children: Maria, Charlotte, Peter,
Michael and William.
    Ex. Elizabeth Jordan. Lancaster Borough.

19 Jan. 1808   7 July 1808
JORDAN, ELIZABETH
    Widow of Owen Jordan. Child: Charlotte (there was no
mention made of the other children — as will be seen in the will
of Owen Jordan, there were others).
    Ex. Jonas Jordan. Lancaster Borough.

23 May 1808   10 Dec. 1808
JOHNS, JACOB
    Wife. Elizabeth Johns. Children: Paul, John, Samuel,
Charlotte and Elizabeth.
    Ex. Elizabeth, Paul and John Johns. Leacock Twp.

21 March 1803 12 May 1810
JENKINS, JOHN
    Wife. Eizabeth Jenkins. Children: George, Mary wife of
Peter Trego, William, Rebecca wife of Thomas Morgan and
Elizabeth.
    Ex. George, William and Elizabeth Jenkins. Caernarvon Twp.

21 Jan. 1812   2 June 1812
JORDAN, MARTIN
    Wife. Elizabeth Jordan. Children: Casper, Catharine wife
of Thomas Wentz, Mary and Elizabeth.
    Ex. Henry Hakelroth. Lancaster Borough.

27 July 1815   17 Aug. 1815
JOHNSON, JOSEPH H.
    Father: James Johnson. Mother: Sarah Johnson. Bro.: John.
    Ex. James Johnson. Marietta Twp.

6 Nov. 1815   25 March 1816
JOHNSON, MARY
    Bros. & sisters: Robert, Rosana wife of --- Barnes and Sarah
Johnson.
    Ex. James and William Barnes. Drumore Twp.

7 May 1816   12 July 1816
JOHNSTON, JOHN
    Children: Isaac and Magdalena wife of Charles Killian.
    Ex. Philip Killian. Earl Twp.

14 Sept. 1815   4 Nov. 1816
JOST, PHILIP
    [should be YOST] Wife. Elizabeth Yost. Children: John,
Mary and Frederick.
    Ex. John Yost. Lancaster Borough.

15 Jan. 1817   15 Feb. 1819
JONSON, WILLIAM
    Wife. Elizabeth Jonson. Children: John, Samuel and James.
Step-daughter: Ann wife of Adam Hart. Stepson: Thomas Davis.
    Ex. Elizabeth Johnson and William Henderson. Twp. omitted.

19 Oct. 1785   30 Feb. 1786
KNEISSLEY, GEORGE
    Children: Samuel, John, George, Catharine wife of Henry
Yordey, Barbara wife of Frederick Berg and Mary wife of John
Mayer.
    Ex. John and George Kneissley. Hempfield Twp.

25 June 1785   25 March 1786
KEEFABER, PETER
    Child: Elizabeth wife of Baltzer Lantz.
    Ex. Baltzer Lantz. Lancaster Borough.

10 Dec. 1785   7 April 1786
KLING, THOMAS
    Wife. (name omitted). Children: James, Michael, Vincent,
Isabella, Margaret, Jane, Mary and Miriam.
    Ex. James and Michael Kling. Twp. omitted.

3 April 1786   7 June 1786
KEYSER, JACOB
    Wife. Mary Keyser. Children: Jacob (there were others,
names and number not given).
    Ex. Mary Keyser and George Matter. Salsbury Twp.

19 May 1785   4 Jan. 1787
KREMER, JOHN
    Children: John, Christina wife of Leonard Ratfon and
Catharine wife of Mathias Dehuff. Grandchildren: Catharine,
Mary, Elizabeth and John Dehuff. N.B. There was a bequest to the
United Brethern of Lancaster.
    Ex. Henry Dehuff. Manor Twp.

18 April 1787   25 May 1787
KENDIG, HENRY
    Wife. Ann Kendig. Children: Daniel, Susanna wife of John
Graff, Barbara wife of Benjamin Graff, Ann wife of John Forree,
Elizabeth and Catharine.
    Ex. Isaac and Christian Herr. Lampeter Twp.

28 May 1787   30 Aug. 1787
KNEISSLEY, JOHN
    Wife. Christiana Kneissley. Children: John, Michael,
Barbara, Christian, Matilda, Elizabeth, Henry, Mary, Daniel and
David.
    Ex. Jacob Byers and Christian Black. Martic Twp.

12 Aug. 1788   30 Aug. 1788
KIRKPATRICK, SAMUEL
    Children: Samuel, Jean, Elizabeth wife of Thomas Barclay and
Margaret.
    Ex. George McLaughlin and Samuel Kirkpatrick. Martic Twp.

30 July 1781   13 June 1789
KLICK, PHILIP
    (This should be GLICK.) Wife. Elizabeth Glick. Children:
(The names and number not given).
    Ex. Samuel Wissler and Daniel Stauffer. Warwick Twp.

11 July 1789   28 July 1789
KAGEY, ISAAC
    Father: John Kagey. Mother: Ann wife of James Jacks
(married second time). Sister: Ann wife of Isaac Neaff. Bro.:
John Kagey.
    Ex. James Jacks. Lancaster Borough.

6 July 1789   12 Aug. 1789
KENDIG, ABRAHAM
    Wife. Mary Kendig. Children: Abraham, Tobias, Samuel,
George, Prudence wife of John Good, Catharine, Mary and
Elizabeth.
    Ex. John Good and Samuel Mayer. Conestoga Twp.

3 Nov. 1789   14 Nov. 1789
KLINE, GEORGE
    Wife. Susanna Kline. Child: Catharine. Father-in-law:
Henry Gross.
    Ex. Henry Gross and Andrew Keise. Lancaster Borough.

19 Aug. 1789   1 Jan. 1790
KILLCREST, ROBERT
    (This should be GILLGREEST.) Brother-in-law: Charles Herrs.
Cousin: Samuel Gillgreest.
    Ex. Robert Campbell. Little Brittain Twp.

25 Aug. 1790   16 Oct. 1790
KINSEY, JACOB
    Wife. Anna Margaret Kinsey. Children: Jacob, David and
Daniel. Son-in-law: Henry Hogh.
    Ex. John Erb and Christian Grebiel. Warwick Twp.

---   24 Nov. 1790
KUCHERLE, JACOB
    N.B. This is a German will - not copied on the records, and
the original records are lost.

Rapho Twp.

7 Feb. 1780   7 April 1790
KENNEDY, FRANCIS
      Children: William and Robert.
      Ex. Willian Kennedy. Martic Twp.

--- 11 Jan. 1791
KAUFMAN, MICHAEL
      N.B. This is a German will - not copied on records, and the
original has been temporarily removed from the office.
      Manor Twp.

13 June 1791   8 Nov. 1791
KISSEL, NICHOLAS
      Children: George, John, Frederick, Anna wife of --- Leib,
Maria wife of --- Kinsey and Anna wife of --- Martin.
      Ex. George Kissel and Casper Grub. Warwick Twp.

9 Aug. 1788   26 May 1792
KURTZ, JACOB
      Wife. Elizabeth Kurtz. Children: Jacob, Christian,
Catharine wife of John Kurtz, Abraham, John, Anna wife of
Christian Weidman and Barbara wife of Jacob Kurtz.
      Ex. Elizabeth, Christian and John Kurtz. Leacock Twp.

3 Aug. 1774   30 May 1792
KNAPP [crossed out and KNOPF inserted], JACOB
      Children: Jacob, John, Valentine, Christian, Anna, Barbara
and Margaretta.
      Ex. Isaac Horsebarger and Jacob Rup. Cocalico Twp.

--- 24 Dec. 1792
KAUFMAN, BENJAMIN
      N.B. This is a German will, not copied on the records, and
the original records are temporarily removed from the office.
      Manor Twp.

28 July 1789   2 Nov. 1792
KLICK, ELIZABETH
      (This should be GLICK.) Children: John, Mary and Elizabeth.
Son-in-law: John Bower (wife's name not stated).
      Ex. John Glick. Warwick Twp.

7 Nov. 1792   9 April 1793
KURTS, PETER
      Wife. Mary Kurts. Children: John, (there were others, names
and number not given). Bros.: Samuel and Christian.
      Ex. Christian Kurts and Peter Planck. Earl Twp.

17 April 1790 1 June 1793
KYSER, MICHAEL
      Wife. Maria Kyser. Children: Philip, Michael, Catharine
wife of Frederick Gantz and Elizabeth wife of Joseph Woulf.
      Ex. Philip and Michael Kyser. Rapho Twp.

24 Nov. 1792   22 July 1793
KLEIN, LEONARD
    Wife. Rosina Klein. Bro.: Henry Klein.
    Ex. Rosina Klein and Stephen Martin. Lancaster Borough.

13 July 1793   19 Aug. 1793
KNEISLY, MICHAEL
    The names and number of children - not given.
    Ex. Jacob and John Mohler. Cocalico Twp.

25 April 1793   25 Aug. 1793
KRIDER, MICHAEL
    Wife. Anne Krider. Children: John and Jonas.
    Ex. John Krider and Christian Over. Donegal Twp.

25 Aug. 1792   10 Sept. 1793
KNIRNSHILT, JOHN CHRISTOPHER
    Wife. Elizabeth Knirnshilt. Child: Christopher.
    Ex. George Lindebergher. Lancaster Borough.

29 Jan. 1802 [sic] --- 1793
KEHLER, PETER
    Children: Maria wife of Nathaniel Powell, Adam, Christina
wife of Frederick Toehterman and Andrew.
    Ex. Albert Dufrine. Lancaster Borough.

23 Nov. 1793   14 Jan. 1794
KAUFFMAN, SAMUEL
    Bros.: Jonas, Jacob, Christian and David. Sister: Feronica
wife of Herman Long and Elizabeth wife of Christian Baughman and
Ann.
    Ex. Christian Frick and Benjamin Landis. Manheim Twp.

17 Aug. 1793   5 April 1794
KALB, HERVEY
    Wife. Susanna Kalb. Children: Jacob, Henry, Catharine,
Christian, Nancy, Susanna, Barbara, David, Samuel and Mariley.
    Ex. Susanna Kalb and John Stoffer. Mt. Joy Twp.

12 Oct. 1794   4 Nov. 1794
KEANO, DENNIS
    Bros. and sisters: Dormick, James and Elizabeth.
    Ex. Joseph Gochnower and Benjamin Hershey. Hempfield Twp.

7 July 1794   29 Sept. 1794
KAUFFMAN, JACOB
    Wife. Magdalena Kauffman.
    Ex. Samuel Hess and Magdalena Kauffman. Donegal Twp.

16 Sept. 1785   20 Oct. 1794
KOBER, CHRISTIAN
    Wife. Sarah Kober. Children: Adam and Jacob.
    Ex. Abraham Gish and Adam Kober. Rapho Twp.

28 July 1794   18 March 1795
KLEIN, ROSINA
    Legatee: Jane wife of Peter Pastor.
    Ex. Peter Pastor. Lancaster Borough.

10 March 1795   16 March 1795
KAUTZ, JOSEPH
    Wife. Barbara Kautz. Children: Frederick, Thomas,
Christian, Jacob, Barbara wife of John Rode and Mary wife of
Lawrence Deterich.
    Ex. Barbara Kautz. Lancaster Borough.

11 April 1795   17 April 1795
KREIDER, GEORGE
    Wife. Susanna Kreider. Children: John, Elizabeth and Mary.
    Ex. Susanna Kreider and John Lind. Lancaster Brough.

26 Feb. 1791   27 May 1795
KNOX, JAMES
    Child: James. Grandchildren: James, Robert, Peggy, Jenny
and Billy Knox.
    Ex. Col. Robert King and James Knox. Drumore Twp.

5 March 1795   7 April 1795
KILCHRIST, WILLIAM
    (This should be GILCHRIST.) Children: Sarah and Samuel.
Son-in-law: James Cummings (wife's name not given).
    Ex. James Cummings and Sarah Gilchrist. Twp. omitted.

10 Dec. 1785   28 March 1796
KOFFROTH, GERHART
    (This should be COFFROTH.) Children: Elizabeth, Barbara,
Catharine, Dorothea, Christina, Henry and Jacob.
    Ex. Henry and Jacob Coffroth. Cocalico Twp.

22 May 1796   2 July 1796
KERN, PETER
    Bros. and sisters: Christopher, Henry, Catharine wife of
Adam Kneck and Michael.
    Ex. Christopher and Henry Kern. Brecknock Twp.

6 July 1795   19 April 1796
KORFFMAN, MICHAEL
    Father: John Korffman. Mother: Margaret Korffman. A
legatee: Charles Rentzheimer (of Kinsington, Philadelphia).
    Ex. Adam Messenkop. Lancaster Borough.

25 Nov. 1789   20 April 1796
KIEFER, JACOB
    Bros.: John and Daniel Kiefer. Nephew: John Hoby.
    Ex. Daniel and Christian Kiefer and John Hoby [Holy?] Mt.
Joy Twp.

26 April 1797   27 May 1797
KILHEFFER, JOHN

Wife. Mary Kilheffer. Children: Jacob, Christian, Ann, Elizabeth, Mary, John and Henry.
Ex. Jacob Kilheffer and John Herr. Manor Twp.

2 June 1797   31 Aug. 1797
KUNTZ, CHRISTIAN
Wife. Christina Kuntz. Child: Mary.
Ex. Christian Nisly. Donegal Twp.

25 July 1796   23 Sept. 1797
KING, JANE
Bro.: Vincent King.
Ex. Joseph Harlan and John Webster. Twp. omitted.

3 May 1797   18 May 1797
KUNTZ, JOHN
Wife. Anna Johanna Kuntz. Children: Henry (there were others, names and number not given).
Ex. Jacob Kuntz and Jacob Light. Mt. Joy Twp.

7 Feb. 1798   30 March 1798
KERCHER, FREDERICK
Wife. Justina Kercher. Children: John, Elizabeth, Catharine and Frederick.
Ex. John Spickler. Warwick Twp.

19 March 1798   7 April 1798
KREBS, PETER
Sisters: Catharine and Barbara Krebs. N.B. There was a bequest made to the Lutheran Congregation at New Holland.
Ex. Jacob Holl. Earl Twp.

---   1 March 1798
KAUFMAN, HENRY
N.B. This is a German will - not copied on the records, and the original records are temporarily removed from the office.
Manor Twp.

14 Feb. 1798   1 March 1798
KAUFMAN, CHRISTIAN
Wife. Ann Kaufman. Children: Magdalena wife of Henry Sherer, Catharine, John, Ann and Rudy.
Ex. Henry Sherer and Joseph Carly. Manor Twp.

15 Aug. 1798   --- 1798
KUHN, MARIA
Children: Adam, John, Frederick, Peter, Jacob, Eve and Maria wife of James Ross.
Ex. Frederick Kuhn and Lewis Heek. Lancaster Borough.

7 Oct. 1797   15 April 1800
KLEISS, PHILIP
Wife. Elizabeth Kleiss. Children: George, John, Philip, Elizabeth, Catharine, Ann and Susanna.
Ex. George and John Kleiss. Lancaster Borough.

17 Oct. 1800   22 Nov. 1800
KOENIG, CONRAD
     Wife. Catharine. Children: Christina wife of Christian
Humrich, George, Catharine wife of Jacob Breaser, Adam, Conrad,
John, Joseph and Magdalena.
     Ex. Christian Humrich. Lancaster Borough.

30 Sept. 1795   3 Jan. 1801
KEGEREIS, AGNESS
     Child: Michael.
     Ex. Michael Kegereis. Cocalico Twp.

25 May 1801   13 June 1801
KINSEY, MARGARET
     Children: Jacob, Sarah, Catharine, Esther, Daniel, David,
Joseph and Elizabeth.
     Ex. John and Peter Erb. Warwick Twp.

22 March 1794   13 Nov. 1801
KING, VINCENT
     Wife. Mary King. Children: James, Joshua, Mary, Vincent and
Jeremiah.
     Ex. Mary King and Jeremiah Brown. Little Brittain Twp.

11 Dec. 1801   3 April 1802
KRALL, CHRISTIAN
     Wife. Catharine. Children: Christian, Jacob, John, Joseph,
Magdalena and Elizabeth.
     Ex. Catharine Krall and Christian Reisser. Elizabeth Twp.

4 Sept. 1799   19 May 1802
KREITER, PETER
     Wife. Anna Maria. Children: Frederick, Andrew, Anna,
Elizabeth, Michael, Sarah and Benjamin. Grandchildren: John,
Jacob, Godfrey and Michael (sons of Michael).
     Ex. Frederick and Adam Kreiter. Warwick Twp.

4 June 1802   26 July 1802
KURTZ, LAWRENCE
     Wife. Catharine Kurtz. Stepson: John Reese. N.B. There was
a bequest to the German Lutheran Church of Lancaster.
     Ex. Godlieb Nauman. Lancaster Borough.

7 May 1794   11 Dec. 1802
KARAGAN, MICHAEL
     Children: Jacob, Susanna and Mary.
     Ex. Christian Shanck. Conestoga Twp.

6 March 1801   3 Aug. 1802
KUNTZ, MARIA
     Children: Michael, George, Peter, Margaret, Barbara,
Christina and Mary.
     Ex. Mary Smith. Lancaster Borough.

20 July 1802   20 Jan. 1803
KOCH, BARBARA
    Bro.: John Koch.   Sisters: Anna Maria, Anna, Christina and
Susanna Koch.
    Ex. John Longenecker and Christian Huber.   Rapho Twp.

--- 1 Feb. 1803
KEENTZLY, JACOB
    Wife. Elizabeth Keentzly.   Children: John, Elizabeth, Sarah,
Martha, Mary, Jacob and Susanna.
    Ex. Jacob Gisch and Abraham Hernly.   Mt. Joy Twp.

18 March 1799   31 March 1803
KEHLER, ANDREW
    Wife. Barbara Kehler.   Children: Mary wife of William Kuntz,
Peter, John, Andrew, Adam and Jacob.
    Ex. Barbara Kehler and Benjamin Shaum.   Lancaster Borough.

2 Dec. 1798   11 April 1803
KENDIG, CATHARINE
    Wife of Jacob Kendig.
    Ex. Jacob Kendig.   Strasburg Twp.

20 Sept. 1790   12 Oct. 1803
KRATZER, PETER
    Wife. Ann Kratzer.   Children: John, Anna, Mary, Abraham,
Susanna, Jacob and Peter.
    Ex. Ann Kratzer and Abraham Myer.   Warwick Twp.

23 Sept. 1803   17 Oct. 1803
KILLIAN, MAGDALENA
    Niece and nephews: Barbara, John, Henry, Joseph and Jacob
Reitzel.
    Ex. Michael Reigal and Joseph Huber.   Hempfield Twp.

22 Nov. 1791   8 Nov. 1803
KEHLER, PETER
    Children: Andrew, Mary wife of Edward Powell, Christina wife
of Frederick Doughterman.   Grandchildren: Jacob, Susanna and
Elizabeth Doughterman.
    Ex. Thomas Foster and Peter Maurer.   Lancaster Borough.

29 Jan. 1802   7 Nov. 1803
KELLER, PETER
    Children: Maria wife of Nathaniel Powell, Adam, Christina
wife of Frederick Tochterman, Andreas and William.
    Ex. Albert Dufrene.   Lancaster Borough.

27 Jan. 1804   1 Feb. 1804
KOENIG, DAVID
    Children: George, Jacob, Charlotte and Mary.
    Ex. George and Jacob Koenig.   Lancaster Borough.

3 March 1804   21 March 1804
KEGERISE, MICHAEL

Wife. Elizabeth Kegerise. Children: Christian, Jacob,
Michael, Elizabeth wife of Jacob Kumber, John and Susanna wife of
Jacob Gerner.
Ex. Michael Kegerise and Bechtolt Vaneda. Cocalico Twp.

10 May 1804   25 Oct. 1804
KITTERA, HANNAH
Widow of Thomas Kittera. Child: John. Grandchildren:
Hannah and John Kittera.
Ex. James Anderson. Earl Twp.

10 Aug. 1804   5 Dec. 1804
KELLER, JACOB
Wife. Barbara Keller. Children: Samuel, Jacob, John (and
four daughters - names not given).
Ex. Jacob and John Keller. Cocalico Twp.

9 Sept. 1804   16 Oct. 1804
KING, SOLOMON
Wife. Feronica King. Children: (The names and number not
given).
Ex. John Smucker and Jacob Honeck. Leacock Twp.

4 Oct. 1803   15 March 1806
KLOPPER, LEONARD
Children: George, Elizabeth wife of John Bowman, Magdalena,
Eva and Susanna.
Ex. Peter Good. Earl Twp.

10 Sept. 1805   10 Oct. 1805
KLEE, JACOB
Wife. Barbara Klee. Children: (the names and number not
given).
Ex. Barbara Klee and John Wummrer. Brecknock Twp.

25 Feb. 1802   22 July 1805
KLOUSE, MICHAEL
Children: Adam, Elizabeth and Jacob.
Ex. Anthony Hains. Donegal Twp.

4 Nov. 1804   28 Jan. 1805
KLINE, ADAM
Wife. Christiana Kline. Children: John, Susanna, David and
Elizabeth.
Ex. Christiana Kline. Donegal Twp.

21 March 1805   28 June 1805
KOENIG, JOHN CHRISTOPHER
Wife. Margaret Koenig.
Ex. Samuel Grosh. Warwick Twp.

3 Dec. 1805   4 Feb. 1806
KAUFMAN, CHRISTIAN
Children: Andrew, Michael, Christian, John, Elizabeth wife
of Henry Lighty and Anna wife of Abraham Stoner.

Ex. Andrew Shenck. Manor Twp.

10 March 1806   26 March 1806
KLEIN, PETER M.
    Children: Peter, Henry, Jacob and Christopher.
    Ex. Jacob Klein and Christian Smith. Manor Twp.

15 Jan. 1798   25 April 1806
KELLEN, CLAUS
    Wife. Elizabeth Kellen. Children: John, Henry and
Christian.
    Ex. Elizabeth Kellen. Warwick Twp.

4 Sept. 1804   24 Sept. 1807
KENDIG, ADAM
    Wife. Alice Kendig. Children: Christian and Ann wife of
Jacob Bear. Grandchildren: Elizabeth, Alice, Nancy and Mary
Bear.
    Ex. Christian Kendig and Jacob Bear. Conestoga Twp.

21 May 1807   9 Nov. 1807
KURTZ, CHRISTIAN
    Children: George, Cornelius, Christian, Jacob, Christopher,
Conrad, Catharine wife of Joseph Weaver, Sophia wife of Michael
Bender and Dorothea wife of George Rudisill.
    Ex. Christopher and Conrad Kurtz. Manheim Twp.

18 April 1807 12 Sept. 1807
KIPP, HENRY
    Wife. Anna. Children: George, Magdalena wife of Frederick
Hipple, Gertrude wife of John Katz [Hatz?] and Catharine wife of
Peter Balsor.
    Ex. Christopher Weaver and Joseph Shenk. Donegal Twp.

3 Nov. 1807   14 Nov. 1808
KREIDER, JOHN
    Wife. Anna Kreider. Children: Elizabeth, Jacob, Abraham,
John, Ann, Daniel and Mary.
    Ex. Tobias Kreider and John Buckwalter. Lampeter Twp.

20 Dec. 1802   9 June 1803
KNOPF, CHRISTIAN
    Wife. Eve Knopf. Children: John, Christian, Michael, Ann,
Susanna, Esther and Elizabeth wife of David Gerber.
    Ex. Peter Gerber. Cocalico Twp.

25 Feb. 1806   10 Nov. 1806
KOLON, JOHN
    Wife. Anna Kolon. The names and number of children omitted.
    Ex. Christian Sherrer and Abraham Longenecker. Rapho Twp.

4 Feb. 1808   14 March 1808
KELLER, SEBASTIAN

Children: Jacob, John, Sebastian, Esther wife of George Bear and Rosina wife of --- Evans. Grandchildren: John and Jacob Keller (sons of Jacob) and Magdalena Evans (daughter of Rosina).
Ex. Samuel Ensminger and John Keller. Rapho Twp.

30 Jan. 1807   14 March 1808
KREITER, MARGARET
Children: Michael, Peter, John, Anna, Barbara, Elizabeth, Susanna, Catharine and Rosina.
Ex. Michael Kreiter and Christian Blickenderfer. Warwick Twp.

3 Oct. 1807   25 Feb. 1808
KINTZER, MICHAEL
Wife. Magdalena Kintzer. Children: George, Jacob, Catharine wife of Jacob Rode, William, Elizabeth, Mary wife of George Pender and Rebecca.
Ex. George and Jacob Kintzer. Earl Twp.

29 April 1810   28 July 1810
KREBILL, JACOB
Wife. Catharine Krebill. Children: Henry, John, Catharine and Anna.
Ex. John Forrer and Henry Krebill. Manor Twp.

13 March 1810   30 April 1810
KUEHNER, ADAM
Wife. Christina Kuehner. Children: Henry, Catharine, Christian, Barbara, John, George, Elizabeth, Susanna, Adam, Magdalena and Samuel.
Ex. Valentine Griner. Warwick Twp.

28 May 1810   29 June 1810
KERLIN, JAMES
The Legatees were - Mother, Brother and Sister - living in Ireland (names not given).
Ex. Henry Kinzer, Amos Slaymaker and Isaac Smith. Salisbury Twp.

7 July 1812   28 July 1812
KNOX, JAMES
Wife. Jane Knox. Children: Robert, James, William, Mary and Martha.
Ex. Joel Lightner and John Lapp. Leacock Twp.

7 Feb. 1811   10 July 1812
KAPP, GEORGE
Wife. Anna Kapp. Bros. and sisters: Christopher, John, Andrew, Michael, Anthony, Peter, Barbara, Susan, Catharine and Christiana Kapp. N.B. There was a bequest of £50 to the Church at Lititz.
Ex. Anna Kapp and Peter Youngman. Warwick Twp.

14 Aug. 1809   4 Jan. 1812
KUNKLE, CHRISTINA

Children: Henry, William, Barbara, Christina wife of Peter Sider, Elizabeth wife of Daniel Eckman, John, George, Peter and Jacob.
Ex. Peter Sider and Daniel Eckman. Bart Twp.

15 March 1810   8 April 1812
KANN, JOHN
Children: Anna, Henry, Catharine wife of Conrad Stormfels and Peter. Grandchildren: John, Elizabeth and Philip (last name not given).
Ex. Henry Kann. Lancaster Borough.

4 June 1811   22 April 1812
KOCH, JOHN
Children: Jacob and John.
Ex. David Diffenderfer and Isaac Ellmaker. Earl Twp.

29 May 1807   5 March 1812
KUNTZ, JOHN
Wife. Elizabeth Kuntz. Children: Catharine, John, Anna, Margaret wife of William Hiell, Barbara, Magdalena and Elizabeth.
Ex. Gerhard Walter and John Brunner. Cocalico Twp.

31 Aug. 1809   30 April 1812
KLUGH, CHARLES
Bro.: Christopher. Sister: Sophia Klugh.
Ex. Christopher Klugh. Lancaster Borough.

13 May 1811   1 Nov. 1812
KINKEAD, JOHN
Wife. Elizabeth Kinkead. Children: David, Elizabeth, Polly and John. Grandchild: Joseph Kinkead (child of John).
Ex. John Kinkead. Bart Twp.

13 Dec. 1811   28 Dec. 1812
KNEISSLY, JOHN
Wife. Magdalena Kneissly. Children: John, George, Samuel, Abraham and Elizabeth wife of Christian Miller. Grandchildren: Christian and Andrew Miller.
Ex. Joseph Gochenauer and Peter Surry. Hempfield Twp.

13 Dec. 1805   5 Feb. 1812
KURTZ, CATHARINE
Widow of Lawrence Kurtz. Child: John.
Ex. John Reese. Lancaster Borough.

10 Nov. 1810   11 Feb. 1812
KREBILL, JACOB
Wife. Elizabeth Krebill. Children: Jacob, Peter, Christian, Catharine and Sterret. Son-in-law: Christian Nissly (wife's name not given).
Ex. Jacob Krebill and Christian Nissly. Donegal Twp.

23 Aug. 1811   19 Sept. 1812
KOEHLER, JACOB

Wife. Elizabeth Koehler. Children: Mary, Elizabeth, Catharine, Margaret and Salome.
Ex. Elizabeth Koehler and Jacob Snyder.

19 Oct. 1811   22 May 1812
KERN, HENRY
Wife. Barbara Kern. Children: George, Abraham, Catharine wife of Philip Stepha, Eve wife of Daniel Allebach, Peter, Margaret, Barbara, Susanna, Henry and Stophel.
Ex. Henry Kern and Stophel Schabach. Brecknock Twp.

3 March 1807   31 July 1812
KAUFFMAN, JACOB
Children: Andrew, Henry, John, Jacob, Joseph, Elizabeth, Magdalena, Adam, Barbara and David.
Ex. Christian Kauffman and Abraham Miller. Manor Twp.

6 Jan. 1812   2 Sept. 1812
KRIDER, MARGARET
Children: Susan, Martha, Paul, John, David and Maria. Bro.: David Jenkins.
Ex. David Jenkins and Henry Kaeffer. Lancaster Borough.

10 Aug. 1005   24 Jan. 1814
KNOLL, JACOB
Wife. Catharine Knoll. Child: Elizabeth.
Ex. Catharine Knoll. Lancaster Borough.

26 Jan. 1814   7 June 1814
KENDIG, JACOB
Wife. Ann Kendig. Children: Jacob, Magdalena wife of Jacob Rish (?), Francis, Elizabeth wife of Christian Musser, Esther wife of John Harman and Henry. Grandchildren: Samuel, Henry, George and Ester Kendig (children of Jacob) and Jacob, Daniel, Susanna and Benjamin Kendig (children of Henry).
Ex. Francis Kendig and Christian Musser. Strasburg Twp.

9 Jan. 1803   25 April 1814
KREBS, CATHARINE
Sister: Barbara wife of Frederick Youn. N.B. There was a bequest of £15 to the German Lutheran Church at New Holland.
Ex. Jacob Stauffer. Earl Twp.

21 April 1814   1 June 1814
KARCH, JOHN
Wife. Eva Karch.
Ex. Eva Karch. Lancaster Borough.

13 April 1814   4 July 1814
KINNARD, EMANUEL
Wife. Mary Kinnard. Children: Esther and Joseph.
Ex. Joseph Kinnard and Jeremiah Copper. Sadsbury Twp.

12 Feb. 1815   5 June 1815
KEHLER, MICHAEL

Children: John, Daniel, Michael, Henry, Joseph, Abraham, Jonas, Catharine wife of John Saltzman, Elizabeth wife of Philip Hoffman, Ann wife of Jacob Martin, Barbara and Magdalena wife of George Spitel.
Ex. Jacob Witmer and Jacob Witmer Jr. Manor Twp.

20 July 1814   11 Aug. 1815
KEAGY, RUDOLPH
Wife. Esther Keagy. Children: Jacob, Rudolph, Isaac, John, Henry, Abraham, Levi and Anna.
Ex. Francis and Emanuel Bowman. Strasburg Twp.

12 April 1814   1 Nov. 1815
KELB, JONATHAN
Bro. and sister: John and Catharine Kelb.
Ex. John and Catharine Kelb. Cocalico Twp.

--- 1804   9 March 1816
KAUFFMAN, CHRISTIAN
Wife. Barbara Kauffman. Children: John, Christian and Elizabeth wife of Michael Houffman.
Ex. Michael and Christian Kauffman. Hempfield Twp.

--- 1814   3 Feb. 1816
KAUFFMAN, MICHAEL
Children: Anna wife of Joseph Gochnauer, Veronica wife of Henry Musselman, Margaret wife of Martin Stauffer, Barbara wife of David Rohrer, David, Andrew and Christian.
Ex. David Kauffman and Joseph Gochnauer. Hempfield Twp.

10 May 1816   28 May 1816
KENDRICK, ISAAC
Wife. (name omitted). Children: Washington and Isaac.
Bro.: John Kendrick.
Ex. John Snyder and John Kendrick. Columbia Borough.

26 June 1817   11 Aug. 1817
KEMBER, CATHARINE
Sisters: Elizabeth wife of Nicholas Lutz and Barbara wife of Jacob Eckert.
Ex. Nicholas Lutz and Jacob Eckert. Earl Twp.

17 Sept. 1817   30 Oct. 1817
KLEPPER, JOSEPH
Wife. Anna Klepper. Children: Joseph (there were others, names and number not given).
Ex. Christian Peck and Henry Hains. Donegal Twp.

10 May 1817   11 April 1818
KOLB, JOHN ADAM
Sister: Catharine.
Ex. Peter Martin. Cocalico Twp.

12 April 1814   11 April 1818
KELB, CATHARINE

Bro.: John Kelb.
Ex. John Kelb. Cocalico Twp.

12 April 1817   14 April 1818
KLINE, DANIEL
    Wife. Maria Kline. Children: Daniel, Elizabeth, Rebecca,
Esther, Hannah wife of John Jackson and Mary. Grandchild: Daniel
Kline (parents' names not stated).
    Ex. Samuel Landis. Earl Twp.

3 Sept. 1811   20 Oct. 1818
KAUFFMAN, CHRISTIAN
    Wife. Catharine Kauffman. Children: Henry and Abraham
(there were nine other children by a former marriage - names not
given).
    Ex. Christian Hershey, John and Jacob Kauffman. Donegal
Twp.

10 April 1811   27 Jan. 1818
KEENER, LAWRENCE
    Wife. Susanna Keener. Children: John, George, Catharine
wife of Christian Hoffer, Eve wife of John Horum, Barbara wife of
Charles Heftey, Susanna wife of Frederick Kercher and Rosina wife
of John Hollinger.
    Ex. Valentine Griner and John Kenner. Warwick Twp.

25 Jan. 1819   21 April 1819
KEIPER, CASPER
    Wife. Ann Elizabeth Keiper. Children: Barbara, Jacob,
Elizabeth wife of Joseph Urich, Mary wife of Jacob Gordy, John
and Sally wife of Jacob Riefenyder.
    Ex. Jacob and John Keiper. Cocalico Twp.

17 Dec. 1818   21 April 1819
KUNTZ, GEORGE
    Children: Margaret wife of Adam Tritch, Nancy and Catharine
wife of James Platt. Grandchild: George Hemphill (parents' names
not given).
    Ex. Daniel Beck. Cocalico Twp.

8 Nov. 1809   22 May 1819
KINGRY, ANN
    Sister: Veronica wife of John Shenck.
    Ex. Christian Ober. Donegal Twp.

3 Oct. 1818   12 June 1819
KAUFFMAN, CHRISTIAN
    Wife. Maria Kauffman. Children: Elizabeth wife of Jacob
Markey, Ann wife of Abraham Long, Barbara wife of Samuel Eby,
Christian, Tobias, Mary, Susanna and Benjamin.
    Ex. David Kauffman and Benjamin Miller. Hempfield Twp.

15 Feb. 1815   20 Dec. 1819
KENDIG, MARY

Children: Tobias, Catharine, Mary, Prudence wife of John Good, Elizabeth wife of Michael Harnish, Samuel and George.
Ex. Michael Harnish and Abraham Huber. Hempfield Twp.

17 Aug. 1819   23 Nov. 1819
KRALL, CATHARINE
Children: Jacob, John, Joseph, Magdalena, Elizabeth and Catharine.
Ex. John Sybert. Manheim Twp.

--- --- 1819 (as indexed)
KEMPER, HENRY
N.B. This will was never finished, and all further records lost.

11 Oct. 1780   25 Aug. 1787
LUTTMAN, JACOB
Wife. Margaretta Luttman. Children: George, John, Margaretta, Mary and Elizabeth.
Ex. Margaretta Luttman. Lancaster Borough.

1 Oct. 1787   25 Nov. 1787
LANDIS, BENJAMIN
Wife. Anna Landis. Children: John, Benjamin, Mary wife of John Greider, Anne wife of John Weaver, Barbara and Elizabeth.
Ex. John and Benjamin Landis. Manheim Twp.

--- June 1786   24 Dec. 1787
LILE, ELIZABETH
Children: Samuel, Alexander, Elizabeth, Isaac, Ann, John, Peter and Margaret.
Ex. Samuel Wilson and George Brassler. Leacock Twp.

17 Jan. 1788   1 April 1788
LEADER, HENRY
Wife. Maria Salome Leader. Children: George (there were others, names and numbers not given).
Ex. Maria Leader and Adam Musser. Cocalico Twp.

8 May 1789   8 May 1789
LUTTMAN, JOHN
Children: John, George and Jacob.
Ex. John Weidle and John Light. Lancaster Borough.

5 July 1788   9 May 1789
LEFEVER, SAMUEL
Children: Samuel, Joseph, Catharine wife of William Randels, Sarah, Lydia and Mary.
Ex. Thomas Evans and William Webb. Strasburg Twp.

1 March 1789   26 Dec. 1789
LANTZ, JOHN
Wife. Anna. Children: Christian, John, Jacob, Samuel, Peter and Henry. Grandchildren: John and Samuel (sons of Samuel).

Ex. Jacob Lantz and John Greagey.   Caernarvon Twp.

30 April 1790   15 June 1790
LEIDIG, LEONARD M.
     Wife. Anna Margaret Leidig. Children: Martin, Michael,
Peter, George, Margaret, Anna, Jacob and Barbara.
     Ex. Frederick Martin and John Barry. Elizabeth Twp.

29 March 1791   27 July 1791
LUTZ, CASPER
     Wife. Eve Lutz. Children: George, Casper, Catharine wife
of Abraham Peter and Elizabeth wife of George Wermly.
     Ex. Michael Musser and Bernard Man. Manor Twp.

20 Sept. 1791   5 Nov. 1791
LEFEVRE, JOHN JR.
     Child: Elizabeth. Step-Mother: Mary Lefevre. Uncles and
Aunt: George, Adam and Jacob Lefevre and Catharine wife of
Nicholas Meck. Brother-in-law: Henry Gunkle.
     Ex. Henry Gunkle and Henry Eckerman. Lampeter Twp.

14 Sept. 1792   23 Jan. 1793
LONGENECKER, ULRICH
     Wife. Feronica. Children: Peter, John, Daniel, Elizabeth,
Jacob, Feronica, Michael, Anna, Maria, Barbara, Magdalena,
Catharine, Abraham, Ulerick and Christian.
     Ex. (nephew) Daniel Longenecker and Daniel Longenecker.
Rapho Twp.

26 July 1793   23 Sept. 1793
LEAR, JOHN
     Bro. and Sisters: Jacob, Ann, Elizabeth and Barbara Lear.
Step-Father: Philip Penter.
     Ex. Philip Penter. Manheim Twp.

29 Nov. 1793   6 Jan. 1794
LONG, CHRISTIAN
     Wife. Mary Long. Child: Elizabeth. Bro.: Jacob Long.
     Ex. Jacob Long and Peter Shindel. Lancaster Borough.

25 Jan. 1794   3 March 1794
LONG, JOHN
     Father: John Long. Bros. and Sisters: Christian, Herman,
Abraham, Anna, Elizabeth and Mary wife of Jacob Wissler.
     Ex. Herman Long and Samuel Wissler. Hempfield Twp.

6 March 1794   12 March 1797
LONG, ANN MARGARET
     Children: Abraham and Sarah wife of --- Fouk (there were
others, names not given).
     Ex. Jacob Long. Earl Twp.

16 July 1794   23 Aug. 1794
LUTTMAN, JOHN
     Aunt: Elizabeth wife of John Ween.

126

Ex. John Hambright and John Ween. Lancaster Borough.

8 April 1794   13 Oct. 1794
LANDIS, JACOB
     Children: John, Abraham, Mary, Elizabeth, Esther, Magdalena
and Barbara. Bro.: Henry Landis.
     Ex. John and Henry Landis. Lampeter Twp.

1 Aug. 1795   10 Oct. 1795
LINVILL, ANN
     Children: William, Ann and Phebe.
     Ex. William Linvill. Salsbury Twp.

6 July 1794   2 Nov. 1795
LESHER, NICHOLAS
     Wife. Dorothea Lesher. Children: Abraham, Christina,
Margaret, Nicholas and John.
     Ex. John Lesher and John Bechdol. Cocalico Twp.

25 June 1785   ---- 1795
LORENTZ, FRANCIS PETER
     Wife. Margaret Lorentz.
     Ex. Abraham Brubacker and Jacob Mayer. Manheim Twp.

21 Aug. 1795   6 Nov. 1795
LANE, HENRY
     Wife. Elizabeth Lane. Children: Abraham, John and Michael.
     Ex. Abraham Lane and John Lane. Manheim Twp.

9 Nov. 1790   18 April 1795
LINE, CHRISTIAN
     Wife. (name omitted). Children: Christian, Henry, Samuel
and Barbara.
     Ex. Jacob Brubacher and John Jacob Brubacher. Martic Twp.

25 Feb. 1796   24 April 1796
LINDENBERGER, JACOB
     Mother: Hannah Lindenberger. Bro. and Sisters: John, Mary
wife of John Hatz, Catharine and Hannah.
     Ex. Hannah Lindenberger. Lancaster Borough.

7 Aug. 1795   29 Oct. 1796
LAUMAN, MARTIN
     Wife. Mary Lauman. Children: Martin, Philip, Ludwig,
Jacob, Mary and Elizabeth.
     Ex. Jacob Krug and Philip Cloninger. Lancaster Borough.

9 Feb. 1797   19 June 1797
LAUMAN, LUDWIG
     Wife. Elizabeth Lauman. Children: John, Lewis, George,
Frederick and Mary wife of John Hubley.
     Ex. Elizabeth and Lewis Lauman. Lancaster Borough.

7 Jan. 1797   27 Oct. 1797
LUTZ, STEPHEN

Children: Henry, John, Peter and Stevens.
Ex. Daniel Keaborth. Lancaster Borough.

16 May 1786   28 Feb. 1798
LEMAN, JOHN
     Children: John, Elizabeth, Jacob, Christian and Catharine.
Sons-in-law: John Stauffer and Adam Shenck (wives' names not
stated).
     Ex. John Leman and Adam Shenck. Mt. Joy Twp.

27 April 1796   8 Dec. 1798
LUTZ, CHRISTIAN
     Wife. Margaret Lutz. Children: Magdalena, Margaret and
Catharine.
     Ex. Harry Brendel and Samuel Adams. Cocalico Twp.

7 Oct. 1794   28 Nov. 1798
LEIBLY, GEORGE
     Wife. Magdalena Leibly. Child: Anna wife of --- Kramer.
Grandchild: Christian Kramer.
     Ex. John Flory. Hempfield Twp.

12 May 1798   22 May 1798
LUTZ, CASPER
     Wife. Mary Lutz. Children: (the names and number not
given).
     Ex. Mary Lutz, John Herr and Henry Paulus. Manor Twp.

1 Oct. 1795   19 May 1798
LYTLE, WILLIAM
     Wife. Ruth Lytle. Stepdaughter: Hannah (last name not
given).
     Ex. Thomas Lytle. Lancaster Borough.

23 Oct. 1798   29 Jan. 1799
LEFEVER, PETER
     Wife. Catharine Lefever. Children: Peter, Joseph and
Elizabeth wife of Valentine Fundersmith.
     Ex. Catharine, Peter and Joseph Lefever. Strasburg Twp.

11 April 1799   10 June 1799
LEWIG, PETER
     Wife. Appolonia Lewig. Children: Elizabeth and Barbara.
     Ex. Appoloma Lewig and David Mayer. Manheim Twp.

9 March 1795   25 March 1799
LONG, ROBERT
     Children: Stephen, Joseph, William, James, John, Robert,
Martha wife of James McPherson, Mary wife of William Long,
Eleanor and Margaret.
     Ex. Steven and Robert Long. Drumore Twp.

8 Feb. 1790   26 Feb. 1800
LONGENECKER, ABRAHAM

Wife. Magdalena Longenecker. Children: Daniel, Esther wife of Jacob Brua and Abraham.
Ex. John Miller and John Longenecker. Lampeter Twp.

13 May 1800   25 July 1800
LUTZ, CASPER
Wife. Margaret Lutz. Children: Nicholas, Henry, John, Philip, Catharine, Elizabeth and Abraham. Grandchild: Catharine Lutz (child of Abraham).
Ex. Nicholas Lutz. Cocalico Twp.

7 March 1800   27 Dec. 1800
LEHN, ABRAHAM
Wife. Mary Lehn. Children: (there were other children mentioned, names not given).
Ex. Benjamin Royer and Christian Hostetter. Manheim Twp.

7 March 1796   25 March 1801
LANDIS, JOHN
Wife. Anna Landis. Children: Abraham, David, (there were seven other children - names omitted).
Ex. Abraham and Jacob Landis. Cocalico Twp.

17 Sept. 1801   7 Oct. 1801
LEMAN, MARTIN
Wife. Christina Leman. Children: Catharine wife of Jacob Hestand, Henry, Christian, George, Mary, Martin and John.
Ex. Christina and Henry Leman. Rapho Twp.

2 April 1781   2 May 1801
LEFEVER, DANIEL
Wife. Mary Catharine Lefever. Children: Christian, Ellis, David, Daniel, Mary wife of David Ferree, Catharine wife of Peter Lefever, Esther wife of Jacob Lutman and Solomon.
Ex. Daniel Lefever, Joel and Isaac Ferree. Lampeter Twp.

23 April 4 Aug. 1802
LEFEVER, CATHARINE
Children: Joseph, Peter and Elizabeth wife of Valentine Fondersmith.
Ex. Joseph and Peter Lefever. Strasburg Twp.

20 July 1802   --- 1802
LARSHEY, PETER
Wife. Mary Larshey.
Ex. Mary Larshey and Thomas McKnaughton. Strasburg Twp.

29 Sept. 1798 8 Jan. 1803
LONG, ISAAC
Wife. Christina Long. Children: Mary, Isaac, Ann wife of Henry Landis and Susanna wife of Samuel Shieck.
Ex. Henry Landis and Daniel Rudy. Manheim Twp.

7 Feb. 1801   13 Aug. 1803
LANE, PETER

Wife. Margaret Lane. Children: Samuel, (there were others, names not given).
Ex. Samuel and John Lane. Manheim Twp.

1 July 1800   22 Dec. 1803
LONG, JAMES
Bros. and Sisters: John, Martha wife of --- Brothertons, Isabella, Elizabeth and Robert.
Ex. Robert Long. Martic Twp.

2 March 1804   5 April 1804
LOCKART, ROBERT
Grandmother: Margaret Lyons (of Parish Urney, Ireland).
Uncles: John Elliot, James Lyons and Isaiah Lyons. Aunt: Jane Lyons.
Ex. Sameul Humes and William Dickson. Lancaster Borough.

3 Feb. 1802   19 Oct. 1804
LANDIS, JACOB
Wife. Salome Landis. Children: John, (there were others, names and number not given).
Ex. Salome and John Landis. Cocalico Twp.

3 Dec. 1804   26 Dec. 1804
LINTON, SAMUEL
Wife. Elizabeth Linton. Children: William, Caleb and Jean.
Ex. Elizabeth and Caleb Linton. Earl Twp.

26 July 1804   13 Oct. 1804
LINDNER, DANIEL
Wife. Veronica Lindner. Children: John, Nancy and Daniel.
Ex. Godfrey Klug. Manor Twp.

18 April 1804 20 May 1804
LANE, ANNA MARIA
Widow of Cornelius Lane. Sisters: Eve, Barbara and Elizabeth (last names not given).
Ex. Michael Lane and Benjamin Royer. Manheim Twp.

6 Jan. 1804   24 Oct. 1804
LONG, HERMAN
Wife. Elizabeth Long. Children: Herman, Joseph, Martin, Samuel, Abraham, Daniel and John. Son-in-law: Michael Hoffman (wife's name not stated). Grandchild: Abraham (son of John).
N.B. A cavet was filed against this will, and it does not appear on records - only on index. The original is very much faded and worn, and very difficult to decipher.
Ex. Abraham Long and Michael Hoffman. Donegal Twp.

24 Sept. 1798 25 Nov. 1805
LINE, JOHN
Children: Henry, John, Jacob, Mary wife of Jacob Warner, Ann wife of Jacob Shallenberger, Christian, Abraham, Barbara wife of Michael Shinck and Elizabeth wife of George Markley.
Ex. Christian and Abraham Huber. Conestoga Twp.

130

22 March 1805   12 April 1805
LONGNECKER, DANIEL
    Children: Barbara, John, Christian, Henry, Anna and
Elizabeth.
    Ex. John Longnecker and David Coble. Donegal Twp.

11 June 1801   27 March 1805
LUDWIG, JACOB
    Children: Jacob, Catharine wife of George Eckert and
Elizabeth wife of John Shaffer. Grandchildren: Mary wife of
Christian Wolf and Magdalena Ludwig (children of Jacob).
    Ex. George Eckert and Philip Diffenderfer. Lancaster
Borough.

19 Oct. 1804   15 Feb. 1805
LEIB, JOHN
    Wife. Catharine Leib. Children: Christian, John, Jacob and
Barbara wife of George Shreiner.
    Ex. Christian and John Leib. Manheim Twp.

18 March 1805   25 April 1805
LINDEMAN, HENRY
    Wife. Mary Lindeman. Children: (the names and number not
given).
    Ex. John Shock. Manor Twp.

4 March 1804   --- 1805
LOWREY, ALEXANDER
    Wife. Sarah Lowrey. Children: Mary wife of Joseph West,
Margaret wife of George Plumer, Lazarus and Frances wife of
Samuel Evans. Grandsons: Alexander Lowrey, John and Lawrey
(parents' names not given).
    Ex. Lazarus Lowrey and Samuel Evans. Donegal Twp.

16 June 1806   18 Aug. 1806
LONG, ROBERT
    Children: Hugh, John, Martha and Margaret.
    Ex. Hugh Long and Hugh Long Jr. Martic Twp.

23 Sept. 1806   14 Oct. 1806
LONGENECKER, ABRAHAM
    Wife. Catharine Longenecker. Children: Elizabeth,
Feronica, John, Catharine and Ann.
    Ex. Christian Shenk and Catharine Longenecker. Rapho Twp.

11 Dec. 1805   7 Jan. 1806
LANTZ, JOHN
    Wife. Regina Lantz. Children: Abraham, John (and three
others, names not given).
    Ex. Christian Houser and Abraham Landis. Lampeter Twp.

19 Aug. 1806   1 Nov. 1806
LECHLER, JOHN

Children: John, George, Christina wife of Adam Gemshorn, Anthony, Catharine wife of John Miller, Joseph and Eve wife of -- - Walter. Grandchild: Catharine Walter.
Ex. George and Henry Lechler. Lancaster Borough.

19 Aug. 1806   13 Oct. 1806
LEMAN, ABRAHAM
Wife. Mary Leman. Children: Joseph, Ann, Abraham, Mary, Barbara and Elizabeth.
Ex. John Leman and Abraham Myers. Mt. Joy Twp.

18 March 1806   19 April 1806
LONG, ABRAHAM
Bros. and sisters: David, John, Elizabeth wife of Joseph Hershy, Susanna wife of David Stauffer, Maria wife of Lewis Metz, Barbara wife of Peter Summy and Ann.
Ex. Peter Summy. Warwick Twp.

30 Aug. 1804   26 Jan. 1807
LEMAN, PETER
Wife. Mary Leman. Sons-in-law: Joseph Buckholder and John Strickler (wives' names not given).
Ex. Abraham Reiff and John Leman. Rapho Twp.

28 Feb. 1807   18 April 1807
LUTZ, MARGARET
Children: Nicholas, Martin, Elizabeth, Maria and Mary.
Ex. Adam Hoe. Cocalico Twp.

1 May 1795   28 July 1807
LEMAN, PETER
Wife. Barbara Leman. Children: Peter, Jacob, John and Daniel.
Ex. Abraham, Peter and Jacob. Mt. Joy Twp.

4 Nov. 1806   14 Jan. 1807
LEMAN, ABRAHAM
Children: Anna wife of Daniel Beem, Abraham, John, Ulerick, Fronica and Elizabeth.
Ex. John Leman and John Leman Jr. Rapho Twp.

14 Sept. 1808   15 Nov. 1808
LONG, JOHN
Wife. (name not given).
Ex. Hugh Long and Samuel Anhrin. Martic Twp.

14 Nov. 1808   10 Dec. 1808
LIGHT, JOHN
Wife. Barbara Light. Children: Henry, John, Jacob, Ann wife of --- Eby, Barbara wife of John Henly, Elizabeth, Susanna and Magdalena.
Ex. Henry Light and John Hernly. Hempfield Twp.

11 Nov. 1803   13 Oct. 1808
LUTHER, CHRISTIAN

132

Wife. Christina Luther. Children: John, Christian and
Catharine wife of Jacob Beck.
Ex. Christina Luther. Ephrata Twp.

9 June 1804   21 June 1808
LONGENECKER, CHRISTIAN
Children: Elizabeth wife of Michael Huber, Abraham, Daniel,
Barbara wife of Peter Hummer, Mary wife of David Ober and Susanna
wife of Valentine Gensel. Grandchildren: Barbara, Elizabeth,
Christina, Mary and Michael Huber (children of Elizabeth).
Ex. Abraham Longenecker and Daniel Fritz. Rapho Twp.

15 Feb. 1806   20 Jan. 1808
LOUDON, ANN
Sisters: Sarah wife of --- Bartlet and Mary wife of ---
Hutton. Nieces: Mary wife of --- Elliot (formerly Mary Coburn)
and Ann Bartlet. Nephews: George Humphreys and Edward Sanders.
Ex. Joseph Pool and Samuel Miller. Columbia.

19 Aug. 1808   1 March 1809
LESHER, JACOB
Wife. Catharine Lesher. Children: Jacob, John, Mary wife
of Joseph Krall, (there were nine children - the names of the
others not given).
Ex. Jacob Lesher and John Wingert. Cocalico Twp.

11 Nov. 1808   8 March 1809
LIGHT, JACOB
Bros.: John, Peter, Benjamin and Christian Light. Sisters:
Anna wife of --- Stoner and Elizabeth wife of --- Lashey.
Nephews: Samuel, John and Martin (children of John Light).
Ex. Samuel and Martin Light. Lancaster Twp.

14 Oct. 1808   16 Oct. 1809
LOCKHART, JOSIAH
Child: Josiah. Bros.: Samuel and Robert. There was a
bequest made to the Presbyterian Church in Lancaster.
Ex. George Simpson and Robert Coleman. Lancaster Borough.
N.B. George Simpson was cashier of the United States Bank in
Philadelphia at the time, and Robert Coleman Judge of the Court
of Common Pleas of Lancaster.

25 May 1808   27 Dec. 1809
LEVY, LAZARUS
Wife. Magdalena Levy. Child: Elizabeth wife of Peter
Snyder.
Ex. George Lohra and Christian Westhaffer. Cocalico Twp.

14 Dec. 1809   12 Jan. 1810
LANDIS, BENJAMIN
Wife. Elizabeth Landis. Children: John, Benjamin,
Elizabeth, Anne, Maria, Barbara, Susanna and Jacob.
Ex. John Landis and John Brackbill. Manheim Twp.

20 May 1810   3 July 1810
LANTZ, PAUL
     Wife. Feronica Lantz. Children: John, Feronica, Christian
and Jacob.
     Ex. Jacob Lantz and Jacob Warfel. Lampeter Twp.

20 Dec. 1805   3 Nov. 1810
LAUMAN, ELIZABETH
     Legatees: Jacob, Barbara and Joshua Shaub. (they are not
spoken of as relatives.)
     Ex. John Hart. Martic Twp.

12 March 1810   16 April 1810
LIGHTNER, MICHAEL
     Children: John, Margaret wife of Frederick Shivel, Catharine
wife of Jonas Frion and Elizabeth.
     Ex. John Lightner. Earl Twp.

22 Feb. 1806   23 Oct. 1810
LEFEVER, JOHN
     Children: George, Elizabeth wife of Joseph Leman, Catharine
wife of --- Keports and Mary wife of John Shultz. Grandchildren:
Daniel, John and George Lefever (parents' names not given) and
Elizabeth and John Keports.
     Ex. George and Joseph Lefever. Strasburg Twp.

12 Sept. 1809   10 Nov. 1810
LEONARD, PHILIP
     Children: Christian, George, John, Mary, Charlotte,
Elizabeth, Henry, Catharine and Susanna.
     Ex. John Leonard. Lancaster Borough.

9 Feb. 1797   27 Dec. 1810
LINDEMAN, JOHN
     Wife. Anna Lindeman.
     Ex. Anna Lindeman. Lancaster Borough.

1 March 1806   16 April 1811
LESSLE, BENJAMIN
     Children: Benjamin and Christian.
     Ex. Christian Lessle and John Hissner. Brecknock Twp.

4 Dec. 1811   21 Dec. 1811
LUTZENBERGER, ADAM
     Wife. Hannah Lutzenberger. Children: Francis and Mary.
     Ex. Valentine Gardner and John Stehman. Manor Twp.

8 Dec. 1805   28 Sept. 1811
LOUDON, CATHARINE
     Sister: Margaret Stake. Aunt: Mary Barber.
     Ex. John Evans and John Barber. Buffalo Valley
(Northumberland Co.)

31 March 1809   29 May 1811
LONG, ELEANOR

Wife. Anne Long. Bro. and Sister: Mary and Joseph. Brother-in-law: William Long.
Ex. William Long and Alexander McFuson. Drummore Twp.

2 June 1810   25 May 1812
LANTZ, BALSER
Children: Elizabeth wife of Terrence Megram, Susanna and Peter. Grandchildren: John and Peter Lantz (children of Peter) and John Haines (parents' names omitted).
Ex. Terrence Megrann and Elizabeth Megrann. Lancaster Borough.

17 Sept. 1811   28 Jan. 1812
LIGHTNER, JOHN
Wife. Barbara Lightner. Children: Nathaniel, John, Joel, Juliana wife of John Sharp, Adam, Ann wife of Samuel Hinkle, Margaret wife of Christian Sharp and Barbara wife of James Magy. Grandchild: Daniel Magy.
Ex. John and Joel Lightner. Leacock Twp.

11 Dec. 1809   28 May 1812
LUTHER, CHRISTINA
Children: Christian and Catharine wife of Jacob Beck.
Ex. Christian Luther. Cocalico Twp.

15 July 1812   19 Aug. 1812
LESLEY, SAMUEL
Wife. Sarah Lesley.
Ex. John Wallace. Earl Twp.

15 Oct. 1803   20 March 1813
LIGHT, HENRY
Wife. Barbara Light. Children: John and Henry.
Ex. John and Henry Light. Manor Twp.

29 April 1813   23 Dec. 1813
LEMAN, HANNAH
Widow of Daniel Leman. Children: Peter, Mary wife of John Ferree, John, Christian, Betsey, Nancy, Hannah and Rebecca.
Ex. John Leman. Strasburg Twp.

13 Aug. 1813   8 March 1814
LEFEVER, PHILIP
Wife. Eliza Lefevre. Children: Daniel, Hetty, George and Samuel.
Ex. Henry Lefever and David Scott. Drumore Twp.

17 May 1811   3 Jan. 1814
LINE, SAMUEL
Bros.: John and Christian Line.
Ex. Jacob Brubaker and Samuel Line. Martic Twp.

27 Nov. 1813   30 March 1814
LANIUS, WILLIAM
Wife. Elizabeth Lanius. Bros.: John and Jacob.

Ex. John Philips and Henry Ranck. Lititz Twp.

14 March 1812   23 April 1814
LONGENECKER, CHRISTIAN
     Children: Christian, Ann wife of Abraham Gish, Elizabeth
wife of Jacob Hurst and Barbara wife of Samuel Bosler.
     Ex. Christian Longenecker and John Cable. Donegal Twp.

11 Jan. 1813   9 June 1813
LINVILL, WILLIAM
     Wife. (name omitted). Sisters: Ann and Phebe. N.B. There
was a bequest made to Salisbury Friends Meeting.
     Ex. William Linville and William Linvill. Salisbury Twp.

18 April 1810   8 Dec. 1814
LEIB, ABRAHAM
     Wife. Maria Leib. Children: John, Isaac, Christian, Anna
wife of Philip Lanor and Maria wife of George Grubb.
     Ex. Christian Hostetter and Charles Rudy. Manheim Twp.

20 July 1814   24 Dec. 1814
LAW, ABRAHAM
     Wife. Martha Law. Bro. and Sister: Thomas and Barbara Law.
     Ex. Martha Law. Twp. omitted.

25 Jan. 1815   4 March 1815
LINE, JUSTINA
     Children: Magdalena, Mary, Godlieb, Frederick and Michael.
     Ex. Godlieb and Michael Line. Lancaster Borough.

4 April 1815   26 Aug. 1815
LAPP, JOHN
     Wife. Maria Lapp. Children: John, Anna, Elizabeth, Maria,
Michael, Barbara, Christian and Sarah.
     Ex. John Lapp and Christian Konig. Leacock Twp.

29 July 1815   23 Dec. 1815
LEFEVER, GEORGE
     Bros. and sisters: Jacob, Adam, Mary wife of Peter Lefever,
Henry, John, Peter, Catharine wife of Henry Wanderbaugh,
Elizabeth wife of Daniel Espenohead, Esther wife of Jacob Rathfon
and Philip.
     Ex. Peter Lefever and Jacob Rathfon. Lampeter Twp.

8 March 1816   8 June 1816
LEMAN, JOHN
     Children: John, Barbara wife of Abraham Burkholder, Abraham,
Peter, Jacob, David and Benjamin.
     Ex. John and Benjamin Leman. Rapho Twp.

7 Aug. 1815   11 Nov. 1816
LINE, HENRY
     Wife. Anna Line. Child: John.
     Ex. Martin Funck and Henry Rush. Conestoga Twp.

16 Feb. 1814   24 May 1817
LONG, JOHN
     Children: Joseph, Christian, John, David, Ann wife of Conrad
Shissler, Barbara wife of Charles Rudy, Mary wife of Daniel Erb
and Elizabeth wife of Martin Shenk.
     Ex. Benjamin Long and Benjamin Long Jr.   Manheim Twp.

22 July 1815   15 Sept. 1817
LONG, ANN
     Children: Catharine wife of Paul Yutz and John.
     Ex. John Long and Paul Yutz.   Donegal Twp.

8 Dec. 1810   12 March 1818
LEHR, ESTHER
     Children: Catharine wife of --- Stauffer and Christiana wife
of --- Rosenbaum.   Grandchildren: Jacob, Magdalena and Catharine
Stauffer and Maria Rosenbaum.
     Ex. Jacob Brubacker.   Donegal Twp.

23 June 1815   31 March 1818
LOVETT, AARON
     Wife. Charity Lovett. Children: Joseph, John, Samuel,
William, James, Thomas, Rodman and Mary.
     Ex. Charity and John Lovett.   Little Brittain Twp.

--- 16 May 1818
LUTZ, HENRY
     Children: (the names and number not given).   N.B. This is a
German will with translation attached.
     Ex. Christian Nissly.   Donegal Twp.

26 Feb. 1816   31 Mach 1819
LANTZ, FERONICA
     Formerly Feronica Diffenbaugh.   Children: Catharine wife of
Isaac Hains, Susanna, John, George, Henry, Andrew and Elizabeth
wife of --- Buckwalter.   Grandchildren: Henry, Ann, Susanna and
Mary Lantz (children of John), Abraham, Joseph, Mary and
Elizabeth Buckwalter.
     Ex. George Diffenbaugh and Henry Diffenbaugh.   Lampeter Twp.

3 Dec. 1815   23 March 1819
LONGENECKER, JOHANNES
     Wife. Susanna Longenecker. Children: Elizabeth wife of
John Easton, Maria wife of Henry Lesher and Barbara wife of David
Eahleman.
     Ex. Christian Reist.   Warwick Twp.

13 Aug. 1804   17 July 1819
LAUMAN, LEWIS
     Legatee: William Hamilton.
     Ex. William Hamilton.   Lancaster Borough.

7 Feb. 1786   14 Feb. 1786
MARTIN, JACOB

Wife. Mary Eve Martin. Children: Jacob, John, George, Catharine and Magdalena.
    Ex. Mary Eve Martin. Lancaster Borough.

8 March 1786   19 April 1786
MAWROR, JACOB
    Wife. Susanna Mawror. Children: Elizabeth, Mary and Susanna. Bro.: John Mawror.
    Ex. Susanna and John Mawror. Lancaster Borough.

6 March 1786   20 April 1786
MEYER, CONRAD
    Wife. Elizabeth Meyer. N.B. There was a bequest of thirty shillings to build and repair a Common School House in New Holland.
    Ex. Christian Bremer and John Engle. Earl Twp.

9 April 1785   29 July 1786
MUMMA, GEORGE
    Wife. Barbara Mimma. Children: Elizabeth wife of John Carle, Magdalena wife of Jacob Strickler, Juliana wife of David Mellinger, Maria Barbara, George, Henry, David and Jacob.
    Ex. John Hertzler and John Shirk. Hempfield Twp.

10 Feb. 1776   23 May 1786
MAURER, PHILIP
    Wife. Anna C. Maruer. Children: Simon, Eva, Catharine, Anna wife of Christopher Brown and George.
    Ex. Anna Maurer and Wendel Bartholomew. Hanover Twp.

22 Nov. 1786   15 Feb. 1787
MUSSER, CHRISTIANA
    There were two children, names omitted. Bro.: John Engle.
    Ex. John Engle and Benjamin Musser. Manor Twp.

2 Oct. 1786   7 Feb. 1787
MILLER, JAMES
    Wife. Jane Miller. Children: Eleanor wife of Francis Bailey and Andrew.
    Ex. Francis Bailey and Andrew Miller. Bart Twp.

17 Feb. 1785   2 May 1787
MARK, CONRAD
    Wife. Catharine Mark. Children: Henry, Conrad, (and two daughters - names omitted).
    Ex. Catharine Mark. Warwick Twp.

6 June 1787   25 Aug. 1787
MILLER, JOHN
    Wife. Mary Miller. Children: Tobias, John and Susanna.
    Ex. John Stauffer and Henry Musser. Manor Twp.

28 Dec. 1787   31 May 1787
MILLER, JOHN

138

Wife. Anna Margaret Miller. N.B. There was a bequest of £5 to the Reform Congregation of Lancaster.
Ex. Anna Margaret Miller. Lancaster Borough.

21 May 1788   28 June 1788
MOUNTGOMERY, MARY
Children: John McClain, Moses McClain and Robert Montgomery.
Ex. Robert Maxwell. Little Brittain Twp.

26 Sept. 1788 20 Oct. 1788
MILLER, WILLIAM
Wife. Isabella Miller. Children: Mary wife of William Allison and James. Son-in-law: Joseph Young (wife's name not given). Grandchild: Jane Young.
Ex. James Miller and Robert Robison. Mt. Joy Twp.

24 Oct. 1788   29 Nov. 1788
MUMMA, BARBARA
Widow of George Mumma. Children: Christian, Henry, Jacob, Magdalena wife of Abraham Hestand, Juliana wife of David Mellinger, Mary wife of Jacob Hertzler, Barbara, George and David.
Ex. David Brubacher. Hempfield Twp.

27 Oct. 1788   17 Feb. 1789
MILLER, JOHN
Wife. Margaret Miller. Children: Henry, Jacob (and another son - name not given).
Ex. Margaret Miller and John Yount. Cocalico Twp.

14 Jan. 1789   11 Feb. 1789
MEYER, JOHN
Wife. (name omitted). Children: John, Samuel, David, Magdalena, Barbara, Frena and Elizabeth.
Ex. Christian Meyer and David Kempfer. Earl Twp.

22 Aug. 1788   6 July 1789
MEIXEL, MARTIN
Wife. Juliana Meixel. Children: John, Jacob, Juliana, Martin, Ann and Andrew.
Ex. Jauliana Meixel and John Brubacher. Leacocok Twp.

21 Sept. 1789 21 Oct. 1789
MULLINS, DANIEL
Wife. Ann Mullins. Children: John, Catharine and Alice.
Ex. Ann and John Mullins. Lancaster Borough.

26 Feb. 1787   9 Dec. 1789
MORRISON, JAMES
Children: William, John, Ann wife of John Nelson, Elizabeth wife of John McPorland, James, Margaret wife of James Knox, Margery wife of Jehu Howell, Jean and Samuel.
Ex. Samuel and James Morrison. Drumore Twp.

7 Oct. 1782   10 Dec. 1789
MILCHSACK, AUGUST
    Wife. Elizabeth Milchsack. Children: George, August,
Philip, Magdalena and Elizabeth.
    Ex. Elizabeth Milchsack. Lancaster Borough.

9 Dec. 1789   14 Dec. 1789
MUSSER, JACOB
    Child: Mary wife of Jacob Byer. Grandchild: Jacob Byer.
    Ex. Henry Byer and Christian Huber. Martic Twp.

20 June 1786   12 Jan. 1790
MC DERMIT, DANIEL
    Children: Archibald, John, Daniel, Mary, Nancy, Joseph and
David.
    Ex. John and David McDermit. Martic Twp.

16 March 1795   6 May 1790
MC MILLAN, JOHN
    Wife. Jean McMillan. Children: Ann wife of James Loag,
Mary wife of William Marling and wife of John Mitchel and Jean
wife of John Patton. Grandchildren: William Gebby (parents'
names not stated), John, Marling and Jean Patton.
    Ex. Jean McMillan and James Loag. Martic Twp.

12 Oct. 1789   24 June 1790
MC KEAN, MARY
    Widow of William McKean. Children: Robert, William and
James. Grandchildren: William, Hugh, Mary and Elizabeth
(children of Robert McKean) and William (son of William McKean).
    Ex. James Moorehead and James Miller. Mt. Joy Twp.

9 April 1790   5 Aug. 1790
METZGER, JACOB
    Wife. Susanna Metzger. Children: Frederick and Jacob.
    Ex. Susanna and Frederick Metzger. Conestoga Twp.

6 Sept. 1790   10 Sept. 1790
MC KINNEY, JAMES
    Children: Samuel, Rosanna, Elizabeth and Agness wife of
George Hunter. Granddaughter: Margaret Linch (parents' names not
given).
    Ex. George Hunter. Little Brittain Twp.

17 Feb. 1786   3 Nov. 1790
MARTIN, JACOB
    Wife. (omitted). Children: John, Rosina, Mary, Elizabeth
and Anna. Son-in-law: George Geyer (wife's name omitted).
    Ex. John Mohler and J. George Geyer. Cocalico Twp.

22 Dec. 1789   2 Dec. 1790
MODDERWELL, THOMAS
    Children: John and Adam. Son-in-law: John Reed (wife's name
not given).

Ex. Adam Modderwell and John Paxton. Drumore Twp.

14 Sept. 1790 6 Dec. 1791
MYER, ABRAHAM
 Wife. Hannah Myer. Children: John, Jacob, Eve wife of
Henry Eaby, Elizabeth, Mary wife of Peter Eby, Catharine,
Christina wife of John Dennis, Susanna, Rebecca and Barbara.
 Ex. Jacob Myer. Leacocok Twp.

5 July 1790   15 Feb. 1791
MICHAEL, JOHN
 Wife. Sarah Michael. Children: John, Susanna and Sarah.
 Ex. Sem Harlacher and Jacob Stees. Cocalico Twp.

8 May 1791   5 Aug. 1791
MILLER, HENRY
 Wife. Christina Miller. Children: Henry, Ulrick,
Elizabeth, Barbara, Susanna, Ann Margaret, Magdalena, Catharine
and Christina.
 Ex. Henry Miller and John Bott. Conestoga Twp.

6 March 1792   22 March 1792
MILLER, CHARLES
 Wife. Agness Miller (this was the second wife - The name of
first not given, nor does it state which was the mother of the
children mentioned). Children: Peter, William, Ursula and
Salome.
 Ex. Andrew and Brand, Adam Diller and Agness Miller. Earl
Twp.

9 July 1792   4 Aug. 1792
MARTIN, CHRISTIAN
 Wife. Susanna Martin. Children: Joseph, David, (there were
others, names not given).
 Ex. Frederick Mumma and John Hammacher. Rapho Twp.

25 July 1792   8 Oct. 1792
MC CARTNEY, ANDREW
 Wife. Margaret McCartney. Children: George and Rebecca.
 Ex. John Caldwell, William Brown and Margaret McCartney.
Colerain Twp.

6 Sept. 1792   31 Oct. 1792
MARTIN, CHRISTIAN
 Bros.: David, Jacob and Isaac Martin. Sisters: Christina
wife of David Herr and Mary wife of Emanuel Herr.
 Ex. Christian Wisler and George Shoman. Manor Twp.

14 Nov. 1792   19 Dec. 1792
MAFFET, JOHN
 Wife. Eleanor Maffet. Children: Josiah, Martha, Mary and
Jenny.
 Ex. Elenor Maffet and Patrick Campbell. Martic Twp.

13 Dec. 1792   17 Jan. 1793
MC FARLAND, JAMES
        Wife. Jean McFarland. Children: James, Samuel, (there were others, names and number not given).
        Ex. Jean McFarland and Joseph Laromore. Drumore Twp.

21 May 1793   26 June 1793
MILLER, JACOB
        Wife. Mary Miller. Children: George, Catharine wife of George Sahm, Jacob, David, John and Barbara wife of Christopher Weisert.
        Ex. Samuel Ensminger and George Sahm. Manheim Twp.

15 March 1793   20 July 1793
MILLER, DANIEL
        Wife. Margaret Miller. N.B. There was a bequest to the Warwick German Lutheran Church.
        Ex. Margaret Miller and Christian Spickeler. Warwick Twp.

14 June 1791   21 Sept. 1793
MC CLURE, RENDAL
        Children: John, William, Margaret and Rendal.
        Ex. John Haldeman and Frederick Bower. Donegal Twp.

7 June 1793   7 Nov. 1793
MAYER, GEORGE
        Wife. Barbara Mayer. Children: Christopher and Susanna. Son-in-law: Frederick Steinman (wife's name not stated).
        Ex. Christopher Mayer, Frederick Steinman and Thomas Turner. Lancaster Borough.

5 Nov. 1793   27 Nov. 1793
MOORE, ANN
        Widow of Hugh Moore. Children: Ann, Mary and Rebecca.
        Ex. Zachariah Moore and James Wilson. Donegal Twp.

24 July 1793   11 Jan. 1794
MEYER, JACOB
        Wife. Ann Meyer (2nd wife). Children: John, Barbara, Abraham (children by 1st wife), Anna, Christian, Jacob, Mary, Martin and Daniel (children of 2nd wife).
        Ex. Christian Meyer and Jacob Brubaker. Manheim Twp.

4 Nov. 1791   27 Feb. 1794
MC LAUGHLIN, JAMES
        Wife. Rachel McLaughlin. Children: James, Mary wife of Dick Thomas, Margaret wife of James Gribben, William, Rachel and Isabella.
        Ex. Rachel and James McLaughlin. Drumore Twp.

28 March 1794   14 April 1794
MARBURG, MARGARET
        Sister: Elizabeth wife of Bernard Grider.
        Ex. Andrew Bausman. Lancaster Borough.

3 Nov. 1785   14 May 1794
MILLER, DAVID
     Bros. and sisters: Abraham, Benjamin and Eve.
     Ex. Jacob Kendrick and Hy Hoober. Strasburg Twp.

5 Sept. 1794   20 Nov. 1794
MEYER, CHRISTIAN
     Children: Jacob, John, Christian, Anna wife of Jacob Lashey,
Barbara wife of Christian Meyer, Maria wife of Abraham Johns,
Magdalena wife of Samuel Grebill.
     Ex. John and Christian Meyer. Earl Twp.

14 Sept. 1793   10 Sept. 1794
MAXWELL, JAMES
     Child: Alies wife of Samuel Ramsey. Grandchildren: James,
Mary, Robert, Moses, William, John, Nathaniel, Martha, Agness,
Jean and Samuel Ramsey.
     Ex. Samuel Ramsey. Drumore Twp.

2 April 1781   3 Oct. 1794
MC KOWN, MALCOM
     Wife. Jean McKown. Children: Mary, Elizabeth, Isabella,
Margaret, William and Moses. Jennet. [sic]
     Ex. Jean McKown and James Colbreth. Colerain Twp.

27 June 1792   12 Nov. 1794
MC SPARRAN, JAMES
     Children: James, John, Samuel, Elizabeth and Martha.
     Ex. James McSparran and James Buchanan. Little Brittain
Twp.

31 Oct. 1794   2 Dec. 1794
MONEY, BARNABAS
     Children: William, George, Daniel, John, Thomas and
Margaret.
     Ex. James Arbuckle and Samuel Dilworth. Little Brittain
Twp.

27 March 1791   8 Nov. 1794
MUMMA, JACOB
     Wife. Catharine Mumma. Children: Jacob and Magdalena.
     Ex. John Ebersole and Frederick Mumma. Donegal Twp.

9 Jan. 1793   26 Oct. 1795
MEAD, PHILIP
     Wife. Catharine Mead (her former husband was John Shotter).
Nephews and nieces: Philip, Casper and John Mead, Mary wife of
John Libhard and Appolonia Libhard.
     Ex. Adam Musser. Cocalico Twp.

2 April 1794   24 Oct. 1795
MAYER, SAMUEL
     Wife. Ann Mayer. Child: Michael. Grandson: Christian
Brenneman (parents' names not given).
     Ex. Ann and Michael Mayer. Conestoga Twp.

20 Nov. 1794   2 Feb. 1795
MC CURDY, ARCHIBALD
    [No relative names given here.]
    Ex. William Brisben, Hannah and Adam McCurdy.

11 March 1795   18 March 1795
MC CLURE, ROBERT
    Bro. and sister: Sarah and Thomas McClure.
    Ex. Thomas McClure and Joseph Walker. Bart Twp.

17 Sept. 1794   9 May 1795
MELLINGER, BENEDICT
    Children: David, Christian, John and Feronica wife of Jacob
Ebersole.
    Ex. David and John Mellinger. Manor Twp.

20 Aug. 1795   9 Oct. 1795
MILLER, SIMON
    Wife. Barbara Miller. Bro.: John Miller.
    Ex. John Miller. Twp. omitted.

6 May 1781   6 May 1795
MC DILL, JAMES
    Wife. Mary McDill. Children: George, James, Elizabeth,
Mary, Nancy and Isaac.
    Ex. Isaac McDill. Salisbury Twp.

22 Oct. 1795   2 Jan. 1796
MILLER, CHRISTIAN
    Wife. (name omitted). Children: Christian and David.
    Ex. David Miller and John Nissly. Hempfield Twp.

20 March 1785   12 May 1796
MICHLER, JOHN
    Wife. Mary Michler. Bro.: Wolfgang Michael [sic].
    Ex. Christian Bleckenderfer and David Tannenberg. Warwick
Twp.

29 June 1796   21 July 1796
MILLER, JACOB
    Wife. Sophia Miller. Children: Elizabeth and Jacob.
    Ex. Sophia Miller. Lancaster Borough.

29 Sept. 1796   ---
MILLER, PETER
    N.B. This will was not proved and therefore not recorded.
    Cocalico Twp.

15 Dec. 1792   13 Feb. 1797
MESSENCOPE, JOHN
    Wife. Elizabeth Messencope. Children: Philip, John, Jacob,
Adam, Magdalena, Elizabeth, Catharine and George. Grandchild:
Elizabeth Messencope (daughter of George).
    Ex. Peter Eckman. Lancaster Borough.

4 Aug. 1797   28 Aug. 1797
MARTIN, WILLIAM
    Uncle: John Foster.
    Ex. John Foster. Strasburg Twp.

5 May 1797   27 Aug. 1797
MC CALMONT, SAMUEL
    Wife. Mary McCalmont. Children: Robert, Samuel, Martha
wife of Matthew Scott, Mary wife of Andrew Heany, Rachel wife of
James Jackson, Jean wife of James Heany, Ann wife of James
Downing and James.
    Ex. Robert and James McCalmont. Colerain Twp.

19 Dec. 1796   1 March 1797
MC CONNAL, DANIEL
    Wife. Mary McConnal. Children: Samuel, Daniel, Hugh,
David, Mary, Elizabeth and Martha.
    Ex. Hugh and Samuel McConnal. Colerain Twp.

---   7 Feb. 1797
MC CLOUGHLIN, BOYD
    Father: Daniel McGloughlin. Mother: Mary McGloughlin.
Bros.: Alexander and Neal McGloughlin.
    Ex. John Moore. Lancaster Borough.

20 Aug. 1793   18 Nov. 1797
MUSSELMAN, JOHN
    Wife. Christiana Musselman. Children: Christian, Abraham,
Jacob, Barbara, John, Margaret and Christina.
    Ex. Christian Frantz and Christian Hostetter. Warwick Twp.

23 March 1794   15 Sept. 1796
MILES, JONAS
    Children: John, Thomas, Joseph, Anna, Sarah and Elizabeth.
Son-in-law: Isaac Coulson (wife's name not stated).
    Ex. Ann Miles and Isaac Webster. Little Brittain Twp.

3 Dec. 1787   5 March 1798
MUSSELMAN, CHRISTIAN
    Wife. Mary Musselman. Children: John, Christian, Joseph,
Barbara, Mary and Christina.
    Ex. John Sensenig and Michael Bear. Earl Twp.

9 Aug. 1795   5 April 1798
MEYER, CHRISTIAN
    Wife. Anna Meyer. Children: John, David, Jacob, Martin,
Christian, Elizabeth wife of Peter Hohl and Mary wife of
Christian Streib.
    Ex. John Meyer and Christian Frick. Manheim Twp.

8 July 1797   25 Aug. 1798
METZGAR, VITUS
    Wife. Elizabeth Metzgar. Children: Anna wife of Daniel
Sheller, Dorothea wife of Michael Shaar. Grandchild: Daniel
Sheller.

Ex. Elizabeth Metzgar and Michael Zartman. Elizabeth Twp.

28 Nov. 1796   7 Sept. 1798
MUSSER, FERONICA
        Child: Daniel.
        Ex. Daniel Musser. Conestoga Twp.

19 Nov. 1798   8 Dec. 1798
MUSSELMAN, JACOB
        Wife. Elizabeth. Children: Christian, John and Jacob
(there were eight others, names omitted).
        Ex. Elizabeth, Christian and John Musselman. Donegal Twp.

23 Jan. 1798   28 Nov. 1798
MORRISON, JOHN
        Bro.: James Morrison. Nephews: James and Robert Knox.
Nieces: Margaret Tomson and Jenny Graham.
        Ex. James Buchanan and James Knox. Drumore Twp.

1 June 1797   9 Jan. 1799
MC CLEERY, JOSEPH
        Wife. Jennet McCleery. Children: John, Mary, Martha and
Jennet. Son-in-law: James McCleery (wife's name not stated).
        Ex. John and James McCloory. Earl Twp.

16 Sept. 1778   8 Jan. 1799
MC CLUNG, MATTHEW Jr.
        Wife. Elizabeth McClung. Children: Charles, Hugh, Martha,
Elizabeth, Jane and Charles.
        Ex. Hugh McClung and James Mercer. Leacock Twp.

24 Jan. 1792   25 Nov. 1799
MC CULLY, JAMES
        Wife. Elizabeth McCully. Children: William, Margaret wife
of John Watt, Fanny wife of John Roland and Thomas.
        Ex. Elizabeth and Thomas McCully. Little Brittain Twp.

10 June 1799   20 Feb. 1800
MC NEAL, MARGARET
        Children: Ann, Mary, Margaret, Rebecca, Jean, Thomas,
Daniel, John and Archibald.
        Ex. Daniel and John McNeal. Salisbury Twp.

6 May 1800   29 July 1800
MAINZER, GEORGE
        Wife. Christiana Mainzer. Children: John, George, Conrad,
Christina wife of Jacob Wolf, Jacob, Michael, Simon, Juliana wife
of George Grim, Catharine wife of Jacob Nagle and Michael.
        Ex. Jacob and Simon Mainzer. Earl Twp.

14 April 1797   13 Aug. 1800
MOHR, MICHAEL
        Wife. Catharine Mohr. Children: Adam, Michael, Peter,
John, Jacob and Catharine.
        Ex. Michael Mohr. Elizabeth Twp.

26 June 1796   6 Dec. 1800
MC CLURE, JEAN
    Children: William, John, James, Thomas and Sarah.
    Ex. Thomas McClure and Joseph Walker. Bart Twp.

20 Jan. 1800   25 July 1800
METZGER, JONAS
    Wife. Eve Metzger. Children: Jonas and Elizabeth wife of
Michael Shallenber (these are the children of the first wife
whose name was Hambright - the last five are of the second wife),
Michael, Mary, Catharine, Salome and Eve.
    Ex. Eve Metzger and Casper Shaffer. Lancaster Borough.

22 Feb. 1798   1 Oct. 1801
MUHLEISEN, JOHN
    Wife. Maria. There were six children - names not given.
Son-in-law: John Moyer.
    Ex. Maria Muhleisen and John Moyer. Rapho Twp.

5 Aug. 1797   10 Nov. 1801
MC GIRR, NATHANIEL
    Wife. Margaret McGirr. Bro.: James McGirr.
    Ex. Samuel Cook and Thomas Bayley. Maytown Twp.

15 June 1801   29 May 1802
MC CALLEY, JAMES
    Children: John and Mary wife of John Galbrath.
Grandchildren: James and John McCalley (sons of John) and
Elizabeth and James Galbreath.
    Ex. John McCalley and John Byers. Salsbury Twp.

20 Oct. 1798   17 May 1802
MC CLUNG, MATTHEW
    Wife. Martha McClung. Children: Matthew, Charles and Hugh.
Grandchildren: Charles and Hugh McClung (children of Matthew).
    Ex. Joseph Lefever, Hugh and Charles McClung. Leacock Twp.

4 March 1788   13 March 1802
MILLER, JOHN
    Children: Elizabeth wife of David Miller, Barbara wife of
David Eshleman, Ann wife of Abraham Hare, John and Jacob.
    Ex. John and David Miller. Lampeter Twp.

17 June 1802   6 July 1803
MC ANTIER, WILLIAM
    Wife. Mary McAntier. Children: Mary, Martha, Isabella,
Samuel and Elizabeth. Grandchildren: William Scott, Mary Black,
Mary McCay and William McAntier (parents' names not stated).
    Ex. Robert King and James Calhoun. Drumore Twp.

2 July 1803   30 July 1803
MILLER, CHRISTIAN
    Wife. Barbara Miller. Child: Fronica wife of Daniel
Kinports.
    Ex. Barbara Miller and Jacob Denlinger. Lampeter Twp.

22 May 1798   6 Aug. 1803
MILLER, ABRAHAM
    Wife. Mary Miller. Children: Abraham, John, Mary and Ann.
    Ex. Abraham and John Miller. Conestoga Twp.

4 July 1796   11 Aug. 1803
MEAD, CATHARINE
    Bros.: John and Jacob Nees.
    Ex. John Nees and Philip Rahn. Cocalico Twp.

3 July 1802   8 Oct. 1803
MC CULLOUGH, JOHN
    Wife. Mary McCullough. Children: Hugh, Isaac, John,
Margaret wife of --- McPherson, James, Mary, Elizabeth and
Catharine.
    Ex. Hugh McCullough and John Steele. Drumore Twp.

26 Jan. 1802   23 Nov. 1803
MC CULLEY, THOMAS
    Wife. Frances McCulley. Bro.: James McCulley.
    Ex. Archibald McCulley. Little Brittian Twp.

26 July 1800   28 March 1804
MILLER, JACOB
    Children: Leonara, Jacob and Anna.
    Ex. Peter Elser. Warwick Twp.

14 Jan. 1804   30 Jan. 1804
MC ENALLY, BERNARD
    Wife. Elizabeth McEnally.
    Ex. Elizabeth McEnally. Rapho Twp.

28 March 1798   10 Jan. 1804
MILLER, HENRY
    Wife. Mary Miller.
    Ex. Christian Hurst. Earl Twp.

22 Jan. 1804   10 March 1804
MARTZALL, WENDLE
    Wife. Anna Martzall. Children: Martin, Christopher,
Elizabeth, Christian, Mary, Philip and John. Grandchild: Leah
Martzall (child of Martin).
    Ex. John Martzall and John Reist. Warwick Twp.

14 Nov. 1799   22 March 1804
MC ELROY, JOHN
    Wife. Elizabeth McElroy. Children: Samuel, George, John
and Margaret.
    Ex. John McCull and Samuel McElroy. Drumore Twp.

2 June 1802   25 May 1804
MARTIN, STEPHEN
    Wife. Catharine Martin.
    Ex. Catharine Martin. Lancaster Borough.

2 Nov. 1803   10 Dec. 1804
MERCER, JAMES
    Children: Samuel, John, Margaret and Alexander.
    Ex. John Mercer, Francis Bailey and Joseph Lefever.
Strasburg Twp.

7 Sept. 1801   31 Aug. 1804
MEYER, CHRISTIAN
    Wife. Barbara Meyer. Children: John, Jacob, Mary wife of
Jacob Eckert and Elizabeth wife of George Miller.
    Ex. Barbara and John Meyer. Leacocok Twp.

4 Oct. 1804   3 Jan. 1805
MILLER, TOBIAS
    Wife. Barbara Miller. Children: Benjamin, Tobias, Mary,
Elizabeth, John and Barbara wife of Christian Kauffman.
Grandchildren: Isaac, Jacob and Susanna Kauffman.
    Ex. Benjamin Miller and Christian Kauffman. Rapho Twp.

15 March 1803 13 Feb. 1805
MILLER, RUDOLPH
    Children: Barbara, Mary, Esther and Rudolph. Nephew:
Abraham Miller.
    Ex. John and Abraham Miller. Conestoga Twp.

20 Feb. 1805   23 Dec. 1805
MUSSER, HENRY
    Wife. Elizabeth Musser. Children: Henry, John and Jacob.
Grandchild: Elizabeth Musser (Henry's child).
    Ex. John and Jacob Musser. Leacock Twp.

7 July 1805   19 Oct. 1805
MARTIN, DAVID
    Wife. Gertrude Martin. Children: Christian, Jacob,
Magdalena, Elizabeth, Barbara and Ann wife of Jacob Stoner.
    Ex. Christian and Jacob Martin. Manor Twp.

25 Feb. 1805   9 April 1805
MOORE, ANDREW
    Wife. Sarah Moore. Children: Elizabeth, Casandra, Sarah,
Rebecca wife of --- Jones and Ann wife of --- Williams. Son-in-
law: Ellis Passmore (wife's name not stated). Grandchildren:
Walter and Andrew Jones. N.B. There was a bequest of £30 to the
Sadsbury Preparative Meeting.
    Ex. Ashel Walker and James Moore. Sadsbury Twp.

7 Aug. 1805   14 Sept. 1805
MYER, CHRISTIAN
    Wife. Ann Myer. Children: Mary wife of Samuel Behm,
Christian, Ann, Susanna, Elizabeth, John, Barbara, Jacob,
Abraham, Catharine and Madgalena.
    Ex. Jacob Myer and Benjamin Hershey. Manheim Twp.

7 July 1804   8 Nov. 1805
MUSSER, PETER

Wife. Magdalena Musser. Children: Jacob, Feronica wife of Christian Johns, Henry and Joseph.
Ex. Jacob Musser and Christian Hartman. Lampeter Twp.

4 April 1797   13 Feb. 1805
MEIXEL, JULIANA
Child: Juliana.
Ex. Peter Eby. Leacocok Twp.

21 Nov. 1804   15 Jan. 1805
MC KINNEY, JOHN
Children: Daniel and Jane.
Ex. John Whitehill. Donegal Twp.

13 Feb. 1804   13 Feb. 1805
MUSSELMAN, HENRY
Children: Maria wife of --- Helden, John, Elizabeth, Magdalena and Henry.
Ex. Christian Kauffman and Henry Musselman. Hempfield Twp.

1 Feb. 1805   16 March 1805
MOSSER, HENRY
Wife. Froney Mosser. Children: Christian, Esther and John.
Ex. Peter Mosser and Abraham Guth. Brecknock Twp.

22 Oct. 1804   5 April 1805
MURRAY, JOSEPH
Legatees: Father and Uncle (names not given).
Ex. B. Owen and R. Lithgow. Leacock Twp.

21 Feb. 1805   9 March 1805
MC CALL, JOHN
Legatees: Michael Dougherty and others.
Ex. Michael Dougherty and Thomas Eagan. Maytown Twp.

17 Feb. 1804   5 May 1805
MONTELIUS, MARCUS
Wife. Christina Montelius. Children: Elizabeth, Charles, William, John, Maria, Sally, Peter and Marcus.
Ex. William Moutelius. Cocalico Twp.

13Feb. 1806   30 May 1806
MC GROURTY, JOHN
Wife. Catharine McGrourty. Children: Charles, Mary, Catharine and Frances.
Ex. John Risdel and Henry Lechler. Lancaster Borough.

10 Jan 1806   22 March 1806
MAYER, JACOB
Wife. Magdalena Mayer. Children: Jacob and Ann.
Ex. Henry Detrich. Conestoga Twp.

20 Feb. 1806   23 May 1806
MARTIN, FREDERICK
Wife. Anna Martin. Children: John, Englehard and Yost.

Ex. Yost Martin and John Martin. Elizabeth Twp.

1 July 1806   1 Sept. 1806
MUSSER, GEORGE
     Wife. Christiana Musser. Children: Rebecca wife of Henry
Derring, Mary wife of John Singer, Sarah, George, Catharine wife
of William Haberstick, Mathias, John, William, Henry, Abraham and
Harriet.
     Ex. Mathias Young and William Webb. Lancaster Borough.

14 April 1806   30 Aug. 1806
METZGER, CATHARINE
     Children: Catharine and Barbara wife of --- Frantz.
Grandchild: Adam Frantz.
     Ex. George Lohra and Peter Heip. Earl Twp.

24 Jan. 1806   11 Feb. 1806
MC CLURE, WILLIAM
     Wife. Elizabeth McClure. Children: John, James and Robert.
Bro.: John McClure.
     Ex. (Bro.) John McClure and Elizabeth McClure. Bart Twp.

13 April 1806   20 Sept. 1806
MINK, JACOB
     Wife. Elizabeth. Children: Jacob, Anna, John, Daniel,
Elizabeth, Simon, Catharine, Magdalena and Susanna.
     Ex. Jacob Mink and John Swer. Hempfield Twp.

30 Oct. 1804   8 April 1806
MC CLELLAN, SAMUEL
     Children: Jean wife of John Kinkade, Sally wife of Joseph
Ewing, Samuel, Katharine, Martha wife of Alexander Morrow, Polly
and James.
     Ex. Samuel McClellan. Colerain Twp.

17 Oct. 1806   --- Nov. 1807
MC CULLOUGH, GEORGE
     Wife. Isabella McCullough. Children: Eleanor wife of Joseph
Morrison, George, Jane wife of James Clark, William, Robert,
Sampson, Bella, Mary, Betsey and Margaret. Sons-in-law: Robert
Sampson, David Evans, Thomas Grier and John Vance (wives' names
not stated).
     Ex. William McCullough and David Evans. Little Brittain
Twp.

28 Aug. 1806   5 June 1807
MC MULLAN, JANE
     Legatees: Cummingham Patton and others.
     Ex. James Brown. Martic Twp.

3 June 1807   18 Nov. 1807
MUSSELMAN, JOSEPH
     Wife. Anna. Children: Abraham, Jacob, Samuel, Christian,
John, Mary and Ann.
     Ex. Christian Shelly and John Nissly. Mt. Joy Twp.

20 May 1805   14 Dec. 1807
MAYERS, JOHN
       Sister: Susanna Hamphferwill.   Brother-in-law: Frederick
Steinman.
       Ex. Frederick Steinman.   Twp. omitted.

26 Nov. 1807 [6.]   6 Jan. 1807
MC CAMANT, ISAAC
       Wife. (name omitted).   Children: Mary, Sarah, Isaac,
Alexander and Elihu.
       Ex. Isaac and Alexander McCamant.   Salisbury Twp.

29 Aug. 1801   20 April 1807
MESSNER, CHRISTIAN
       Wife. Catharine Messner.   Children: Barbara, Eve, Philip,
Catharine, Rosina and Christian.
       Ex. Philip Messner.   Brecknock Twp.

12 Sept. 1807   25 Sept. 1807
MC ILVAIN, GEORGE
       Wife. Rebecca McIlvain.   Children: Robert, Mary, Jean and
Elizabeth.
       Ex. Robert McIlvain and John Slaymaker.   Salsbury Twp.

26 Oct. 1805   29 April 1807
MILCHSACK, ELIZABETH
       Widow of August Milchsack.   Children: Magdalena wife of John
Meeling and George,.   Daughter-in-law: Catharine Milchsack (the
name of her husband not given).
       Ex. Henry Swentzel and Nicholas Groll.   Lancaster Borough.

8 Sept. 1802   5 Dec. 1807
MUSSER, MARTIN
       Wife. Mary Musser.   Children: Elizabeth wife of John Landis,
Peter, Mary wife of Joseph Buckwalter, Esther wife of Joseph
Yordy and Barbara.
       Ex. Joseph and Henry Buckwalter.   Lampeter Twp.

4 Feb. 1805   19 Oct. 1807
MEYERS, MARIA
       Children: Magdalena wife of Henry Gryder, Susanna wife of
Christian Shenck and Barbara wife of George Hide.   Grandchildren:
Abraham, Susanna, David and Daniel Gryder; Abraham, Christian,
Barbara and Daniel Shenck; and David and Henry Hide.
       Ex. Christian Habeeker and Henry Gryder.   Lampeter Twp.

16 May 1808   25 Oct. 1808
MC KENNEY, DAVID
       Wife. Esther McKenney.   Children: Samuel and Mary.
Grandchildren: David Ferree and Margaret McFarland (parents'
names not given).
       Ex. Esther and Samuel McKenney.   Donegal Twp.

7 March 1808   22 March 1808
MUSSELMAN, CHRISTIAN

152

Wife. Susanna Musselman. Child: Henry.
Ex. Christian Smith and Susanna Musselman. Hempfield Twp.

20 March 1808   3 May 1808
MILNER, NATHAN
Wife. Mary Milner. Children: Daniel, Cyrus, Jehu,
Catharine, Esther, Rachel, Mary and Eliza.
Ex. Cyrus and David Milner. Colerain Twp.

22 Dec. 1801   15 Feb. 1809
MILLER, MARGARET
Niece: Mary Lambert.
Ex. Mary Lambert. Lancaster Borough

21 Dec. 1808   4 March 1809
MAYER, SAMUEL
Bros.: George, Lewis and Michael Mayer.
Ex. George Mayer. Lancaster Borough.

27 May 1809   9 June 1809
MANART, JACOB
Children: Frederick, Mary wife of Jacob Goodman, Ann wife of
Abraham Warfell and Jacob. Grandchildren: Jacob Manart (son of
Jacob), Ann, Mary, Barbara and Susanna Manart (children of
Frederick).
Ex. Christian and John Stauffer. Conestoga Twp.

7 Feb. 1809   20 June 1809
MC DILL, GEORGE
Wife. Margaret McDill. Children: James, Hugh, George,
Catharine, Margaret, Jane and Jacob.
Ex. Jacob McDill. Salsbury Twp.

28 April 1804   20 July 1809
MC NAUGHTON, JAMES
Wife. Mary McNaughton. Child: James.
Ex. Mary McNaughton. Lancaster Borough.

21 Jan. 1807   9 Aug. 1809
MOORE, JAMES
Children: Jeremiah, John, James, Rebecca wife of --- Cooper,
Ann wife of Ashel Walker and Andrew. Grandchildren: James Cooper
and Jesse Moore (father's name not given). N.B. There was a
bequest of £100 to the Sadsbury Friends' Meeting to establish a
school.
Ex. John Moore and Ashel Walker. Sadsbury Twp.

2 May 1809   19 Aug. 1809
MEYERS, MARTIN
Children: Abraham, Martin and Ann wife of Benjamin Hershey.
Ex. Christian Frantz and Benjamin Hershey. Manheim Twp.

23 May 1805   28 Aug. 1809
MEYER, MARTIN

Wife. Catharine Meyer. Children: Henry, Catharine, Elizabeth, Jacob, John and Susanna wife of David Stam.
Ex. John Sherdle and John Albert. Donegal Twp.

3 Feb. 1808   25 Sept. 1809
MC LAUGHLIN, WILLIAM
    Wife. Mary McLaughlin. Children: James, John and Jean.
    Ex. Mary McLaughlin and John McKesseck. Martic Twp.

20 Feb. 1808   17 Jan. 1809
MC CAMANT, ALEXANDER
    Brothes: Isaac and Elihu McCamant.
    Ex. Isaac and Elihu McCamant. Salisbury Twp.

11 Feb. 1810   15 Aug. 1810
MURPHY, JOHN
    Wife. Catharine Murphy. Children: Francis, John, William, Eleanor, Ann and Mary wife of --- Bard.
    Ex. Francis Murphy and George Daly. Bethel Twp.

10 Oct. 1805   22 Aug. 1810
MISHEY, JACOB
    Children: Jacob, Ann, Elizabeth and Barbara.
    Ex. Abraham Shelly and Abraham Reiff. Rapho Twp.

17 March 1809   5 Sept. 1810
MILLER, JOHN
    Wife. Margaret Miller. Children: Anna wife of Philip Shaffer, George, John, Susanna wife of Philip Eberman, Elizabeth and Catharine wife of Henry Hibsham. Son-in-law: Michael Weidler (wife's name not stated).
    Ex. Margaret Miller, Henry Hibsham and Peter Gouter. Lancaster Borough.

5 Sept. 1806   11 Oct. 1810
MARTIN, REBECCA
    Nieces: Mary Graham, Rebecca Wallace and Elizabeth McIlvain.
    Ex. George Tompson and John Wallace. Earl Twp.

24 June 1809   12 May 1810
MONDORFF, ELIZABETH
    Child: Rachel. Grandchild: Elizabeth Qury (parents' names not stated).
    Ex. Isaac Mondorff and Samuel Miers. Conestoga Twp.

1 Dec. 1808   20 Oct. 1810
MAYER, CATHARINE
    Children: Catharine wife of Adam Oberly and Peggy.
    Ex. Adam Oberly. Lampeter Twp.

7 Sept. 1805   22 Oct. 1810
MEYER, MARTIN
    Wife. Barbara Meyer. Brother: Paul Meyer. Sister: Hannah Magdalena Meyer.
    Ex. Peter Bollinger and David Royer. Cocalico Twp.

2 March 1809   7 Jan. 1811
MENGEL, GEORGE
    Wife. Catharine Mengel.
    Ex. Catharine Mengel. Cocalico Twp.

5 Nov. 1807   29 Jan. 1811
MEYER, SAMUEL
    Children: Samuel, Cornelius, Henry, Abraham, Elizabeth wife
of Christian Shelly, Catherine wife of Benjamin Bear and Mary
wife of George Kneissly.
    Ex. Samuel and Henry Meyer. Mt. Joy Twp.

25 Feb. 1811   27 June 1811
MORRIS, WILLIAM
    Wife. Mary Morris. Child: William.
    Ex. James Wright. Columbia.

14 June 1790   7 June 1811
MORRISON, SAMUEL
    Bros.: James and Joseph Morrison. Nephews: Daniel, Joseph
and Col. James Morrison (sons of Joseph); James, John and William
Morriston (sons of James).
    Ex. Col. James Morrison. Drumore Twp.

4 Jan. 1808   8 Feb. 1811
MARTIN, MARTIN
    Wife. Barbara Martin. Children: David, Barbara wife of
Christian Witmer, Anna wife of John Mosser, Elizabeth wife of
Andrew Leckron, Jacob, John, Susanna wife of Peter Krubb, Fronica
wife of John Frick and Martin. Grandchildren: Barbara, Elizabeth
and John (children of Elizabeth); Mary, John, David, Ann and
Elizabeth (children of Martin).
    Ex. Christian Martin and Christian Witmer. Earl Twp.

7 April 1805   18 Feb. 1811
MUSSELMAN, MATHIAS
    Wife. Magdalena Musselman. Children: Christian, Elizabeth,
Catharine, Maria, Magdalena and Barbara.
    Ex. Christian Musselman. Brecknock Twp.

29 June 1810   28 May 1811
MEYER, JACOB
    Wife. Susanna Meyer. Children: Conrad, Jacob, Daniel,
Catharine, John, Barbara, Rosina, George, Samuel and Susanna.
    Ex. Valentine Greiner. Warwick Twp.

7 Nov. 1811   15 Nov. 1811
MASLICK, GODLIEB
    Wife. Justina Maslick. Children: Ignatus, Gottfried and
Timotheus.
    Ex. Peter Huber. Warwick Twp.

---   (as indexed) 1811
MC NEIL, DANIEL

N.B. This will has not copied on records and the original records are lost.

27 May 1803   27 Jan. 1812
MESSERSMITH, GEORGE
   Wife. Elizabeth Messersmith. Children: Catharine wife of Martin Miller, Elizabeth wife of Jonathan Foltz, Mary, Jacob, George, Susanna, Margaret, John and Philip.
   Ex. Elizabeth and George Messersmith. Lancaster Borough.

15 Oct. 1812   16 Nov. 1812
MC PHERSON, ALEXANDER
   Parents: James and Martha McPherson. Sisters: Elizabeth and Mary McPherson and Martha wife of William Ritchy. Bros.: William and James.
   Ex. John Buchanan and Dr. James Ankrim. Drumore Twp.

27 Dec. 1811   8 Jan. 1812
MC ENELLY, ELIZABETH
   Bros.: Jacob, Michael and Christian Judy. Sister. Ann.
   Ex. Mathias Judy and Christopher Schoner. Manheim Twp.

6 Jan. 1812   18 Feb. 1812
MAY, ARTHUR (DR.)
   Bros.: John, David and Samuel May. Brothers-in-law: Robert Reed and Joseph Coudin.
   Ex. Henry Slaymaker and Dr. Abraham Carpenter. Lancaster Borough.

12 March 1808   17 April 1812
MARCK, CATHARINE
   Widow of Conrad Marck. Children: Catharine wife of Peter Shiffer, Rosina wife of Joshua Moyer, Conrad and Henry.
   Ex. Conrad Marck. Warwick Twp.

18 May 1812   29 Oct. 1812
MARCKEL, GEORGE
   Wife. Sabina Marckel. Children: Adam, George, John, Jacob and Daniel. Grandchildren: Sally wife of Samuel Mohler, John, Elizabeth, Catharine and George Marckel (children of George).
   Ex. Sabina and Jacob Marckel. Cocalico Twp.

25 Sept. 1812   17 March 1813
MC FARLIN, JAMES
   Mother: Jean McFarlin. Brother: Samuel. Sister: Margaret wife of Robert Rush.
   Ex. William Strrls (?) and Robert Rush. Drumore Twp.

2 April 1813   19 April 1813
MARTIN, ABRAHAM
   Wife. Eva Martin. Children: Ann, Mary, Susan, Abraham, John and Eve.
   Ex. George Stouffer and Samuel Martin. Caernarvon Twp.

5 Feb. 1812   14 April 1813
MILLER, LEONARD
     Wife. Barbara Miller. Children: John, George, Elizabeth
wife of Peter Feller (and seven others, names not given).
     Ex. Barbara and Leonard Miller. Warwick Twp.

--- April 1813 1 May 1813
MALO, ADAM
     Stepchildren: Jacob, George, Elizabeth and Peter Young.
     Ex. Jacob Neff. Strasburg Twp.

27 May 1800   25 May 1813
MILLER, PETER
     Wife. Mary Miller. Children: Abraham, Daniel, Peter,
Tobias, Ann, Esther and Susanna wife of Peter Eby.
     Ex. Daniel, Peter and Tobias Miller. Leacock Twp.

19 March 1798 4 June 1813
MURRAY, SUSANNA
     Child: Mary wife of --- Ledley.
     Ex. Samuel Morrison. Twp. omitted.

4 March 1794   10 June 1813
MINNIG [sic.], JOHN
     Children: Adam and Jacob. Son-in-law: Jacob Keemer (wife's
name not stated).
     Ex. Jacob Keemer and John Minning Jr. Rapho Twp.

3 June 1813   18 June 1813
MC CLOUD, ALEXANDER
     Wife. Elizabeth McCloud.
     Ex. Elizabeth McCloud and Jeremiah Mosher. Lancaster
Borough.

28 Aug. 1810   16 Aug. 1813
MOONEY, GEORGE
     Wife. (name omitted). Children: George, Mary wife of Elias
Simmons, Martha wife of Joseph Simmons and Hannah wife of Robert
Simmons. Grandchild: Sarah Moore (parents' names not given).
     Ex. George Mooney. Sadsbury Twp.

3 June 1813   18 June 1813
MC CLOUD, ALEXANDER
     Wife. Elizabeth McCloud.
     Ex. Elizabeth McCloud and Jeremiah Mosher. Lancaster
Borough.

28 Aug. 1810   16 Aug. 1813
MOONEY, GEORGE
     Wife. (name omitted). Children: George, Mary wife of Elias
Simmons, Martha wife of Joseph Simmons and Hannah wife of Robert
Simmons. Grandchild: Sarah Moore (parents' names not given).
     Ex. George Mooney. Sadsbury Twp.

28 July 1813   6 Oct. 1813
MC LAUGHLIN, GEORGE
        Nephews: George McLaughlin, Robert and George King and James
McLaughlin. Nieces: Rachel Calvin, Isabella wife of James White
and Mary wife of Thomas Dick.
        Ex. Robert King and James McLaughlin. Drumore Twp.

31 Dec. 1805   24 Nov. 1813
MILLER, PETER
        Wife. Magdalena Miller. Children: Barbara wife of George
Steagh, Martin, Frederick, Magdalena wife of Philip Wyant, Peter
and Michael.
        Ex. Martin Miller. Lancaster Borough.

11 May 1814   6 Sept. 1814
MARTIN, JOHN
        Wife. Salome Martin. Children: John, George, (and four
others, names not given).
        Ex. John and George Martin. Cocalico Twp.

8 Feb. 1799   25 Feb. 1814
METZGER, JACOB
        Children: Adam and Christina wife of John Shreiber.
        Ex. Conrad Swartz and Jacob Stall. Lancaster Borough.

13 May 1813   10 Jan. 1814
MILLER, ADAM
        Wife. Anna Maria Miller. Children: Adam, David, Pete, John,
George, Samuel, Mary wife of Martin Shaffer, Catharine wife of
David Huber, Elizabeth wife of Benjamin Longenecker and Isaac.
        Ex. Anna Maria Miller and David Benter. Earl Twp.

29 March 1811 26 Feb. 1814
MUMA, FREDERICK
        Wife. Elizabeth Muma. Children: Jonas, Maria, Jacob and
Elizabeth.
        Ex. Andrew Beeker, Jacob and Joseph Muma. Donegal Twp.

20 June 1809   15 April 1814
METZLER, JACOB
        Wife. Maria Metzler. Children: Jacob, Mary, Elizabeth,
Anna, Barbara and Veronica.
        Ex. Maria and Christian Metzler. Earl Twp.

6 Oct. 1813   2 April 1814
MC CANN, BERNARD
        Legatee: The Rev. Michael Joseph Byrne - for the use of the
Roman Catholic Church of Lancaster.
        Ex. Michael Joseph Byrne. Twp. omitted.

7 Feb. 1799   7 April 1814
MC CLEERY, JAMES
        Wife. Eals McClerry. Child: James.
        Ex. James McCleery. Earl Twp.

4 May 1814   28 May 1814
MARTIN, JACOB
        Wife. Mary Martin. Children: George and Jacob.
        Ex. Mary Martin and Henry Landis. Cocalico Twp.

31 Oct. 1813   30 May 1814
MARTIN, ISAAC
        Wife. Susanna Martin. Child: Jacob.
        Ex. Christian Niswanger and Jacob Martin. Drumore Twp.

17 April 1813   12 Aug. 1814
MUMMA, CATHARINE
        Children: Esther, Abraham and David.
        Ex. John Strickler and Abraham Reiff. Rapho Twp.

3 Nov. 1813   14 July 1814
MOSSER, MICHAEL
        Wife. Mary Mosser. Children: William, John, Mary wife of
Michael Barnitz and Catharine wife of Samuel White.
        Ex. Samuel White. Lancaster Borough.

11 May 1814   6 Sept. 1814
MARTIN, JOHN
        Children: John and George.
        Ex. John and George Martin. Cocalico Twp.

28 April 1814   26 Nov. 1814
MANTLE, CHRISTOPHER
        Wife. (name omitted). Children: Frederick and William.
        Ex. Frederick Mantle. Earl Twp.

6 May 1806   3 Dec. 1814
MILLER, MICHAEL
        Wife. Maria Miller. Children: Michael, Elizabeth, Barbara
wife of --- Shaffer, Mary wife of Henry Strohm and Anna wife of
David Royer.
        Ex. David Royer and Peter Martin. Warwick Twp.

29 June 1814   10 Dec. 1814
MOERIG, JOHN WILLIAM
        Wife. Hannah Moerig. Children: George, William, John,
Elizabeth and Maria.
        Ex. John and George Bard. Leacock Twp.

19 Dec. 1813   23 Feb. 1815
MOHLER, JOHN
        Wife. Catharine Mohler. Children: John, Daniel, Samuel,
Jacob, Henry, Elizabeth wife of Leonard Weaver, Catharine wife of
Jacob Thrill and Mary.
        Ex. Jacob Hagy and John Mohler. Cocalico Twp.

22 May 1815   5 June 1815
MILNER, JEHU

Mother: Mary Wilson. Stepbrother and sister: Catharine and John Wilson. Bros. and sisters: Daniel, Rachel, Mary and Eliza Milner.
Ex. William Brown and Daniel Milner. Colerain Twp.

3 Oct. 1814   10 April 1815
MILLER, SOPHIA
Children: Jacob and Elizabeth wife of --- Jefferies. Grandchildren: Charlotte, Sarah, Sophia, Susanna and Elizabeth Jefferies.
Ex. John Baker and Jacob Brubaker. Donegal Twp.

28 March 1812   8 June 1815
MEISTER, JOHN
Children: Henry, Conrad, Margaret wife of Charles Obitz and John. Grandchildren: John, Conrad, Mary and Christian Meister (children of John).
Ex. Henry and Conrad Meister. Manheim Twp.

5 May 1815   5 July 1815
MILLER, MARTIN
Wife. Magdalena Miller. Bros. and sisters: Henry and Samuel Miller and Susanna wife of Christian Rohrer.
Ex. Magdalena Miller and Martin Barr. Martic Twp.

27 April 1812   29 July 1815
MARTIN, ABRAHAM
Wife. Mary Martin. Children: Abraham, David, Jacob, Barbara wife of Samuel Good and Mary wife of John Sollenberger.
Ex. David and Jacob Martin. Brecknock Twp.

10 May 1815   8 Aug. 1815
MAYER, CHRISTOPHER
Wife. Susanna Mayer. Children: George, Jacob, John, Maria wife of Thomas Beverly, Randolph, Susanna, Margaret and Juliana.
Ex. Susanna and George Mayer. Lancaster Borough.

11 Oct. 1814   9 Sept. 1815
MUHLENBERG, HENRY (REV.)
Wife. Catharine Muhlenberg. Children: Henry, Philip, (and six others, names not given).
Ex. Henry Augustus and Philip Muhlenberg. Lancaster Borough.

7 Jan. 1815   19 Sept. 1815
MC CLUNG, ELIZABETH
Bros. and sisters: Charles, Hugh and Jane McClung.
Ex. Nathaniel Watson and Jane McClung. Leacocok Twp.

5 Sept. 1814   6 Nov. 1815
MILLER, CHRISTOPHER
Children: Samuel and George. Sons-in-law: George Hacker and Henry Habacher (wives' names not given).
Ex. John and Christopher Miller. Cocalico Twp.

21 March 1812   9 Nov. 1815
MILLER, PHILIPINA
     Children: Mary, Andrew and Philip. Grandchildren: George
Miller (son of Andrew).
     Ex. Daniel Hahn and Peter Stipe. Earl Twp.

11 Nov. 1815   1 Dec. 1815
MAXWELL, JOHN
     Wife. Elizabeth Maxwell. Children: Robert, William, Anna,
Eliza, George, Sally, John and Joseph.
     Ex. William Maxwell. Donegal Twp.

25 July 1804   13 Dec. 1815
MURRAY, LECKEY
     Wife. Elizabeth Murray. Children: Nancy, Joshua, Leckey,
Elizabeth, James, Bartrem and Samuel.
     Ex. William Boyd, Nancy and Joshua Murray. Lancaster
Borough.

22 Feb. 1813   23 Dec. 1815
MACKEY, THOMAS
     Sister: Sarah.
     Ex. James Brown and Samuel Stevenson. Martic Twp.

28 Aug. 1815   22 Nov. 1815
MC CREADY, ARCHIBALD
     Wife. Agness McCready. Children: Agness, Elizabeth, Martha,
James, Margaret, Sarah, Mary and Annias.
     Ex. Agness and Annias McCready. Bart Twp.

1 July 1816   23 July 1816
MILLER, JACOB
     Wife. Mary Miller. Children: (The names and number not
given.)
     Ex. Henry Miller. Earl Twp.

7 Feb. 1814   13 Dec. 1816
MC CREARY, JOHN
     Wife. Rebecca McCreary. Children: John, William, Joseph,
James, Rebecca, Mary, Margaret and Elizabeth.
     Ex. John and William McCreary. Martic Twp.

--- May 1816   2 Nov. 1816
MURRAY, RACHEL
     Children: Betsey, (There were other children - names and
number not given).
     Ex. Robert McIlvain and Maxwell Kennedy. Salisbury Twp.

21 Oct. 1816   3 Jan. 1817
MILLER, GEORGE
     Wife. Catharine Miller. Children: Peter, (There were three
others, names not given).
     Ex. Samuel Miller and Peter Weidman. Elizabeth Twp.

20 March 1816 28 Jan. 1817
MARTZALL, CATHARINE

Sister: Magdalen.
Ex. John Gebel. Twp. omitted.

18 April 1817   28 April 1817
METZAR, JONAS
     Wife. Mary Metzgar. Children: Jonas, Elizabeth, Henry, Mary
and Susanna.
     Ex. Mary Metzgar and John Hoff. Lancaster Borough.

26 March 1817   30 April 1817
MC KOWN, WILLIAM
     Wife. Jane McKown. Children: John, Mary, Samuel, William
and Jane.
     Ex. Philip Feilshu and William Buck. Lancaster Borough.

3 Oct. 1815   1 May 1817
MILLER, JOHN
     Wife. Esther Miller. Children: John, Samuel, Mary wife of
Henry Hartman, Esther wife of John Taylor and Elizabeth wife of
Nicholas Hoffman.
     Ex. Nicholas Hoffman. Strasburg Twp.

25 Jan. 1810   14 July 1817
MANN, BERNHARD
     Wife. Anna Mann. Children: Bernard, John, George and
Elizabeth wife of Jacob Wermly.
     Ex. Bernhard and John Mann. Manor Twp.

15 Nov. 1810   27 Nov. 1817
MUMA, LEONARD
     Wife. Catharine Muma. Children: Elizabeth and Henry.
     Ex. Henry Fry and Henry Hambright. Earl Twp.

21 Sept. 1817   7 Oct. 1817
MUSSELMAN, JOSEPH
     Wife. Anna Musselman. N.B. The names and number of children
not given.
     Ex. Christian Steman. Manheim Twp.

4 Aug. 1817   3 Nov. 1817
MARTIN, ALEXANDER
     Wife. Jane Martin. Children: Hugh and Catharine.
     Ex. William Robinson. Earl Twp.

30 July 1817   24 June 1818
MICHAEL, PHILIP
     Children: Jacob, Frederick, Anna wife of Robert Bell and
Mary wife of John Pretz.
     Ex. John Sensenig and Peter Eberman. Warwick Twp.

16 June 1818   4 Aug. 1818
MYERS, JOHN
     Wife. Elizabeth Myers. Children: (The names and number not
given.)
     Ex. John Neff and Henry Bremman. Strasburg Twp.

162

26 Sept. 1818   9 Oct. 1818
METZGER, CHRISTIAN
    Legatee: John Sheaff.
    Ex. John Sheaff. Lancaster.

26 July 1804   20 Jan. 1819
MILLER, MARY
    Widow of Henry Miller. Legatee: Christiana wife of Adam
Oberly.
    Ex. Adam Betzer. Earl Twp.

15 Jan. 1817   20 Jan. 1819
MELLINGER, JOSEPH
    Wife. Dorothea Mellinger. Children: Joseph, William, John,
Anthony, Samuel, Christopher, Jacob and Molly.
    Ex. Anthony and Samuel Mellinger. Cocalico Twp.

4 Nov. 1818   2 Feb. 1819
MISHLER, JOSEPH
    Wife. Margaret Mishler. Children: Jacob, (There were eight
others, names omitted.)
    Ex. John Mohler and Abraham Bear. Cocalico Twp.

5 Nov. 1812   18 Feb. 1819
MC CULLOUGH, MARY
    Children: Margaret wife of--- McPherson, Mary, Elizabeth,
Catharine, Isaac, John, James and Hugh. Grandchildren: Mary
McPherson (child of Margaret), Catharine, Eleanor, John and Ann
McCullough (children of Isaac) and Mary S. Michael (parents'
names not given).
    Ex. James Johnson. Drumore Twp.

7 Jan. 1817   8 March 1819
MISHEY, JACOB
    Wife. Anna Mishey. Children: John, Jacob and Elizabeth.
    Ex. John Leaman and John Mishey. Rapho Twp.

24 Sept. 1808   30 Jan. 1819
MARTIN, DAVID
    Children: Mark, David, Christian, Abraham, Samuel, Susanna
wife of --- Wenger and Mary. Grandchild: Anna Wenger.
    Ex. David and Abraham Martin. Earl Twp.

18 Dec. 1818   21 May 1819
MC INTIRE, DINAH
    Legatee: Jacob Getz.
    Ex. Jacob Getz. Lancaster.

20 Sept. 1810   2 June 1819
MAYER, ANN
    Children: Ann wife of --- Brenneman and Michael.
Grandchildren: Cristian and Jacob Brenneman (sons of Ann),
Samuel, Nathaniel, Rudolph, Socrates, Ann wife of Jacob Lichy,
Mary wife of Christian Thomas and Margaret (children of Michael).
    Ex. Samuel Mayer. Conestoga Twp.

29 March 1819   3 June 1819
MAYER, JACOB
     Wife. Mary Mayer.   Children: John, (There were nine others,
names not given.)
     Ex. John Mayer and Jacob Brown.   Manheim Twp.

27 Jan. 1819   26 July 1819
MC CAMMOND, REBECCA
     Widow of Isaac McCammond.   Children: John Smith, Isaac and
Elihu McCammond, Mary wife of David Jenkins and Sarah wife of
Samuel Bun.   Grandchildren: Rebecca Jenkins and Rubria (?)
Anderson Bun.
     Ex. Robert Jenkins and John Wallace.   Salsbury Twp.

5 Sept. 1818   28 Aug. 1819
MARKLEY, MARTIN
     Wife. Anna Markley.   Child: Martin.
     Ex. (Brother) Daniel Markley.   Earl Twp.

29 Aug. 1819   8 Sept. 1819
MOORE, JOHN
     Children: Robert, Ashel and James.   Grandchildren: John,
Elizabeth, Rebua and Susanna (children of James).
     Ex. Robert and Ashel Moore.   Sadsbury Twp.

23 Aug. 1819   10 Sept. 1819
MILLER, JACOB
     Wife. Elizabeth Miller.   Children: George, Elizabeth wife of
John Pim, Daniel, Mary wife of Michael Stambacher, Jacob and
Samuel.
     Ex. George Miller and William Echtesnacht.   Strasburg Twp.

21 June 1816   6 Nov. 1819
MURRAY, JOHN
     Wife. Rebecca Murry.   Children: Jacob, John, Elizabeth wife
of John Peters and Catharine.
     Ex. Christian Grosh.   Warwick Twp.

1 April 1812   14 May 1819
MARTIN, HENRY
     Wife. Barbara Martin.   Children: Henry, John, Anna wife of
Henry Root, Barbara wife of David Martin, Elizabeth wife of John
Root, Mary wife of Jacob Stauffer, Jacob, Judith wife of Henry
Martin and Samuel.
     Ex. George Stauffer and Henry Root.   Earl Twp.

---   (as indexed) 1819
MC CURDY, HANNAH
     N.B. This will was unfinished and was not copied on records.
The original records are lost.

15 March 1786   3 April 1786
NISSLY, HENRY
     Wife. Elizabeth Nissly.   Children: Henry, Abraham, Martin,
Barbara wife of Michael Brandt, Mary, Catharine and Ann wife of
Jabez Shoe.

Ex. Abraham Reist and Michael Brandt. Rapho Twp.

15 March 1789   29 May 1789
NAGEL, JOHN
    Wife. Margaret Nagel. Children: Philip (There were others,
names and number not given).
    Ex. Margaret Nagel. Cocalico Twp.

8 June 1784   19 July 1789
NISSLEY, JOHN
    Wife. Mary Nissley. Children: Feronica, Michael, John,
Jacob, Abraham, Samuel and Martin.
    Ex. Michael Nissley and Jacob Eversole. Donegal Twp.

6 March 1797   4 Jan. 1790
NEFF, JACOB
    Wife. Elizabeth Neff. Children: Jacob, John, Barbara,
Elizabeth, Susanna wife of George Ruth, Magdalena wife of Jacob
Sener, Henry, Anna wife of John Sware, Catharine and Polly.
    Ex. John Huber and Henry Acker. Hempfield Twp.

10 Nov. 1783   31 May 1792
NEEL, JOHN
    Children: Thomas, John, James, Joseph, Darius, Adam and
William. Grandchildren: Mary, John and William Neel (children of
Adam); Adam and William Neel (sons of William).
    Ex. Thomas and John Neel. Martic Twp.

7 May 1790   24 July 1793
NEFF, ISAAC
    Wife. Anna Neff (formerly Kagey). Father: Isaac Neff.
    Ex. Isaac Neff. Manor Twp.

6 Oct. 1793   15 Oct. 1793
NEFF, ISAAC
    Wife. Anna Neff. Children: Ann and Elizabeth. Brother:
John Neff. Sister: Magdalena.
    Ex. Christian Habecker and Henry Neff. Manor Twp.

12 Sept. 1793   22 Oct. 1793
NININGER, JACOB
    Mother: Barbara Nininger. Brother: George.
    Ex. John Rohrer. Lampeter Twp.

18 Sept. 1793   27 Sept. 1794
NEWCOMER, ABRAHAM
    Child: Christian.
    Ex. Christian Newcomer. Conestoga Twp.

17 Aug. 1794   29 Sept. 1794
NISLY, ELIZABETH
    Widow of Henry Nisly. Bros.: Jacob, David and Abraham
Gingrich. Sisters: Fornica wife of John Shenck, Barbara and Anna
Gingrich.
    Ex. David Gingrich and John Shenck. Rapho Twp.

16 Jan. 1794   22 Nov. 1794
NINNGER, BARBARA
      Legatee: Catharine Haber.
      Ex. John Rohrer. Lampeter Twp.

19 Feb. 1793   18 April 1797
NEHER, MARTIN
      Wife. Ursula Neher. Children: Martin, Mary, Agness,
Catharine and Christina.
      Ex. Martin Neher and Andrew Herter. Earl Twp.

6 March 1797   7 Dec. 1798
NEFF, JACOB
      Wife. Elizabeth Neff. Children: John, Barbara wife of Peter
Henneberger, Elizabeth wife of Christian Miller, Susanna wife of
George Ruth, Magdalena wife of Jacob Sener, Jacob, Anna wife of
John Swar, Catharine, Polly and Henry.
      Ex. John Huber and Henry Acker. Hempfield Twp.

28 Jan. 1799   28 May 1800
NEWKOMER, CHRISTIAN
      Wife. Barbara Newkomer. Child: John. Grandchild: John
Newkomer (son of John).
      Ex. Jacob Eborly and Jacob Haugy. Cocalico Twp.

13 Aug. 1800   30 Sept. 1800
NOTZ, MICHAEL
      Wife. Anna Notz. Children: Catharine, Elizabeth, Anna,
Leonard and Magdalena.
      Ex. Joseph Shenck and Leonard Negly. Rapho Twp.

8 March 1796   26 Dec. 1801
NESSLEY, MARY
      Child: Freney.
      Ex. Christian Cobel and Martin Missly. Donegal Twp.

22 June 1802   27 Aug. 1802
NELSON, ISAAC
      Brother: John Nelson. Nephew and niece: Abraham and
Margaret Nelson.
      Ex. David Brown and Richard Smith. Drumore Twp.

30 Sept. 1802   30 Sept. 1802
NERIUS, JOHN
      Legatee: Dietrich Fahnstock.
      Ex. Dietrich Fahnstock. Cocalico Twp.

5 Oct. 1803   20 Jan. 1804
NAGLE, JOACHIN
      Wife. Juliana Nagle. Children: George, Joseph, Henry and
Jacob.
      Ex. Juliana Nagle and William Reichenbach. Lancaster
Borough.

9 Dec. 1804   12 Feb. 1805
NICHOLAS, MICHAEL
    Wife. Eve Nicholas. Children: John, Henry, Elizabeth wife
of --- Ream, Jacob, Frederick, Mary, Susanna, Esther, Ann, George
and Daniel.
    Ex. Peter Bishop and Peter Lindemuth. Donegal Twp.

8 Jan. 1799   19 March 1815 [1805?.]
NEWKOMET, CHRISTIAN
    Wife. Barbara Newkomet. Grandchild: John Newkomeb (parents'
names not given).
    Ex. Jacob Eberly and Jacob Ilayg. Cocalico Twp.

6 March 1799   --- 1805
NEWCOMER, CATHARINE
    Legatee: Catharine Keagy.
    Ex. John Hart. Conestoga Twp.

10 Nov. 1804   2 March 1805
NOLTE, MARIA
    Children: Anna wife of Casper Sheck, Elizabeth wife of David
Miller, Susanna wife of Andrew Gerber, Jonas and Barbara wife of
Joseph Rerf.
    Ex. Christian Kauffman. Hempfield Twp.

2 Jan. 1804   20 March 1805
NOLL, JOHN HENRY
    Wife. Barbara Noll. Children: John, Susanna wife of Isaac
Hoffman, Elizabeth wife of George Baughman Sr., Catharine wife of
Michael Horse, Joseph, George, Henry, and Mary wife of Matthew
Bartholomew.
    Ex. Matthew Bartholomew. Bart Twp.

23 Oct. 1802   16 Feb. 1805
NEWCOMER, JOHN
    Children: Elizabeth wife of Daniel Forrer, Mary, Ann wife of
Jacob Hershey, Susanna wife of Peter Reitzel and John.
    Ex. John Newcomer and John Hertzler. Hempfield Twp.

30 Jan. 1806   18 April 1806
NOBLE, JAMES
    Wife. Margaret Noble. Children: James, Andrew, Peggy,
Eliza, Nancy wife of --- Henderson and William.
    Ex. William and James Noble. Sadsbury Twp.

16 March 1803   3 Jan. 1806
NEES, ADAM
    Wife. Margaret Nees. Children: John, George, Adam, Samuel,
Catharine wife of Jacob Stover, Hannah wife of Conrad Meinser and
Susanna.
    Ex. John and George Nees. Rapho Twp.

21 Aug. 1793   5 Nov. 1807
NEES, JOHN

Wife. Salome Nees. Bros.: Adam and Jacob Nees. Nephew:
John Nees (son of Adam).
    Ex. Salome Nees and William Dishong. Lancaster Borough.

25 April 1811 12 Dec. 1812
NAGLE, CHRISTOPHER
    Wife. Margaret Nagle.
    Ex. Margaret Nagle and Benjamin Hershey. Lancaster Borough.

4 April 1807 28 May 1813
NEWCOMET, ANNA
    Children: Anna wife of David Mellinger, Christian, John,
Jacob, Peter, Abraham, Barbara, Elizabeth and Magdalena.
    Ex. John Newcomet and David Mellinger. Manor Twp.

11 June 1806 27 Dec. 1813
NEWSWANGER, ANNA
    Children: Abraham, Mary, Ann, Elizabeth, Christian, David
and Jacob.
    Ex. Christian and Jacob Newswanger. Drumore Twp.

9 May 1810 21 March 1814
NEFF, JACOB
    Wife. Anna Neff. Children: Jacob, John, Esther wife of
Jacob Weaver, Anna wife of Francis Kendig and Veronica wife of
Martin Barr.
    Ex. Jacob and John Neff. Strasburg Twp.

18 July 1814 12 Sept. 1814
NIGH, NICHOLAS
    Legatee: Christopher Denny.
    Ex. Jacob Kauffman. Hempfield Twp.

23 March 1815 28 April 1815
NAUMAN, GEORGE
    Wife. Salome Nauman. Children: Charles, George, (There were
four others, names not given).
    Ex. Salome Nauman. Lancaster Borough.

11 June 1815 9 Sept. 1815
NEWCOMMER, CHRISTIAN
    Wife. Susanna Newcommer. Children: John, Ann and Susanna.
    Ex. Joseph Newcommer and Jacob Stribge. Hempfield Twp.

7 Feb. 1817 11 March 1817
NEWWANGER, EMANUEL
    Wife. (name omitted). Children: Joseph, Jacob and Nancy.
    Ex. Jacob Newswanger and Henry Hoffman. Carnarvon Twp.

20 March 1817 7 April 1817
NEHVE, CHRISTIAN
    Wife. Susanna Nehve.
    Ex. Susanna Nehve and Jacob Snyder. Lancaster Borough.

17 April 1817   10 May 1817
NESSINGER, NICHOLAS
    Wife. Catharine Nessinger.   Children: (the names not given).
    Ex. Samuel Gerber.   Leacock Twp.

9 May 1817   13 May 1817
NETZLY, HENRY
    Wife. Anna Maria Netzly.   Children: Henry, George, John,
Jacob, Susanna and Feronica wife of John Swartz.
    Ex. Henry Netzly and John Netzly.   Warwick Twp.

6 Aug. 1816   12 Aug. 1816
NUN, HENRY
    Wife. Catharine Nun.   Children: Susanna, Henry and David.
Grandchild: Susanna Nun (child of David).
    Ex. Adam Wenger and Henry Nun.   Leacock Twp.

18 Sept. 1817   11 Oct. 1817
NETZLY, JOHN
    Wife. Susanna Netzly.   Children: Jacob and John.
    Ex. Francis Netzly and John Musselman.   Warwick Twp.

29 March 1816   19 July 1819
NEASER, NICHOLAS
    Wife. Hannah Neaser.   Children: Daniel, Jacob, Catharine
wife of Daniel Schwigert, Mary wife of John Emig, Elizabeth wife
of Philip Killian and Hannah wife of Frederick Fultz.
    Ex. Jacob Masser and Philip Killian.   Earl Twp.

9 Aug. 1819   17 Nov. 1819
NISSLY, JOHN
    Children: Martin, Henry, Abraham, Samuel, Gertrut wife of
David Ebersol, Ann, Elizabeth wife of Peter Graybill and Mary
wife of Christian Graybill.
    Ex. Martin Nissly and David Ebersol.   Mt. Joy Twp.

26 Aug. 1747   14 Nov. 1747
OYSTER, CHRISTIAN
    Wife. Margaret Oyster.   The names and number of children not
stated.
    Ex. Margaret Oyster.   Twp. omitted.

--- 1748   2 May 1748
OVERHOLZER, SAMUEL
    Wife. Elizabeth.   Children: Martin and Jacob.
    Ex. Jacob Cedy and Henry Keepeffer.   Twp. omitted.

10 March 1762   7 May 1762
OFFNER, MARTIN
    Wife. Barbara Offner.   Children: John, Mathias and
Catharine.
    Ex. Michael Waidler.   Lancaster Borough.

23 April 1768   1 June 1768
OMOBERSTEG, ABRAHAM

(This should be OBERSTEG.) Children: John and Benjamin.
Ex. William Bersh and Everhart Michael. Hempfield Twp.

20 Oct. 1767   11 July 1768
OBEL, CHRISTOPHER
Wife. Catharine Obel.
Ex. Philip Gerber and Andrew Eshbach. Lebanon Twp.

22 Oct. 1768   8 Nov. 1770
OLIFANT, CHARLES
Child: John. Grandchildren: Catharine and Bentin McCorkle
(parents' names not stated).
Ex. John and Daniel McCornnel. Colerain Twp.

25 Aug. 1770   1 Oct. 1770
ONEIL, CHARLES
Children: William, Elizabeth and Prudence.
Ex. Alexander Johnson, William McClure and John Barnett.
Paxton Twp.

1 April 1777   28 Dec. 1780
OBERLANDER, PETER
N.B. This is a German will and was never completed.
Ex. ---

13 April 1782   6 May 1782
OVERKVISH, MICHAEL
Wife. Barbara Overkvish. Children: Baltzer, Barbara, Jacob
and Michael.
Ex. Jacob Keller and John Shaffer. Bethel Twp.

15 March 1784   4 April 1786
OWEN, BENJAMIN
Wife. Elizabeth Owen. Children: Ann, Jonathan and Benjamin.
Ex. Elizabeth, John and Benjamin Owen. Leacock Twp.

17 May 1787   23 Oct. 1788
OBERLIN, MICHAEL
Wife. Christina Barbara Oberlin. Children: Adam, Margaret,
Jacob, Christina, Rebecca, Anna, Elizabeth, Catharine wife of
John Rein. Son-in-law: Jacob Oberlin (wife's name not stated).
Ex. Adam Ness and Jacob Oberlin. Earl Twp.

18 July 1785   7 Aug. 1789
OBERHOLTZER, CHRISTIAN
Children: Christian, Anne, Molly and Barbara. Son-in-law:
George Huber (wife's name not given).
Ex. George Huber. Hempfield Twp.

6 Jan. 1792   10 April 1792
ODENWALT, GEORGE
Wife. Elizabeth Odenwalt. Children: Christian, George,
John, Catharine wife of Daniel Slighter, Christina wife of ---
Messersmith and Maria wife of --- Bard. Grandchildren: Mary and
Elizabeth Messersmith and Elizabeth Bard.

Ex. Elizabeth and Christian Odenwalt. Lancaster Borough.

1 Feb. 1792   21 May 1792
OKELY, JOHN
    Children: John and Elizabeth.
    Ex. George and John Moore. Lancaster Borough.

22 Aug. 1792   --- 1793
OLWILLER, JACOB
    Wife. Anna Olwiller. Children: Anna, Elizabeth, Philip and
two other daughters - names not given.
    Ex. Philip Olwiller. Donegal Twp.

26 Sept. 1795 22 Oct. 1795
ORTH, DANIEL
    Children: Barbara wife of --- Foglesong, Catharine wife of -
-- Blazer, Rosina and Elizabeth wife of --- Kollinger.
Grandchild: Matalina Kollinger.
    Ex. Ulerich Engle. Donegal Twp.

20 March 1797 2 Nov. 1797
OTTO, CATHARINE
    Legatees: Jonathan Roland and others.
    Ex. Jonathan Roland. Earl Twp.

--- 27 Dec. 1790
OBLINGER, CHRISTIAN
    N.B. This is an administration.
    Ex. Jacob Koffroth and John Souter. Warwick Twp.

16 March 1798 26 Feb. 1805
OWEN, ELIZABETH
    Children: Anna wife of John Williams, Lydia, Benj., and
Jonathan. Grandchild: Elizabeth (child of Benj.).
    Ex. Jonathan and Benjamin Owen. Leacock Twp.

10 Dec. 1802   7 June 1806
OVERHOLTZER, JACOB
    Wife. Catharine Overholtzer. Children: Jacob, Mary wife of
John Shumacher, Ann wife of Jacob Ober and Catharine wife of
Michael Ober. Grandchildren: Catharine, Elizabeth, Magdalena and
John Shumacher (children of Mary by her first marrige with Philip
Shumacher).
    Ex. Jacob Overholtzer and Christian Frick. Manheim Twp.

6 Sept. 1809   5 Feb. 1810
OSTER, HENRY
    Wife. Louisa Oster. Children: Catharine, John, Christian,
Magdalena and Susanna.
    Ex. George Peters. Lancaster Borough.

21 March 1814 29 March 1814
OWENS, ARCHIBALD

Wife. Elizabeth Owens. Bros. and sisters: Thomas, Margaret
wife of --- Faulkner, Ann wife of --- Russel and Jane wife of ---
Sharp.
  Ex. Samuel Houston and Robert McIlvain. Salisbury Twp.

20 May 1815   1 Aug. 1815
OBER, MICHAEL
  Wife.Catharine Ober. Brother: Christian Ober. Brother-in-
law: John Shartle.
  Ex. Christian Ober and John Shartle. Warwick Twp.

14 Nov. 1809   29 Dec. 1815
OLWEILER, PHILIP
  Children: Frederick, Jacob and Barbara wife of Philip Sauer.
Grandchildren: Jacob, George, Leonard and Elizabeth Olweiler
(children of Jacob), Jacob, Frederick, Mary and Catharine
Olweiler (children of Frederick).
  Ex. Adam Vonderau Jr. and Ulerich Bott. Manor Twp.

1 May 1816   10 June 1816
ORR, ROBERT
  Bros.: Thomas and Joshua Orr.
  Ex. Thomas and Joshua Orr. Lampeter Twp.

28 April 1814 10 June 1818
OBERLIN, MICHAEL
  Wife. Anna Oberlin. Children: John, Jacob, Michael,
Susanna, George, Adam and Christian.
  Ex. Jacob Hagy. Cocalico Twp.

1 Jan. 1734   14 March 1734
PATTERSON, JAMES
  Wife. (names not given). Children: Jean, Mary and
Elizabeth.
  Ex. Jean Patterson. Twp. omitted.

3 Oct. 1735   11 Nov. 1735
PATTERSON, JAMES
  Wife. Susanna Patterson. Children: James, Thomas, Sarah,
Susanna and Rebecca.
  Ex. Susanna Patterson. Hempfield Twp.

14 July 1739   27 Aug. 1739
POOR, ALEXANDER
  Wife. Margaret Poor.
  Ex. James Harris and James Morrison. Twp. omitted.

7 Sept. 1740   6 May 1741
PARRY, ROGER
  Wife. Elizabeth Parry. Children: Guin, Thomas, William and
David.
  Ex. Morgan Morgans and Iaccheus David. Earl Twp.

1 Sept. 1744   2 Oct. 1744
PARKESON, RICHARD

Wife. Agness Maxwel Parkeson. Children: Mary wife of Francis Cunningham, Agness, William and John.
Ex. William Parkeson and John Milehan. Twp. omitted.

23 Sept. 1745   22 Oct. 1745
PATTERSON, WILLIAM
Children: Samuel, Francis, Anna, Caytron, Jayn and Mary.
Ex. Robert Taylor and Robert Baker. Paxton Twp.

--- 9 Sept. 1745
PORTER, ROBERT
Wife. Mary Porter. Children: Robert, John, James, Samuel and Jannet.
Ex. Mary Porter. Drumore Twp.

15 Sept. 1746   23 Sept. 1746
PATTON, JAMES
Wife. Mary Patton.
Ex. Thomas Patton and John Byers. Donegal Twp.

6 Jan. 1746   10 Jan. 1746
PATTON, MARY
Legatees: Isabella Miller and Mary Casseny and William Allison.
Ex. James Allison and David Byers. Donegal Twp.

4 June 1740   3 Aug. 1746
PARKHOFFER, CONRAD
Wife. (name omitted). Child: Balthaser (and a daughter, name not given).
Ex. Balthaser Parkhoffer. Twp. omitted.

29 Feb. 1747   13 March 1747
PATTERSON, ROBERT
Child: Robert
Ex. Samuel Smith and Isaac Saunders. Lancaster Borough.

19 March 1747   29 Jan. 1744
PUGH, EDWARD
Wife. Mary Pugh.
Ex. Mary Pugh. Twp. omitted.

14 March 1748   14 April 1748
PRATOR, MARY
Legatees: Elias Ellmaker and Adam Lightner. The Church of England in Lancaster Borough, The Lutheran Church in Earl Twp., The Dutch Presbyterian Church in Lancaster Borough.
Ex. Leonard Ellmaker. Earl Twp.

1 June 1748   2 June 1748
PALSPACKER, PETER
Wife. (name omitted). Thee were six children - names omitted.
Ex. Jacob Houke. Lancaster Borough.

23 Nov. 1748   29 Nov. 1748
POWELL, JOHN
    Wife. Margaret Powell. Children: Nancy, (There were others,
names and number not stated).
    Ex. Margaret Powell, Thomas McKee and John Allison.   Paxton
Twp.

31 Oct. 1749   ---
POOLMAN, CHRISTIAN
    Wife. Christiana Poolman. There were two sons-in-laWife.
names not stated. N.B. This will is in a very bad condition, can
scarcely be read and part of it lost - it has never been copied
on records as it was never proved.
    Ex. Jacob Sigrist and Christina Poolman. Twp. omitted.

21 March 1747   26 March 1748
PATTERSON, GEORGE
    Wife. Margaret Patterson. Children: William, Mary, James,
John, Margaret, Eleanor and Agness.
    Ex. Robert Ellison and Hugh Barkley. Twp. omitted.

7 Oct. 1749   ---
POSSARD, HENRY
    N.B. This is a German will, not proved, and the translation
lost.

17 Nov. 1749   --- 1749
PAGAN, ARCHIBALD
    Wife. Agness Pagan. Child: James.
    Ex. James Duncan and Andrew Pagan. Martic Twp.

15 Jan. 1749   15 Jan. 1749
PARKER, JOHN
    Wife. Margaret Parker. Children: Richard, Mary, Elizabeth,
Nancy, John, Margaret, Esther and Alexander.
    Ex. Margaret and Richard Parker. West Pennsborough Twp.

29 May 1750   ---- (no probate indorsed)
PERSINGER, CASPER
    Wife. Audelheid Persinger. N.B. There was a bequest to the
Reformed Calvin Church in the borough.
    Ex. Casper Shaffer, Jacob Hollinger and Jacob Metzgar.
Lancaster Borough.

9 June 1752   24 July 1752
PERRY, WILLIAM
    Wife.Janet Perry. Children: John, Matthew, James and
Esther.
    Ex. Janet Perry. Bart Twp.

4 Aug. 1752   15 Aug. 1752
PERRY, JANET
    Child: John.
    Ex. John Perry and Moses McCarter. Bart Twp.

3 March 1752   26 March 1752
PRATER, ANTHONY
    Wife. Mary Prater.
    Ex. Leonard Ellmaker and John Shetz. Earl Twp.

13 Oct. 1752   1 May 1753
PARK, ROBERT
    N.B. The names and number of his family not given. The
estate was left to the executors to divide among them (his
family) as they thought best.
    Ex. Joseph Wilson and James Riddel Jr. Hanover Twp.

10 Feb. 1755   28 Feb. 1755
PATTEN, JAMES
    Wife. (name omitted). Children: Martha (There were others,
names not given).
    Ex. Martha Patten and Hugh Paden. Manor Twp.

18 July 1755   5 Aug. 1755
PAXTON, SAMUEL
    Wife. Agness Paxton. Children: Samuel, Margaret and Jean.
Brother: Andrew Paxton.
    Ex. Andrew Paxton. Bart Twp.

25 Oct. 1755   4 Dec. 1755
PATTON, ROBERT
    Children: Mary, Esther, Jean, Margaret and Lattis. Sons-in-
law: Joseph Joans, Thomas Jenney, Joshua Ewing and David Craig
(wives' names not given).
    Ex. James Whitehill and John Byers. Sadsbury Twp.

6 May 1757   2 July 1757
PLATNER, MICHAEL
    Wife. Lena Platner. Children: Lena, Agness, Catharine and
Mary.
    Ex. Jacob Bruah. Strasburg Twp.

17 Aug. 1758   30 Aug. 1758
PEEPELS, JAMES
    Brother: John Peepels.
    Ex. Joseph McKiney and John McCracken. Strasburg Twp.

3 Sept. 1759   12 Oct. 1759
PEAK, SAMUEL
    (This should be POAK.) Wife. (name omitted). Children:
Samuel and Sarah. Bros.: John and William Poak.
    Ex. John and William Poak. Little Brittain Twp.

14 Sept. 1758   7 June 1759
PRITCH, PETER
    Wife. Sabina Pritch. Children: John and George.
    Ex. Sabina Pritch. Lancaster Borough.

25 Jan. 1759   13 Nov. 1759
PLUM, JAMES

Wife. Mary Dorothea Plum. Children: Amoba, Catharine and Catgen.
Ex. James Jenning and Michael Hartman. Twp. not given.

24 Feb. 1759   --- 1759
PREES, THOMAS
Wife. Mary Prees. Children: Johannas, Thomas, Joseph, David, Richard, Hannah, Mary and Elizabeth.
Ex. Mary and Thomas Prees. Derry Twp.

6 Aug. 1753   17 June 1759
PRENNIMAN, ADAM
Wife. Mary Penniman. Children: Adam, Henry, Anna, John, Phebe, Maria, Isaac, Magdalena and Eva.
Ex. Benedict Eshleman and Christian Friney. Conestoga Twp.

4 Dec. 1760   --- 1760
PURCAT, CHARLES
Wife. Anna Purcat. Children: Paul, (There were two daughters - names omitted). Son-in-law: Frederick White.
Grandchild: Catharine Purcat.
Ex. Frederick White. Strasburg Twp.

16 Aug. 1760   1 Sept. 1760
PATTERSON, CHRISTIAN
Brother and sisters: Daniel, Susanna and Catharine Patterson.
Ex. John Jacob Loeser and Jacob Hilderbrand. Lancaster Borough.

9 March 1748   1 Nov. 1762
PATTON, JOHN
Wife. Mary Patton. Children: Robert, Elizabeth, Margaret and John.
Ex. Mary Patton. Twp. omitted.

29 Dec. 1760   25 May 1761
PRICKER, PETER
(This should be BRICKER.) Wife. Elizabeth Bricker. Children: Peter, Christian, Jacob, John and David.
Ex. Christian Eby and Detrich Pauelin. Cocalico Twp.

27 June 1761   --- 1761
PFEIL, PETER
Wife. Mary Pfeil. Children: Leonard, Catharine and John.
Ex. Jacob Enk (Senr.). Warwick Twp.

26 Sept. 1763 30 Sept. 1763
PERSINGER, HENRY
Brother: Andrew Persinger.
Ex. Andrew Kline and Abraham Myer. Lancaster Borough.

--- 7 Feb. 1763
PLOUGH, JOHN

(This should be BLOUGH.)   N.B. This is a German will, and translation lost.

16 Nov. 1763   7 June 1765
PORTER, JOHN
     Wife. Rebecca Porter.   Children: Thomas, William and Violet. Grandsons: John Porter and John Price (parents' names not stated).
     Ex. Joseph Morrison and Samuel Morrison.   Drumore Twp.

10 Aug. 1764   23 Aug. 1765
PLEES, JACOB
     Legatees: Elizabeth Haggetsville and the four Switzer boys. N.B. He gives his chest, and guns with lead, to the above, providing they give the ships crew an anchor of brandy.
     Ex. Jacob Wenger.   (Late of Hamburg in the Canton of Bern, Switzerland).

8 July 1767   4 Aug. 1767
PENNY, WILLIAM
     Wife. Eleanor Penny.   Children: James, Hugh, Joseph, William and Grissall.
     Ex. John McDowel and Thomas Whill.   Drumore Twp.

23 Nov. 1767   13 March 1768
POH, WENDEL
     Wife. Mary Poh.   Sons-in-law: Christopher Shub and --- Halteman (wives' names omitted).   Grandchildren: Jacob, Christian and Adam Halteman.
     Ex. Mary Pok and Christian Shaub.   Derry Twp.

16 May 1769   13 June 1769
PFOUTZ, MICHAEL
     Wife. Catharine Pfoutz.   Children: Jacob, Michael, John and Catharine.
     Ex. Catharine Pfoutz and John Zug.   Warwick Twp.

21 Sept. 1767   7 Nov. 1769
POTTS, ROBERT
     Wife. Sarah Potts.   Children: Rachel, Peggy, Jean and Ann. Sister: Jean Potts.
     Ex. Sarah Potts.   Paxton Twp.

23 Dec. 1768   2 Aug. 1769
PAXTON, JOHN
     Wife. Grissel Paxton.   Child: John.
     Ex. John Paxton and John Miller.   Bart Twp.

7 Sept. 1769   6 May 1771
PECK, SAMUEL
     (This should be BECK.)   Wife. Magdalena Beck.   Child: Martin.
     Ex. George Matter.   Earl Twp.

24 March 1772   8 Dec. 1772
PATTERSON, SAMUEL
    Wife. Mary Patterson.   Children: James, Martha, Mary,
Elizabeth and Isabella.
    Ex. Mary and William Patterson.   Twp. omitted.

11 April 1772   13 May 1772
POWELL, JOHN
    Wife. Mary Powell.   Child: William.
    Ex. George Burger.   Lancaster Borough.

9 Aug. 1773   15 Sept. 1773
PEEBEL, DANIEL
    (This should be BEEBEL.)   Wife. Margaret Beebel.   Children:
Jacob, (There were others, names and number not given.)
    Ex. Casper Snevely and Margaret Beebel.   Lebanon Twp.

5 Dec. 1765   28 Aug. 1774
PERSINGER, ANDREW
    (This should be BERSINGER.) Wife. Mary Persinger.   N.B.
There was a bequest to John Wistar of the City of Philadelphia.
    Ex. Mary Bersinger and Jacob Carpenter.   Lampeter Twp.

9 Sept. 1765   25 May 1774
PATTON, THOMAS
    Wife. Janet Patton.   Children: William, Nathan, Jean,
Elizabeth and Rebecca.
    Ex. Samuel Wilson and William Miller.   Mt. Joy Twp.

5 April 1774   20 June 1774
PLANTZ, MATHIAS
    (This should be BLANTZ.]   Wife. Elizabeth Blantz.   Children:
George, Barbara, Margaret, Elizabeth, Juliana, Rosina, Ann and
Catharine.
    Ex. John Meef and Elizabeth Blantz.   Elizabeth Twp.

11 Nov. 1774   14 Dec. 1774
PREECE, DAVID
    Wife. Dorothea Preece.   Children: Elizabeth and Anna.
    Ex. (This will was declared null and void at above date).
Hanover Twp.

11 May 1775   7 June 1775
PORTER, SAMUEL
    Children: Jacob and Elizabeth.
    Ex. James Patterson.   Drumore Twp.

1 Aug. 1775   11 Nov. 1775
PEDEN, JOHN
    Wife. Martha Peden.   Child: Isabella.
    Ex. Hugh Peden and James Patterson.   Hempfield Twp.

6 Jan. 1776   4 March 1776
PEDEN, MARTHA
    Child: Isabella.   Brother: William Wallace.

178

Ex. Robert Spear and Samuel Rankin. Hempfield Twp.

16 March 1776   9 April 1776
PATTON, ROBERT
     Wife. Jane Patton. Sister: Merion Patton.
     Ex. Jane Patton and James Turbett. Manheimer Twp.

24 April 1777   29 May 1777
PETRY, ANTHONY
     Wife. Elizabeth Petry. Children: Catharine, John, Ann,
Anthony, Henry and Margaret.
     Ex. William Bush and Henry Rung. Lancaster Borough.

12 Nov. 1775   16 June 1777
PATTERSON, SAMUEL
     Wife. Rebecca Patterson. Children: Matthew, Samuel,
William, John, Janet wife of Archibald Tweed and Sarah wife of --
--. Grandchild: Samuel (child of Sarah - last name not given).
     Ex. Rebecca and Samuel Patterson. Sadsbury Twp.

20 Aug. 1776   31 Oct. 1777
PRICE, JAMES
     (This should be BRICE.) Mother: Jean Gunnion. Sister: Mary
Corse.
     Ex. Joseph McCrery. Twp. omitted.

12 March 1778   17 April 1778
POLLOCK, SAMUEL
     Children: Jean, Agness, Mary, Margaret and Martha. Stepson:
Gilbert Anderson. Grandchildren: Margaret Anderson and Margaret
Woodburn (parents' names omitted).
     Ex. John Johnson and Andrew Caldwell. Drumore Twp.

14 Jan. 1778   19 May 1778
PATRICK, HUGH
     Children: William, Robert, John, Elizabeth wife of James
Carruthers and Jane wife of Alexander Ewing. Grandchildren:
Hugh, James, William, Ebenezer, Martha and Jean (children of
Patrick) [sic.], Hugh, John, Elizabeth and Mary Patrick (children
of Robert).
     Ex. Stephen Herd and William Arbuckle. Little Brittain Twp.

5 Feb. 1779   12 May 1779
PFLIEGER, TOBIAS
     Ex. Anna Christina Pflieger. Children: Anna wife of Adam
Hickman, John, Magdalena wife of Dietrich Heiss and Catharine
wife of Peter Wien.
     Ex. Anna Pflieger and Jacob Stahl. Lancaster Borough.

30 Dec. 1778   22 July 1779
PAYNE, JASPER
     Wife. Phebe Payne. Children: Jasper and Nathaniel.
     Ex. Phebe Payne. Warwick Twp.

1 Oct. 1778   28 July 1781
PETZ, GEORGE
     Wife. Ann Petz. Sons-in-law: John Huber, Ernst Operman and
John Sile (wives' names not given).
     Ex. John Huber. Warwick Twp.

18 Jan. 1780   22 March 1781
PRINISHOLTZ, ELIZABETH
     Bros.: John, Christian, Ulerich and Jacob Stehly. Sister:
Christina Stehly. Stepdaughter: Anna Zwally.
     Ex. Christian Weber. Cocalico Twp.

12 July 1781   4 Aug. 1781
PFEIFFER, EMANUEL
     Wife. Barbara Pfeiffer. Children: Emanuel, Fredig, George
and Sally.
     Ex. Benjamin Lesle and John Miller. Brecknock Twp.

23 July 1776   10 Dec. 1781
PATTERSON, WILLIAM
     Wife. Elizabeth Patterson. Children: Arthur, Alexander and
Eleanor.
     Ex. Elizabeth, Samuel and James Patterson. Rapho Twp.

24 March 1781   14 May 1782
POORMAN, STEPHEN
     Wife. Ann Poorman. Children: Chrisly, John, Stephen,
Barbara wife of Elis Neglee, Mary wife of John Roop, Addy wife of
Jacob Roop, Freny wife of Christly Stopher, Ann wife of Henry
Landis and Elizabeth wife of Michael Poorman.
     Ex. Conrad Woolfby and Jacob Rook. Paxton Twp.

8 Jan. 1784   23 Jan. 1784
PYLE, MOSES
     Children: Rutha, Phebe, Lydia, Hannah, Abraham and Amos.
     Ex. Abraham and Amos Pyle. Little Brittain Twp.

9 Dec. 1784   18 Feb. 1784
POORMAN, JACOB
     Wife. Mary Poorman. The names and number of children
omitted.
     Ex. Conrad Pope, Bernard Shope and Mary Poorman. Paxton
Twp.

20 June 1784   18 Aug. 1784
PETTICREW, DAVID
     Wife. Elizabeth Petticrew. Children: John, James, Rosy,
Margaret, Catharine and Elizabeth.
     Ex. James Byers. Hanover Twp.

19 Aug. 1784   11 Sept. 1784
PLETES, JOHN
     Wife. Elizabeth Pletes. Children: John (and others, names
omitted).
     Ex. Elizabeth Pletes. Hempfield Twp.

17 Feb. 1783   5 Oct. 1784
PATTON, ROBERT
    Wife. Elizabeth Patton.   Children: Abraham and Robert.
    Ex. Elizabeth Patton.   Lebanon Twp.

23 July 1783   19 Oct. 1784
PATTON, DAVID
    Wife. Rebecca Patton.   Children: David, John, Elizabeth,
Rebecca, Jane, Joseph and Sarah wife of John Hatfield.
    Ex. David Patton.   Paxton Twp.

20 Sept. 1784   30 Oct. 1784
PLETZ, JOHN ADAM
    Mother: Ann Elizabeth Pletz.   Brother: John.   Sister: Ann
Pletz.
    Ex. William Pletz and John Smith.   Warwick Twp.

11 Dec. 1780   30 Oct. 1784
PLETZ, FREDERICK
    Wife. Ann Elizabeth Pletz.   Children: John, William, Adam,
Elizabeth and Ann.
    Ex. Abraham Huber and John Bletz [sic.].   Warwick Twp.

23 Sept. 1779   6 June 1783
PATTON, NATHAN
    Bros. and sisters: William, Jean, Elizabeth, Rebecca and
Martha wife of John Wilson.
    Ex. John Wilson and James Cunningham.   Mt. Joy Twp.

4 Dec. 1784   10 Jan. 1785
PHITE, GEORGE
    (This should be FEIT.]   Children: Peter, Jacob, John,
Abraham and Eve.
    Ex. John Jacob Brubacher.   Martic Twp.

23 Jan. 1778   18 April 1785
PEIFER, BERNARD
    Wife. Sybilla Piefer.   Children: Jacob, Ann, Maria and
Catharine.
    Ex. Jacob Peifer.   Lebanon Twp.

11 Jan. 1785   10 May 1785
PENNY, JOSEPH
    Bros.: James, Hugh and William Penny.   Sister: Eleanor
Penny.   Brother-in-law: Thomas Neill.
    Ex. Thomas Neill.   Drumore Twp.

2 April 1776   7 Aug. 1785
PUGH, GEORGE
    (This should be BUGH.]   Wife. Mary Elizabeth Bugh.
Children: John, Henry, George, Susan and Philip.
    Ex. Henry Bugh.   Manheim Twp.

23 Jan. 1775   21 Oct. 1785
PORTER, JAMES

Wife. Eleanor Porter. Children: William, Andrew, Stephen, James, Samuel, Elizabeth, Eleanor and Mary.
Ex. Stephen and William Porter. Octarara Hundred, Cecil Co. MD.

10 Sept. 1782   3 Dec. 1785
PATTERSON, JAMES
Wife. Mary Patterson. Children: Sarah, John, Mary, Robert, Jane, Elizabeth and James.
Ex. James Porter and William Calhoon. Drumore Twp.

12 Jan. 1786   6 June 1786
PORTER, JAMES
Wife. Mary Porter. Children: John, Jane, Margaret, Janet, William, David and Samuel.
Ex. John and David Porter. Drumore Twp.

21 Aug. 1781   29 Aug. 1786
PATTERSON, PETER
Children: Mary wife of John Thompson, Margaret wife of Samuel Patterson and Hannah wife of James Mitchel. Son-in-law: Robert Kirkpatrick (wife's name omitted).
Ex. Andrew Caldwell and Joseph Larimor. Drumore Twp.

9 Sept. 1788   13 Jan. 1789
PEGAN, ANDREW
Children: John, James, Andrew, Jean, Margaret wife of --- Herron and Mary. Grandchild: Ann Pegan (child of James).
Ex. John Caldwell and James Pegan. Martic Twp.

18 May 1789   6 June 1789
PATTERSON, JAMES
Wife. Margaret Patterson. Children: Arthur, Martha, James, William, Samuel, Margaret, Rebecca and Ann.
Ex. Margaret and Arthur Patterson. Rapho Twp.

3 Dec. 1782   18 Jan. 1790
PLANK, JOHN
(This should be BLANK.] Wife. Magdalena Blank. Children: John, Barbara, Catharine, Anne and Yoder. Sons-in-law: Christian Zug and Jacob Yoder (wives' names not given).
Ex. Christian Zug and Jacob Yoder. Salisbury Twp.

20 April 1783   4 May 1790
PICKLE, LEONARD
CHildren: Peter, Jacob, Elizabeth, Leonard, Adam and Susanna.
Ex. Frederick White. Sadsbury Twp.

15 April 1791   18 April 1791
PATTEN, THOMAS
Wife. Summer Patten. Children: John (There were others, names not given). Son-in-law: Philip Gaulher. Grandchildren: John, Eleanor and Thomas Rogers Jr. (parents' names not given).
Ex. Philip Gaulher. Patten Twp.

15 Sept. 1791   24 Oct. 1791
PETRIE, CHRISTOPHER
      Wife. Sarah Petrie. Brother: Christian Petrie.
      Ex. Sarah Petrie. Lancaster Borough.

20 Dec. 1791   30 Dec. 1791
PATTERSON, JAMES
      Children: Hannah, William, John, Samuel, Isabella, Mary,
Thomas, Jean and James. Grandchildren: James and Martha
(children of Samuel) and Nathan and Elizabeth (children of
Thomas).
      Ex. John McCullough and John Eckman.   Little Brittain Twp.

10 Dec. 1789   20 May 1792
PATTERSON, ANN
      Widow of Arthur Patterson.   Children: Samuel, Jane, Rebecca,
William, James, Eleanor wife of --- Moore, Catharine wife of ---
Hays and Elizabeth wife of --- Tom.   Grandchildren: Eleanor
(child of William) and Arthur (son of James).
      Ex. Samuel Rankin. Rapho Twp.

24 Jan. 1793   26 Feb. 1793
PARKESON, JOSEPH
      Wife. Margaret Parkeson. Mother: Mary McManus. Sister:
Mary Clark.
      Ex. Margaret Parkeson and William Hambleton. Salisbury Twp.

13 Aug. 1789   28 Feb. 1793
PETRY, CATHARINE
      Widow of George Petry.   Children: George, Ann and Catharine
wife of Philip Becher.   Grandchildren: Rudy Bear and Magdalena
wife of Philip Measner (parents' names omitted).
      Ex. Philip Measner. Cocalico Twp.

26 June 1774   25 July 1794
PETERS, LEWIS
      Wife. Catharine Peters. Children: George, Lewis and
Margaret wife of John Sneider.
      Ex. Catharine Peters and Adam Wilhelm. Lancaster Borough.

2 Aug. 1794   26 Aug. 1794
PLANK, JOHN
      (This should be BLANK.] Wife. Mary Blank. Children: Jacob,
Catharine wife of John Konig and Peter.
      Ex. Peter and Jacob Blank. Cocalico Twp.

---   18 April 1795
PETER, FRANCIS
      N.B. This is a German will, not copied on the records and
the original will missing.
      Ex. ---   Manheim Twp.

17 Sept. 1799 26 Dec. 1799
PRINTZEL, GEORGE

Wife. Margaret Printzel.   Nephews: George Kautz and George Hertzell.
Ex. Peter Brunner and Godlieb Nauman.   Lancaster Borough.

2 Jan. 1800   16 Jan. 1800
PORTER, JOHN
Children: Richard, Charles, Martha, Lidice and Grace.
Ex. William Moore.   Lancaster Borough.

8 March 1794   27 Sept. 1800
PETER, MICHAEL
Wife. Magdalena Peter.   Child: Catharine.
Ex. John Eshleman and Christopher Ox.   Mt. Joy Twp.

17 April 1800   6 Nov. 1800
PEDEN, HUGH
Wife. Sarah Peden.   Children: John, Samuel, Grace, Jean, Margaret, Sarah, Martha, Mary, Nancy and Elizabeth.
Ex. John Peden and Henry Strickler.   Rapho Twp.

21 June 1791   21 June 1791
POUTS, JACOB
(This should be FOUTS.]   Children: Jacob, Catharine wife of John Eckman, Elizabeth wife of William Cunkle, Michael and Martin.
Ex. Martin Fouts and John Eckman.   Strasburg Twp.

8 Aug. 1787   12 March 1801
PETREE, ANDREW
Children: Vallentine and Barbara.   Son-in-law: Christian Gates.
Ex. Vallentine Petree.   Earl Twp.

21 March 1801   5 June 1801
PLATT, WILLIAM
Bros.: John and George Platt.   Sister: Martha.
Ex. Thomas Platt.   Earl Twp.

4 May 1802   26 May 1802
PINKERTON, JOHN
Children: Mary, Elizabeth, Jean, William, James and Hannah.
Ex. Joseph Pinkerton and William Gibbons.   Twp. omitted.

14 July 1802   30 July 1803
PRATT, JAMES
Children: John, James, Elizabeth wife of Philip Brenner, Sarah wife of Peter Sybert, Eleanor wife of John Hooper and David.   Grandchildren: Elizabeth, Catharine and John Pratt.
Ex. Christian Stauffer and Christian Stauffer Jr.   Manor Twp.

5 Oct. 1801   22 Aug. 1803
PENNAL, WILLIAM

Children: Robert, Thomas, Margaret wife of --- Irvin, John, William and Hugh. Grandchildren: William and Mary Pennal (children of Robert).
Ex. Robert Pennal. Little Brittain Twp.

10 May 1774   --- 1803
PINKERTON, DAVID
Wife. Margaret Pinkerton. The names and number of children omitted. N.B. This will has not been copied on the records.
Ex. Margaret and Thomas Pinkerton. Earl Twp.

31 Aug. 1803   24 May 1804
PENNY, MARY
Legatees: Anna Margaret Kreiger and "The Sisters House" at Lititz and Bethlehem.
Ex. Anna Margaret Kreiger. Lititz Twp.

--- Aug. 1801 5 Aug. 1805
PATTERSON, REBECCA
Bros.: Samuel and William Patterson. Sisters: Jane, Eleanor wife of --- Moore and Elizabeth wife of --- Thom. Nephews: Arthur and Samuel Patterson.
Ex. Arthur and Samuel Patterson. Rapho Twp.

6 Dec. 1804   5 Jan. 1805
PHYFER, JOHN
Wife. Mary Phyfer. Children: Catharine, Mary, Magdalena, John and Elizabeth.
Ex. Peter Baughman and Andrew Kauffman. Manheim Twp.

28 March 1805 4 May 1805
PAULUS, ELIZABETH
Children: Jacob, John, Elizabeth, Ann, Henry and Feronica Eshleman. N.B. These are children by a former marriage, but no mention of such is made in will.
Ex. Andrew Kauffman and Abraham Herr. Twp. omitted.

3 March 1806   12 May 1806
PLANCK, JOHN
(This should be BLANK.] Wife. Ferena Blank. Children: Nicholas, Martha, John, Catharine, Barbara and Jane.
Ex. John Black and Christian Omby. Salisbury Twp.

24 Feb. 1806   8 March 1806
PROSEY, JOHN
(This should be BROSEY.] Wife. Barbara Brosey. Children: Henry, John, Catharine, Elizabeth, Maria wife of Jacob Judy and Barbara wife of Henry Whitson.
Ex. Barbara Brosey and Henry Whilson. Rapho Twp.

1 Sept. 1807   --- 1807
PRICE, WILLIAM
Wife. Eve Price. Brother-in-law: Joseph Clapper.
Ex. Anthony Haines. Doengal Twp.

28 April 1807   12 May 1807
PINKERTON, THOMAS
    Sister: Jane Caldwell.
    Ex. Andrew Caldwell and Watson McCurdy. Leacock Twp.

29 June 1807   15 Aug. 1807
PLOUTZ, GEORGE
    Wife. Barbara Ploutz.
    Ex. Barbara Ploutz and John Hoyle. Warwick Twp.

8 Oct. 1808   14 Aug. 1809
PENNY, HUGH
    Wife. Sarah Penny. Children: Joseph, James and William.
Uncles: William and James Calhoon.
    Ex. Joseph and James Penny. Martic Twp.

-- Nov. 1809   5 Dec. 1809
PATTERSON, MARY
    Children: Geney wife of David Bowers, Jane, William, John,
Margaret wife of --- Harris and Mary.
    Ex. John McClure and Mary Patterson. Sadsbury Twp.

3 Oct. 1809   22 Feb. 1810
PATTON, JOHN
    Wife. Jane Patton. Children: Mary wife of --- Moffet, Jane,
Ann, William, Cunningham and John.
    Ex. John Patton and James Brown. Martic Twp.

20 July 1810   22 Aug. 1810
PENNAL, ROBERT
    Wife. Anna Pennal. Children: William, Robert, Mary and Ann.
    Ex. Ann and William Pennal. Little Brittain Twp.

10 June 1810   21 Nov. 1810
PLATT, THOMAS
    Wife. Margaret Platt. Children: Isaac, Catharine, Mary and
Harriet.
    Ex. John Lightner and John Slaymaker. Strasburg Twp.

16 Feb. 1810   16 April 1811
PETRIE, CHRISTIAN
    Children: Julianna wife of John Shaffer and Catharine wife
of Michael Gross.
    Ex. Michael Gross and William Reichenbach. Lancaster
Borough.

21 Jan. 1806   8 Aug. 1811
PECK, PETER
    (This should be BECK.] Wife. Margaret Beck. Children:
John, Peter, George, Henry, Adam, David, Daniel, Susanna,
Catharine and Elizabeth.
    Ex. omitted. Twp. omitted.

6 July 1812   25 Aug. 1812
POUTS, MICHAEL

(This should be FOUTS.) Sisters: Catharine wife of Henry Eckman and Elizabeth wife of William Cunkle. Bros.: Martin and Jacob Fouts. N.B. There was a bequest of two hundred dollars to the Lutheran Church being built in the village.
 Ex. Daniel Eckman and John Cunkle. Strasburg Twp.

6 Sept. 1807 16 Jan. 1812
PARKER, ROBERT
 Wife. Susanna Parker. Children: Mary and Robert.
Ex. Robert Parker and Jacob Musser. Leacock Twp.

9 Oct. 1811 17 Aug. 1812
PATTON, THOMAS
 Children: William, Mary, Agness, James and William.
Grandchild: Isabelle Patton (child of William).
 Ex. William and James Patton. Salisbury Twp.

24 April 1813 17 May 1813
PHYFER, GEORGE
 Wife. Margaret Phyfer. Children: George, Elizabeth wife of Sep Swigert, Jacob, Catharine wife of Philip Witmer, Daniel, John, Dorothea, Peter, Frederick and Sally.
 Ex. Margaret and Daniel Phyfer. Brecknock Twp.

13 May 1813 4 June 1813
POWELL, PETER
 Wife. Christina Powell. The name and number of children not given.
 Ex. Christina Powell and David Burkholder. Lampeter Twp.

18 Dec. 1812 10 June 1813
PORTER, SAMUEL Jr.
 Wife. Jane Porter.
 Ex. Jane Porter and William McMahon. Donegal Twp.

2 May 1812 27 Aug. 1814
PARR, GRACE
 Widow of William Parr. Sister: Mary Reed. Stepchildren: Ann Reigart and Mary Hubley.
 Ex. Richard Stockton and William Jenkins. Lancaster Twp.

14 Nov. 1815 5 June 1816
PINKERTON, HENRY
 Wife. Elizabeth Pinkerton. Children: Mary wife of Conrad Shwartz, Henrietta and Henry.
 Ex. Elizabeth Pinkerton and Conrad Shwartz.

8 Sept. 1816 24 Sept. 1816
PHILIPS, GEORGE
 Wife. Catharine.
 Ex. Philip Schisler. Manor Twp.

15 Sept. 1812 31 May 1817
PETERS, ARNOLD
 Wife. Rosina.

Ex. Rosina Peters. Lancaster Borough.

28 March 1818   17 Nov. 1817
PORTER, JAMES
    Wife. (name omitted). Brother: Robert Porter. Nephews:
John, James and Samuel Porter (children of Robert). N.B. There
was a bequest of £100 to the Presbyterian Church at Chestnut
Level.
    Ex. Robert Anderson and Samuel Pusey. Colerain Twp.

15 Feb. 1818   12 March 1818
PETER, ABRAHAM
    Wife. Catharine Peter. Children: Abraham, John, Catharine
wife of --- Bear, Elizabeth wife of John Bausman, Maria wife of
Jacob Klug, Nancy and George. Grandchild: Catharine Bear.
    Ex. John Bausman and Abraham Peter. Manor Twp.

15 April 1819 25 Sept. 1819
PETERMAN, JOAKIM
    Wife. Elizabeth Peterman. Children: George, Sarah, William,
Jacob, John, Frederick, Joseph, Catharine and Elizabeth.
    Ex. Elizabeth and George Peterman. Lancaster Twp.

20 May 1776   22 July 1786
REED, ROBERT
    Wife. Hannah Reed. Children: James, Samuel, Jean wife of -
-- Snodgrass and Hannah. Grandchild: Robert Snodgrass.
    Ex. James and Samuel Reed. Drumore Twp.

15 Jan. 1781   22 Nov. 1786
RAMSEY, JAMES
    Children: William and Rebecca wife of --- Montgomery.
Grandchildren: James, Joseph, Ephraim and John (children of
William), Jane and Lena Montgomery (children of Rebecca) and Jane
Stewart (parents' names not given).
    Ex. James Sterret and John Ramsey. Drumore Twp.

11 Nov. 1785   28 March 1787
REAH, JOHN
    Wife. Janet Reah. Children: Samuel, John, Rebecca, Agness
and Andrew.
    Ex. Samuel and John Reah. Little Brittain Twp.

26 Dec. 1785   13 Oct. 1787
REILEY, JOHN
    Children: Margaret wife of James Vogan, Jean, Elizabeth and
Mary.
    Ex. George Rein. Earl Twp.

2 Aug. 1782   15 Oct. 1787
RICHARDSON, EZEKIEL
    Wife. Isabella Richardson. Child: Mary. N.B. (Extract
from will) - "I, Ezekiel Richardson, late Drum Major of the Third
Pennsylvania Regiment of infantry, being sick and " - There is

menton made in the will of real estate due him for public
service, which he wished sold.
Ex. John Light and Adam Messencope. Lancaster Borough.

29 May 1787   24 May 1788
ROHRER, ELIZABETH
     Children: Isaac, Christian, Henry, David, Magdalena and
John.
     Ex. John Stoffer. Lampeter Twp.

20 Nov. 1786   19 Aug. 1788
REIFF, ABRAHAM
     Wife. (name omitted). Children: David, Samuel, Joseph,
Anna and Abraham, (there were other daughters - names not given).
     Ex. Christian Hurst and David Reiff. Earl Twp.

8 Sept. 1774   5 Nov. 1788
RICHWINE, GEORGE
     Wife. Susanna Richwine. Children: Henry, (there were four
other children - names not given).
     Ex. Leonard Stein, Susanna Richwine and Anthony Ellinaker.
Earl Twp.

13 Jan. 1789   4 Feb. 1789
REAM, MATHIAS
     Wife. Magdalena Ream. Children: Barbara, Frederick,
Abraham, Daniel, Catharine, Molly and Susanna. Son-in-law: Jacob
Roth (name of wife omitted).
     Ex. Magdalena and Abraham Ream. Cocalico Twp.

1 Feb. 1789   10 Aug. 1789
RINGWALT, JACOB
     Wife. Barbara Ringwalt. Children: Jacob and Martin.
     Ex. Frederick Seeger and Henry Road. Earl Twp.

31 July 1789   13 Aug. 1789
RAMSEY, ROBERT
     Children: Martha wife of John Richards and Robert.
     Ex. John Richards and John McClure. Bart Twp.

27 June 1785   5 Oct. 1789
REID, GEORGE
     Children: John, Mary and Ann. Son-in-law: William Bingham
(wife's name omitted).
     Ex. John Reid and William Bigham. Martic Twp.

24 Oct. 1789   23 Nov. 1789
RITTER, PETER
     Wife. Barbara Ritter. Children: Peter, (there were others,
names and number not given).
     Ex. Christian Wissler and Ulerick Engle. Donegal Twp.

19 Nov. 1789   1 Feb. 1790
ROCKEY, HENRY

Wife. Elizabeth Rockey. Children: Jacob, George, Barbara wife of --- Lotman, Henry, William, Frederick, John and Philip.
Ex. Philip and Henry Rockey. Bart Twp.

15 March 1790   20 April 1790
ROLAND, JOHN
Wife. Anna Roland. Children: John, Samuel, George, Catharine, Ann, Mary, Elizabeth and Fronica.
Ex. Benjamin Witmer, Anna and John Roland. Leacock Twp.

9 April 1786   24 Jan. 1791
ROESER, SUSANNA
Widow of Mathias Roeser. Child of former marriage, Abraham Stub. Grandchild: John Stub. Stepchildren: Jacob, Peter, Margaret wife of --- Fetter, Christiana, Catharine wife of --- Kraft and Elizabeth wife of --- Eberman (all children of Mathias Roeser by a former marriage).

30 May 1791   13 March 1792
RENNER, JOHN WENDLE
Child: John. Brother-in-law: George Adam Frantz.
Ex. George Adam Frantz. Cocalico Twp.

21 Sept. 1792   12 March 1793
RESSEL, JOHN
Wife. Eve Ressel. Children: Henry, Michael, Rachel wife of John Christ, Rebecca wife of Jacob Kock and Susanna.
Ex. Eve Ressel and Christian Daffy. Bart Twp.

3 March 1793   1 April 1793
REINHOLD, CHRISTOPHER HENRY
Wife. Sophia Reinhold. Children: Henry, Frederick, John, Regina, Sophia and Christopher.
Ex. Henry, Frederick and John Reinhold. Cocalico Twp.

13 March 1793   22 Aug. 1793
RUNG, HENRY
Wife. Ann Rung. Children: Catharine, William and George.
Ex. George Hoff and Godlieb Nauman. Lancaster Borough.

11 July 1792   2 Nov. 1793
RUSHER, HENRY
Mother: Elizabeth Rusher. Sisters: Elizabeth wife of John Weaver, Margaret wife of George Foust and Barbara wife of Jacob Foreign. Uncle: Peter Lazarus.
Ex. Peter Lazarus. Lancaster Twp.

11 April 1793   18 May 1793
ROAD, PETER
Children: Henry, John, Anna wife of Anthony Stormback, Mary wife of John Tharon, Veronica wife of Jacob Baltzly and Barbara wife of --- Horsh.
Ex. Henry Road and Martin Barr. Strasburg Twp.

9 July 1789   5 May 1794

RITTER, MICHAEL
     Wife. Ann Ritter. The names of children omitted.
     Ex. Ulerich and John Engle. Donegal Twp.

18 May 1790   4 Feb. 1795
RIDDLE, WILLIAM
     Children: Peggy, Elizabeth, William, James, Mary, David and
John.
     Ex. Michael Peter and George Rambaugh. Mt. Joy Twp.

30 March 1795   9 May 1795
REDICK, AGNESS
     Children: Sarah wife of --- Barton and Agness wife of John
Henry. Grandchilden: Robert Barton and Agness Henry.
     Ex. Thomas McCosland. Lancaster Borough.

2 Feb. 1782   28 Jan. 1796
RUSHER, HENRY
     Wife. Elizabeth Rusher. Children: Henry, Catharine,
Elizabeth and Margaretta. Son-in-law: Jacob Fahrim (wife's name
not given).
     Ex. Jacob Fahrim. Lancaster Borough.

3 Feb 1796   12 Feb 1796
ROST, GEORGE
     Bro.: Mathias. Sister: Catherine wife of Francis Witmyer.
     Ex. Mathias Rost. Cocalico Twp.

12 Dec. 1793   22 Mar 1796
REIGER, EVE CATHARINE
     Widow of Bartholomew Reiger. Children: John, Peter, Maria
wife of Christian Ish, Benjamin and Abraham. Grandchild: Mary
Catharine Reiger (child of Peter).
     Ex. Abraham Reiger. Lancaster Borough.

24 Oct. 1796   23 Nov. 1796
RAUCH, HENRY
     Wife. Mary Elizabeth Rauch. Children: (of the first wife)
Henry and Jonannah, (children of·the second wife) John,
Christian, William and Mary Rauch.
     Ex. William Lahnius and George Getner. Warwick Twp.

19 April 1795   29 July 1796
RADMACHER, MICHAEL
     Wife. Christina Radmacher. N.B. There was a bequest of £6
to the German Reformed Congregation in the borough of Lancaster.
     Ex. Christina Radmacher. Lancaster Borough.

2 Sept. 1796   29 Sept. 1796
RICHEBACH, JOHN
     Wife. Anna Richebach. Bros.: Henry, Adam, Jacob and David
Richebach. Sisters: Mary, Ann, Elizabeth, Barbara, Betty,
Catharine and Margaret Richebach.
     Ex. John Kurtz and Christian Hess. Salisbury Twp.

25 Jan. 1787   30 April 1796
RICHISON, ELEANOR & MARGARET
       Bro.: Adam Richison.
       Ex. John Patterson and William Richison. Colerain Twp.

12 April 1796   14 June 1796
REDICK, AGNESS
       Sister: Sarah wife of John Barton.
       Ex. Adam Reigart and Henry Pinkerton. Lancaster Borough.

19 Jan. 1795   30 Sept. 1797
REMLY, FREDERICK
       Wife. Anna M. Remly. Children: Elizabeth, John, Frederick
and Christopher.
       Ex. Anna M. Remly. Lancaster Borough.

1 April 1786   18 Sept. 1797
RAMSEY, ELIZABETH
       Sisters: Agness, Jane, Isabella Ramsey and Jane wife of
Andrew Work.
       Ex. Andrew Work. Bart Twp.

3 July 1785   5 Feb. 1797
ROTH, PHILIP
       Wife. Maria Roth. Children: John, Philip, Jacob, Henry,
George, Catharine wife of David Ream, Maria and Susanna wife of
Martin Bowman.
       Ex. Jacob Roth and Jacob Shirk. Earl Twp.

12 Jan. 1788   18 Sept. 1797
RAMSEY, SAMUEL
       Father: Samuel Ramsey. Bros.: James, John and William
Ramsey. Sisters: Agness, Jane and Isabella Ramsey. Nephews:
Samuel Ramsey and Samuel Work.
       Ex. James Ramsey and Andrew Work. Bart Twp.

10 Dec. 1791   20 March 1797
ROOT, HENRY
       Wife. (name omitted). Children: Henry and Jacob. Bro.:
Christian Root.
       Ex. Christian and Henry Root. Earl Twp.

9 Dec. 1797   17 April 1798
RUNSHAW, WILLIAM
       Wife. Mary Runshaw. Children: James, William, Mary, Jan
wife of --- Wilson, Margaret wife of --- Landis, Edward,
Elizabeth wife of --- Gilmore, Samuel, Isaac, Joseph, David and
John. N.B. The first three mentioned are the youngest - the age
of those mentioned later is not clear.
       Ex. Samuel Runshaw and James McCarnout. Salisbury Twp.

8 June 1780   26 June 1798
RICHARDSON, JOHN

192

Mother: Alice Richardson. Bros.: William and Isaac
Richardson. Sisters: Rebecca and Hannah Richardson. Nephew:
William Atlee (son of Samuel Atlee).
Ex. Cornelius Cox. Salisbury Twp.

26 Sept. 1799   20 Nov. 1799
ROATH, THEOBALD
Children: Margaret, John, Anthony, Mary and Maxton.
Ex. Jacob Strickler, John and Anthony Roth. Hempfield Twp.

15 July 1799   24 Sept. 1799
REITZEL, GEORGE
Wife. Eve Reitzel. Children: John, Christopher, Ann wife
of Rev. Daniel Wagner, Jacob and Catharine.
Ex. John and Christopher Reitzel. Lancaster Borough.

22 April 1799   4 May 1799
RADINGER, JOHN
Legatee: Joseph Clinton.
Ex. John Longnecker. Lampeter Twp.

11 Feb. 1799   22 April 1799
RONNER, AUTON
Wife. Ann Ronner. Sister: Thorethea wife of --- Huber.
Ex. George Capp, Christian Blickenderfer Jr. and Peter
Leuert. Warwick Twp.

14 June 1797   28 May 1800
RIPPEY, MATTHEW
Children: John, Hugh, Isabella wife of --- McAntire and
Rebecca.
Ex. Hugh Long and William Calhoon. Drummore Twp.

3 Sept. 1800   15 Oct. 1800
RAMSEY, SAMUEL
Wife. Alice Ramsey. Children: John, Nathaniel, Jane and
Samuel.
Ex. Alice and John Ramsey. Drumore Twp.

27 Aug. 1800   11 Nov. 1800
ROBINSON, HUGH
Wife. Jean Robinson. Children: William, John, Mary,
Eleanor, Jane, Margaret, Elizabeth, Martha and Agness.
Ex. Jane and William Robinson. Salisbury Twp.

13 March 1799   18 Nov. 1800
REIGART, CHRISTOPHER
Mother: Susanna Edwards. Bros.: Henry and John Reigart.
Ex. Susanna Edwards, John and Henry Reigart. Lancaster
Borough.

21 June 1798   21 June 1798
RAMSAY, ELIZABETH
Children: James, John, William, Agness, Jane wife of Andrew
Work and Isabella wife of --- Boyd.

Ex. James Ramsay and Andrew Work. Bart Twp.

19 July 1797   17 April 1800
RHULE, GEORGE
     Children: George, Christian, Michael, Philip, Elizabeth wife
of Frederick Nauman, Mary wife of Samuel Cox and Peter.
     Ex. Frederick Nauman. Warwick Twp.

26 May 1800   6 March 1801
REIFF, ISAAC
     Wife. Rebecca Reiff. Bro.: Christian.
     Ex. Rebecca Reiff and David Bear. Leacock Twp.

16 July 1800   20 April 1801
REED, ROBERT
     Children: Thomas, John and James. Grandchildren: Robert,
Jean and Susanna Reed (children of James).
     Ex. John Reed and Samuel McElroy. Drumore Twp.

--- 28 Sept. 1801
REYNOLDS, WILLIAM
     Wife. Catharine Reynolds. Children: Samuel, William, John
and Lydia.
     Ex. Catharine, Samuel and William Reynolds. Strasburg Twp.

25 March 1802   16 June 1802
REID, WILLIAM
     Children: Mary wife of --- Caldwell and Jean wife of James
Caldwell. Grandchildren: William and John Caldwell (parents'
names not stated).
     Ex. Mary and John Caldwell. Drumore Twp.

12 March 1803   7 May 1803
ROHRER, JACOB
     Wife. Feronica Rohrer. Children: John, Elizabeth wife of
Jacob Souder, Jacob, Mary wife of Christian Huber. Bro.: John
Rohrer.
     Ex. Christian and (bro.) John Rohrer. Lampeter Twp.

20 May 1803   26 July 1803
REED, WILLIAM
     Wife. Mary Reed. Children: William, Elizabeth wife of
Matthew Welch, Nancy, Joseph, Jenny and Polly.
     Ex. Mary and William Reed. Drumore Twp.

20 May 1803   24 Jan. 1804
ROOT, CHRISTIAN
     Wife. Anna Root. Children: Christian, Peter, Barbara wife
of Christian Carpenter, Jacob, Magdalena wife of Jacob Weaver,
Susanna wife of John Senseney. Son-in-law: David Martin (wife's
name not stated). Grandchild: Elizabeth Martin.
     Ex. John Senseney and Peter Martin. Earl Twp.

20 March 1802   15 Oct. 1804
ROYER, PHILIP

Wife. Elizabeth Royer. Children: Abraham, Philip and
Jonathan. (there were two other sons - names omitted).
Ex. Abraham, Philip and Jonathan Royer. Menheim Twp.

29 Sept. 1804   6 Oct. 1804
ROHRER, ISAAC
Wife. Elizabeth Rohrer. Children: John, Ephraim, Joel,
Christiana wife of Abraham Frick, Rebecca, Salome and Mary wife
of --- Singer. Grandchildren: John, Susanna and Mary Singer.
Ex. William Webb, David Graff and Martin Rohrer. Lampeter
Twp.

17 June 1797   6 Nov. 1805
RUT, PETER
Wife. Ann Rut. Children: George, Jacob, Peter, Henry,
Barbara wife of Christian Eversole, Ann wife of John Wilhelm,
Magdalena wife of Samuel Weaver and Elizabeth.
Ex. Henry Rut and Christian Eversole. Donegal Twp.

13 June 1805   20 Aug. 1805
RUDISILLY, MELCHOIR
Wife. Christiana Rudisilly. Children: Jacob, Adam, Mary,
Christiana wife of John Metzgar and Catharine wife of Adam
Eshleman. Grandchild: Philip Metzgar.
Ex. Jacob and Adam Rudisilly. Lancaster Borough.

17 May 1801   17 May 1805
ROE, MATHIAS
Legatee: Rev. Robert Matineux (Priest of the Lancaster Roman
Catholic Church at Lancaster).
Ex. Rev. Lewis Barth. Twp. omitted.

30 Oct. 1804   5 Nov. 1805
RIPLEY, PETER
Legatees: Margaret Reissel and Margaret Whiteside.
Ex. Abraham Whiteside. Colerain Twp.

31 Dec. 1804   2 Feb. 1805
RICKENBACK, JACOB
Sister: Margaretta wife of Samuel Bear. Bros.: Adam, John
and Henry Rickenback. Niece: Anna Bear.
Ex. John Bear and Christian Smith. Manor Twp.

1 July 1806   13 Oct. 1806
RUNNER, WILLIAM
Children: George, William, Christiana, Margaret and John.
Ex. William Runner. Little Brittian Twp.

6 Oct. 1805   6 Feb. 1806
RICKSEKER, JACOB
Wife. Elizabeth Rickseker. Children: Peter, Mary wife of -
-- Krider, Rachel, Elizabeth and Abraham.
Ex. Elizabeth Rickseker and Andrew Krider. Warwick Twp.

8 Jan. 1806   13 Jan. 1806
ROW, FRANCIS
    Wife. Catharine Row. Children: John, George, Wendel and
Sarah.
    Ex. John, George and Wendel Row. Strasburg Twp.

9 Feb. 1805   10 April 1806
RESSLER, JOHN
    Children: John, George, Henry, Jacob, Philip, Juliana,
Elizabeth, Barbara, Catharine and Mary.
    Ex. George Ressler and Mark Groff. Earl Twp.

8 Jan. 1807   20 Oct. 1807
REAM, TOBIAS
    Wife. Juliana Ream. Children: Henry, Ann, Barbara wife of
William Wheeler, Juliana, George, Catharine wife of Samuel
Werdenberger, Christian, Frederick, John and Susanna.
    Ex. George and Frederick Ream. Twp. omitted.

12 Aug. 1803   8 June 1807
REIN, ELIZABETH
    Widow of George Rein. Bros.: David, Abraham, Joseph and
Jonathan Roland. Sister: Barbara wife of --- Hinkle.
    Ex. John and Henry Roland. Earl Twp.

7 May 1807   15 June 1807
RUTTER, GEORGE
    Wife. Margaret Rutter. Children: Nathaniel, Adam, Rebecca,
Margaretta, Joseph, Elizabeth wife of --- Williamson and Mary
wife of William Cowan. Grandchildren: George, Thomas and Harriet
Williamson.
    Ex. Nathaniel Rutter. Salsbury Twp.

10 Sept. 1801   16 May 1807
ROLAND, JONATHAN
    Wife. Catharine Roland. Children: John, Henry, Elizabeth
wife of Peter Diller, Susanna wife of Isaac Diller and Catharine
wife of --- Lemon. Grandchildren: John and Henry Lemon.
    Ex. John and Henry Roland. Earl Twp.

18 Nov. 1807   10 Dec. 1807
RUDY, EMICH
    Wife. Catharine Rudy. Children: Conrad, John, Andrew,
Henry, Catharine and Elizabeth wife of Joseph Irwin.
    Ex. Christian Carpenter. Earl Twp.

15 May 1807   11 June 1807
ROLAND, DAVID
    Wife. Susanna Roland. Children: Susanna and Elizabeth.
Sons-in-law: Peter Beck and Peter Martin (wives' names not
stated).
    Ex. Peter Beck and Peter Martin. Earl Twp.

24 Aug. 1805   24 Feb. 1808
RESH, HENRY

Wife. Susanna Resh. Children: Magdalena, Barbara, Maria and Henry. Son-in-law: Jacob Brenneman (wife's name not stated).
Ex. Jacob Brenneman, Henry Resh and Henry Hess. Conestoga Twp.

17 Dec. 1808   21 Feb. 1809
REYNOLDS, HENRY
Wife. Mary Reynolds. Children: Henry, Emanuel, Sarah, Joshua, Jacob, Elijah, Nathaniel and Samuel. Grandchildren: Mary Miller and Lydia Reynolds (parents' names not stated).
Ex. Jacob and Emanuel Reynolds. Little Brittain.

20 Feb. 1809   21 March 1809
ROBISON, DUNKIN
Wife. (name not given). Children: Susanna, Sarah, Mary, Jane, James, John, William and Alexander.
Ex. James Robison. Leacock Twp.

19 Feb. 1800   28 March 1809
ROCKEY, PHILIP
Wife. Mary Rockey. Children: Jacob, Peter and Elizabeth wife of --- Ritz.
Ex. Jacob Baughman and Henry Rickel. Sadsbury Twp.

25 July 1808   18 May 1809
ROBERTS, JOHN
Wife. (name omitted). Bros. and sisters: Daniel, Ann, Molly and Elizabeth. Stepson: William Powell.
Ex. Eliza Jones. Lancaster Borough.

2 Oct. 1809   14 Oct. 1809
REA, JOHN
Bro.: Andrew Rea. Sister: Mary Rea.
Ex. Andrew and Mary Rea. Leacock Twp.

16 Sept. 1809 2 Nov. 1809
RINE, LEONARD
Wife. Catharine.
Ex. Catharine Rine. Hempfield Twp.

20 May 1809   17 Jan. 1810
REAM, SAMUEL
Children: Samuel, Esther and Catharine.
Ex. Samuel Ream and John Patimer. Mt. Joy Twp.

10 July 1810   11 Aug. 1810
ROYER, PHILIP
Wife. Elizabeth Royer. Children: Samuel, John, Philip and Elizabeth.
Ex. John Becker, John and Samuel Royer. Cocalico Twp.

23 June 1811   24 Aug. 1811
RICKERT, LEONARD
Wife. Barbara Rickert. Children: John, Jacob, Daniel, Abraham, Barbara wife of John Shaffer, Ann wife of Henry Behm and

Elizabeth wife of --- Albert. Grandchildren: Daniel, John, Jacob and Ann Albert.
    Ex. Frederick Byrod. Donegal Twp.

9 Nov. 1811   3 Dec. 1811
RUTTER, HENRY
    Wife. Elizabeth Rutter. Children: John, Joseph, George, Anna wife of Benjamin Miser, Daniel, Jacob, Henry, Benjamin, Elizabeth wife of Conrad Evits, Mary wife of David Trout, Andrew, Hannah wife of Samuel Miller, Catharine wife of John Miser and Isaac.
    Ex. Joseph, Andrew and Isaac Rutter. Leacock Twp.

4 June 1807   30 March 1811
ROTH, JOHN
    Wife. Barbara Roth. Children: Mary wife of Jacob Winauer, Margaret wife of George Milchrack, Catharine wife of John Lewis, George, Jacob and John.
    Ex. Barbara Roth and Jacob Kautz. Lancaser Borough.

11 May 1811   1 July 1811
RUSH, HENRY
    Sister: Nancy wife of Henry Kendrick. Bros.: Jacob and John Rush.
    Ex. Henry Shearer. Twp. omitted.

14 March 1811 8 Oct. 1811
REICHENBACK, SUSANNA
    Wife of William Reichenback. Children: William, Henry and Edward.
    Ex. John Youngman, Henry and Edward Richenback. Lancaster borough.

3 May 1812   27 July 1812
REESE, HENRY
    Wife. Margaret Reese. Children: John, Jacob and Daniel.
    Ex. Henry Bowman. Martic Twp.

19 Oct. 1807   30 Jan. 1813
REIST, JOHN
    Children: John, Peter, Abraham, Christian (and three daughters - names not given). Son-in-law: Christian Hostetter.
    Ex. Peter Reist and Christian Hostetter. Warwick Twp.

7 Aug. 1810   16 March 1813
REIST, ABRAHAM
    Wife. Elizabeth Reist. Children: John, Nancy, Elizabeth, Abraham, Barbara wife of Christian Bamberger and Christian.
    Ex. Abraham Reist and Christian Hershey. Warwick Twp.

19 Feb. 1813   27 March 1813
RANK, VALENTINE
    Wife. (name omitted). Children: Michael, Mary, Jacob and Susanna.
    Ex. Michael, Mary, Jacob and Susanna Rank. Salisbury Twp.

5 Feb. 1813   22 June 1813
REIGART, ADAM
    Wife. Susanna Reigart. Children: Adam, Emanuel, Catharine
wife of Philip Albright, Mary wife of --- Frisler.
Grandchildren: Catharine, Adam, Emanuel, Maria, Elizabeth,
Susanna and Rebecca Frisler.
    Ex. Adam and Emanuel Reigart. Lancaster Borough.

21 April 1813   27 July 1813
RICKSECKER, JOHN
    Wife. Rachel Ricksecker. Children: John, Frederick and
Anna.
    Ex. Rachel and John Ricksecker. Warwick Twp.

6 Nov. 1813   2 Feb. 1814
ROHRER, JOHN
    Wife. Mary Rohrer. Children: John, Mary wife of Christian
Herr, Barbara wife of George Diffenbach, Elizabeth and Ann.
    Ex. John Rohrer and Christian Herr. Lampeter Twp.

12 April 1810   9 Feb. 1814
RICHARDSON, JOSEPH
    Wife. Dinah Richardson. Children: Samuel, Isaac, Lydia,
Hannah wife of Samuel Embre, Mary wife of Joshua Webster, Joel,
Joseph and Caleb.
    Ex. Samuel and Isaac Richardson. Little Brittain Twp.

7 April 1800   13 June 1814
RIEGEL, MAGDALENA
    Children: Christian, Henry, Martin, David, John, Barbara and
Magdalena wife of John Otto. Grandchild: Elizabeth Reigel (child
of John).
    Ex. Peter Summy. Hempfield Twp.

2 Jan. 1808   29 Nov. 1814
REIST, CHRISTIAN
    Wife. Barbara Reist.
    Ex. Barbara Reist and Christian Hoover. Warwick Twp.

19 Feb. 1811   27 March 1815
ROAD, PHILIP
    Wife. Elizabeth Road. Children: William, Daniel, Sally,
Philip, George, Lydia, Abraham, David and Joel.
    Ex. Elizabeth and Daniel Road. Cocalico Twp.

20 March 1812   6 May 1815
REESE, JAMES
    Wife. Elizabeth Reese. Children: Henry, Susanna wife of
Joseph Gray, Mary wife of William Jefferies, John and Jacob.
    Ex. Elizabeth and Peter Reese. Lancaster Borough.

7 Aug. 1810   6 June 1815
RANCK, SAMUEL
    Children: Anna, Elizabeth, John, Peter, Samuel and Anna.
    Ex. John and Peter Ranck. Warwick Twp.

20 March 1806   7 July 1815
REIHM, MAGDALENA
    Children: Susanna, (there were others, names and number not given).
    Ex. Henry Hershberger and David Landis. Cocalico Twp.

7 Aug. 1815   24 Nov. 1815
RALSTON, JOHN
    Mother: Lettice Ralston.
    Ex. Lettice Ralston. Columbia Borough.

18 June 1804   6 Dec. 1815
RANEK, PHILIP
    Wife. Anna Barbara Renck. Children: Michael, Barbara wife of --- Schnall, John, Anna wife of --- Kluge, Elizabeth wife of --- Grosh, Philip, George and Mathias.
    Ex. Mathias Tshudy and Christian Blickenderfer. Warwick Twp.

4 Oct. 1811   2 Jan. 1816
RUMEL, VALENTINE
    Children: Valentine, Catharine wife of Conrad Kerrer, Elizabeth wife of Adam Burtzfield, Sabina wife of Philip Stech, Louisa wife of Christian Kneissly, Peter and Frederick. Grandchild: John Runnel (son of Peter).
    Ex. Valentine Runnel and Jacob Witmer. Manor Twp.

2 Feb. 1816   28 Feb. 1816
REINHARD, MARGARET
    Children: John and Michael.
    Ex. Michael Reinhart. Conestoga Twp.

10 May 1815   22 April 1816
ROLAND, BARBARA
    Children: Elizabeth and Eve wife of Charles Shaffer.
    Ex. Christian Meyer. Cocalico Twp.

4 Feb. 1816   11 March 1816
RUDY, JOHN
    Wife. Dorothea Rudy.
    Ex. Godfrey Zahn. Lancaster Borough.

30 May 1810   10 July 1816
ROYER, JOHN
    Wife. Barbara Royer. Children: Joseph, Elizabeth, Barbara, Ann and Magdalena wife of Ephraim Holl.
    Ex. Joseph Royer and David Boyer. Cocalico Twp.

16 May 1816   7 Jan. 1817
RANCK, ELIZABETH
    Bros.: Peter and John Ranck. Niece: Elizabeth Ranck (child of Peter). N.B There was a bequest of £20 to the sick room of the Sisters' House at Lititz.
    Ex. John Ranck. Warwick Twp.

28 May 1816   31 March 1817
ROSS, COL. GEORGE Late of the City of New Orleans and Col. of the
44 Regt. of the U.S.
    Wife. Henrietta Ross. Children: Alonzo and George.
Father: Col. James Ross. Aunt: Susanna wife of John Kuhn.
Nieces: Maria and Sarah Kuhn and Polly Bird. N.B. (Extract from
will) - "I request my friend John Dick to use every means in his
power with the officers and all concerned in the land and naval
force under my command, and that of Capt. Daniel Patterson, in
capturing the vessels and cargo near the Island of Barataria, and
which the Honorable Congress have relinquished in favor of the
said George J. Ross and Capt. Daniel Patterson and their
officers, etc ... . " He also made an especial request to have
his body shipped to New Orleans in a hogshead of strong rye
brandy.
    Ex. Henrietta Ross.

5 Feb. 1816   17 Oct. 1817
REDSECKER, ANN MARY
    Widow of George Redsecker. Children: Catharine wife of
Michael Balmer, Susanna wife of Reinhart Houser, Magdalena wife
of Philip Negley and Ann wife of Andrew Kergher. Grandchildren:
Catharine, Andrew, Mary and George Kergher.
    Ex. Frederick Byroad. Mt. Joy Twp.

24 April 1816   5 April 1817
REINEHART, CHRISTINA
    Daughter-in-law: Nancy Reinehart (husband's name not given).
Grandchild: Andrew Sites.
    Ex. Andrew Sites. Columbia Borough.

16 April 1816   21 Nov. 1817
RAMSEY, WILLIAM
    Wife. Rebecca Ramsey. Children: James and Anna.
    Ex. James and Robert Ramsey. Bart Twp.

4 Jan. 1817   13 Dec. 1817
REAH, SAMUEL
    Wife. (name omitted). Children: John, Robert, Samuel, Adam
and James.
    Ex. John Reah. LIttle Brittain Twp.

6 Dec. 1817   7 Jan. 1818
RINE, GEORGE
    Children: Michael, John, Margaret, Catharine wife of John
Plitt, Daniel, Mary wife of Henry Greiss. Grandchildren: Davis
Rine (child of Daniel) and Henry Greiss (son of Mary).
    Ex. Isaac Ellmaker and Samuel Kurtz. Earl Twp.

18 Aug. 1815   30 Jan. 1818
RITCHEY, WILLIAM
    Children: William, Hugh, John and Jane. Grandchild: William
Ritchey (son of John).
    Ex. William Ritchey. Drumore Twp.

16 March 1818   20 April 1818
RUPP, GEORGE
    Wife. Catharine Rupp. Children: Catharine (there were others, names omitted).
    Ex. Philip Vonnieda and Peter Hartman. Cocalico Twp.

19 June 1818   1 Aug. 1818
ROHRER, ELIZABETH
    Sisters: Nancy, Maria wife of Christian Herr and Barbara wife of George Diffenbach. Bro.: John Rohrer.
    Ex. Christian Herr and George Diffenbach. Lampeter Twp.

10 May 1815   14 Aug. 1818
RUPP, NICHOLAS
    Wife. Anna Rupp. Children: Margaret, Elizabeth, Barbara, Anna, George, Catharine, Juliana, Anna and Peter.
    Ex. John Waldshmith and Andrew Fleisher. Cocalico Twp.

3 April 1817   30 Sept. 1818
RUDY, DANIEL
    Wife. Barbara Rudy. Children: George, Christian, Daniel, Henry, Barbara, Mary, Susanna, Elizabeth wife of John Landis and Nancy.
    Ex. Charles Rudy and Christian Frantz. Manheim Twp.

15 Oct. 1817   26 Jan. 1819
ROTH, HENRY
    Wife. Mary Roth. Child: Daniel. Stepson: John Young.
    Ex. Mary Roth and Peter Kline. Lancaster Borough.

25 April 1814   26 Jan. 1819
ROWLAND, CATHARINE
    Widow of Jonathan Rowland. Children: Elizabeth wife of Peter Diller, John, Henry, Catharine wife of George Yohe and Susanna wife of Isaac Diller. Grandchild: Catharine Rowland (child of Henry).
    Ex. Henry Rowland. Earl Twp.

20 April 1815   23 April 1819
REINERT, FREDERICK
    Wife. Catharine Reinert.
    Ex. Catharine Reinert. Lancaster Borough.

5 Sept. 1818   1 June 1819
ROTH, LUDWIG
    Wife. Anna Roth.
    Ex. John Florey. Rapho Twp.

20 April 1785   12 Feb. 1786
SHULTZ, CHRISTIAN
    Wife. Mary Shultz. Children: Christian, John, Fronica and Anna.
    Ex. Christian and Isaac Hare and Mary Shultz. Strasburg Twp.

30 Aug. 1784   3 April 1786
SHELLY, ABRAHAM
    Wife. Anne Shelly. Children: Jacob and Christian.
    Ex. Michael Horst and Jacob Shelly. Mt. Joy Twp.

28 April 1784   17 April 1786
SHEAFFER, ALEXANDER
    Wife. Catharine Sheaffer. Children: Henry, Sabina wife of
Michael Hake, Anna wife of Christian Meyer, Catharine wife of
John Meyer, John and Margaret wife of John Bright.
    Ex. Henry Sheaffer. Heidleberg Twp.

10 Aug. 1781   5 July 1786
STUCKEY, JOHN
    Wife. Anna Catharine Stuckey. Children: John, Anna wife
of --- Hushar, Elizabeth wife of --- Harnig and Mary wife of ---
Caquetin. Grandchildren: Pater, Henry and Joseph Hushar.
    Ex. John Stuckey and Martin Bear. Elizabeth Twp.

26 July 1785   19 Oct. 1786
STARR, MOSES
    Wife. Sarah Starr. Children: Jeremiah, Rebecca wife of ---
Downing, Hannah and Sarah.
    Ex. Jeremiah Starr. Sadsbury Twp.

30 Nov. 1786   29 Jan. 1787
SALTZMAN, FRANCIS
    Wife. Barbara Saltzman. Children: John and Catharine.
    Ex. Barbara and John Saltzman. Manor Twp.

26 March 1787   12 April 1787
SCOTT, ALEXANDER
    Wife. Sarah Scott. Sisters: Grizel wife of --- Peden, Ann
wife of --- Patterson (and one married to --- Lowrey - name not
given). Bros.: Samuel, Josiah and Abraham Scott.
    Ex. Hugh Peden, James Patterson and Abraham Scott.
Hempfield Twp.

14 Feb. 1787   7 April 1787
SHEARER, MICHAEL
    Child: Elizabeth wife of John Carpenter.
    Ex. John Carpenter. Earl Twp.

16 Jan. 1787   11 July 1787
SEIDENSPINNER, JOSEPH
    Wife. Magdalena Seidenspinner.
    Ex. Magdalena Seidenspinner. Lancaster Borough.

2 Nov. 1787   20 Dec. 1787
STOUFFER, PETER
    Wife. Mary Stouffer. Children: Mathias, George, Peter,
Jacob, Madlin, Fanney, Christian and Samuel
    Ex. Peter Carpenter and George Stouffer. Earl Twp.

23 July 1776   6 Feb. 1788
SWEITZER, JOHN
     Wife. Gertraut Sweitzer.
     Ex. Gertraut Sweitzer. Heidleberg Twp.

30 Dec. 1786   8 March 1788
SHELLY, CHRISTIAN
     Wife. Magdalena Shelly. Children: Jacob, Abraham, Barbara
wife of --- Snevely, Anna wife of Mark Martin, Magdalena wife of
Martin, Christian, Peter and Elizabeth.
     Ex. Jacob Shelly and Mark Martin. Rapho Twp.

4 March 1788   2 May 1788
SHRECK, JACOB
     Children: Mary, Susanna, Joseph, Jacob, John, David and
Christian.
     Ex. Joseph Shreck and Henry Neff. Hempfield Twp.

7 Dec. 1787   26 Aug. 1788
SHREIBER, JOHN
     Wife. Anna Mary Shrieber. Children: Elizabeth wife of
Christian Herman, Susanna wife of Frederick Weidle and Margaret
wife of Jacob Grubb.
     Ex. Anna Mary Sherieber and Christian Herman. Lancaster
Twp.

2 Aug. 1788   27 Sept. 1788
SUMMERS, CHRISTIAN
     Wife. Fronica Summers. Children: Christian, Mary and
Joseph.
     Ex. John Kenege and Yost Yotter. Earl Twp.

23 May 1786   4 Oct. 1788
SELTENREICH, GEORGE
     Wife. Anna Mary Seltenreich. Children: John, Baltzar,
George, Martha wife of Nicholas Weaver, Magdalena and Anna wife
of John Ewe.
     Ex. Adam Miller and John Seltenreich. Leacock Twp.

18 Jan. 1785   5 Nov. 1788
SMITH, WILLIAM
     Stepchildren: Jacob and Christian Breidenstone and Froney
wife of Benja. Lyle, Margaret wife of Michael Rank, Mary wife of
Valentine Rank and Anna wife of Jacob Durnbach. N.B. He states
in his will that he has no children of his own.
     Ex. Martin Fry and John Miller. Brecknock Twp.

21 Sept. 1788   5 Nov. 1788
SOWDER, JOHN
     Wife. Anna Sowder. Children: Benjamin, Jacob, David,
Joshua, Mary wife of David Miller, Elizabeth, Anna wife of John
Spentz, Susanna and Esther.
     Ex. Anna Sowder and Christian Hare. Lampeter Twp.

25 Jan. 1785   28 Jan. 1789
SHILER, JULIANA
    Children: Barbara wife of Michael Horn, Eva wife of James
Freeny. Grandchildren: William Meas (parents' names not stated)
and Mary Horn (child of Barbara).
    Ex. Christian App and George Lendenberger. Lancaster
Borough.

1 Oct. 1785   13 March 1789
SHLOTT, JOHN
    Children: John and Margaret.
    Ex. Adam Grill and John Miller. Cocalico Twp.

7 March 1789   7 April 1789
SHALLENBERGER, GEORGE
    Children: John, Jacob, Mary, Henry, Peter and Elizabeth.
    Ex. John Shallenberger and Christian Kaffman. Manor Twp.

12 Aug. 1784   13 Oct. 1789
SHULTZ, ANDREW
    Wife. Barbara Shultz. Children: John, Elizabeth wife of
Jacob Rees, Anna wife of John Christ, Christina wife of Jacob
Byers, Barbara wife of Henry Byers, Susanna wife of Andrew Mentz,
Mary wife of John Rohrer and Catharine.
    Ex. Henry Kendrick, John Forrer and John Christ. Lampeter
Twp.

17 April 1787   10 Nov. 1789
SHITZ, MAGDALENA
    Bros.: Englehard and Frederick Yeizer. Niece and nephews:
Frederick Yeizer (parents' names not stated), Englehard, Philip
and Mary Yeizer (children of Fred).
    Ex. Englehard Yeizer. Lancaster Borough

24 April 1788   12 Nov. 1789
SIMONE, JOHN JACOB
    Wife. Eve Simone. Child: Reyal.
    Ex. Reyal Simone. Warwick Twp.

5 June 1789   25 Nov. 1789
SCOTT, THOMAS
    Wife. Margaret Scott. Children: Thomas, Margaret wife of
Thomas Clark, Mary wife of John Roose, Matthew, Andrew and
Gebrel. Grandchildren: Violet, Jean and Mary Clark and Thomas
Scott (son of Matthew).
    Ex. Alexander Scott and James Bigham. Little Brittain Twp.

17 Jan. 1785   1 Feb. 1785
SHWARTZ, BARBARA
    Children: Abraham, John, David and Christian Hess. N.B. The
above children must have been by a former marriage, but no
mention of such is made in the will.
    Ex. David and Michael Hess. Conestoga Twp.

17 Dec. 1789   3 Feb. 1790
SHIRK, JOHN
     Wife. Barbara Shirk. Children: Feronica wife of Nicholas
Wolf, Barbara wife of Christian Showalter and Ann wife of John
Wenger. Grandchild: Christian Wenger.
     Ex. Ulerich and John Shirk. Cocalico Twp.

4 Sept. 1782   29 Jan. 1790
SCHNIERER, JACOB
     Wife. Catharine Schnierer. Children: Michael, John,
Margaret wife of Andrew Besch and Catharine wife of Martin Bear.
     Ex. Michael and John Schnierer. Cocalico Twp.

17 Jan. 1790   6 March 1790
SHIRK, BARBARA
     Bros. and sisters: Christian, Jacob, Michael and John
Fother, Catharine wife of --- Kauffman, Magdalena Anna wife of --
- King and Veronica wife of John Hertzler.
     Ex. John Hertzler and Jacob Jothor. Cocalico Twp.

22 July 1788   23 March 1790
SHIRE, CONRAD
     Wife. Nancy Shire. Children: Susy, Polly and John.
     Ex. Nancy Shire and John Wolfly. Elizabeth Twp.

8 Feb. 1790   5 June 1790
SHITTS, JOHN
     Wife. Barbara Shitts. Child: Christiana wife of John
Bauchman.
     Ex. Barbara Shitts and Christian Burkholder. Earl Twp.

9 Aug. 1788   22 May 1790
SHENCK, MICHAEL
     Wife. Mary Shenck. Children: John, Ann wife of John Mayer
and Barbara wife of Rudy Mayer.
     Ex. Christian Weiss. Heidleberg Twp.

9 Aug. 1789   27 Sept. 1790
SHAEFER, MARTIN
     Wife. (name omitted). Children: Abraham, Samuel, John,
Martin, Isaac, Christina, Elizabeth wife of Adam Miller and
Margaret wife of David Miller.
     Ex. John Shaefer. Earl Twp.

19 Jan. 1790   7 March 1791
SCHREINER, PHILIP
     Wife. Eve Catharine Schreiner. Children: Michael, Catharine
wife of Nicholas Hess, Margaret wife of Frederick Hoffman, Mary
wife of Henry Fehmer, Philip and Martin. Grandchildren:
Catharine, Philip, Mary, Ann, Elizabeth and Michael Hess; Philip,
Henry, Frederick, Elizabeth and Margaret Hoffman.
     Ex. Henry Fehmer and Michael Hess. Manheim Twp.

13 Aug. 1786   18 April 1791
SHUMACHER, PHILIP

Wife. Magdalena Schumacher. The names and number of children not given.
Ex. Henry Ober and Michael Shelly. Mt. John Twp.

9 March 1791   2 May 1791
STRICKLER, GEORGE
Wife. Rosina Strickler. Children: George, Daniel, Jacob, Catharine wife of Julius Groves, Mary, Ludwig, Rosina, Barbara, Veronica, Magdalena and Elizabeth.
Ex. Rosina Strickler and Peter Frankhouser. Brecknock Twp.

5 April 1791   7 June 1791
SUMEY, PETER
Wife. Mary Sumey. Children: John, Barbara, Peter, Jacob, Samuel, Daniel, Christian and Henry.
Ex. Mary and Jacob Sumey. Earl Twp.

8 Dec. 1791   4 Feb. 1792
SLEMMONS, THOMAS
Wife. Margaret Slemmons. Children: William, John, Thomas, James, Sarah and Robert.
Ex. Margaret and William Slemmons. Salisbury Twp.

13 April 1791   13 March 1792
SEES, EMANUEL
Wife. Susanna Sees. Children: Belthazar, Susanna wife of Paul Brietenbach, Leonard, Catharine wife of George Mengel, Christopher, Barbara, Jacob, Christina, Emanuel and John. Grandson: Philip (son of Leonard).
Ex. Susanna Sees and Leonard Miller. Warwick Twp.

3 Jan. 1792   6 March 1792
SNODGRASS, JOHN
Wife. (name not given). Children: James, Joseph, Alexander, Margaret, Janet and Mary.
Ex. William and James Snodgrass. Martic Twp.

8 Dec. 1787   15 April 1792
SMITH, ABRAHAM
Legatee: Catharine Bear, formerly Catharine Iuigle.
Ex. John Kilhefner. Manor Twp.

27 Aug. 1791   21 Aug. 1792
STEMAN, JOHN
Children: Joseph, John, Jacob, Samuel, Abraham, Ann wife of Henry Neff and Elizabeth wife of Christian Kauffman.
Ex. Jacob and Abraham Steman. Manor Twp.

5 April 1792   1 June 1792
SWEANY, AMBROSE
Legatee: Miles Sweany, of Donegal County, Ireland.
Ex. Joseph Lefever and William Arvin. Twp. omitted.

10 Aug. 1792   13 Sept. 1792
SHOWALTER, JOHN

Wife. Jane Showalter. Children: Elizabeth, John, Joseph,
Christian and Isaac.
     Ex. Jane Showalter and George Ryne. Earl Twp.

7 July 1792   17 Dec. 1792
STUMP, ELIAS
     Bro.: George Stump. Nephews: John and Jacob Stump (sons of
George Stump).
     Ex. Bernard Man and David Barr. Leacock Twp.

---- (omitted) 31 Dec. 1792
SEEGRIST, EVE
     Children: Laurence, Susanna and Bartholomew and John.
Grandchildren: John and Solomon (sons of John) and Catharine
Seegrist (daughter of Bartholomew).
     Ex. Laurence Seegrist. Earl Twp.

24 Jan. 1792   11 Jan. 1793
SHEIBLE, JOHN
     Wife. Margaret Sheible. Children: John, Elizabeth wife of
Jacob Busar and Margaret.
     Ex. Henry Sheible and Christopher Grosh. Earl Twp.

16 June 1789   1 Feb. 1793
SNEDER, CHRISTIAN
     Children: Jacob, Christian, Philip, Michael, Margaret and
Elizabeth.
     Ex. John Brubacher and John Luther. Earl Twp.

10 Jan. 1793   28 Feb. 1793
STEEGLER, JACOB
     Children: Jacob, George, Catharine and Mary.
     Ex. Christian Lessle and Christopher Hess. Brecknock Twp.

8 March 1785   11 March 1793
SNODGRASS, WILLIAM
     Wife. Sarah Snodgrass. Children: William, Mary, James,
Martha and Jane. Grandchildren: William and Mary Snodgrass
(parents' names not given).
Ex. John Boyd and James Snodgrass. Martic Twp.

29 Oct. 1787   7 March 1793
SITES, PETER
     Wife. Barbara Sites. Children: Jacob, Eva, Barbara, John,
Peter, Christine wife of Henry Sweesher, Henry, Elizabeth wife of
Martin Eckman and Catharine wife of Conrad Hoffman.
     Ex. Henry and John Eckman. Bart Twp.

28 May 1762   18 May 1793
SHAUP, BARBARA
     Children: John, Christian and Henry.
     Ex. Martin Bare and Jacob Graff. Strasburg Twp.

4 Oct. 1786   19 July 1793
SMITH, MATHIAS

Wife. Juliana Smith. Children: George, Martin, Barbara, John, Elizabeth, Susanna and Mathias.
Ex. Juliana Smith and Henry Stouffer. Lancaster Borough.

8 March 1790   26 Nov. 1793
SCHNEIDER, JOHN
Wife. (name omitted). Children: Christian, John, Abraham, Michael and Elizabeth.
Ex. John Stern and Isaac Wagoner. Mt. Joy Twp.

3 Jan. 1793   29 Aug. 1793
SCHLABACH, HENRY
Wife. Elizabeth Schlabach. Children: George, Christopher, Catharine wife of Henry Weith, Dorothea wife of Jacob Zeller, Elizabeth wife of Peter Blaser, Barbara, Philip and John.
Ex. John and Christopher Schlabach. Brecknock Twp.

7 Nov. 1793   10 Dec. 1793
STRUNK, WYMAR
Children: Jacob, Wymar, Elizabeth wife of --- Chopper, Susanna and Catharine.
Ex. Adam Musser. Cocalico Twp.

1 Nov. 1793   17 Dec. 1793
SIDWELL, ISAAC
Wife. Ann Sidwell. Children: Isaac, Lydia, Rebecca, Elizabeth, Rachel, Ann, and Ellenor. Son-in-law: Samuel Coopock (wife's name omitted).
Ex. Samuel Coopock, Isaac and Ann Sidwell. Little Brittain Twp.

1 Nov. 1793   9 Nov. 1793
SHUMAN, GEORGE
Wife. Catharine Shuman. Children: Michael, John, Henry, Adam, Catharine, Andrew, Christian, Elizabeth, Jacob, Mary, Frederick and George.
Ex. Christian Wissler and Christian Herr. Manor Twp.

19 Jan. 1790   4 Jan. 1794
SCHANTZ, MAGDALENA
Bro.: Jacob Neff. Sisters: Catharine wife of Jacob Kendrick and Elizabeth wife of Martin Kendrick.
Ex. Jacob Neff. Lampeter Twp.

18 Feb. 1792   5 Feb. 1794
SHERTZER, JACOB
Children: Philip, John, Leonhard and Jacob. Grandchildren: Jacob, John, Joseph, Elizabeth, Susanna, Mary and Philip Shertzer (children of Jacob).
Ex. John Grosh and Jacob Shertzer. Warwick Twp.

23 Sept. 1793 26 Feb. 1794
SHARRER, ABRAHAM
Wife. Annally Sharrer. Children: John, Jacob, Samuel, Elizabeth, Nancy, Mary and Barbara.

Ex. Annally and John Sharrer. Donegal Twp.

12 Dec. 1793   11 March 1794
SNEIDER, JACOB
    Wife. Mary Sneider. Children: Christian, Barbara,
Elizabeth, Mary, Jacob, Peter, Freney, John, Joseph, Ann,
Catharine and Henry (children of Jacob and Mary Sneider).
    Ex. Martin Nissly and Christian Sneider. Rapho Twp.

8 Aug. 1793   18 June 1794
SHEFFEL, JOHN
    Wife. Catharine Sheffel. Children: Christian and Mary.
    Ex. Catharine Sheffel. Lancaster Borough.

7 Nov. 1794   13 Dec. 1794
STOUFFER, JACOB
    Wife. Elizabeth Stouffer. Children: Christian, Jacob,
Daniel and Magdalena.
    Ex. John Stouffer and Martin Mellinger. Lampeter Twp.

1 March 1793   26 July 1794
STOUFFER, JACOB
    Wife. Freany Stouffer. Children: John, Freany, Barbara (and
two others, names not given).
    Ex. John and Chrisley Stouffer. Mt. Joy Twp.

25 Sept. 1793   6 Sept. 1794
SIGNER, THOMAS
    Children: Melchoir, (There were others, names not given).
    Ex. Peter Shweitzer and Peter Baker. Brecknock Twp.

25 Sept. 1794   2 Oct. 1794
SMITH, SAMUEL
    N.B. The legatees were his mother and Bro. (names omitted),
living in Coldrain, County of Entram and parish of Dinachen, in
Ireland.
    Ex. James and John Forsyth. Twp. omitted.

12 Aug. 1793   27 Aug. 1794
STAMBACH, HENRY
    Bro.: Jacob Stambach.
    Ex. Abraham Carpenter and Jacob Stambach. Strasburg Twp.

18 June 1794   27 Aug. 1794
STRUNK, WEIMAR
    Wife. Sally Strunk. Child: Rebecca.
    Ex. Peter Diller. Earl Twp.

16 Oct. 1793   30 Oct. 1795
SNEBER, GEORGE
    Wife. Anna Sneber. Child: Mary wife of --- Strayly.
Grandchildren: Eliza, Catharine and Mary Sneber (parents' names
not given), Mary and Susanna Strayly.
    Ex. William Kelly and Anthony Hains. Donegal Twp.

10 Sept. 1795   27 Nov. 1795
SCHNEIDER, JOHN
    Wife. Hannah Schneider. Children: John, Margaret wife of
Michael Lauterbach, Elizabeth wife of Michael Berger, Andrew,
Philip, Barbara wife of John Hess and Peter.
    Ex. John Miller and Gotlieb Nauman. Manheim Twp.

25 Oct. 1794   15 Jan. 1795
SHELLER, JOHN
    Wife. Rosina Sheller. Children: Elizabeth, Catharine and
Dorothea.
    Ex. George Prinzell. Lancaster Borough.

29 Jan. 1794   21 Jan. 1795
SCOTT, ANDREW
    Children: John, Matthew, David, Ann wife of --- Kenedy,
Margaret wife of --- Brown and Jean wife of --- Donaldson.
    Ex. John and Matthew Scott. Colerain Twp.

7 May 1794   24 Jan. 1795
SWARTZ, JOHN
    Wife. Mary Swartz. Children: Abraham, John and Mary wife of
Abraham Witmer.
    Ex. John Stern and John Kauffman. Mt. Joy Twp.

4 March 1795   3 April 1795
SHANNON, JOHN
    Children: John, James, Sarah and Jannet. N.B. There was a
bequest of two hundred pounds to the Middle Octorara
Meetinghouse.
    Ex. John and James Shannon. Bart Twp.

12 Jan. 1795   3 Sept. 1795
SAMPLE, WILLIAM
    Wife. Ann Sample. Child: Elizabeth wife of William
Robinson.
    Ex. Ann Sample. Colerain Twp.

6 Dec. 1780   27 Oct. 1795
SOWTER, ANN
    Children: Anna wife of Jacob Bare and John.
    Ex. John Sowter and Anna Bare. Strasburg Twp.

19 Oct. 1793   13 May 1795
SHNYDER, CHRISTIAN
    Wife. Elizabeth Shnyder. Children: Anna wife of Peter
Reeser, Mary wife of Christian Bauchman, Elizabeth wife of
Christian Hersh, Catharine wife of Samuel Huber, Feronica and
Barbara wife of Henry Stouffer.
    Ex. Jacob Shnyder and Martin Necely. Londonderry Twp.

21 Sept. 1795   4 April 1796
SLAYMAKER, JOHN
    Wife. (name omitted). Children: William, John, Mathias,
Jean, Elizabeth, Margaret, Mary, Anne, Catharine and Alexander.

Ex. William and John Slaymaker. Strasburg Twp.

13 May 1796   29 Oct. 1795
SHAEFFER, MICHAEL
     Wife. Elizabeth Shaeffer. Children: Elizabeth wife of Adam
Minig, Magdalena wife of Jacob Hiller, Sivila wife of Adam
Grashard, Maria wife of Stoffel Shenk, Susanna wife of Peter
Minig, Catharine wife of John Canade, Michael and John.
     Ex. Elizabeth Shaeffer and Henry Asher. Rapho Twp.

16 May 1796   21 May 1796
SMUCK, JACOB
     Children: Jacob, Solomon, Catharine, Magdalena and
Elizabeth.
     Ex. Philip and Joseph Stergis. Warwick Twp.

3 April 1789   1 June 1796
STRICKLER, HENRY
     Children: Henry, Ann wife of John Horst, Barbara, Frances,
Maria and Magdalene.
     Ex. Henry Strickler and John Horst. Rapho Twp.

28 July 1795   15 Aug. 1796
SPICKLER, MARTIN
     Wife. Barbara Spickler. Children: John, Elisabeth, Anna,
Barbara, Mary, Susanna and Catharine. Bro.: John Spickler.
     Ex. Barbara and [Bro.] John Spickler. Warwick Twp.

23 Jan. 1796   4 March 1796
STOUTER, CATHARINE
     Bro. and sister: Henry Stouter and Eve wife of Jonas
Metzger.
     Ex. Peter Prong. Lancaster Borough.

11 April 1796   11 April 1796
SCOTT, JANNETT
     Sisters: Agness wife of --- Stewart, Jean wife of --- Beety,
Sarah Scott and Mary wife of --- McGee.
     Ex. Alexander Scott. Little Brittain Twp.

24 Dec. 1787   23 April 1796
SENGER, CHRISTIAN
     Wife. Eliza Senger. Children: Christopher, Philip, David,
Martin, Elizabeth and Jacob.
     Ex. Christian Hoover. Manheim Twp.

7 Dec. 1785   20 April 1796
SHOEMAKER, PHILIP
     Wife. Mary Shoemaker. Children: Anthony, John, Philip,
Daniel and David. Son-in-law: Adam Hamacher (wife's name not
stated).
     Ex. John Shoemaker and Adam Hamacher. Rapho Twp.

6 Nov. 1792   13 April 1796
SHELLY, MAGDALENA

Children: Jacob, Abraham, Christian, Barbara, Magdalena, Elizabeth, Ann wife of Christian Martin and Mary wife of Mathias Myer.
Ex. Abraham and Christian Shelly.   Rapho Twp.

4 Feb. 1786   25 July 1797
STONER, CATHARINE
Children: Barbara wife of Tobias Greider, Jacob and Catharine wife of John Shuck.
Ex. Tobias Grider and Jacob Stoner.   Conestoga Twp.

20 Oct. 1795   23 Nov. 1797
STEMAN, SAMUEL
Wife. Mary Steman.   Child: Francis.
Ex. Jacob Stranler and William Wright.   Manor Twp.

25 Feb. 1795   28 Aug. 1797
SANDERS, JACOB
Wife. Anna Sanders.   Children: Jacob, John, George, Tidoves, Peter, Henry, Michael and Anna.
Ex. Anna and Jacob Sanders.   Elizabeth Twp.

10 May 1797   10 June 1797
SHELLY, BARBARA
Mother: Maria Bowman.   Bro. and sister: Jacob, Maria wife of --- Kraus and Catharine Shelly.
Ex. Maria Bowman.   Hempfield Twp.

9 Feb. 1795   12 Dec. 1798
STAYMAN, BARBARA
Children: John, Henry, Elizabeth, Anna, Barbara, Mary, Susanna and Martha.
Ex. Christian Shenck and John Burkholder.   Conestoga Twp.

23 Feb. 1798   13 March 1798
SHIRTS, JOHN
Children: Christian, Hannah wife of Samuel Ferree and Susanna.   Bros.: Jacob and Christian Shirts.
Ex. Jacob and Christian Shirts.   Strasburg Twp.

24 Aug. 1798   22 Sept. 1798
SINGER, PHILIP
Wife. Margaret Singer.   Children: Martha and Elizabeth.
Bro.: David Singer.
Ex. David Singer and Christian Huber.   Manheim Twp.

7 Feb. 1798   16 March 1798
SCHANTZ, ANNA MARIA
Widow of Jacob Schantz.   Children: Barbara wife of --- Levy, Philip, Anna wife of --- Baurenmeester and Jacob.
Ex. Jacob Schantz.   Hempfield Twp.

27 Nov. 1798   27 Dec. 1798
STAUFFER, JOHN

Wife. Margaret Stauffer. Children: John, David, Peter, Margaret, Anna and Magdalena.
    Ex. Margaret and John Stauffer. Martic Twp.

11 Feb. 1795   31 May 1798
SPRIGEL, JACOB
    Children: Joseph, Michael, Mary and George.
    Ex. Joseph and Michael Sprigel. Cocalico Twp.

2 May 1798   11 Jan. 1799
STAUFFER, JACOB
    Wife. Anna Stauffer. Children: Anna, John, Jacob and Barbara. Son-in-law: John Flory (wife's name not given).
    Ex. John Stauffer and John Flory. Rapho Twp.

15 June 1796   16 March 1799
SHOEWALTER, CHRISTIAN
    Children: Jacob and John.
    Ex. Jacob Shoewalter. Earl Twp.

28 Nov. 1785   9 March 1799
SHWARTZ, ANN
    Bro.: Peter Shwartz. Sister: Catharine wife of --- Musser.
Nephew and nieces: Christian, Barbara, Ann and Elizabeth Shwartz (children of Peter).
    Ex. John Nissley. Mt. Joy Twp.

14 March 1794   5 June 1799
SHARP, PETER
    Wife. Mary Sharp. Children: Peter, Moses, John, Jacob, Elizabeth, Barbara and Anna.
    Ex. Christian Sharp. Leacocok Twp.

29 May 1799   15 March 1799
SHERTZ, JOHN
    Wife. Christina Shertz. Children: Jacob, Barbara wife of Samuel Chapman.
    Ex. Daniel Keeports and Michael Greider. Lancaster Borough.

29 Aug. 1799   5 Nov. 1799
STAUFFER, MARGARET
    Children: Peter, Margaret, Anna, Magdalena, John and David.
    Ex. John Stauffer and John Lyne. Martic Twp.

20 May 1799   13 June 1799
SNEIDER, PHILIP
    Wife. Dorothea Sneider. Children: Catharine, Sophia, Dorothea, Susanna, Elizabeth, Philip, Christina, Eleanor, Mary, Peter and Rebecca.
    Ex. Dorothea and Philip Sneider. Earl Twp.

26 Dec. 1798   1 Feb. 1799
STAUFFER, JOHN
    Wife. Barbara Stauffer. Children: Catharine wife of Daniel Hollinger, John, Jacob, Joseph, Martin, Barbara wife of Christian

Knoll, Mary wife of Henry Acker and Ann. Grandchildren: Anna and
Barbara Hollinger.
    Ex. John and Jacob Stauffer. Warwick Twp.

11 Sept. 1794   11 Nov. 1799
SCHWARTZ, GEORGE
    Children: Jacob, George, Susanna wife of William
Reichenbach, Catharine wife of Godlieb Iungman and Anna.
    Ex. Anna Schwartz and William Reichenbach. Lancaster
Borough.

17 Sept. 1797   19 Oct. 1799
STEHMAN, JACOB
    Wife. Barbara Steman. Children: John, Nancy, Elizabeth and
Jacob.
    Ex. Abraham Steman and Jacob Brenneman. Manor Twp.

3 Jan. 1799   26 Feb. 1799
STOLER, RACHEL
    Sister: Anna Stoler. Bro.: Frederick Stoler.
    Ex. Frederick Stoler. Mt. Joy Twp.

3 May 1796   13 April 1799
SOWER, HENRY
    Wife. Maria Dorothea Sower. Children: Philip, Jonas,
Michael, Christopher, Juliana wife of Justus Hauck, Barbara wife
of John Smith, Margaret wife of Frederick Roadacker and Anna wife
of John Road.
    Ex. Justus Hauck and John Breneisen. Earl Twp.

12 Aug. 1797   15 April 1800
SEEGRIST, MICHAEL
    Wife. Magdalena Seegrist. Children: John, Michael, Jacob,
Ann wife of Henry Wissler and Barbara wife of Herman Long.
    Ex. Michael Baughman and Martin Greider. Hempfield Twp.

10 May 1800   5 June 1800
SWEITZER, HENRY
    Wife. Margaret Sweitzer. Children: Catharine wife of
Frederick Hess, Eve wife of Henry Sheffer. Stepdaughter: Susanna
wife of Peter Beder.
    Ex. Casper Shaffner Jr. Lancaster Borough.

11 Nov. 1799   11 Nov. 1800
SPEAR, ROBERT
    Wife. Isabella Spear. Children: Robert, Mary wife of ---
Cook, Hugh, Catharine, Elizabeth, John and William.
    Ex. Isabella and Robert Spear. Hempfield Twp.

13 Aug. 1800   13 Dec. 1800
SHOFF, FREDERICK
    Wife. Magdalena Shoff. Children: Frederick, Abraham,
Martha, Barbara, Freany, Jacob, John, Christian, Ann and Susanna.
    Ex. Frederick and Abraham Shoff. Conestoga Twp.

215

29 July 1793   2 Aug. 1800
STEINER, HENRY
     Bros.: John, Abraham, Isaac, Jacob and Frederick Steiner.
Sister: Magdalena wife of Henry Acker.
     Ex. Isaac Long. Manheim Twp.

10 Nov. 1800   19 Jan. 1801
SHICK, LEONARD
     Wife. Elizabeth Shick. Children: John and Susanna.
     Ex. Henry Acker and Christian Metz. Rapho Twp.

14 Feb. 1801   23 March 1801
STEFFE, PHILIP
     Wife. Catharine Steffe. The names and number of children
not given.
     Ex. Daniel Allebach. Brecknock Twp.

24 Feb. 1799   6 Oct. 1801
SIDWELL, ANN
     Children: Ellen, Rebecca, Elizabeth, Rachel and Ann. Son-
in-law: Nathan Webster (wife's name not stated).
     Ex. Nathan and John Webster. Little Brittain Twp.

26 Jan. 1801   11 Nov. 1801
SCHUCK, MARTIN
     Children: John, Susanna wife of John Rubert, Joseph, Esther
wife of Joseph Gengrich, Abraham and Salome.
     Ex. John and Joseph Schuck. Rapho Twp.

1 June 1799   8 Dec. 1801
SMITH, JOHN
     Children: Jacob, Elizabeth wife of Moses Bower, John, Peter
and Elizabeth. Son-in-law: Joseph Holl (name of wife not
stated). Grandchildren: Henry, Elizabeth, Susanna and Mary Holl.
     Ex. David Diffenderfer and Christian Bremer. Earl Twp.

6 June 1774   --- 1801
SLAYMAKER, DANIEL
     Wife. Geils Slaymaker. Children: Daniel, Mathias and Geils.
Bros.: Mathias and John Slaymaker.
     Ex. (Bros.) Mathias and John Slaymaker. Strasburg Twp.

12 March 1802   26 April 1802
SANDER, DANIEL
     Wife. Elizabeth Sander. Children: David, Jacob, Catharine
and Christian.
     Ex. Bernard and Frederick Waggoner. Donegal Twp.

30 March 1802   15 May 1802
SCHONER, JOHN
     Wife. Anne Schoner.
     Ex. Peter Summy and Joseph Newkomet. Twp. not given.

23 April 1802   31 May 1802
STOUTSEBERGER, JOHN

Wife. Margaret Stoutseberger. Bro.: Jacob Stoutseberger.
Nephew: John (son of Bro. Jacob).
Ex. Jacob Stoutseberger and Jacob Eshleman. Strasburg Twp.

27 Aug. 1802   30 Sept. 1802
STAUFFER, PETER JR
Bros. and sisters: Mary wife of David Weaver, Catharine,
Christian, Barbara and Elizabeth wife of Philip Rank.
Ex. David Weaver. Caernarvon Twp.

10 Aug. 1802   10 [18?] Nov. 1802
SHREINER, MATHIAS ANDREW
Wife. Maria Shreiner. Children: Henry, John and Elizabeth.
Ex. Peter Reitenback. Manheim Twp.

31 July 1797   30 Sept. 1802
SHAEFFER, FREDERICK
Wife. Margaret Shaeffer.
Ex. Adam Messencope. Lancaster Borough.

4 May 1773   2 April 1802
SOEHNER, GODLIEB
Wife. Maria Soehner. Children: Godlieb, Jacob, Frederick,
John, Catharine and Elizabeth.
Ex. Maria and Godlieb Soehner. Lancaster Borough.

26 Nov. 1795   16 Feb. 1803
SHENCK, CHRISTIAN
Wife. Barbara Shenck. Children: John, Christian, Feronica
wife of Abraham Miller, Elizabeth wife of Christian Shaup,
Barbara wife of John Brenneman and Mary wife of George
Steinbecker. Grandchildren: Barbara, Christian, Martin, John,
Henry, Mary, Jacob and Joseph Shaup.
Ex. John and Christian Shenck. Martic Twp.

19 Feb. 1803   18 March 1803
SCHNEIDER, HENRY
Wife. Elizabeth Schneider. Children: Jacob, Elizabeth wife
of Casper Kieper, Henry, Margaret and John.
Ex. Adam Musser and John Henry Schneider. Cocalico Twp.

8 Nov. 1802   27 April 1803
SHITZ, DANIEL
Wife. Christina Shitz. Children: John and Elizabeth.
Ex. Abraham Shelly and Henry Strickler. Rapho Twp.

2 May 1793   17 June 1803
SMITH, MARGARET
Children: Frederick and Elizabeth wife of John German.
Ex. Frederick Smith. Cocalico Twp.

30 Dec. 1784   1 Aug. 1803
SANDOE, JACOB
Wife. Margaret Sandoe. Children: George, Jacob, Charles,
John, Peter, Abraham, David and Catharine.

Ex. Margaret Sandoe. Lancaster Borough

7 Aug. 1801   26 Aug. 1803
SHENCK, JOHN
     Children: Joseph, John, Magdalena wife of Andrew Snavely,
Barbara and Esther.
     Ex. Jacob Hostetter and Benjamin Hershey. Lancaster Borough

6 Aug. 1796   1 Oct. 1803
STAUFFER, DANIEL
     Wife. Susanna Stauffer. Children: Christian, David and
Abraham.
     Ex. Susanna Stauffer. Warwick Twp.

13 Feb. 1801   10 Sept. 1803
STONER, ABRAHAM
     Children: Henry, David, Abraham, Jacob, Magdalena and
Elizabeth wife of John Hoffert.
     Ex. Christian Frick and John Longenecker. Manheim Twp.

15 Sept. 1803   28 Nov. 1803
STEER, PHILIP
     Wife. Dorthea Steer.
     Ex. Dorothea Steer. Lancaster Borough.

21 March 1803   12 Oct. 1803
SHULTZ, JOHN
     Wife. Margaret Shultz. N.B. There was a bequest to the
German Reformed Church of Lancaster.
     Ex. John P. Hellenstein. Lancaster Borough.

15 Sept. 1797   14 Jan. 1804
SEWEITZER, STEPHEN
     Wife. Mary Magdalena Seweitzer. Children: John, Louisa wife
of Henry Oster, Eve wife of Arnold Hebelman and Magdalena wife of
Jacob Shot.
     Ex. Mary Magdalena Seweitzer and Henry Oster. Lancaster
Borough.

14 Feb. 1804   14 Feb. 1804
SHENK, MICHAEL
     Children: John, Barbara, Michael, Christian, Henry, Jacob,
Andrew, Elizabeth wife of Emanuel Herr, Mary wife of Jacob
Bassler and Ann wife of Jacob Harnish.
     Ex. Michael Shenk and Jacob Hostetter. Lancaster Borough

13 Jan. 1804   27 Feb. 1804
SCHNEIDER, MICHAEL
     Wife. Catharine Schneider. Children: Elizabeth, Catharine,
Barbara, John and Jacob.
     Ex. Catharine Schneider and Michael Bender. Manor Twp.

26 Oct. 1799   23 Dec. 1804
SIMON, JOSEPH

Children: Moses, Myer, Esther, Shinah, Belah, Mariam and Leah wife of Levi Philips.
Ex. Levi Philips and Belah Simon. Lancaster Borough.

1 Sept. 1802   30 March 1804
SHNEIDER, GEORGE
Children: Peter, Maria, (There were two others, names omitted).
Ex. Peter Shneider. Cocalico Twp.

14 March 1801   27 Jan. 1804
SOHL, HENRY
Wife. Catharine Sohl. Bro.-in-law: Henry Tiemer.
Ex. Catharine Sohl and Henry Tiemer. Cocalico Twp.

1 Oct. 1803   3 April 1804
SHOPF, HENRY
Children: John, Barbara wife of Christian Steiner and Ann.
Ex. Henry Shenck and Jacob Carly. Manor Twp.

29 Aug. 1804   29 Nov. 1804
STRICKLER, ULRICH
Wife. Elizabeth Strickler. Children: John, Abraham, Henry, Barbara wife of John Leaman, Maria wife of Jacob Bretz and Elizabeth wife of Abraham Hostetter.
Ex. John and Henry Strickler. Rapho Twp.

25 May 1804   12 June 1804
SOUDER, BARBARA
Widow of Rudolph Souder. Children: Esther wife of Henry Gram, Rudolph and Eve.
Ex. Henry Gram. Twp. omitted.

23 May 1797   19 Nov. 1804
SMITH, THEOBALD
Wife. Elizabeth Smith. Children: George, Rosina, Frederick, Mary wife of Henry Philips, Jacob, Elizabeth, John and Michael.
Ex. Elizabeth Smith and Michael Bartle. Lancaster Borough.

2 March 1803   7 Feb. 1804
SLAYMAKER, MATHIAS
Children: John, Rachel, Elizabeth, Rebecca and Mary.
Grandchildren: Mary McCompsey and Barbara Pickel (parents' names not stated).
Ex. John and William Slaymaker. Strasburg Twp.

12 Dec. 1797   13 Nov. 1804
SHAEFFER, ABRAHAM
Children: John, Susanna, Abraham, Maria, Elizabeth, Samuel and Christian and Martin (There was one other, name not given).
Ex. John Shaeffer and Conrad Ziegler. Donegal Twp.

2 May 1804   13 Oct. 1804
SWEIGART, JACOB

Wife. Mary Sweigart. Children: Juliana wife of Peter Weis, John, Mary wife of Jacob Hoyl, Catharine wife of Henry Foster, Philip, Barbara wife of Peter Zinn, Christina wife of Jacob Redig, Elizabeth wife of Jacob Hornberger and Peter.
Ex. Philip and Peter and Sweigart. Cocalico Twp.

27 March 1804   3 Jan. 1805
STOLTZ, JACOB
Wife. Juliana Stoltz. Children: Maria and Margaret wife of William Steffen. Grandchildren: Maria and Margaret Steffen.
Ex. Jost Hieneman and Abraham Hamacher. Hempfield Twp.

18 May 1805   27 May 1805
STAUFFER, HENRY
Wife. Catharine Stauffer. Children: Christopher, George, Catharine wife of Henry Schneider, Mary wife of Thomas Burns, Sabina wife of John Pratt and Salome.
Ex. Conrad Schwartz and John Light. Lancaster Borough.

10 April 1805   24 April 1805
SHULTZ, JOHN
Mother: Mary wife of Henry Westly (second marriage). Bro.: Christian Shultz. Sister: Franey wife of --- Herr.
Ex. Henry Westly and Christian Shultz. Twp. omitted.

14 Aug. 1805   24 Aug. 1805
SANDER, JOHN
Wife. Magdalena Sander. Child: John. N.B. There was a bequest of three pounds to the Evangelic Lutheran Church in Heidelberg Township.
Ex. Michael Mohr. Elizabeth Twp.

10 June 1805   25 July 1805
STIESS, JACOB
Wife. Margaret Stiess. Child: John.
Ex. Elias Wolf and John Shrautz Jr. Warwick Twp.

8 Oct. 1801   31 July 1805
SHOBER, ANDREW
Wife. Rosina Shober. Children: John, Johanna, Susanna, Andrew, Samuel, William, Jacob and Maria.
Ex. Rosina Shober. Warwick Twp.

23 July 1801   26 March 1805
SHAEFFER, JACOB
Wife. Elizabeth Shaeffer. Children: Jacob, Margaret wife of Christian Kline, Mary wife of Ludwig Diffenderfer, Catharine, Sophia and Mary.
Ex. Elizabeth Shaeffer and William Haverstick. Lancaster Borough.

1 March 1803   11 March 1805
SIMONY, EVA
Child: Rachel wife of --- Yundt. Grandchild: Susanna Yundt wife of --- Miller.

Ex. Christian Erb and Susanna Miller. Warwick Twp.

30 Nov. 1805   15 Dec. 1806
SENSENICH, MICHAEL
    Wife. Barbara Sensenich. Children: Peter, Mary, Barbara,
Magdalena and Michael. Bro.: John.
    Ex. John Sensenich and John Overholtzer. Earl Twp.

3 Jan. 1806   3 May 1806
STOLL, MARTIN
    Bros. and sisters: Jacob, George, John, Maria wife of
Godlieb Schack and Barbara Stoll (all living in Europe).
    Ex. John Barr. Martic Twp.

28 July 1804   22 Aug. 1806
STONER, JACOB
    Wife. Ann Stoner. Stepchildren: John Binkley and Ann wife
of Abraham Huber. Bros.: John, Christian and Henry Stoner.
Sisters: Ann, Elizabeth and Barbaa (all married, but last names
not given). Brothers-in-law: John and Martin Mylin.
    Ex. John and Martin Mylin. Lampeter Twp.

3 March 1806   4 March 1806
SYBERT, HENRY
    Wife. Susanna Sybert. Children: John and David.
    Ex. Susanna Sybert, Abraham Metz and Jacob Shoemaker. Rapho
Twp.

14 Nov. 1806   17 Dec. 1806
SMITH, WILLIAM
    Children: Edward, William, Mary wife of --- Henderson, Sarah
wife of --- Slowens, Margaret, Rebecca and Lydia wife of ---
Wallace. Grandchildren: Rachel Henderson wife of --- Davis,
Harriet Slowens and William Wallace.
    Ex. Edward Smith and John Wallace. Earl Twp.

16 Nov. 1805   26 July 1806
SNYDER, LORENTZ
    Legatee: John Klein. N.B. This will was contested, and an
administrator appointed.
    Ex. John Klein. Cocalico Twp.

23 Jan. 1806   22 June 1806
SMITH, GEORGE
    Children: Jacob, John, Mary wife of Jacob Brubacher,
Elizabeth wife of John Kendik. Grandchild: Nancy Kendik.
    Ex. Jacob Brubacher and Daniel Smith. Donegal Twp.

5 Nov. 1805   7 March 1806
SHENCK, ROSINA
    Bros.: George and Christopher Shenck.
    Ex. Christian Bliensderfer. Lititz Twp.

15 Sept. 1806 31 Oct. 1806
SHENCK, MICHAEL

Wife. Anna Shenck. Children: Jacob, Benjamin, Joseph, Michael, Elizabeth, Barbara, Feronica, Ann and Susanna.
Ex. Jacob Shenck and Abraham Warfel. Conestoga Twp.

9 Nov. 1805   23 April 1806
SWEIGART, GEORGE
Wife. Elizabeth Sweigart. Children: Jacob, Daniel, Samuel, Susanna wife of Andrew Betzer, George, Catharine wife of John Keller, Elizabeth wife of Henry Kemper and Salome wife of Daniel Royer. Grandchild: Elizabeth Keller.
Ex. Henry Kemper and Christian Meyer. Earl Twp.

10 Dec. 1805   22 Feb. 1806
SMITH, CHRISTOPHER
Wife. Catharine Smith. Children: Christian (There were others, names and number not given).
Ex. Catharine Smith and Jacob Garner. Cocalico Twp.

13 Sept. 1804   25 Aug. 1807
SUMMY, JACOB
Wife. Margaret Summy. Children: Margaret, Anna wife of Martin Markley and Barbara. Son-in-law: Abraham Gittinger (name of wife not stated). Grandson: Abraham Witwer (parents' names not given).
Ex. David Witwer and Michael Brubacher. Earl Twp.

17 Oct. 1806   21 Jan. 1807
SCOTT, JOHN
Bros.: James and William Scott. Sisters: Jane Scott and Mealy wife of Thomas Woods. Nephews and nieces: Martha, Sarah, Rebecca, Margaret, Mary, David and Thomas (children of Mealy Woods) and Jane Stewart wife of Thomas Stewart.
Ex. David Woods. Lampeter Twp.

21 May 1800   11 Sept. 1807
SMITH, ANNA MARIA
Godlieb Hill (first husband). Grandchildren: Godlieb and Michael Hill, Magdalena wife of Jacob Dubbs and Mary wife of John Young (parents' names not given).
Ex. Godlieb Hill. Lancaster Borough.

14 Nov. 1805   17 Aug. 1807
SPONHOUR, JACOB
Children: Anna wife of Jacob Michel and John.
Ex. John Smith and George Geyer. Warwick Twp.

9 May 1803   13 June 1807
STEIGELMAN, JACOB
Wife. Barbara Steigelman. Children: Jacob, Eve wife of Mathias Dillinger, John and George.
Ex. Barbara and Jacob Steigelman. Manor Twp.

2 May 1807   19 Oct. 1807
SHERB, CHRISTOPHER

Wife. Catharine Sherb. Children: Adam, John, Susanna wife of Isaac Gushard, Christopher, Jacob and Elizabeth wife of Jacob Young.
Ex. Michael Oberlin. Cocalico Twp.

22 April 1807   23 May 1807
STEIGERWALT, EVERHARD
Wife. Susanna Steigerwalt. Children: Abraham, Frederick, Susanna, Michael and Christian.
Ex. Susanna Steigerwalt. Lancaster Borough.

28 Aug. 1807   5 Oct. 1807
STEEL, FRANCIS
Wife. Mary Steel. Stepdaughter: Barbara wife of Robert Rush. N.B. There was a bequest of twenty dollars to German Reformed Church in Lancaster Borough.
Ex. Peter Reed. Lancaster Borough.

26 Feb. 1805   11 Sept. 1807
SHIRE, ANN
Children: Susanna wife of Joshua Felton, Mary wife of Henry Brenneman, Elizabeth and John.
Ex. Peter Bishop. Mt. Joy Twp.

15 April 1805   23 Nov. 1807
SIECHRIST, JACOB
Wife. Magdalena Siechrist. Children: Jacob, Anna, Magdalena wife of Charles Dougherty, Elizabeth, Mary, Barbara, Jacob, Esther, Susanna and Veronica.
Ex. Christian Hershey and John Newcomer. Hempfield Twp.

25 Dec. 1806   22 April 1807
SHIRK, JOSEPH
Children: Joseph, Jacob, Catharine, John, Henry and Christian.
Ex. Andrew Gerber and Christian Shirk. Hempfield Twp.

17 Nov. 1794   21 Feb. 1807
SHREINER, MARTIN
Children: Philip, Mary wife of Michael Rudy, Catharine wife of Michael Lore and Margaret wife of Leonard Bellmyer.
Grandchildren: Margaret, Catharine, Mary, Leonard, Martin, Andrew and Jacob Billmyer.
Ex. Michael and George Shreiner. Manheim Twp.

7 June 1796   8 Jan. 1808
STOUFFER, SUSANNA
Bros.: Peter and Christian. Nephews and nieces: Mathias, George, Peter, Magdalena, Frany, Jacob, Christian and Samuel (children of Peter Stouffer); Anna, Mathias, Susanna, Frany, Esther, Mary, Catharine, Christian, Peter, Barbara, Elizabeth and Sarah Stouffer (children of Christian).
Ex. Mathias and Jacob Stouffer. Earl Twp.

5 Feb. 1801   6 June 1808
SOLLENBERGER, ABRAHAM
     Wife. Barbara Sollenberger. Children: John, (There were
others, names and number not given). Son-in-law: John Criley.
     Ex. John Criley. Cocalico Twp.

6 June 1806 28 April 1808
STAUFFER, CHRISTIAN
     Wife. Anna Stauffer. Children: Christian, John, Peter,
Elizabeth wife of Daniel Brubacher, Ann wife of Peter Weist and
Jacob. Grandchildren: Michael, Ann and Jacob Stauffer (children
of Jacob).
     Ex. Christian Stauffer and John Erb. Warwick Twp.

29 May 1808   12 July 1808
STEINMAN, CHRISTIAN F.
     Wife. Maria Magdalena Steinman. N.B. There was a bequest of
thirty poiunds to "The Society for the Propagation of the Gospel
among the Heathen," established at Bethelham.
     Ex. Maria Magdalena Steinman and Christian Blickenderfer.
Warwick Twp.

5 March 1808   23 May 1808
SHOELEIN, LEONARD
     Wife. Margaret Shoelein. Children: John and Rachel wife of
Samuel Grosh.
     Ex. John Shoelein and Samuel Grosh. Warwick Twp.

10 May 1807   25 May 1808
STUBBS, DANIEL
     Children: Joseph, Vincent, Daniel, Thomas, Hannah, Betsy,
Orpha, Mary, Sarah, Ruth wife of --- Pile, Idah and Isaac.
     Ex. Vincent and Joseph Stubbs. Little Brittain Twp.

16 March 1808 1 Aug. 1808
SWEIGART, SEBASTIAN
     Wife. Maria Sweigart. Children: Maria, Felix, Margaret,
Barbara, John, Hannah wife of Adam Barget, Henry and George.
     Ex. Maria and Felix Sweigart. Martic Twp.

30 Jan. 1808   8 Oct. 1808
SWOBE, HENRY
     Wife. Barbara Swobe. Children: George, John, Mary,
Catharine wife of John Bart and Elizabeth wife of George Bart.
     Ex. John and George Bart. Leacock Twp.

12 July 1797   30 May 1809
STAHLEY, CHRISTIAN
     Wife. Elizabeth Stahley. Children: Christian, Jacob, John,
Benjamin, Abraham, Anna wife of Abraham Day, Catharine wife of
John Illig.
     Ex. Christian, Jacob, John, Benj. and Abraham Stahley.
Elizabeth Twp.

9 Jan. 1809   9 March 1809
STUTENSROAD, HENRY
    Wife. Susanna Stutensroad. Children: John (There were others, names and number not given).
    Ex. George Weidman and Peter Elser. Cocalico Twp.

20 June 1801   4 April 1809
STERN, JOHN
    Wife. Esther Stern. Children: Mary wife of Peter Adams, Phebe wife of James Hagar, Thomas, William and Esther.
    Ex. Esther Stern. Lancaster Borough.

16 Jan. 1809   13 April 1809
SHOWALTER, JACOB
    Wife. Barbara Showalter. [Children?]: Christian, Elizabeth wife of Peter Good, Barbara wife of Samuel Kurtz, Jacob, David, Catharine wife of John Kurtz, Henry, Maria, Anna, Christina, Daniel, Susanna, Joseph, Samuel and Lydia.
    Ex. Jacob Showalter and Samuel Kurtz. Earl Twp.

10 April 1809   27 April 1809
SINGHAAS, CASPER
    Wife. Elizabeth Singhaas. Children: Catharine wife of --- Beck, Eve wife of Philip Brenner, Elizabeth and Esther.
    Ex. Elizabeth Singhaas, Jacob Shaffer and Peter Beer. Mt. Joy Twp.

15 Sept. 1806   3 Sept. 1809
STEWART, JOHN
    Children: Isabella wife of --- McCord, Hugh and Elizabeth wife of --- Barcley. Grandchildren: John and Anna Stewart (children of Hugh). N.B. Martha Stewart was the wife of Hugh, who was deceased at the time the will was made.
    Ex. George Black and Martha Stewart. Strasburg Twp.

-- Sept. 1807   22 Nov. 1809
STAUFFER, BARBARA
    Children: John, Joseph, Martin, Barbara wife of Christian Knoll and Mary wife of Henry Aches.
    Ex. Samuel Ensminger. Warwick Twp.

31 Dec. 1805   16 Feb. 1810
SHPPEN, JOSEPH
    Children: John, Robert, Mary wife of Samuel Swift, Margaret, Joseph and Henry. Bro.: Edward Shippen. Brother-in-law: Col. James Burd. Grandson: Edward Burd Yates Shippen (parents' names not stated).
    Ex. Edward Burd, Robert Shippen, Samuel Swift, Joseph and Henry Shippen. Lancaster Borough.

9 Aug. 1808   2 May 1810
STERRETT, JAMES
    Wife. Sarah Sterrett. Children: James, Fanny wife of Samuel Woods, William, David, John and Charles. Grandson: James Sterrett (son of James).

Ex. Robert and John Sterrett. Rapho Twp.

7 Oct. 1808   3 May 1810
SIEGEL, ADAM
    Grandchildren: Isaac and Magdalena Johnson (parents' names
not given).
    Ex. George Merkel and George Lorah. Earl Twp.

3 Feb. 1810   6 March 1810
STOLTZFUSE, JACOB
    Wife. Mary Stoltzfuse. The names and number of children not
given. Bro.: John Stoltzfuse.
    Ex. John and Christian Stoltzfuse. Leacock Twp.

7 Oct. 1809   24 March 1810
SCOTT, ALEXANDER
    Wife. Mary Scott.
    Ex. Mary Scott. Twp. omitted.

11 Sept. 1810 27 Sept. 1810
SIDWELL, JOHN
    Wife. Elizabeth Sidwell. The names and number of children
not given.
    Ex. Elizabeth Sidwell and Timothy Hains. Little Brittain
Twp.

10 Aug. 1810   24 Oct. 1810
SHIRK, DAVID
    Wife. Elizabeth Shirk. Child: Barbara.
    Ex. John Shirk and Joseph Landis. Earl Twp.

20 Oct. 1810   12 Dec. 1810
SAHM, GEORGE
    Wife. Catharine Sahm. Children: George, David, John, Jacob,
Catharine wife of Conrad Mark and Barbara wife of Jacob Kettel.
    Ex. George and David Sahm. Warwick Twp.

22 Sept. 1809 29 Dec. 1810
SCOTT, JANE
    Sister: Mary wife of --- Woods.
    Ex. David Woods. Lampeter Twp.

17 Oct. 1810   26 Jan. 1811
SWOPE, JACOB
    Wife. Sabina Swope. Children: Jacob, George, Mathias,
Emanual, Frederick, Catharine and Elizabeth.
    Ex. George and Mathias Swope. Leacock Twp.

2 March 1810   2 March 1811
SHENK, MICHAEL
    Wife. Susanna Shenk. Children: Christian, Michael, Henry,
John, Jacob, Barbara, Catharine, Ann and Elizabeth wife of ---
Eshbach.
    Ex. Benjamin Hershey. Twp. omitted.

16 May 1808   25 April 1811
SHULER, JACOB
    Wife. Regina Shuler.
    Ex. Regina Shuler. Lancaster Borough.

12 March 1811   9 May 1811
STOFFER, DAVID
    Wife. Mary Stoffer.
    Ex. Mary Stoffer and John Shanke. Drumore Twp.

16 Sept. 1805   3 Aug. 1811
STAUFFER, ELIZABETH
    Children: Daniel and Magdalena Stauffer. Bro.: John
Stauffer. Nephew: Daniel (son of John Stauffer).
    Ex. (nephew) Daniel Stauffer. Lampeter Twp.

8 Aug. 1811   11 Sept. 1811
SPICKLER, BARBARA
    Children: Mary, Barbara, Elizabeth, Anna, John, Mary,
Susanna and Catharine.
    Ex. Abraham Reist Jr. Warwick Twp.

18 March 1807   15 Sept. 1811
STOWLER, ANN
    Widow of George Stowler. Legatee: Magdalena wife of Jacob
Klein of Tennessee. N.B. There was a bequest to Dunkers (near
Middle Creek, Lancaster Co.)
    Ex. John Klein and Christian Royer. Elizabeth Twp.

16 July 1811   15 Oct. 1811
STAHLE, JACOB JR
    N.B. The legatees are his father, mother, bro., sisters -
names not given.
    Ex. Henry Snyder and Samuel Eberly. Cocalico Twp.

14 Sept. 1811   4 Nov. 1811
SAPP, MESSACH
    Wife. Piercey Sapp. N.B. This was a nuncupative will.
    Ex. (names omitted). Philadlephia, PA.

13 April 1812   28 April 1812
SHIRK, PETER
    Wife. Mary Shirk. Children: John, Samuel and Esther wife of
John Horst.
    Ex. John Shirk and John Horst. Earl Twp.

5 Aug. 1811   22 Jan. 1812
STRICKLER, JACOB
    Wife. Sarah Strickler. Children: Henry, Jacob, Joseph,
Catharine, Emile, Susanna, Elizabeth, Nancy wife of --- Spear,
Mary wife of --- Weaver and Sarah wife of --- McCorkle. Son-in-
law: Samuel J. Atlee (name of wife not stated).
    Ex. Jacob Strickler, Christian Brenneman, Andrew Gerber and
John Furry. Hempfield Twp.

25 Nov. 1811   24 Jan. 1812
SHIRK, JOHN
  Wife. Elizabeth Shirk. Children: David and Ann.
  Ex. Peter Shirk and Joseph Landis. Earl Twp.

7 Aug. 1802   22 Feb. 1812
STAUFFER, JOHN
  Wife. Feronica Stauffer. Children: Magdalena wife of Tobias
Wanner, Ann, Jacob, Daniel, Christian and Feronica wife of Tobias
Greider.
  Ex. Abraham Buckwalter and Martin Mellinger. Lampeter Twp.

13 Aug. 1808   3 Aug. 1812
SMEDLEY, JOSEPH
  Wife. Rebecca Smedley. Children: Lewis, Eli, Joseph,
Thomas, Joel, Lydia, Sarah and Rebecca.
  Ex. Rebecca and Lewis Smedley. Little Brittain Twp.

31 May 1802   28 April 1812
SUMMY, JOHN
  Wife. Anna Summy. Children: Peter, Elizabeth, John,
Christian, Jacob, David, Maria, Anne and Henry. Son-in-law:
Joseph Long (wife's name omitted).
  Ex. Peter Summy and Peter Becker. Warwick Twp.

6 Nov. 1811   18 April 1812
SHIFFER, HENRY
  Bros. and sisters: John, Elizabeth wife of --- Shoemaker,
Molly wife of --- Howarter, Peter and Joseph Shiffer.
  Ex. Richard Ream and John Diehl. Cocalico Twp.

15 Aug. 1812   5 Sept. 1812
SMITH, CHRISTIAN
  (First Wife) Magdalena Smith. (Second wife) Elizabeth
Smith. Children of 1st wife: Samuel, Christian and Jacob.
Children of 2nd wife: Joseph, (There were others, names not
given).
  Ex. John Wisler and John Shock. Manor Twp.

11 Sept. 1805 5 Nov. 1812
SHALLENBERGER, JACOB
  Wife. Ann Shallenberger. Children: Andrew, Jacob,
Christian, Ulrich, Mary wife of John Musser, Ann wife of John
Stouffer, Matty wife of John Bradley, Catharine wife of Philip
Lutz and Barbara [wife of] Jacob Weilandt.
  Ex. Andrew Shallenberger and Jacob Strickler. Hempfield
Twp.

13 Aug. 1812   13 Oct. 1812
SHREINER, GEORGE
  Wife. Barbara Shreiner. Children: Catharine wife of John
Grosh, Elizabeth wife of John Shugert, Magdalena wife of Samuel
Lehn, Michael, John, Adam, Eve wife of Leonard Miller, Susanna
wife of Philip Rudisil and Jacob.
  Ex. John Shreiner and Peter Baughman. Manheim Twp.

23 Sept. 1807   17 Oct. 1812
SHANTZ, JOHN
    Wife. (name omitted). Children: Magdalena and Henry. Son-
in-law: Isaac Graybill (wife's name not stated).
    Ex. John Shantz and Isaac Graybill. Twp. omitted

15 May 1811   19 Jan. 1813
SHULER, REGINA
    Child: Margaret.
    Ex. Nathaniel Smith. Lancaster Borough.

12 May 1812   20 Feb. 1813
SHALLENBERGER, JOHN
    Bros. and sisters: Henry, Maria, Elizabeth and Jacob
Shallenberger.
    Ex. Adam Shallenberger and Christian Newcomer. Manor Twp.

2 Dec. 1811   3 May 1813
SHENCK, MARTIN
    Wife. Anna Shenck. Children: John, (There were eight other
children, names omitted). Grandchild: John Shenck (son of John).
    Ex. Peter Martin and Moses Rosenberger. Warwick Twp.

9 July 1812   7 April 1813
SPECK, BERNARD
    Wife. Magdalena Speck. Children: Barbara and Mary.
    Ex. Peter Lintemute and Jacob Hastings. Donegal Twp.

14 May 1813   10 June 1813
STRICKLER, JOSEPH
    Wife. Elizabeth Strickler. Children: Samuel, David, Jacob,
Henry, Benjamin, Elizabeth and John.
    Ex. Christian Hershey and Benjamin Miller. Rapho Twp.

28 July 1808   5 Aug. 1813
SMITH, EPHRAIM
    Wife. (name omitted). Children: Ephraim, Samuel (there
were others, names not given).
    Ex. Ephraim and Samuel Smith. Sadsbury Twp.

18 April 1805   29 Oct. 1813
SHELLY, JACOB
    Wife. Ann Shelly. Bro. and sister: Christian Shelly and
Anna wife of --- Musselman.
    Ex. David Horst and Christian Shelly. Mt. Joy Twp.

15 June 1812   12 March 1814
SENSENIG, JACOB
    Wife. Barbara Sensenig. Children: Mary, Elizabeth, Anna,
Esther, Sarah, Feronica, Daniel and John.
    Ex. Daniel and John Sensenig. Earl Twp.

16 Dec. 1809   9 April 1814
SPECK, CHRISTOPHER
    Wife. Lewis Sharlotte Sophia Speck. Bro.: John Speck.

Ex. Lewis Sharlotte, Sophia Speck and Abraham Keagy.
Strasburg Twp.

13 Nov. 1800   19 April 1814
SHELLENBERGER, JOHN
     Sisters: Catharine wife of David Geimer and Barbara wife of
Jacob Yoder.
     Ex. Jacob Yoder and Jacob Kurtz. Manheim Twp.

17 March 1800   26 April 1814
SHOBER, ROSINA
     Children: John, Samuel, Jacob, Maria, Susanna, Andrew and
William.
     Ex. John and Samuel Shober. Twp. omitted.

13 June 1814   1 Aug. 1814
SENER, JOHN
     Wife. Catharine Sener. Children: John, Godleib, Jacob,
Catharine, Frederick and Elizabeth.
     Ex. Gotlieb Sener. Lancaster Borough.

1 Aug. 1808   1 Aug. 1814
STEMAN , MARY
     Children: John, Christian, Ann wife of --- Greider, and Mary
wife of --- Gish. Grandchildren: Anna Brenneman, Mary, John,
Elizabeth, Frederick, Jacob and Abraham Galbouch (parents' names
not given).
     Ex. Christian Steman and John Brenneman. Donegal Twp.

12 Nov. 1813   22 July 1814
SAUDER, JOHN
     Wife. Mary Sauder. Children: Jacob, Anna wife of Henry
Martin, John, Christine wife of John Graff and Feronica wife of
Peter Huber.
     Ex. John Beam and John Brenneman. Manor Twp.

2 April 1815   8 May 1815
SMITH, DANIEL
     Bro.: John. Nephew: John Smith Jr. (son of Bro. John).
     Ex. (nephew) John Smith. Dongeal Twp.

14 Nov. 1814   12 May 1815
SHAUM, PHILIP
     Wife. Mary Shaum. Children: John, George and Philip.
     Ex. Benjamin Shaum. Lancaster Borough.

25 Feb. 1806   25 May 1815
SWISHER, JOHN
     Children: Henry, Elizabeth, Barbara, Mary and Philip.
     Ex. Robert Anderson, Henry and John Swisher. Colerain Twp.

10 June 1815   1 Nov. 1815
STAKE, GEORGE R.
     Mother: Catharine Stake.
     Ex. Catharine Stake. Lancaster Borough

2 Oct. 1812   20 Nov. 1815
STEEL, MARY
    Granddaughter: Mary Remly (parents' names not given).
    Ex. Peter Reed. Lancaster Borough.

5 Sept. 1815   19 Jan. 1816
SWEIGART, ELIZABETH
    Children: Susanna wife of Andrew Bitzer, Elizabeth wife of
Henry Kemper, Salome wife of Daniel Royer and Samuel.
    Ex. Daniel Royer. Earl Twp.

2 July 1812   22 Jan. 1816
STEIGELMAN, LUDWIG
    Wife. Rachel Steigelman. Children: Elizabeth, Catharine,
and Sarah.
    Ex. John Stoner. Hempfield Twp.

3 Feb. 1816   23 March 1816
SMITH, PHILIP
    Bro.: William Smith.
    Ex. Peter Summy. Hempfield Twp.

11 April 1816   22 April 1816
SMITH, HANNAH
    Bro.: John Smith.
    Ex. John Smith. Donegal Twp.

29 June 1816   10 Aug. 1816
STONER, CHRISTIAN
    Children: Anna wife of John Steman, Barbara wife of David
Heyd, Catharine wife of David Longenecker and Mary. Bro.: John
Stoner.
    Ex. John Stoner and David Longenecker. Manor Twp.

20 Jan. 1817   8 Feb. 1817
SCHNEIDER, PETER
    Children: Magdalena, Catharine wife of Gerhart Brenner and
Henry.
    Ex. Jacob Witmer. Manor Twp.

27 Aug. 1816   15 Oct. 1816
SCOTT, ROBERT
    Mother: Ann Scott. Bros. & sisters: John, Isabella wife of
George Foster, Archibald, Mathias, Ann and Obadiah Scott.
    Ex. Mathias and Ann Scott. Lancaster Borough.

9 Jan. 1816   5 Aug. 1816
SIDWELL, JOSEPH
    Wife. Rachel Sidwell. Children: Levi, Prudence wife of Abel
Green and Jess.
    Ex. Rachel and Levi Sidwell. West Nottingham, Cecil Co.,
Maryland.

14 Nov. 1814   28 Jan. 1816
STEMAN, TOBIAS

Wife. (name omitted). Child: John. Grandchildren: Tobias, Christian, John and Jacob Steman (sons of John).
Ex. Tobias Steman and Frederick Fehl. Conestoga Twp.

20 Jan. 1817   8 Feb. 1817
SCHNEIDER, PETER
Children: Magdalena wife of --- Brenneman, Catharine wife of Gerhart Brenner, Henry, George and Philip. Grandchildren: Christian and Martin Brenneman.
Ex. Jacob Witmer and Christian Martin. Manor Twp.

20 Aug. 1813   12 April 1817
SEHINECKEL, SOLOME
Children: Mary wife of Casper Shaffner Jr., Elizabeth wife of George Ford and Salome wife of George Nauman.
Ex. Casper Shaffner. Lancaster Borough.

30 Nov. 1813   17 May 1817
STOVER, JOHN
Children: Philip, John, Adam, Benjamin, Elizabeth, Anna, Catharine, Margaret, Susanna, Eve and Barbara.
Ex. Philip and John Stover. Brecknock Twp.

8 July 1817   25 Aug. 1817
SCOTT, JAMES
Wife. Catharine Scott.
Ex. Catharine Scott. Lancaster Borough.

20 June 1816   9 Nov. 1817
STEINMAN, MAGDALENA
Sister: Louisa wife of --- Miller. Bro.: Lorentz Steinman.
Ex. Mathias Tschudy. Lititz Twp.

7 Aug. 1813   1 Dec. 1817
SCOTT, JOHN
Wife. Jane Scott. Children: Nancy wife of John McConnel, Elizabeth and Jane.
Ex. John Hill and Robert Clark. Little Brittain Twp.

10 Feb. 1816   2 Jan. 1818
SHOCK, JACOB
Wife. Esther Shock. Children: Jacob, John, Henry, Abraham, Christian, Joseph, Esther and Anna.
Ex. Jacob and Henry Shock. Manor Twp.

19 March 1817   9 Feb. 1818
SHEIBLEY, HENRY
Wife. Elizabeth Sheibley. Children: Henry, Elizabeth, Nancy wife of David Meyers and Sarah.
Ex. David Bear and David Meyers. Leacocok Twp.

5 Sept. 1813   30 May 1818
SPADE, GEORGE

232

Wife. Anna Maria Spade. Children: Catharine wife of Samuel
Mellinger, Elizabeth wife of Emanuel Meily, Anna wife of John
Mellinger, Susanna, George, John and Christian.
Ex. George Spade and Jacob Hibshman. Cocalico Twp.

15 Dec. 1814   1 June 1818
SMITH, JOHN
Wife. Salome Smith. Children: Henry, Rebecca wife of
Abraham Smith, Mary wife of George Mayer, Elizabeth wife of David
Erb and Susanna wife of Charles Fahnestock.
Ex. Samuel Carpenter, Abraham and Henry Smith. Lancaster
Borough.

16 July 1818   4 Aug. 1818
SMITH, ALEXANDER
Child: Lewis. N.B. There was a bequest of one hundred
dollars to the Roman Catholic Church of Lancaster Borough.
Ex. William Haugey and John Houry. Strasburg Twp.

2 June 1818   17 Aug. 1818
SMOKER, JOHN
Wife. Christiana Smoker. Children: Samuel, Isaac, Maria,
Barbara, Elizabeth, Harriet and John.
Ex. Christiana Smoker and Isaac Eby. Strasburg Twp.

27 Oct. 1813   16 Oct. 1818
SNYDER, EMICK
Wife. Christiana Snyder. Children: John, Polly, and Sally
wife of C. Newman. Grandchildren: Jacob Newman and Rachel Newman
wife of --- Strunk.
Ex. Benjamin Diffenderfer. Earl Twp.

9 Nov. 1817   20 Oct. 1818
SHENCK, JOHN
Wife. Magdalena Shenck. Children: Peter, Christian, John,
Anna wife of John Rohrer and Elizabeth wife of Henry Miller.
Ex. John Stoner and John Shenck. Hempfield Twp.

7 Nov. 1817   19 Jan. 1819
STAUFFER, HENRY
Children: Jacob, Mathias, Daniel, Barbara wife of Jacob
Rechel, Catharine wife of Ludwig Rank, John, Peter and Samuel.
Grandson: David Bealer (parents' names not stated).
Ex. Samuel Stauffer. Earl Twp.

19 Dec. 1806   30 Jan. 1819
SMITH, GEORGE
Wife. Anna Smith. Stepchildren: Mary wife of Martin
Brubacher and Elizabeth wife of Francis Bowman.
Ex. Henry Brenneman and Martin Bear. Strasburg Twp.

21 Aug. 1812   20 March 1819
SHEAFFER, JOHN
Wife. Magdalena Sheaffer. Children: John, Samuel, Susanna
wife of Peter Beck, Magdalena wife of Samuel Cerfoss, Elizabeth

wife of Jacob Miley, Catharine wife of Jacob Martin, Maria wife
of George Kline and Hannah.
    Ex. Magdalena and John Sheaffer. Cocalico Twp.

14 March 1819   23 March 1819
STEINIKE, SAMUEL
    Wife. Ann Steinike. Children: Christina wife of George
Shuster, Samuel, Catharine wife of John Krause and Mary. N.B.
There was a bequest of two hundred dollars to the "Congregation
Deacony" at Lititz.
    Ex. Ann Elizabeth Steinike and John Krauser. Warwick Twp.

12 Nov. 1804   9 April 1819
SENSENIG, JOHN
    Wife. Margaret Sensenig. Bros.: Abraham and Joshua
Sensenig.
    Ex. Christian Zwally and Margaret Sensenig. Earl Twp.

17 Feb. 1817   15 April 1819
STEMAN, JOHN
    Wife. Barbara Steman. Children: John, Henry, Peter,
Christian, Elizabeth, Barbara wife of Martin Miller, Anna and
Magdalena.
    Ex. Joseph Gochenour. Hempfield Twp.

19 Feb. 1819   26 [?] April 1819
SHAUER, ROSINA
    Children: John, Elizabeth, George, Susanna wife of Peter
Blatenberger, Jacob, Catharine and Henry.
    Ex. Peter Blatenberger. Rapho Twp.

7 April 1819   26 April 1819
SPANGLER, CATHARINE
    Children: John and Susanna wife of David Hain.
    Ex. David Hain. Mt. Joy Twp.

17 April 1819   15 May 1819
SHENK, JOHN
    Wife. Elizabeth Shenk. Children: John and Barbara.
    Ex. John Shenk and Christian Habecker. Manor Twp.

19 Dec. 1809   17 June 1819
SHWAHR, ELIZABETH
    Widow of Christian Shwahr. Children: John, Barbara wife of
John Steman, Elizabeth wife of John Gissy and Ann wife of John
Kauffman.
    Ex. John Shwahr. Hempfield Twp.

21 Aug. 1813   7 June 1819
SAUER, PHILIP
    Wife. Barbara Sauer. Children: Catharine wife of Adam
Derstler and Margaret wife of Jacob Wither.
    Ex. Barbara Sauer and Adam Derstler. Manor Twp.

4 July 1819   27 July 1819
SMITH, MARY
    Legatee: John Ortman.
    Ex. John Ortman. York Co.

4 Jan. 1817   15 Nov. 1819
SLOUGH, CHRISTIAN
    Wife. Elizabeth Slough. Child: Isaac.
    Ex. Henry Flickinger. Cocalico Twp.

10 Aug. 1818   20 Dec. 1819
STOFFT, MARY
    Children: Susanna wife of George Roat, Catharine wife of
Philip Shertzer, Mary wife of William Franck, George, Margaret
wife of David Bradey and Jacob. Grandchildren: Jacob, George and
Michael Stofft (sons of Jacob).
    Ex. Jonas Dorwart. Lancaster Borough

11 Nov. 1786   8 Feb. 1788
TEMPLE, ELIZABETH
    Children: William, Mary, Margaret, Jennet and John.
    Ex. John Temple. Colerain Twp.

4 April 1788   10 June 1788
TREISH, LEONARD
    Wife. Margaret Treish. Children: Adam, Barbara wife of
Philip Wolfhiel, Margaret, Catharine, Elizabeth and Michael.
    Ex. Margaret Treish. Cocalico Twp.

7 Aug. 1788   1 April 1789
THOMAN, JOHN
    Wife. (name omitted). Children: Susanna, Elizabeth wife of
--- Lowe and Ann.
    Ex. John Messenkop. Mt. Joy Twp.

8 Aug. 1786   5 July 1789
TROUTMAN, GEORGE
    Legatees: George Eley and the Lutheran Church.
    Ex. George Eley. Earl Twp.

28 March 1789   13 Aug. 1789
TALBOTT, ELIZA
    Sister: Sarah wife of --- Cuthberston. Nephews: Dr. John
and Walter Cuthberston (sons of Sarah). Niece: Sarah Cuthberston
(daughter of Sarah).
    Ex. Dr. John Cuthberston. Bart Twp.

13 April 1773   18 May 1791
TOMPSON, WILLIAM
    Wife. Eleanor Tompson. Children: Nathan, James, Mary wife
of --- Ramsey, Margaret wife of --- Walker, Sarah wife of ---
Longhead, Andrew and Robert.
    Ex. Robert Tompson. Sadsbury Twp.

16 May 1794   12 June 1794
TROUT, PAUL
    Wife. Mary Trout. Children: George, Abraham, Isaac, Jacob,
Paul, David, Hannah and Mary.
    Ex. Mary Trout and Joseph Lefever. Strasburg Twp.

13 June 1796   11 July 1796
TURBETT, SAMUEL
    Wife. Dolly Turbett. Bros.: Thomas and John Turbett.
    Ex. Dolly Turbett and John Moore. Lancaster Borough.

5 July 1792   9 April 1799
THOMPSON, JAMES
    Wife. Agness Thompson. Children: George, Hugh, Margaret
wife of James Johnson, Elizabeth, Mary, John, Sarah and Agness.
Grandson: Patterson Johnson (son of Margaret).
    Ex. Agness, George and Hugh Thompson. Earl Twp.

30 May 1801   26 Sept. 1801
TRUMP, JOHN
    Wife. Margaret Trump. Children: William, Andrew, Samuel,
Barbara wife of Jacob Dussinger, Mary and John.
    Ex. William and Andrew Trump. Warwick Twp.

16 Aug. 1801   10 Feb. 1802
TOMPSON, AGNESS
    Children: Hugh, George, Elizabeth, Mary, John, Agness and
Sarah.
    Ex. Hugh and George Tompson. Earl Twp.

6 April 1799   24 March 1803
THOMAS, JOHN
    Wife. Mary Salome Thomas. Children: Maria, John, Godfried
and Rosina.
    Ex. George Kapp and John Grosch. Warwick Twp.

23 April 1803   15 Oct. 1803
TEPLY, JOHN
    Wife. Elizabeth Teply.
    Ex. Samuel Lefever. Leacock Twp.

9 Oct. 1796   25 June 1804
TANNEBERG, DAVID
    Children: David, Anna wife of William Cassler, Elizabeth
wife of John Shropp and Maria wife of John Philip Bachman.
    Ex. John Shropp, William Cassler and John Philip. Warwick
Twp.

19 July 1805   6 Jan. 1806
TEMPLETON, ANDREW
    Wife. Rosina Templeton. Children: John, Mary, Betsey,
Andrew, Sarah and James.
    Ex. John Neff. Drumore Twp.

3 April 1808   27 Aug. 1808

TEPLEY, ELIZABETH
    Bro.: John Bowman.
    Ex. Benjamin Verner. Leacock Twp.

28 Nov. 1810   15 Jan. 1811
TRITCH, CHARLES
    Wife. Justina Tritch. Children: Magdalena, Catharine,
William, John, Philip and Eve.
    Ex. John Frymeyer and William Tritch. Cocalico Twp.

6 Dec. 1811   20 Feb. 1812
TRIMBLE, WILLIAM
    Wife. Rebecca Trimble. Child: Samuel.
    Ex. Rebecca Trimble and Samuel Pusey. Drumore Twp.

-- Oct. 1813   23 Nov. 1813
TOMPSON, NATHAN
    Wife. Jane Tompson. Children: Miller, Nathan, Rachel and
Ellen.
    Ex. Jane and Miller Tompson. Sadsbury Twp.

31 Dec. 1808   8 March 1814
TWEED, AGNESS
    Children: John, Ann, Grisel, Robert, Agness, Catharine,
Margaret, James, Archibald, William and Joseph. Son-in-law:
Robert Richey (wife's name not given). Grandchildren: John and
Anna Tweed (children of James), Ebenezer and Levi Gumof (parents'
names not given).
    Ex. William Tweed and William Browne. Sadsbury Twp.

--- 1814 19 May 1814
TAYLOR, ISAAC
    Children: Jacob, Samuel, James, Enoch, Jane wife of John
Powell, William, Sarah wife of --- Wilson, Isaac and Joseph.
Grandchildren: Jacob and Phebe Taylor wife of John Sillymon
(children of William). Bulah Wilson (child [of] Sarah, Ann and
Elizabeth Taylor (daughters of Isaac).
    Ex. Ashael Walker and Isaac Walker. Salisbury Twp.

11 March 1810 8 May 1815
TWEED, WILLIAM
    Bro.: James Tweed. Nieces: Elizabeth, Margaret and Ann
Tweed.
    Ex. James Steele and John McGlaughlen. Sadsbury Twp.

18 July 1813   20 Dec. 1815
THOMAS, PHILIP
    Wife. Juliana Thomas.
    Ex. Juliana Thomas. Lancaster Borough.

23 Dec. 1815   30 Dec. 1815
THOMAS, JULIANA
    (Husband) - Philip Thomas. Children: Juliana wife of Jacob
Middlekauff, George and Mary wife of --- Walker.
    Ex. Jacob Middlekauff. Lancaster Borough.

10 April 1811   3 May 1816
TRAGER, JACOB
    Wife. Maria Trager. Children: Elizabeth, Maria wife of
John Gochenower, Ann and Catharine wife of John Barr.
    Ex. John Guchenower and John Barr. Martic Twp.

14 June 1817   15 Sept. 1817
TWEED, JAMES
    Wife. (name omitted). Children: John, Mary wife of ---
Graham, Anna, Elizabeth and Robert.
    Ex. John Tweed and Mary Graham. Sadsbury Twp.

13 May 1818   25 May 1818
TAYLOR, WILLIAM
    Legatee: George Petters.
    Ex. George Petters [Pettero?]. Strasburg Twp.

2 Aug. 1818   28 June 1819
THUMHARDT, GODFRIED
    Wife. Anna Thumhardt. Bro.: John P. Thumhardt.
    Ex. John Levering and Godfried Treager. Lititz Twp.

4 Sept. 1819   27 Oct. 1819
THUMA, JOHN
    Wife. Catharine Thuma. Children: Ann, John, Barbara,
Catharine, Elizabeth, George, Maria, Sarah, Peter and Feronica.
    Ex. David Singer and Catharine Thuma. Warwick Twp.

4 Aug. 1818   6 Dec. 1819
TREISH, ADAM
    Wife. Magdalena Treish. Children: Adam, (there were five
other children - names not given).
    Ex. Henry Hish and Adam Treish. Elizabeth Twp.

8 March 1811   17 April 1811
URBAN, LUDWICK
    Wife. Dorothea Urban. Children: George, Lewis, Joseph,
John, Philip, Jacob and Elizabeth wife of Michael Shuman.
    Ex. Samuel Maier and George and Lewis Urban. Conestoga Twp.

16 Oct. 1800   13 Nov. 1803
VINEGAR, CHRISTIAN
    Wife. Anna Maria Vinegar. Children: Christian, David,
George, John and Elizabeth.
    Ex. Jacob Long. Maytown Twp.

24 May 1802   29 Aug. 1802
VINEGAR, DAVID
    Wife. (name omitted). Children: Susanna and Mary.
    Ex. Anthony Haines and Christian Nisley. Donegal Twp.

1 Aug. 1804   16 Oct. 1804
VONKENNEN, CATHARINE
    Widow of Balser Vonkennen. Children: Barbara wife of
Michael Forney, Hannah wife of Enoch Abraham, Margaret wife of

238

(name omitted), Catharine wife of Andrew Shower and Jacob. Bro.:
Michael Withers.
Ex. Michael Withers. Leacock Twp.

29 March 1810   4 Dec. 1810
VENEGER, ANNE MARIA
[The will is signed WENEGER.) Children: George, Andrew,
John and Jacob Peterman, Catharine wife of --- Lefever, Rachel
wife of ---- Strominger, Ann wife of --- Millhoofe and Elizabeth
wife of David Henderson. Stepson: David Weneger. Grandson:
Jacob Hollinger (parents' names not given).
Ex. Jacob Hollinger. Twp. omitted.

10 March 1810   27 Dec. 1811
VOGAN, THOMAS
Wife. Margaret Vogan. Stepchildren: Joseph, William, James
and Mary Russel.
Ex. Margaret Vogan and Philip Heitshu. Lancaster Twp.

26 Dec. 1811   18 May 1813
VOGHT, CHRISTIAN
Legatee: Jacob Strein.
Ex. Jacob Strein. Lancaster Twp.

2 April 1785   13 Jan. 1786
WHITE, JANE
Widow of William White. Children: Alexander and Joseph.
Ex. Alexander and Joseph White. Strasburg Twp.

22 Nov. 1785   7 March 1786
WHOLGEMUTH, ABRAHAM
Wife. Elizabeth Wholgemuth. Children: Henry, Christian,
Abraham, Mary, Barbara and Salome.
Ex. Abraham Sherer and Abraham Gisch. Mt. Joy Twp.

6 Sept. 1786   17 Nov. 1786
WENGER, STEPHEN
Wife. Anna Wenger. Children: Christian, Henry, Stephen and
Ann.
Ex. Christian Wenger and Peter Foox. Rapho Twp.

6 June 1787   7 July 1787
WERNER, WILLIAM
Wife. Anna Mary Werner. Children: Frederick, Anna, Mary,
Elizabeth, Rosina, Nathaniel, John, Mathias, Ludwick and
Wilhelmina.
Ex. William Cassler and John Recksecker. Warwick Twp.

5 Sept. 1787   3 Oct. 1787
WEAVER, HENRY
Father: George Weaver. Wife. Elizabeth Weaver. Children:
Henry, Christian, Benjamin, Mary, Elizabeth and Ann.
Ex. Henry Martin and Henry Weaver. Earl Twp.

1 Aug. 1787   12 Oct. 1787

WENGER, JOSEPH
    Wife. Mary Wenger. Children: John, Elizabeth, Ann, Mary
and Barbara, Catharine, Susanna, Salome and Jacob. Son-in-law:
Christian Hernly (wife's name not given).
    Ex. John Wenger and Christian Hernley [?]. Cocalico Twp.

3 Jan. 1788   5 Jan. 1788
WAGGONER, HENRY
    Children: George and Barbara. N.B. There was a bequest of
ten pounds to the Lutheran Church in Lancaster Borough.
    Ex. Michael App. Lancaster Borough.

12 Jan. 1788   5 March 1788
WHARRY, THOMAS
    Wife. Martha Wharry. Children: James, Thomas, Mary wife of
Robert Steven, Sarah wife of Robert McCullough, Jean wife of John
Pegan and Martha wife of Benjamin Winter.
    Ex. James and Thomas Wharry. Martic Twp.

29 Jan. 1788   2 July 1788
WEIMAN, GEORGE
    Children: Jacob, George, Agness wife of --- Yuncker and
Maria wife of --- Bernhard.
    Ex. Jacob and George Weiman. Elizabeth Twp.

29 Jan. 1787   28 April 1788
WEAVER, CHRISTOPHER
    Wife. Maria Weaver. Child: Christopher. Stepchildren:
Adam Hostetter, Christiana wife of George Finfrock and Margaret
wife of Christopher Weaver. Grandson: John Weaver (name of
parents omitted).
    Ex. Christopher Weaver. Leacock Twp.

12 June 1787   8 July 1788
WOLFFSKEIL, HENRY
    Wife. Catharine Wolffskiel. Child: Kilian. Grandchild:
Margaret (daughter of Kilian).
    Ex. Joseph Heafly and Wendel Hilsman. Earl Twp.

26 Sept. 1786   4 Feb. 1789
WOLF, REGINA
    Widow of Andrew Wolf. Children: Andrew, George, Jacob,
Henry, Leonard, Valentine, Nicholas, Michael, Regina and Abraham.
    Ex. Nicholas Wolf. Cocalico Twp.

20 Feb. 1787   12 Aug. 1789
WHISTLER, JACOB
    Wife. Anna Whistler. Children: Christian, Magdalena wife
of Joseph Mosser, Elizabeth wife of Mathias Miller. Bro.:
Richard Whistler.
    Ex. Joseph Mosser, Richard and Christian Whistler. Manor
Twp.

27 Aug. 1789   13 Oct. 1789
WITMER, MICHAEL

Wife. Anna Witmer. Children: John, Abraham and Herman.
Son-in-law: Joseph Eberle (wife's name not given).
Ex. Herman Witmer, Jacob Eberle and Jacob Frantz. Manor
Twp.

(omitted) 1790 21 June 1790
WENGER, EVE
Children: Magdalena, John, Christian, Mary, Eve, Michael,
Elizabeth, Joseph and Henry.
Ex. John Wenger. Earl Twp.

5 Jan. 1779   9 Aug. 1790
WOODS, THOMAS
Wife. Mary Woods. Children: David, Thomas, Martha, Jane
wife of Thomas Stewart, Sarah, Rebecca, Margaret, Adam, Mary,
John and Hannah. Bro.: Adam Woods.
Ex. Mary and (brother) Adam Woods. Leacock Twp.

1 June 1790   12 Oct. 1790
WEIDMAN, JOHN
Children: Mary wife of George Ilick and Catharine wife of
Philip Meinhard.
Ex. Jacob Weidman. Cocalico Twp.

24 June 1790   18 Oct. 1790
WALTER, JOSEPH
Wife. Christina Walter.
Ex. Christina Walter. Lancaster Borough.

7 April 1790   28 July 1791
WILLSON, JOHN
Legatees: The widow and children of James Hutchison, living
in Rapho Twp.
Ex. James Cook and John Whitehill. Donegal Twp.

27 June 1788   28 Dec. 1791
WEAVER, GEORGE
Wife. Maria Elizabeth Weaver. Children: George, Christian
and Margaretta. Son-in-law: John Apple (wife's name omitted).
Ex. Jacob Beck and Jacob Oberle. Cocalico Twp.

25 July 1790   24 Sept. 1791
WERNER, JACOB
Wife. Barbara Werner. Children: Casper, Mary, Elizabeth,
Margaret and Barbara.
Ex. Peter Guckerly and Barbara Werner. Rapho Twp.

19 Oct. 1789   21 March 1792
WEINLAND, CHRISTIAN
Mother: Ann Weinland. Bros. and sisters: John, Jacob,
Catharine, Christian and Elizabeth Weinland.
Ex. Ann Weinland and John Lichty. Twp. omitted.

12 March 1792   14 April 1792
WEINHOLT, NICHOLAS

Wife. Barbara Weinholt. Children: Michael, Margaret, Barbara, Anna, Philip, Peter, Elizabeth and Apolonia.
Ex. Michael and Philip Weinholt. Cocalico Twp.

9 May 1792   8 May 1792 [sic]
WHITE, THOMAS
Wife. Abigail White. Children: John, Mary and Margaret.
Ex. James Glen and John Eckman. Colerain Twp.

6 June 1782   3 April 1792
WEBSTER, WILLIAM
Children: John, Isaac, William, Nathan, Joshua and Rebecca.
Ex. John and Isaac Webster. Little Brittain Twp.

20 Nov. 1784   28 July 1792
WITMER, PETER
Wife. Catharine Witmer. Children: Peter, John, Henry, Abraham, Jacob, David, Daniel, Elizabeth, Magdalena, Mary, Ann, Catharine, Christina, Esther, Barbara, Susanna and Ferena.
Ex. Benjamin Musser and Christian Stouffer. Manot Twp.

5 Dec. 1789   28 Aug. 1792
WARNOCK, JOHN
Wife. Isabella Warnock. Children: Margaret wife of Alexander Reyburn. Grandchildren: John and James Reyburn.
Ex. Alexander Snodgrass, Alexander Scott and Isabella Warnock. Little Brittain Twp.

7 Nov. 1792   6 Dec. 1792
WILLIAMSON, WILLIAM
Wife. Margaret Williamson. Children: John, Samuel, Jean, William, David, Margaret and Mary.
Ex. Margaret Williamson and Robert King. Little Brittain Twp.

4 Nov. 1791   4 March 1793
WITMER, ANN
Widow of Michael Witmer. Children: John, Herman, Abraham, Ann wife of Jacob Everly and Elizabeth wife of Jacob Knop. Grandchild: Jacob Knop.
Ex. Jacob Everly. Manor Twp.

5 Feb. 1793   10 Aug. 1793
WALLACE, WILLIAM
Children: Robert, James, Hannah wife of --- Calhoon, Mary wife of --- Lennegan, Margaret, Josiah, William and Thomas.
Ex. Robert and James Wallace. Leacock Twp.

14 Aug. [no year given] 11 May 1793
WEAVER, JACOB
Wife. Magdalena Weaver. Children: Jacob, John, Elizabeth wife of Jacob Rohrer and Elizabeth [Barbara] wife of Abraham Herr. Grandchildren: John, Jacob, Christian, Martin, Daniel, David, Elizabeth and Mary Rohrer.
Ex. Jacob Hartman. Lampeter Twp.

7 Nov. 1793   23 Nov. 1793
WOODS, ADAM
    Wife. Margaret Woods. Bros.: David, Thomas and Adam.
Nephews: David Woods and John Scott. Sister: Janet wife of ---
Stewart.
    Ex. (nephews) David Woods and John Scott. Leacock Twp.

22 July 1793   10 Aug. 1793
WENGER, MICHAEL
    Children: Joseph, Jacob and Christian, (there were two
others, names not given).
    Ex. Henry Martin and Jabaez Shuh. Twp. omitted.

13 Aug. 1793   21 Feb. 1794
WALLACE, ROBERT
    Wife. Martha Wallace. Children: William, Thomas, James,
Isaac and John.
    Ex. Isaac McCommon and Isaac Davis. Earl Twp.

24 Jan. 1793   30 Jan. 1794
WOHLFART, GEORGE
    Children: Peter, John and Maria wife of David Reiff.
Stepchildren: Barbara wife of Peter Wohlfart and Elizabeth wife
of John Eberly.
    Ex. David Bruecker. Cocalico Twp.

7 Jan. 1793   12 April 1794
WRIGHT, WILLIAM
    Wife. Elizabeth Wright. Children: John, Mary, Benjamin,
Elizabeth, James, Ann and William.
    Ex. Elizabeth Wright and Benjamin Musser. Manor Twp.

30 May 1785   2 July 1794
WERNTZ, GEORGE
    Children: Valentine, Philip, Conrad, Jacob, John, Daniel,
Magdalena, Martin and Ann.
    Ex. Valentine Werntz. Earl Twp.

---   28 May 1794
WOLGEMUTH, ELIZABETH
    This is a German will and the translation lost.

20 March 1777   10 Dec. 1794
WEIDMAN, CHRISTOPHER
    Wife. Anna Maria Weidman. Children: Christopher, John,
Catharine and Anna.
    Ex. Christopher and John Weidman. Cocalico Twp.

9 April 1790   13 Nov. 1794
WITMER, JOHN
    Children: Benjamin, John, Abraham, Henry, David, Annale wife
of John Kendig and Daniel.
    Ex. Benjamin and Henry Witmer. Lampeter Twp.

8 May 1794   9 Oct. 1794
WEILAND, CHRISTIAN
    Wife. Anne Weiland. Children: John, Christina and Susanna.
Ex. Jacob Eberlie. Cocalico Twp.

13 Feb. 1795   17 Nov. 1795
WILHELM, JACOB
    Wife. Elizabeth Wilhelm. Children: Jacob, Adam, Barbara
and Catharine.
    Ex. Elizabeth Wilhelm, Michael and Jacob Haberstick.
Lancaster Borough.

4 Sept. 1792   --- 1795
WISSLER, CHRISTIAN
    Wife. Barbara Wissler. Children: Barbara wife of Joseph
Flickinger, Ann wife of Samuel Overholser, Mary wife of Jacob
Over and Magdalena wife of John Musser.
    Ex. Samuel Overholser and John Musser. Warwick Twp.

6 Jan. 1795   7 Feb. 1795
WIDDER, GEORGE
    Wife. Ann Widder. Children: George, Henry, John, Jacob,
Susanna, Ann, Elizabeth, Mary and Sarah.
    Ex. Ann Widder. Earl Twp.

16 Jan. 1795   12 Feb. 1795
WOLFESBARGER, FREDERICK
    Wife. Elizabeth Wolfesbarger. Children: John, Frederick,
George, Philip and Elizabeth. Bro.: George Wolfesbarger.
    Ex. George Wolfesbarger and George Weinman. Elizabeth Twp.

19 Dec. 1789   7 April 1795
WOLFINGTON, ELEANOR
    Child: Margaret.
    Ex. James Bigham and James Greer. Drumore Twp.

15 Jan. 1796   20 Feb. 1796
WEIDEL, JOHN
    Wife. Ann Weidel. Children: Margaret, Magdalena, John,
Elizabeth, Sophia and Adam. Friend: Frederick Weidel.
    Ex. Ann Weidel and Frederick Weidel. Lancaster Borough.

30 Jan. 1791   22 March 1796
WILSON, JAMES
    Wife. Elizabeth Wilson. Children: Ann wife of Samuel
Hathorn, James and Samuel. Grandchildren: Agness, Elizabeth,
Margaret, John, Mary, Ann, Samuel, Sarah and Abigail Hathorn.
    Ex. Elizabeth and Samuel Wilson. Bart Twp.

20 April 1797   22 May 1797
WHITESIDE, ABRAHAM
    Wife. Rebecca Whiteside. Children: Hannah, Mary wife of
James Cannon, Isabella, John, Thomas and William. Son-in-law:
Samuel Neiper (the name of wife omitted). Bro.: Thomas
Whiteside.

Ex. Samuel Neiper and Adam Black. Little Brittain Twp.

1 July 1797   19 July 1797
WEITZEL, JACOB
    Bro.: George Weitzel.
    Ex. George Weitzel. Lancaster Borough.

7 July 1795   16 Feb. 1798
WISLER, RUDOLPH
    Wife. Catherine Wisler. Children: Jacob, Magdalena wife of
Benjamin Hostetter and Catharine.
    Ex. Jacob Wisler and Benjamin Hostetter. Manor Twp.

18 Aug. 1795   22 March 1798
WANNER, JOHN
    Children: Jacob, Henry, Tobias, John, Mary wife of --- Eby
and Ann wife of --- Wenger.
    Ex. Tobias and John Wanner. Lampeter Twp.

3 Jan. 1798   2 Oct. 1798
WALKER, JOHN
    Children: John, Hannah, Joseph, Andrew, Sarah, Ann, Rebecca
and Martha. Grandchildren: John and Joseph Walker (parents'
names not given).
    Ex. Joseph and Andrew Walker. Colerain Twp.

17 March 1798   26 March 1798
WHITE, FREDERICK
    Wife. Susanna White. Child: Frederick.
    Ex. Susanna White and Jacob Carns. Strasburg Twp.

26 Jan. 1789   28 Feb. 1798
WALTER, JACOB
    Children: Andrew, Margaret, Magdalena, Peter, Balser,
Barbara, Jacob and Dorothea.
    Ex. Peter and Jacob Walter. Rapho Twp.

(omitted) 14 March 1798
WILSON, SAMUEL
    Mother: Elizabeth Wilson. Sister: Ann wife of S. Hethorn.
Bro.: James Wilson.
    Ex. Samuel Hethorn and Cornelius Collins. Talbot Co.,
Maryland.

1 Nov. 1799   20 Nov. 1799
WOLFKEEL, WILLIAM
    Wife. Elizabeth Wolfheel. Child: John.
    Ex. Elizabeth Wolfkeel. Lancaster Borough.

11 Nov. 1789   20 March 1799
WEBER, GEORGE
    Wife. Elizabeth Weber. Children: George, Adam, Sophia wife
of Abraham Eichert, Henry, Catharine, Elizabeth and Frederick.
    Ex. Jacob and Adam Weber. Earl Twp.

1 Aug. 1789   27 Nov. 1799
WILSON, JOHN
      Wife. Jane Wilson. Children: Margaret wife of --- Hamilton
and Mary wife of --- Peters.
      Ex. John Wilson and Robert Hamilton. Leacock Twp.

(omitted) 20 March 1800
WILSON, SAMUEL
      Mother: Elizabeth Wilson. Bro.: James Wilson. Sister: Ann
wife of Samuel Haethorn.
      Ex. Samuel Haethron and Cornelius Collins. Talbot Co.,
Maryland.

10 June 1795   19 May 1800
WELSH, JAMES
      Legatees: Sarah Evans and children.
      Ex. William Smith. Twp. omitted.

18 Sept. 1798 12 April 1800
WISSLER, CATHARINE
      Widow of Rudolph Wissler. Children: Jacob, Magdalena wife
of Benjamin Hostetter and Catharine wife of Jacob Musser.
      Ex. Benjamin Hostetter. Manor Twp.

19 June 1800   1 Aug. 1800
WALKER, WILLIAM
      Father: James Walker. Bro.: John Walker.
      Ex. John McFarland. Pequea Twp.

16 Oct. 1800   13 Nov. 1800
WINEGAR, CHRISTIAN
      (This should be VINEGAR.) Wife. Anna Maria Vinegar.
Children: Christian, David, George, John and Elizabeth.
      Ex. Jacob Long. Donegal Twp.

1 May 1799   21 Feb. 1800
WENGER, JOHN
      Children: Christian, John, Joseph, Mary wife of Michael
Eberly, Feronica wife of Peter Weaver, Eve wife of Abraham
Martin, Ann wife of Joseph Sassman, Barbara, Elizabeth, Michael,
Feronica wife of Peter Weaver and Eve wife of A. Martin.
      Ex. Christian Wenger and Henry Weaver. Earl Twp.

17 Oct. 1800   20 Nov. 1800
WEISS, GEORGE
      Wife. Margaret Weiss. Children: Christian, George, Jacob,
Catharine wife of John Conner, Elizabeth wife of Thomas Hamilton,
Mary wife of Abraham East and Justina.
      Ex. Margaret Weiss. Lancaster Borough.

17 Dec. 1797   24 May 1800
WISSLER, JACOB
      Wife. Catharine Wissler. Children: Magdalena and John
(there were three other sons, names not given). Son-in-law:
Michael Kapleffer (wife's name not given).

Ex. John Wissler. Donegal Twp.

29 Jan. 1798   10 Aug. 1801
WHARRY, JOHN
    Wife. Jean Wharry. Children: John, Martha wife of ---
Chambers and Mary wife of --- Chambers.
    Ex. James Porter and Samuel McElroy. Drumore Twp.

20 May 1800   11 Feb. 1801
WOODS, MARGARET
    Sister: Sarah Scott. Nieces and nephews: Mary Woods, Martha
Sterret, Jane Stewart, Jane Scott and Thomas Woods (parents'
names not given).
    Ex. Mary Woods and David Woods. Leacock Twp.

9 Sept. 1789   19 Sept. 1801
WATSON, DAVID
    [A negro.] Wife. Elizabeth Watson.
    Ex. Elizabeth Watson. Millersburg Twp.

24 May 1802   11 June 1802
WINEGAR, DAVID
    Wife. (name omitted). Children: Susanna and Mary.
    Ex. Anthony Haines and Christian Nisley. Donegal Twp.

27 July 1799   27 July 1802
WENGER, HENRY
    Children: Christian, Mary, Barbara wife of Peter Bushung,
Eve wife of Joseph Miller, Salome wife of Peter Reidebach, Henry,
Abraham and Adam.
    Ex. Adam Wenger and David Eby. Leacock Twp.

1 Nov. 1800   9 Nov. 1802
WILSON, ELIZABETH
    Child: Ann wife of --- Harthorn.
    Ex. Cornelius Collins. Twp. omitted.

30 Sept. 1800 10 Nov. 1802
WALKER, JOSEPH
    Children: Andrew, John, Isaac, Mary and Rebecca.
Grandchildren: Rebecca and Hannah Walker (children of John).
    Ex. James Patterson and Joseph Walker. Little Brittain Twp.

19 Jan. 1799   3 Dec. 1802
WEAVER, JOHN
    Wife. Feronica Weaver. Children: Samuel, Mary wife of
Christian Yenowine, George, David, Barbara wife of Christian
Zimmerman, Magdalena, Elizabeth wife of Henry Roott, Catharine,
Susanna, Aidda and Anna wife of John Swartz.
    Ex. Christian Zimmerman and David Weaver. Earl Twp.

2 Feb. 1803   14 March 1803
WERFEL, PETER
    Wife. Mary Werfel. Child: Henry. Uncle: Abraham Werfel.
    Ex. Abraham Werfel. Conestoga Twp.

14 Sept. 1802   11 May 1803
WACHTER, GEORGE
     Wife. Catharine Wachter. Children: Frederick, George,
Catharine, John and Elizabeth wife of Peter Elser.
     Ex. Frederick and George Wachter. Cocalico Twp.

28 Aug. 1794   27 Sept. 1803
WEIBRIGHT, ELIZABETH
     Child: Christina wife of John Kremer.
     Ex. John Kremer. Lancaster Borough.

1 Feb. 1804   2 Feb. 1804
WATT, JAMES
     Sisters: Mary wife of Joseph Howard and Nancy Watt.
     Ex. Samuel Bethel. Hempfield Twp.

4 Aug. 1802   30 July 1804
WITMER, MICHAEL
     Wife. Ann Witmer. Children: John, Elizabeth wife of William
Couley, Barbara, Anna and Magdalena.
     Ex. John Erb. Warwick Twp.

20 Feb. 1804   10 March 1804
WISTLER, JACOB
     Wife. Elizabeth Wistler. The names and number of children
not given.
     Ex. John Brenneman and John Stauffer. Manor Twp.

10 Aug. 1797   30 March 1804
WOLF, MICHAEL
     Wife. Elizabeth Wolf. Children: Michael, Elizabeth wife of
John Seiller, John, Susanna, George, Catharine, Samuel, Salome,
Nancy, Polly and Henry.
     Ex. Elizabeth and Michael Wolf. Cocalico Twp.

19 Feb. 1798   9 Oct. 1804
WELSH, PHILIP
     Children: Jacob, Nicholas and Magdalena.
     Ex. Benjamin Hershey. Hempfield Twp.

30 May 1804   7 Nov. 1804
WESTHEFFER, CONRAD
     Wife. Catharine Westheffer. Children: Jacob, Leonhard,
Abraham, Conrad, Godfrey, William, Elizabeth, Catharine wife of -
-- Apple and Sally. Grandchild: Elizabeth Westheffer (child of
Jacob).
     Ex. John Hess and Peter Youngman. Warwick Twp.

9 March 1802   8 June 1804
WISSLER, ANDREW
     Wife. Magdalena Wissler. Children: John and Jacob.
     Ex. John and Jacob Wissler. Warwick Twp.

5 April 1802   9 Oct. 1804
WERFEL, GEORGE

Children: Peter, John, Henry, Abraham. Grandchildren: Christian, John, Barbara, George, Catharine and Jacob Werfel (children of John); Barbara wife of John Duncan Campbell, Adam and Ann Werfel (children of Peter) and George, Jacob, Barbara wife of John Bassert, Esther wife of Joseph Hush and Elizabeth wife of Joseph Hersh (children of Henry Werfel).
Ex. Abraham Werfel and Christian Shenck. Conestoga Twp.

26 Nov. 1799   5 Nov. 1804
WHITEHILL, MARGARET
Children: Elizabeth wife of --- Lyon, Agness wife of --- Crawford, Margaret and Rachel.
Ex. Thomas Lyon and William Crawford. Leacock Twp.

14 Nov. 1805   28 Dec. 1805
WOELFLING, HENRY
Legatees: The children of Dr. John Luther and Jacob Bucks and also the widow of --- Kisselman (living in Philadelphia). N.B. (extract from will) - "I give and bequest to Jacob Bucks' three daughters, each thirteen dollars and thirty three cents, to be paid as soon as a collected, out of my bonds and notes, for the house I owned on Market Street, in the City of Philadephia, which was confiscated in the last Revolutionary War."
Ex. Peter Diller. Earl Twp.

29 March 1802   7 June 1805
WESTENBERGER, CHRISTOPHER
Children: Henry, Samuel, Elizabeth, Susanna and Maria.
Ex. Christian Meyer and Jacob Stees. Cocalico Twp.

28 Oct. 1805   10 Dec. 1805
WILSON, MARY
Bro.: Joseph Wilson. Nieces: Mary Wilson and Olivia wife of --- McCall.
Ex. Samuel Humes. Lancaster Borough.

12 Dec. 1805   31 Dec. 1805
WATSON, DAVID
Wife. Sarah Watson. Children: Nathaniel, John, Jane wife of William Huston, Maria wife of Emes Jefferson, Margaret wife of John Cooper and Samuel. Grandchildren: David Watson (son of John) and Sallie Jefferson.
Ex. John and Nathaniel Watson. Strasburg Twp.

2 Dec. 1804   4 Feb. 1805
WEIDLER, MICHAEL
Wife. Magdalena Weidler. Children: Catharine wife of Samuel Carpenter, Jacob, John, George, Elizabeth wife of George Roland, Polly wife of Martin Meyer, Susanna wife of Jacob Stauffer, Michael, William, Samuel and David.
Ex. Magdalena Weidler and Samuel Carpenter. Leacock Twp.

12 March 1804   5 Nov. 1805
WHITESIDE, THOMAS

Wife. Jean Whiteside. Children: Rebecca wife of ---
McConnel, Mary wife of --- Elder, Martha wife of ---McConnel,
Violet wife of --- McConnell, Elizabeth, John, Abraham and James.
Grandchild: Mary Homes (parents' names not given).
 Ex. Alexander Morrison and James Patterson. Colerain Twp.

5 June 1806 30 June 1806
WARFLE, MARGARET
 Child: George. Grandchildren: Barbara wife of --- Bushart,
Jacob, Susanna wife of Jacob Hersh, Elizabeth wife of Abraham
Hersh and Esther wife of Joseph Hersh (all children of George).
 Ex. Abraham Warfle. Bart Twp.

19 April 1803 28 May 1806
WILE, PETER
 Children: Eve wife of John Gredy, Margaret wife of John
Gerdon, Christian, Catharine wife of Henry Good and Elizabeth
wife of (name omitted).
 Ex. Elizabeth Wile. Lancaster Twp.

5 Dec. 1805 12 April 1806
WISSLER, ANN
 Bros.: John and Henry Wanner. Sisters: Feronica wife of ---
Hollor and Mary wife of --- Eby.
 Ex. Jacob Musser and Henry Wanner. Lampeter Twp.

25 Aug. 1806 --- 1806
WHITE, JULIANA
 Legatee: James Todd.
 Ex. William Park. Twp. omitted.

7 June 1803 28 Nov. 1807
WITMER, JACOB
 Wife. Feronica Witmer. Children: John, Anna wife of ---
Herr, Elizabeth, Jacob, Abraham, Feronica and Magdalena.
Grandchildren: Feronica, Mary, Elizabeth, Abraham, Anna and
Magdalena Herr.
 Ex. John and Jacob Witmer. Manor Twp.

3 Aug. 1807 25 Sept. 1807
WHITESIDE, MARY
 Bro: Samuel Gilchrist. Sister: Eleanor wife of Robert
McMilan.
 Ex. Samuel Gilchrist and Daniel Kenny. Little Brittain Twp.

6 March 1805 12 Aug. 1807
WISSLER, SAMUEL
 Wife. Margaret Wissler. Children: David, Solomon, Jacob,
Elizabeth wife of Andrew Boyer, Ann and Hannah.
 Ex. Solomon Wissler. Manheim Twp.

1 Sept. 1804 6 Feb. 1808
WRIGHT, JAMES
 Wife. Dorothea Wright. Child: Eleanor. Stepchildren:
Elizabeth, Mary, Jacob, Susanna and Ann Wagoner.

Ex. Dorothea Wright and Dr. Albert Dwfresne. Manor Twp.

7 Dec. 1807   28 Jan. 1808
WEIDLER, MICHAEL
    Wife. Elizabeth Weidler. Children: Ann, John and Daniel.
    Ex. Jacob Weidler and Samuel Carpenter. Manheim Twp.

26 Oct. 1808   17 Nov. 1808
WILSON, JANE
    Widow of John Wilson. Children: Robert (there were others,
names not given). Grandchildren: Jane Hamilton, Ann Witmer, Jane
Weaver, Hugh Williams, John and Robert Hamilton.
    Ex. Hugh Wallace and Joseph Brinton. Leacock Twp.

29 Feb. 1808   9 Dec. 1808
WEBSTER, RACHEL
    Children: Isaac, Rebecca and Pamela.
    Ex.Isaac Webster. Little Brittain Twp.

8 Jan. 1807   20 Jan. 1808
WRIGHT, JOHN
    Wife. Elizabeth Wright. Children: Polly wife of John Gross
and Ann.
    Ex. John Gross and Elizabeth Wright. Earl Twp.

22 Feb. 1805   18 Feb. 1809
WHITSON, THOMAS
    Wife. Elizabeth Whitson. Children: Benj., Thomas, Mary wife
of --- Eby, Ann wife of --- Starr, Elizabeth wife of Moses
Brinton, Deborah wife of --- Eby, John, Henry, Margaret and Burt.
    Ex. Thomas Whitson and Levi Pownall. Sadsbury Twp.

5 Aug. 1806   30 March 1810
WHITCRAFT, GEORGE
    Wife. Mary Whitcraft. Children: John, Ann and George.
    Ex. John Huston. Warwick Twp.

13 April 1809   13 April 1810
WITHERS, ELIZABETH
    Bros.: George, John and Michael Withers.
    Ex. Michael and John Withers. Strasburg Twp.

4 April 1808   18 May 1810
WEAVER, CONRAD
    Children: John, Conrad, Barbara wife of --- Luther,
Catharine wife of --- Lester and Elizabeth wife of ---Kreig.
Grandchildren: Conrad Weaver (son of Conrad) and Margaret wife of
John Faust (daughter of Catharine).
    Ex. Dr. Jacob Koenigmacher. Cocalico Twp.

4 May 1810   18 May 1810
WEAVER, ADAM
    Wife. Rosana Weaver. Children: George, Susanna wife of
William Michael, Elizabeth wife of Michael Slagle and Rosanna.
    Ex. William Michael. Lancaster Borough.

29 March 1810   4 Dec. 1810
WENGER, ANN MARIA
     Children: George, Andrew, John and Jacob Peterman and
Catharine wife of --- Lefever, Rachel wife of --- Straminger, Ann
Maria wife of --- Millhoofe and Elizabeth wife of David
Henderson. Stepson: David Wenger. Grandson: Jacob Hollinger
(parents' names not given).
     Ex. Jacob Hollinger. Twp. omitted.

27 Aug. 1808   3 Nov. 1810
WITMER, PETER
     Children: Mary, John, Jacob, Elizabeth and Peter.
     Ex. John Gehman and Michael Eberly. Warwick Twp.

2 Jan. 1804   24 Dec. 1810
WOHLFART, LUDWICK
     Wife. Margaret Wohlfart. Children: Martin, Ludwick, John,
Jacob, Elizabeth wife of John Waechter, Mary wife of Bernard Getz
and Catharine wife of Peter Elser. Grandchildren: David and
Samuel Getz and George and John Elser.
     Ex. Christian Meyer and Adam Brown. Earl Twp.

10 March 1810   27 Dec. 1811
WOGAN, THOMAS
     (Should be VOGAN.) Wife. Margaret Vogan. Stepchildren:
Joseph, William, James and Mary Russel.
     Ex. Margaret Vogan and Philip Heitshu. Lancaster Twp.

1 March 1807   21 Aug. 1811
WHITEHILL, JOHN SANDERSON
     Wife. Mary Whitehill. Children: Samuel, Sarah, John and
George.
     Ex. Samuel Huston. Salisbury Twp.

11 June 1811   21 Aug. 1811
WITMER, JACOB
     Wife. Catharine Witmer. Children: Jacob and Catharine wife
of William Lewis. Friend: Abraham Witmer.
     Ex. Abraham Witmer and Christian Kauffman. Manor Twp.

4 June 1806   29 Nov. 1811
WARDEN, GEORGE
     Wife. Margaret Warden. Children: Robert, William, George,
James, Mary, Elizabeth and Margaret.
     Ex. Robert and William Warden. Little Brittain Twp.

18 June 1806   16 Sept. 1811
WILHELM, CATHARINE
     Widow of Jacob Wilhelm. Children: Barbara, Magdalena,
Esther, Elizabeth, John, Jacob and Catharine.
     Ex. Christian Streite and Jacob Wilhelm. Twp. omitted.

12 May 1810   5 April 1811
WORK, JAMES

Children: Joseph, Mary and Barbara wife of --- Galbraith.
Grandchildren: Rosetta, Jane and Barbara Work (children of
Joseph) and Jane Moore (parents' names not given).
Ex. John Peden and James Maize. Donegal Twp.

5 Jan. 1812   20 Feb. 1812
WILSON, JOHN JR.
Bro. and sister: Ruth and James Wilson.
Ex. James Wilson and David Scott. Drumore Twp.

13 July 1812   25 Aug. 1812
WAY, FAITHRULL
Mother: Hannah Way. Sisters: Amelia, Ann and Matilda Way.
Ex. Hannah and Matilda Way. Bart Twp.

12 Nov. 1812   4 Dec. 1812
WINAUER, HENRY
Children: Elizabeth wife of Frederick Remly, George, Henry,
Jacob, Peter and Dorothea wife of Abraham Gibbs.
Ex. George Winauer and George Matter. Lancaster Borough.

12 Feb. 1812   17 Dec. 1812
WILSON, JOHN
Wife. Ruth Wilson. Children: Margaret, Mary, Jean, Sarah,
Ruth and Josiah. Son-in-law: John Lane (wife's name not stated).
Ex. John Lane. Drumore Twp.

30 March 1811   25 March 1812
WILL, JOHN
Wife. Elizabeth Will. Children: George, Elizabeth and John.
Ex. Elizabeth Will and Jonas Dorwarth. Lancaster Borough.

27 April 1812   15 Aug. 1812
WEINLAND, JOHN
Wife. Maria Weinland. Children: Anna, John, Susanna, Jacob,
Esther, Barbara and Catharine.
Ex. Benjamin Hershey and John Harnly. Hempfield Twp.

26 Dec. 1811   13 Oct 1812
WITMYER, CHRISTIAN
Wife. Elizabeth Witmyer. Children: Jacob, Elizabeth,
George, Joseph, John, Anna, Maria and Samuel.
Ex. David Senger. Warwick Twp.

2 July 1813   10 Aug. 1813
WILLIS, JOSEPH
Wife. Mary Willis. Children: Henry, Mary and George.
Ex. Henry Willis and John Deshong. Earl Twp.

13 April 1811   4 Sept. 1813
WOHLGEMUTH, CHRISTIAN
Wife. Ann Wohlegemuth. Children: David, Feronica, Daniel,
Christian, Elizabeth wife of Jacob Starn, Ann wife of --- Bauman,
Barbara wife of --- Groff and Catharine wife of David Meyer.
Ex. David and Christian Wohlgemuth. Mt. Joy Twp.

10 Feb. 1806   27 Nov. 1813
WITMER, CHRISTIAN
    Wife. Mary Witmer. Children: John, Ann, Abraham and
Christian. Grandchild: Mary Witmer (child of Christian).
    Ex. Christian Nissly and Jacob Hershey. Mt. Joy Twp.

7 March 1814   15 April 1814
WIELAND, MICHAEL
    Wife. Barbara.
    Ex. Barbara Wieland. Earl Twp.

13 May 1812   4 May 1814
WEAVER, JACOB
    Wife. Anna Martha Weaver. Children: Elizabeth wife of John
Clarke, Susanna wife of --- Mathiot, John, George, Margaret wife
of --- Smith and Catharine wife of --- Weaver.
    Ex. Anna Martha and John Weaver. Lancaster Borough.

21 Feb. 1814   16 March 1814
WALKER, JAMES
    Bros.: Joseph and Andrew Walker.
    Ex. Joseph Walker. Colerain Twp.

8 June 1814   25 Aug. 1814
WILLIAMSON, STEWART
    Father: David Williamson. Child: Sallie Maria Williamson.
Bro.: William Williamson. N.B. The estate was in Worcester Co.,
Maryland.
    Ex. William Williamson. Twp. omitted.

30 Dec. 1814   25 Jan. 1815
WYAND, MAGDALENA
    Children: Catharine and Elizabeth. Bro.: Martin Miller.
    Ex. Martin Miller. Lancaster Twp.

21 May 1814   24 Feb. 1815
WIEST, CHRISTIAN
    Wife. Catharine Wiest. Children: John, Jacob, Benjamin,
Daniel, Christian and Samuel.
    Ex. Jacob and Benjamin Wiest. Cocalico Twp.

9 March 1812   11 March 1815
WEIDLER, ELIZABETH
    Widow of John Weidler. Child: Barbara wife of Henry Swope.
    Ex. Adam Wenger. Leacock Twp.

21 March 1803   14 April 1815
WRIGHT, MARY
    Children: Thomas, William, Mary wife of John May and Joseph.
Grandchildren: Ann and Elizabeth Wright (children of William).
    Ex. Thomas Wright. Manor Twp.

29 Oct. 1812   28 April 1815
WOLFARD, MARTIN
    Sister: Elizabeth wife of John Waihler.

Ex. John Waihler and George Elser. Cocalico Twp.

1 Sept. 1815   21 Sept. 1815
WHITEHILL, JOHN
    Children: James, John, George and Margaret wife of ---
Armor. Grandchildren: Samuel, John and George (children of John)
and Sarah Whitehill (parents' names not given).
    Ex. James Whitehill and John Robison. Salisbury Twp.

25 Oct. 1815   22 Nov. 1815
WAGNER, JOHN
    Wife. Mary Wagner. Children: Catharine, Elizabeth, Samuel
and Maria.
    Ex. Emanuel Deyer and Frederick Smith. Manheim Twp.

6 Oct. 1813   22 March 1815
WAGONER, JOHN
    Wife. Barbara Wagoner. Children: Jacob, Elizabeth wife of
Adam Nair, John, Mary wife of Daniel Lehman, Isaac, Catharine,
Susanna, Martin and George.
    Ex. Henry Brackbill, Barbara and Jacob Wagoner. Bart Twp.

2 June 1816   19 June 1816
WADE, JOHN
    Wife. Mary Wade. Children: John, (there were others, their
names and number not given). Bro.: Daniel Wade.
    Ex. Daniel Wade. Strasburg Twp.

6 June 1816   24 Aug. 1816
WISSLER, ELIZABETH
    Children: Rudy, Elizabeth wife of Peter Hestand, Jacob,
John, Catharine and Henry. Bro.: Henry Brenneman.
    Ex. Henry Bremmeman and Rudy Wissler. Manor Twp.

14 Feb. 1814   26 Nov. 1816
WEAVER, CHRISTIAN
    Wife. Anna Weaver. Children: John, Henry, Susanna wife of
Peter Reist, Elizabeth wife of Philip Young and Jacob.
    Ex. John and Henry Weaver. Brecknock Twp.

6 Nov. 1816   26 Nov. 1816
WEIMAR, CHRISTOPHER
    Wife. Catharine Weimer.
    Ex. Christian Huber. Manheim Twp.

--- ---
WITHERS, JOHN
    N.B. All records of this will lost.

29 Dec. 1816   5 Feb. 1817
WADE, CHARLES
    Wife. Catharine Wade. Children: Andrew, John, Elizabeth,
Mary, Jacob, Catharine and Ignatus.
    Ex. Elizabeth Wade and Henry Groce. Elizabeth Twp.

23 Dec. 1812   18 June 1817
WENGER, CHRISTIAN
    Wife. (name omitted). Children: Christian, Samuel, Abraham,
Magdalena and Eve. Grandchildren: John and Samuel Rup (parents'
names not given).
    Ex. Christian and Abraham Wenger. Earl Twp.

10 May 1815   28 Aug. 1817
WEIDLER, MAGDALENA
    Children: George, William, Catharine wife of Samuel
Carpenter, John, Elizabeth wife of George Roland, Susanna wife of
Martin Shreiner, Michael, Samuel, Polly wife of Martin Meyer,
Jacob and David.
    Ex. Samuel Carpenter. Leacock Twp.

7 Dec. 1816   19 July 1817
WITMER, JOHN
    Wife. Fanny Witmer. Children: Henry and Magdalena wife of
Stephen Cornelius.
    Ex. Andrew Kauffman and Jacob Witmer. Manor Twp.

23 Oct. 1717 [sic]   18 Dec. 1817
WHITEHILL, ROBERT
    Bro.: David Whitehill. Sisters: Ann, Abigail, Margaret,
Kitty, Jane and Sarah Whitehill.
    Ex. David Whitehill. Donegal Twp.

30 July 1816   7 Feb. 1818
WEAVER, GEORGE
    Wife. Margaret Weaver. Children: John, Christina wife of
Henry Steiner and wife of --- Wolf and Peter. Grandchildren:
George and Christian Wolf (children of Christina) and George and
Peter Weaver (sons of Peter).
    Ex. George Stober and Peter Martin. Elizabeth Twp.

14 April 1818   11 July 1818
WEIDLER, JACOB
    Wife. Ann Weidler. Children: John, Elizabeth wife of Martin
Gross, Catharine wife of John Graybill and Jacob.
    Ex. John Weidler, Martin Gross and John Graybill. Manheim
Twp.

4 June 1818   28 July 1818
WITMER, ABRAHAM
    Wife. (name omitted). Children: John, Abraham, Polly wife
of John Groff and Elizabeth wife of Patton Ross. Bro.: David
Witmer. Brother-in-law: Christian Herr.
    Ex. David Witmer, Christian Herr and John Neff. Lancaster
Twp.

28 April 1818   1 Sept. 1818
WRIGHT, WILLIAM
    Sisters: Anna wife of --- Huston and Eliza wife of [---] and
Amelia Wright. Uncle: William Wright.
    Ex. William Wright. Columbia Borough.

13 Aug. 1817   19 Sept. 1818
WATSON, NATHANIEL
 Wife. (name omitted). The names and number of children not
given.
 Ex. John Cooper and Andrew Caldwell. Leacock Twp.

1 Aug. 1817   19 April 1819
WAGONER, GEORGE
 Wife. Sarah Wagoner. Sister: Catharine Wagoner.
 Ex. Christian Houser and Jacob Rudisill. Lampeter Twp.

--- 29 Oct. 1819
WEITZEL, MARGARET
 N.B. This is a German will, the original and the translation
are missing. The will has been copied in German on the records.
 Ex. ---.

17 Feb. 1786   5 Aug. 1786
YORDY, ULRICH
 Wife. Magdalena Yordy. Children: Jacob, Mary wife of
Ulerich Shupp, Elizabeth wife of Samuel Plitcher, Feronica wife
of John Thomas and Ulerich.
 Ex. John Thomas and Isaac Hare. Martic Twp.

21 Sept. 1787   6 Feb. 1788
YOUNGBLOOD, NICHOLAS
 Wife. Ann Margaret Youngblood. Children: Daniel, Casper,
Susanna, Ann and Charlotte.
 Ex. George Kapp. Warwick Twp.

13 Jan. 1794   4 Oct. 1796
YOUNG, MARCUS
 Wife. Christiana Young. Children: Mathias, Margaret, Mary
wife of John Graeff and Catharine wife of --- Graeff.
 Ex. Christiana and Mathias Young. Lancaster Borough.

6 Jan. 1797   2 June 1797
YOUNG, JACOB
 Wife. Catharine Young. Children: John, Elizabeth wife of
John Frick and Rebecca wife of Thomas Minshel.
 Ex. Catharine Young and Jacob Frey. Lancaster Borough.

20 Aug. 1800   8 Nov. 1800
YOUNG, CHRISTIANA
 Children: Mathias, Catharine wife of --- Graeff and Mary
wife of John Graeff.
 Ex. Mathias Young. Lancaster Borough.

23 March 1804   30 April 1804
YETTER, MARTIN
 (Should be IETTER.) Wife. Margaret Ietter. Children:
Margaret, Susanna wife of Abraham Andrew, John, Barbara,
Magdalena and Elizabeth. Grandchild: Margaret Andrew wife of ---
Moyer.
 Ex. Margaret Ietter. Manheim Twp.

14 Oct. 1805   19 Oct. 1805
YOUNG, JOHN
     Wife. Mary Young. Child: John.
     Ex. Henry Swentzel and Godlieb Hill. Lancaster Borough.

30 July 1806   30 Aug. 1806
YOUNG, FREDERICK
     N.B. This is a German will and translation missing.
     Ex. John Frantz. Warwick Twp.

16 Feb. 1802   21 Dec. 1809
YUND, MARY
     Children: John, Nicholas, Catharine wife of George Houck,
(and four others, names not given). Son-in-law: Adam Diller.
Grandchildren: Anna Yund (child of John) and Catharine Yund
(child of Nicholas).
     Ex. Adam Diller and Jacob Mohler. Earl Twp.

11 July 1813   24 Aug. 1813
YERLETS, MARY
     Children: Peter and Jacob.
     Ex. Abraham Greider. Lancaster Twp.

9 Aug. 1816   26 Aug. 1816
YOUNG, MATHIAS
     Nieces: Catharine wife of David Barton and Mary wife of
George Musser.
     Ex. David Barton and George Musser. Lancaster Borough.

14 Sept. 1815   4 Nov. 1816
YOST, PHILIP
     Wife. Elizabeth Yost. Children: John, Mary and Frederick.
     Ex. Elizabeth and John Yost. Lancaster Borough.

16 Sept. 1816   27 March 1817
YEATES, JASPER
     Wife. Sarah Yeates. Children: Mary, John, Elizabeth wife of
Redmond Conyngham, Margaret and Catharine. Son-in-law: Charles
Smith (wife's name not stated). Grandchildren: Jasper Yeates
Conyngham (son of Elizabeth) and Jasper Yeates Smith (son of
Charles Smith). Sister: Sarah Ewing. Brother-in-law: Edward
Burd (living in Philadelphia). Nephew: Edward Shippen Burd (son
of Edward Burd).
     Ex. Sarah and John Yeates. Lancaster Borough.

29 Aug. 1818   --- 1818
YOUNG, MARTHA
     Bro.: Benjamin Young.
     Ex. Michael Young. Columbia Borough.

2 March 1811   6 Nov. 1818
YORDY, CHRISTIAN
     Wife. Barbara Yordy. Children: Jacob, Joseph, Christian,
Peter, Daniel, Mary wife of David Binkley, Elizabeth wife of

Christian Hershey and Susanna wife of --- Herr. Grandchildren:
Christian and Abraham Herr.
 Ex. Jacob Yordy and Christian Hershey. Lampeter Twp.

9 Jan. 1786   22 Feb. 1786
ZIMMERMAN, JOHN [alias JOHN CARPENTER]
 Children: Henry, Barbara wife of Henry Martin, Ann wife of
Mathias Springer, Elizabeth wife of Peter Lance, Mary wife of
John Tulce and Esther.
 Ex. Henry Martin and Peter Carpenter. Earl Twp.

6 Oct. 1787   19 Dec. 1787
ZIMMERMAN, ADOLPH
 Wife. Anna Zimmerman. Children: John, Henry, Mary and
Juliana.
 Ex. John Kurtz and John Zimmerman. Cocalico Twp.

30 Oct. 1787   1 Feb. 1788
ZIMMERMAN, CHRISTIAN
 Wife. (name omitted). Children: Christian, Elizabeth,
Barbara, Mary, Catharine, Magdalena and Esther wife of Emanuel
Newswanger.
 Ex. Christian Zimmerman and Emanuel Newswanger. Earl Twp.

11 Feb. 1788   13 April 1788
ZANDERN, ANNA CHRISTINA
 Bro.: Anthony Zandern. Niece: Elizabeth (daughter of
Anthony). N.B. There was a bequest to the choir of single women
in Lititz.
 Ex. David Zannaberger. Lititz Twp.

2 Nov. 1785   7 Oct. 1790
ZIMMERMAN, PETER
 Wife. (second wife) Ann Zimmerman. Children: (of first
wife) Elizabeth, Ann and Barbara. (Child of second wife): Peter.
 Ex. George Wohlfarthan and Christopher Henry. Cocalico Twp.

3 March 1790   6 Nov. 1790
ZIMMERMAN, ANTHONY
 Wife. Mary Zimmerman. Children: Jacob, Cornelius, Andrew,
Mary and Catharine.
 Ex. Jacob and Cornelius Zimmerman. Cocalico Twp.

--- ---
ZWECKER, WENDLE
 This is a German will and translation lost.

6 May 1790   4 Nov. 1791
ZERBEN, JONATHAN
 Wife. Christina Zerben. Bros. and sisters: Michael and
Peter Zerben, Mary wife of --- Hilman and Elizabeth wife of ---
Meanser.
 Ex. Christina Zerben and Adam Miller. Leacock Twp.

15 July 1797   8 June 1801

ZANCK, HENRY
Children: Jacob, Barbara wife of --- Ferree, Elizabeth wife
of Rudolph Haberstick and Catharine wife of George Peters. Bro.-
in-law: Adam Wilhelm.
Ex. George Peters and Adam Wilhelm. Lancaster Borough.

5 Sept. 1810   17 Dec. 1803
ZARTMAN, ALEXANDER
Wife. Magdalena Zartman. Children: Michael, Alexander and
Emanuel.
Ex. Michael and Alexander Zartman. Warwick Twp.

6 Nov. 1806   12 June 1807
ZELLER, ANDREW
Children: (of first wife) Barbara wife of Henry Hamrich, Eve
wife of Soloman Shaeffer, Anna, Maria and Elizabeth; (children of
second wife) Samuel and Molly.
Ex. John Pfoutz. Cocalico Twp.

8 Oct. 1808   20 Oct. 1808
ZEHMER, SOPHIA
Children: Henry, Maria wife of J. Meder, John and Charles.
Ex. John Wien. Lancaster Borough.

8 March 1810   28 May 1810
ZEHMER, HENRY
Wife. Mary Zehmer. Children: Mary wife of Michael
Schreiner, Sophia wife of John Meiley and Catharine. Brother-in-
law: Martin Schreiner.
Ex. Martin Schreiner and George Matter. Lancaster Borough.

20 Oct. 1810   12 Dec. 1810
ZAHM, GEORGE
(Should be SAHM.) Wife. Catharine Sahm. Children: George,
David, John, Jacob, Catharine wife of Conrad Mark and Barbara
wife of Jacob Kettel.
Ex. George and David Sahm. Warwick Twp.

3 Oct. 1815   12 Feb. 1816
ZANCK, JACOB
Wife. Elizabeth Zanck. Nephew: Henry Schwartz (son of
Conrad Schwartz).
Ex. Elizabeth Zanck and Conrad Schwartz. Lancaster Borough.

8 March 1815   24 Aug. 1816
ZIMMERMAN, ANN
Child: Christian. Grandchild: Elizabeth wife of ---
Summerman (daughter of Christian).
Ex. Elizabeth Zimmerman. Cocalico Twp.

BEAR, Abraham, 29, 162; Adam, 30; Alice, 118; Andrew, 8, 25, 28; Ann, 9, 10, 13, 18, 118; Anna, 8, 14, 194; Anne, 26; Barbara, 9, 13, 14, 24, 25, 31; Benjamin, 9, 13, 15, 18, 26, 154; Catharina, 25; Catharine, 23, 29, 31, 154, 187, 205, 206; Christian, 13, 95; Daniel, 31; David, 8, 25, 28, 31, 193, 231; Elizabeth, 8, 9, 14, 25, 28, 29, 31, 95, 118; Esther, 119; Feronica, 25, 31; Freany, 8; George, 54, 119; Hannah, 8; Henry, 9, 13, 25, 26, 29, 30, 31; Jacob, 10, 118; John, 9, 16, 25, 27, 28, 30, 54, 194; Julian, 29; Juliana, 30; Katharine, 15; Lydia, 30; Magdalena, 8, 25, 26; Margaret, 9, 27; Margaretta, 194; Maria, 30; Martin, 8, 9, 13, 14, 25, 26, 202, 232; Mary, 8, 13, 25, 30, 31, 54, 118; Michael, 144; Nancy, 118; Polly, 15; Rudolph, 61; Rudy, 182; Salome, 25; Samuel, 27, 194; Susanna, 29, 31
BEASHORE, John, 8; Mary, 8
BEATY, James, 42; Jean, 42
BECHDOL, John, 2, 126
BECHER, Cathrine, 182; Philip, 182
BECHTOLT, Catharine, 27; John, 23; Magdalena, 23; Mary, 23; Philip, 23; Polly, 23; Samuel, 23; Susanna, 23; William, 23, 27
BECK, Adam, 24, 185; Catharine, 24, 132, 134, 185, 224; Daniel, 24, 123, 185; David, 24, 185; Elizabeth, 24, 185; George, 24, 185; Henry, 24, 185; Jacob, 132, 240; John, 24, 134, 185; Magdalena, 176; Margaret, 24, 185; Martin, 176; Mary, 7; Peter, 24, 185, 195, 232; Samuel, 176; Susanna, 24, 185, 232
BECKER, Barbara, 16, 31; Catharine, 20, 31; Christian, 15, 54; Christiana, 31; Daniel, 31; Elizabeth, 16;

Henry, 16, 20; Jacob, 16, 20; John, 16, 20, 31, 47, 196; Ludwig, 20; Magdalena, 20; Mary, 16; Peter, 16, 20, 54, 227; Philipina, 47; Regina, 16; Salome, 20; Samuel, 31; William, 31
BECKTOL, John, 61
BECKTOLL, John, 2
BEDER, Peter, 214; Susanna, 214
BEEBEL, Daniel, 177; Jacob, 177; Margaret, 177
BEEKER, Andrew, 157
BEEM, Anna, 131; Daniel, 131
BEEMERSDOERFER, Barbara, 9; Elizabeth, 9; George, 9; John, 9; Mary Elizabeth, 9; Salome, 9
BEER, Elizabeth, 14, 15; Peter, 14, 15, 224
BEETY, Jean, 211
BEGHTHOLT, Elizabeth, 6; John, 6; Margaret, 6; Philip, 6
BEHM, Ann, 196; Henry, 196; Mary, 148; Samuel, 148
BEIDLER, Jacob, 9; John, 9
BEILER, Ann, 24; Anna, 17; Barbara, 24; Christian, 17, 24; Frenie, 24; Henry, 24; Jacob, 17, 24; John, 24; Joseph, 24; Lizzy, 24; Magdalena, 24; Maria, 24
BEISEL, Conrad, 49
BEITLER, Ann, 17; John, 17
BELL, Anna, 161; Catharine, 11; John, 11; Robert, 161; Walter, 11
BELLMYER, Leonard, 222; Margaret, 222
BELTZ, Elizabeth, 95; William, 95
BENDER, Ann, 29; Anna, 9; Catharine, 22; David, 22; Eve, 29; George, 29; Isaac, 22; Jacob, 20; John, 9, 20, 22, 29, 94; Joseph, 22; Leonard, 20; Margaret, 29; Mary, 22, 94; Michael, 20, 21, 25, 29, 64, 118, 217; Sarah, 22; Sophia, 118; Susanna, 20, 22
BENNEMAN, George, 30; John, 30; Maria, 30
BENNET, Elizabeth, 20; Henry, 20; Sarah, 20

Simon, 5; Valentine, 5
BRENNEMAN, Abraham, 25, 27;
Adam, 28, 30; Ann, 10, 17,
22, 28, 91, 162; Anna, 19,
229; Barbara, 10, 22, 216;
Benjamin, 27; Catharine, 20,
22; Christian, 17, 18, 22,
142, 226, 231; Cristian, 162;
David, 10; Elizabeth, 10, 22,
28, 68; Esther, 17; Eve, 10;
Feronica, 17, 91; Henry, 10,
11, 20, 22, 25, 27, 28, 61,
68, 101, 222, 232, 254;
Isaac, 10, 17; Jacob, 10, 17,
19, 20, 27, 162, 196; Jenny,
30; John, 10, 19, 22, 25, 28,
30, 56, 216, 229, 247;
Jonathan, 27; Joseph, 30;
Magdalena, 231; Margaret, 10,
27, 28; Martin, 17, 231;
Mary, 17, 20, 22, 25, 28, 68,
222; Mary Feronica, 17;
Melchoir, 10, 20, 22, 30, 68;
Michael, 18; Nancy, 27;
Peter, 10; Rebecca, 30;
Sally, 27; Samuel, 19;
Solomon, 27; Susanna, 22;
Veronica, 60
BRENNER, Adam, 65; Ann, 6;
Anna, 10; Betsey, 25;
Catharine, 6, 10, 25, 65,
230; Christopher, 25, 76;
Elizabeth, 6, 25, 76, 183;
Eva, 224; George, 10, 25;
Gerhart, 10, 230; Jacob, 25,
214; John, 25; John Adam, 25;
Margaret, 10; Peggy, 25;
Philip, 6, 183, 224; Polly,
10, 25; Susanna, 6
BRESSLER, Catharine, 19;
Charlotte, 19; Elizabeth, 19;
Fanny, 19; George, 19;
Harriet, 19; Mary, 19; Peter,
19; Rebecca, 19; Veronica, 19
BRETZ, Andrew, 28; Ann, 28;
Barbara, 28; Catharine, 28;
Elizabeth, 28; Hannah, 28;
Jacob, 28, 218; John, 28;
Magdalena, 28; Margaret, 28;
Maria, 28, 218; Philip, 28;
William, 28
BRICE, James, 178
BRICKER, Anna, 20; Benjamin,
20; Christian, 98, 175;
David, 57, 175; Elizabeth,

175; Jacob, 175; John, 20,
175; Joshua, 20; Magdalena,
57; Mary, 98; Peter, 175;
Samuel, 20
BRIEN, Dorothea, 28; Edward,
28; Henry, 28; John, 28;
Sarah, 28
BRIESIN, William, 32
BRIETENBACH, Paul, 206;
Susanna, 206
BRIGAM, James, 16; Judith, 16;
Margaret, 16
BRIGHT, John, 202; Margaret,
202
BRINEMAN, Henry, 39
BRINTON, Abigail, 6; Elizabeth,
250; Joseph, 6, 250; Mary, 6;
Moses, 6, 250; William, 6
BRINTZEL, George, 13
BRISBEN, David, 24; Elizabeth,
24; Henry, 24; James, 24;
John, 24; Mary, 24; William,
24, 72, 143
BRISBIN, William, 33
BRITZIUS, Catharine, 31;
Elizbeth, 31; Isaac, 31;
Magdalena, 31
BROCKERT, John, 84
BRODHEAD, Daniel, 22
BRONG, Margaret, 30; Philip, 30
BROSEY, Barbara, 19, 184;
Catharine, 19, 184;
Elizabeth, 19, 184; Henry,
19, 184; Jacob, 19; John, 19,
184; Maria, 19, 184
BROTHERTONS, Martha, 129
BROUG, Margaret, 30; Philip, 30
BROWN, Abner, 13; Abraham, 31;
Adam, 43, 251; Agness, 5;
Andrew, 31; Ann, 21; Anna,
13, 14, 137; Archibald, 15;
Catharine, 21, 25; Christiana,
21, 25; Christopher, 137;
David, 21, 165; Elisha, 13;
Elizabeth, 5, 31; Ezra, 13;
Fillah, 13; Frederick, 81;
Isaak, 13; Jacob, 163; James,
5, 14, 31, 150, 160, 185;
Jeremiah, 13, 107, 115; John,
5, 31; Joseph, 31; Joshua,
13, 91; Juliana, 31; Lydy,
13; Margaret, 5, 31, 210;
Maria, 31; Martin, 48; Mary,
5, 12, 13, 14, 31, 48;
Patience, 13; Rachel, 13;

DOSH, Eve, 45; George, 45;
Magdalena, 45
DOUGHERTY, Charles, 222;
Magdalena, 222
DOUGHTERMAN, Christina, 116;
Elizabeth, 116; Frederick,
116; Jacob, 116; Susanna, 116
DOUGHTERTY, Michael, 149
DOUGLASS, George, 56; James,
44; Thomas, 44
DOWNING, Ann, 144; Hannah, 42;
James, 144; Jean, 42;
Margaret, 42, 46; Rachel, 46;
Rebecca, 202; Ruth, 42;
Samuel, 42, 72; Thomas, 42;
William, 42
DOYLE, Elizabeth, 43; John, 43;
Nancy, 43; Prudence, 43;
Thomas, 43
DRAGER, Jacob, 48
DREISH, Adam, 49
DRITCH, Charles, 47
DRUCKENMILLER, Catharine, 46;
Elizabeth, 46; Emanuel, 46;
George, 46; Jacob, 46; John,
46; Lewis, 46
DUBBS, Jacob, 221; Magdalena,
221
DUCK, George, 44; Jacob, 44;
Nicholas, 44
DUFFY, Patrick, 33
DUFRENE, Albert, 116
DUFRINE, Albert, 112
DULL, Conrad, 62
DUNCAN, James, 173
DUNLAP, Margaret, 5; William, 5
DURNBACH, Anna, 203; Jacob, 203
DURNBACK, Jacob, 46; John, 46;
Mary, 46
DUSSINGER, Barbara, 235; Jacob,
235
DUTT, George, 66
DWFRESNE, Albert, 250
DYER, Catharine, 99; Emanuel,
99

-E-

EABY, Eve, 140; Henry, 140
EAGAN, Thomas, 42, 149
EAHBACH, John, 98
EAHLEMAN, Barbara, 136; David,
136
EAKN, David, 57; Elizabeth, 57;
Hannah, 57; John, 57; Kitty,
57; Susanna, 57; William, 57

EALEY, George, 58; John, 58;
Michael, 58
EAST, Abraham, 245; Mary, 245
EASTON, Elizabeth, 136; John,
136
EBERLE, Jacob, 240; Joseph, 240
EBERLIE, Jacob, 243
EBERLY, Abraham, 56; Anna, 55,
56; Barbara, 56, 64;
Catharine, 29; David, 29, 55;
Elizabeth, 55, 57, 242; Eve,
65; Henry, 23, 56, 57, 65;
Jacob, 55, 165, 166; John,
55, 56, 64, 242; Joseph, 55;
Maria, 56; Mary, 245;
Michael, 23, 56, 245, 251;
Samuel, 29, 55, 226; Susanna,
29, 55; Ulrich, 56; Veronica,
56
EBERMAN, Abraham, 53; Dorothea,
55; Elizabeth, 53, 55, 60,
65, 89, 189; Godlieb, 53, 55;
Hannah, 55; Jacob, 53, 55,
65, 89; Jasper, 65; John, 46,
48, 55, 60, 65, 91; Mary, 48,
55; Mathias, 65; May, 53;
Philip, 55; Philipina, 55;
William, 65
EBERSOL, Barbara, 30; Benjamin,
30; David, 168; Gertrut, 168;
Jacob, 72
EBERSOLE, Elizabeth, 14;
Feronica, 143; Jacob, 143;
John, 14, 142
EBY, Abraham, 58, 59; Andrew,
51, 55; Ann, 58, 59, 131;
Anna, 51, 59; Barbara, 51,
58, 123; Benjamin, 25, 51,
55; Catharine, 55; Christian,
49, 51, 54, 55, 59, 175;
Christiana, 54; Daniel, 51,
59; David, 51, 246; Deborah,
250; Elizabeth, 51, 54, 58,
59; Esther, 58, 59; Feronica,
25; Hannah, 51; Isaac, 54,
232; Jacob, 51, 59; John, 9,
25, 29, 51, 54, 55, 58, 59;
Joseph, 51, 59; Magdalena,
51, 58; Margaret, 9; Maria,
58; Martin, 59; Mary, 54, 55,
140, 244, 249, 250; Michael,
19; Moses, 58; Peter, 15, 50,
51, 59, 140, 149, 156;
Rosina, 60; Salome, 25;
Samuel, 51, 58, 123; Susanna,

ENTRICIAN, Samuel, 52
EPPLER, Ann, 54; David, 54;
Maria, 54
ERB, Abraham, 57; Ann, 13, 57;
Barbara, 32, 54, 57, 96;
Catharine, 57, 60; Christian,
13, 57, 220; Daniel, 29, 136;
David, 57, 59, 232;
Elizabeth, 57, 232; Emanuel,
59; Isaac, 57; Jacob, 57, 59,
60; John, 27, 32, 54, 57, 58,
59, 78, 90, 91, 95, 110, 115,
223, 247; Joseph, 54, 57;
Joshua, 58; Judith, 57, 90;
Louisa, 60; Magdalena, 57;
Marai, 57; Maria, 54; Mary,
57, 136; Nancy, 59; Peter,
57, 96, 115; Salome, 58, 60;
Samuel, 57, 58, 59, 60
ERBB, John, 19
ERBY, Peter, 59
ERFORT, Anna, 50; Anna M., 50;
Anthony, 50; Barbara, 50;
Catharine, 50; Dewalt, 50;
Frederick, 50; Henry, 50;
Jacob, 50; John, 50
ERHARD, Ann, 56; Barbara, 56;
Catharine, 50; Christian, 50,
56; Daniel, 57; Elizabeth,
50, 57, 59; Jacob, 50, 56,
57; John, 56; Mary, 50, 56;
Susanna, 59
ERISHMAN, George, 102; Polly,
102
ERISMAN, Abraham, 50;
Christian, 50; Elizabeth, 50;
Esther, 50; Jacob, 50; John,
50; Mary, 50; Ottilia, 50
ERNST, Catharine, 50;
Christiana, 54; Elizabeth,
54; Herman, 50; John, 54;
John F., 54; Margaret, 54;
Maria, 54; William, 54
ERVEN, Margaret, 33, 72;
Samuel, 33, 72; William, 33,
72
ERVINS, David, 52; James, 52;
John, 52
ERWIN, Elizabeth, 59, 106;
George, 59, 106; Jacob, 106;
John, 59, 106; Joseph, 59,
106
ESBEN, David, 56; Lydia, 56
ESHBACH, Andrew, 169;
Elizabeth, 79, 225

ESHLEMAN, Abraham, 53, 54, 55,
56; Adam, 194; Ann, 49, 51,
55, 184; Anna, 49, 53, 56;
Barbara, 49, 51, 53, 56, 84,
146; Benedict, 51, 175;
Benjamin, 49, 97; Catharine,
53, 54, 56, 57, 194;
Christian, 53, 54, 55;
Christiana, 55; David, 49,
51, 55, 56, 146; Elizabeth,
49, 51, 53, 54, 55, 56, 79,
184; Esther, 97; Fanny, 97;
Feronica, 56, 184; Frena, 49;
Henry, 51, 55, 56, 184;
Isaac, 55; Jacob, 51, 53, 56,
57, 79, 84, 184, 216; John,
49, 51, 53, 55, 56, 183, 184;
Margaret, 56; Maria, 54;
Martin, 51, 56, 97; Mary, 49,
55, 56; Nancy, 56; Peter, 53;
Rosina, 54; Samuel, 56;
Susanna, 56; Ulrich, 53, 57
ESPENOHEAD, Daniel, 135;
Elizabeth, 135
ETTER, Abraham, 58; Anna, 33;
Catety, 54; Catharine, 57;
Christian, 33; Christiana,
57; Daniel, 58; Elizabeth,
57, 58; George, 57, 58;
Hannah, 57; Henry, 58; Jacob,
58; Magdalena, 57; Margaret,
54; Mary, 57, 58; Philip, 58;
Sebella, 57; Susanna, 58
EUTENEYER, Anna Maria, 50;
Betsey, 50; Catharine, 50;
Christiana, 50; Jacob, 50;
Polly, 50; Sally, 50; Susy,
50
EVANS, Abner, 56; Amos, 51, 58;
Caleb, 53; Charles, 59;
Christiana, 51, 59; David,
52, 53, 150; Elizabeth, 53,
92; Frances, 130; Jacob, 52;
James, 53; John, 52, 53, 58,
133; Joseph, 92; Joshua, 50,
51, 52, 58; Magdalena, 119;
Margaret, 10, 58; Mary, 52,
53; Nathan, 52, 53; Philip,
51, 58; Rosina, 119; Ruth,
51; Samuel, 130; Sarah, 245;
Susanna, 51; Thomas, 124;
William, 53, 56
EVERHART, Barbara, 1; George, 1
EVERLY, Ann, 241; Jacob, 241
EVERSOHL, Ann, 50; Benjamin,

50; Catharine, 50; Elizabeth, 50; Jacob, 50, 51; John, 50; Magdalena, 50; Maria, 50; Susanna, 50

EVERSOLE, Abraham, 51; Barbara, 194; Christian, 51, 194; Elizabeth, 51; Feronica, 51; Jacob, 51, 164; Peter, 51; Salome, 51; Yost, 51

EVITS, Conrad, 197; Elizabeth, 197

EWE, Anna, 203; John, 203

EWING, Alexander, 41, 49, 56, 178; Elizabeth, 49, 56; Jane, 178; John, 2, 56; Joseph, 150; Joshua, 174; Margaret, 56; Mary, 56; Patrick, 49; Sally, 150; Sarah, 257; Sinclear, 41; William, 2

-F-

FAAS, Adam, 60; David, 60; Elizabeth, 60; Jacob, 60; Peter, 60; Veronica, 60

FAHNESTOCK, Charles, 232; Daniel, 68; Dietrick, 68; Esther, 68; John, 68; Joseph, 68; Margaret, 68; Mary, 68; Peter, 68; Samuel, 68; Susanna, 68, 232

FAHNSTICK, Catharine, 67; Hannah, 67; Henry, 67; Jacob, 67; John, 67; Peter, 49; Rebecca, 67

FAHNSTOCK, Andrew, 65; Ann, 65; Conrad, 65; Dietrich, 165; Elizabeth, 65; Hannah, 65; Margaret, 65; Obed, 65; Peter, 52, 65; Samuel, 65; Sarah, 65

FAHRIM, Jacob, 190

FAINOT, Catharine, 69; Frances, 69; Frederick, 68

FALKNER, Jesse, 42; Ruth, 42

FANNON, Catharine, 62; James, 62; Nancy, 62

FASS, David, 62; Elizabeth, 62; Jacob, 62

FASSNACHT, Margaret, 62; Philip, 62

FAULKNER, Margaret, 171

FAUSSET, Ann, 63; Anna, 63; Charles, 63; Eleanor, 63; Elizabeth, 63; Francis, 63; John, 63; Margaret, 63;

William, 63

FAUST, John, 250; Margaret, 250

FEATHER, Bernhard, 68; Christiana, 68; Elizabeth, 62, 68; George, 66; Gretraut, 62; Hannah, 66; Henry, 66; Juliana, 68; Mary, 68; Peter, 68; Salome, 66; Susanna, 68

FECHTLY, Barbara, 69; Henry, 69; Jacob, 69

FEGLEY, Ann, 62; Barbara, 62; Elizabeth, 62; John, 62; Mary, 62; Paul, 62

FEHL, Catharine, 68; Elizabeth, 68; Frederick, 231; George, 68; Jacob, 68; John, 68; Mary, 68

FEHMER, Henry, 205; Mary, 205

FEILSHU, Philip, 161

FEIT, Abraham, 180; Eve, 180; George, 180; Jacob, 180; John, 180; Peter, 180

FELLER, Elizabeth, 156; Peter, 156

FELTON, Joshua, 222; Susanna, 222

FENSTEMACHER, Magdalena, 65; Philip, 65

FEREE, John, 72

FERGUSON, Andrew, 41; Margaret, 41; William, 41

FERNTZLER, Mary, 65

FERREE, Abraham, 63; Andrew, 63; Ann, 63; Barbara, 259; Daniel, 13; David, 27, 128, 151; Elijah, 64; Elizabeth, 26, 63, 64; Ephraim, 65; Hannah, 63, 212; Isaac, 64, 128; Jacob, 63; James, 63; Jane, 64; Joel, 63, 64, 128; John, 63, 134; Leah, 64; Mary, 27, 63, 128, 134; Peter, 63; Philip, 63; Rachel, 63, 64; Rebecca, 64; Reuben, 64; Richard, 26, 63; Sally, 13; Samuel, 63, 212; Sarah, 44, 64; Tamer, 63; Uriah, 64; William, 63

FETHER, Barbara, 95; Susanna, 95

FETTER, Catharine, 69; Frederick, 69; Jacob, 69; Margaret, 189; Mary, 69; Rebecca, 69; Sophia, 69

FETTERS, Mary, 245

186; Jacob, 64, 67, 183, 186;
Martin, 64, 67, 183, 186;
Michael, 64, 67, 183, 185
FOX, Jacob, 52
FRANCISCUS, Anna, 67;
Catharine, 64, 65, 67;
Charles, 64; Christopher, 67;
Elizabeth, 64; George, 64;
Jacob, 67; John, 64, 67;
Magdalena, 64; Margaret, 64,
67; Rosina, 65; Stophel, 64;
William, 64
FRANCK, Ann, 63; Catharine, 63,
68; Christiana, 63;
Elizabeth, 63, 68; George,
63, 68; Henry, 62; John, 63,
68, 105; Mary, 234; Susanna,
63; William, 234
FRANK, Catharine, 64, 66;
Daniel, 60; David, 66;
Elizabeth, 60, 64, 66;
George, 66; Jacob, 60, 64;
John, 64; Margaret, 60, 66;
Maria, 60; Martin, 66; Molly,
66; Susanna, 64; Valentine,
64
FRANKFASTER, Barbara, 82; John,
82
FRANKHOUSER, Catharine, 66;
Christian, 61, 65, 66; Henry,
27, 66; Jacob, 66; Margaret,
61, 65, 66; Peter, 66, 206;
Susanna, 66
FRANKS, Daniel, 65; Elizabeth,
65; Jacob, 65; Mary, 64
FRANTZ, Adam, 69, 150; Anna,
63; Baltzer, 69; Barbara, 69,
150; Christian, 60, 63, 73,
82, 87, 95, 144, 152, 201;
David, 69; Elizabeth, 60, 69;
Eve, 69; George Adam, 69,
189; Jacob, 11, 27, 60, 63,
240; John, 60, 63, 257;
Maria, 63; Martha, 98;
Martin, 98; Michael, 60
FRANZT, Jacob, 13
FRAZER, Susanna, 41; William
C., 41
FREDERICK, Abraham, 60, 61;
Anna, 61; Anna Maria, 61;
Barbara, 61; Christiana, 80;
Christopher, 61; Elizabeth,
61; Eva, 61; John, 61, 63,
69; Maria, 61; Noah, 61;
Peter, 61; Philip, 61;

Rachel, 61
FREE, Agness, 61; Barbara, 61;
Christiana, 61; Elizabeth,
61; Margaret, 61; Mary, 61;
Peter, 61; Richard, 61
FREENY, Eva, 204; James, 204
FREY, Adam, 65; Anna, 63;
Barbara, 63; Catharine, 65,
69; Christiana, 63; Dorothea,
65; Elizabeth, 65, 69; Eve,
63, 65, 69; Frederick, 65,
67; George, 65, 67, 68;
Henry, 65, 69; Jacob, 65, 67,
68, 69, 256; John, 63, 65,
67, 69; Joseph, 65, 67;
Magdalena, 63, 65; Margaret,
65, 68; Martin, 65; Mary, 65;
Mathias, 63; Peggy, 67;
Peter, 65, 69; Peters, 67;
Rachel, 69; Rechena, 69;
Regina, 65; Rudy, 63;
Susanna, 65; Veronica, 63
FREYMEYER, Catharine, 64;
Elizabeth, 64; Henry, 64;
Jacob, 64; John, 64
FRICK, Abraham, 67, 194; Anna,
67; Anna Maria, 26; Barbara,
67; Christian, 67, 112, 144,
170, 217; Christiana, 194;
Elizabeth, 67, 256;
Frederick, 35; Fronica, 154;
John, 67, 154, 256; Maria, 67
FRINEY, Christian, 175
FRION, Catharine, 133; Jonas,
133
FRISLER, Adam, 198; Catharine,
198; Elizabeth, 198; Emanuel,
198; Maria, 198; Mary, 198;
Rebecca, 198; Susanna, 198
FRITCH, Catharine, 47; Charles,
47; Eve, 47; John, 47;
Justina, 47; Magdalena, 47;
Philip, 47; William, 47
FRITZ, Daniel, 132
FRY, Catharine, 61; Dorothea,
61; Elizabeth, 61; Henry,
161; Jacob, 61; John, 61;
Juliana, 61; Martin, 61, 203;
Peter, 61
FRYE, John, 16; Regina, 16
FRYMEYER, John, 47, 236
FRYMYER, Elizabeth, 62; John,
62
FUCHS, Abraham, 60; Barbara,
60; Catharine, 60; Esther,

Maria, 82; Veronica, 82
GEHR, Elizabeth, 83; George, 83
GEIB, Barbara, 99; Christian,
    99
GEIGER, Bernard, 70
GEIMER, Catharine, 229; David,
    229
GEISTWEID, Magdalena, 11;
    Martin, 11
GEITNER, Elizabeth, 88; Jacob,
    88; John G., 88; Maria, 88;
    Maria Elizabeth, 88; Rosina,
    88; Susan, 88
GELBACK, Anna, 76; Barbara, 76;
    Catharine, 76; Frederick, 76;
    John, 76
GEMSHORN, Adam, 131; Christina,
    131
GENGRICH, Esther, 215; Joseph,
    215
GENRICH, Abraham, 78; Annie,
    78; David, 78; Freny, 78;
    Jacob, 78
GENSEL, Susanna, 132;
    Valentine, 132
GENSEMER, Christiana, 84;
    Daniel, 84; George, 84;
    Henry, 84; Margaret, 84;
    Sophia, 84
GEORGAS, John, 63
GERBER, Abraham, 57, 72; Adam,
    75; Adi, 77; Andrew, 25, 77,
    80, 166, 222, 226; Ann, 72,
    77, 88; Anna, 80, 87; Anne,
    73; Barbara, 72, 88;
    Catharine, 72, 73, 77, 80,
    88; Charles, 88; Christian,
    72, 77, 80, 82, 87;
    Christiana, 73; David, 118;
    Elizabeth, 9, 57, 72, 73, 82,
    88; Elziabeth, 118; Eve, 73;
    Felix, 71, 72; Henry, 9, 82;
    Jacob, 59, 72, 77, 87; John,
    72, 76, 77, 87, 88;
    Magdalena, 88; Mary, 72, 77;
    Michael, 72, 73; Nancy, 59;
    Peter, 76, 88, 118; Philip,
    169; Samuel, 168; Susanna,
    166
GERDON, John, 249; Margaret,
    249
GERHARD, Barbara, 82;
    Catharine, 82; Christian, 82;
    Elizabeth, 82; Frederick, 82;
    Jacob, 82; John, 82; Peter,

82; Susanna, 82; William, 82
GERINGER, Elizabeth, 75; Jacob,
    75
GERMAN, Dorothea, 74;
    Elizabeth, 216; George, 74;
    John, 74, 216
GERNER, Anna, 70; Catharine,
    70, 89; Christiana, 89; Eve,
    70; Frederick, 89; Jacob, 89,
    117; Margaret, 70; Maria, 70;
    Mark, 89; Mathias, 70;
    Michael, 70, 89; Susan, 70;
    Susanna, 117
GERTEL, Anna, 83; Barbara, 83;
    Elizabeth, 83; Margaret, 83
GESSLER, Elizabeth, 88; Henry,
    88; John, 88; Mary, 88;
    Michael, 88
GESSY, Anna, 83; Barbara, 83;
    Christian, 83; Elizabeth, 83;
    John, 83; Joseph, 83; Philip,
    83
GEST, Benjamin, 87; Deborah,
    87; Elizabeth, 87; Hannah,
    87; John, 87; Joseph, 87;
    Margaret, 87
GETNER, George, 190
GETTICH, Christian, 70;
    Elizabeth, 70
GETTINGER, Abraham, 81;
    Barbara, 81
GETZ, Barbara, 79; Bernard,
    251; Catharine, 75, 79;
    Daniel, 75; David, 251;
    Elizabeth, 79; Frederick, 75;
    George, 75; Jacob, 75, 79,
    162; John, 75, 79, 88;
    Juliana, 79; Magdaline, 79;
    Mary, 75, 251; Peter, 75, 79;
    Samuel, 251
GEYER, Andrew, 86; Barbara, 86;
    Catharine, 86; David, 86;
    Elizabeth, 86; George, 86,
    139, 221; Gertrude, 86; J.
    George, 139
GIBBEL, Abraham, 88; Christian,
    88; Christiana, 88; Daniel,
    88; Elizabeth, 88; Henry, 88;
    John, 88; Joseph, 88; Mary,
    88; Salome, 88; Samuel, 88;
    Susanna, 88
GIBBLE, John, 97
GIBBONS, Abraham, 76; Daniel,
    82; Deborah, 82; Elizabeth,
    76; Hannah, 76; James, 82;

HOUSER, Ann, 79; Christian, 21,
130, 256; Jacob, 79; Martin,
79; Reinhart, 200; Susanna,
200
HOUSTON, Samuel, 59
HOWARD, Joseph, 247
HOWARTER, Molly, 227
HOWE, Adam, 69; Catharine, 69
HOWELL, Jehu, 138; Margery, 138
HOWSER, Christian, 25
HOYL, Anna, 103; Catharine,
103; Christina, 103;
Elizabeth, 103; George, 103;
Jacob, 219; John, 103; Mary,
219; Philibina, 103
HOYLE, Barbara, 95; George, 95;
John, 20, 95, 185; Philibina,
95
HUBER, Abraham, 124, 129, 180,
220; Ann, 79, 97, 220; Anna,
90, 92, 93; Barbara, 13, 92,
93, 97, 132; Catharine, 157,
210; Christian, 13, 79, 84,
90, 92, 98, 99, 116, 139,
193, 212, 254; Christina, 90,
132; Daniel, 98; David, 90,
157; Elizabeth, 90, 92, 93,
98, 99, 132; Feronica, 79,
229; George, 15, 79, 169;
Hannah, 99; Henry, 90; Jacob,
58, 90, 92, 97, 99; Johanna,
90; John, 50, 90, 91, 99,
164, 165, 179; Joseph, 90,
98, 116; Margaret, 58;
Martin, 97, 98; Mary, 50, 90,
92, 93, 98, 132, 193;
Michael, 90, 99, 132; Nancy,
99; Peter, 90, 154, 229;
Samuel, 210; Sarah, 99;
Sophia, 99; Susanna, 90, 93,
97, 98; Thoretha, 192;
Veronica, 98
HUBERT, Gertraut, 100
HUBLEY, Adam, 91, 92; Ann, 91;
Barbara, 91; Bernard, 91;
Charles, 91; Eliza, 91;
Elizabeth, 91, 92; Frederick,
91; Hannah, 91; Isaac, 91;
Jacob, 91; John, 6, 26, 92,
126; Magdalena, 91; Mary, 91,
126, 186; Michael, 91, 92;
Rosenna, 92; Sabina, 92;
Samuel, 91; Sarah, 91;
Sophia, 91; William, 91
HUCHINSON, Robert, 37

HUCKY, John, 76; Salome, 76
HUELL, Barbara, 105
HUFFNAGLE, Catharine, 96;
Elizabeth, 96; George, 96;
Magdalena, 96; Michael, 96;
Peter, 96
HUMES, Agness, 39; Elizabeth,
95; Elziabeth, 52; Hamilton,
95; James, 39, 82; Mary, 95;
Michael, 52; Samuel, 52, 95,
129, 248
HUMMER, Abraham, 97; Barbara,
132; Catharine, 97;
Elizabeth, 97; Feronica, 97;
Froney, 97; Jacob, 97, 99;
John, 97; Mary, 97; Michael,
97, 99; Peter, 132; Rachel,
97, 99; Sarah, 97
HUMPHREYS, George, 132
HUMRICH, Christian, 115
HUNTER, Agness, 139; George,
139
HUNTSPERGER, Abraham, 73;
Feronica, 73
HURST, Christian, 88, 147, 188;
Elizabeth, 135; Jacob, 135;
John, 92; Joseph, 92;
Michael, 92
HUSH, Esther, 248; Joseph, 248
HUSHAR, Anna, 202; Henry, 202;
Joseph, 202; Pater, 202
HUSTON, Anna, 255; Jane, 248;
John, 34, 58, 250; Samuel,
251; William, 248
HUTCHINSON, Joseph, 39
HUTCHISON, James, 240
HUTENBEECHER, Clement, 67
HUTTENSTEIN, Henry, 97; Jacob,
97; William, 97
HUTTON, Mary, 132
HYDE, Elizabeth, 95; George, 95

-I-

IETTER, Barbara, 256;
Elizabeth, 256; John, 256;
Magdalena, 256; Margaret,
256; Martin, 256; Susanna,
256
IHLING, Catharine, 106;
Christopher, 106; George,
106; John, 106; Magdalena,
106; Mary, 106; William, 106
ILICK, George, 240; Mary, 240
ILLAYG, Jacob, 166
ILLIG, Barbara, 106; Catharine,

Catharine, 132, 134;
Christian, 131, 132;
Christina, 132, 134;
Elizabeth, 48; John, 48, 132,
207, 248
LUTMAN, Esther, 128; Jacob, 128
LUTTMAN, Elizabeth, 124, 125;
George, 124; Jacob, 124;
John, 124, 125; Margaretta,
124; Mary, 124
LUTZ, Abraham, 128; Ann, 18;
Bernard, 18; Casper, 125,
127, 128; Catharine, 125,
127, 128, 227; Christian,
127; Elizabeth, 6, 122, 125,
128, 131; Eve, 125; George,
125; Henry, 127, 128, 136;
John, 127, 128; Magdalena,
127; Margaret, 127, 128, 131;
Maria, 131; Martin, 131;
Mary, 127, 131; Nicholas, 6,
55, 122, 128, 131; Peter,
127; Philip, 128, 227;
Stephen, 126; Stevens, 127
LUTZENBERGER, Adam, 133;
Francis, 133; Hannah, 133;
Mary, 133
LYLE, Benjamin, 203; Froney,
203
LYNE, John, 213
LYON, Elizabeth, 71, 248; John,
71; Thomas, 38, 242
LYONS, Isaiah, 129; James, 129;
Jane, 129; Margaret, 129;
Mary, 45; Thomas, 45
LYTLE, Hannah, 127; Ruth, 127;
Thomas, 127; William, 127

-M-

MCANTIER, Elizabeth, 146;
Isabella, 146; Martha, 146;
Mary, 146; Samuel, 146;
William, 146
MCANTIRE, Isabella, 192
MCCALL, John, 149; Olivia, 248
MCCALLAN, Thomas, 6
MCCALLEY, James, 146; John,
146; Mary, 146
MCCALLY, John, 34; Sarah, 34
MCCALMONT, Ann, 144; James,
144; Jean, 144; Martha, 144;
Mary, 144; Rachel, 144;
Robert, 38, 144; Samuel, 144
MCCAMANT, Alexander, 151, 153;
Elihu, 151, 153; Isaac, 151,

153; Mary, 151; Sarah, 151
MCCAMMOND, Elihu, 163; Isaac,
163; Mary, 163; Rebecca, 163;
Sarah, 163
MCCANN, Bernard, 157
MCCARNOUT, James, 191
MCCARTER, Moses, 173
MCCARTNEY, Andrew, 140; George,
140; Margaret, 140; Rebecca,
140
MCCAY, John, 42; Mary, 146
MCCLAIN, John, 138; Moses, 138
MCCLEARY, William, 5
MCCLEERY, Eals, 157; James,
145, 157; Jennet, 145; John,
145; Joseph, 145; Martha,
145; Mary, 145
MCCLELLAN, James, 150; Jean,
150; Katharine, 150; Martha,
150; Polly, 150; Sally, 150;
Samuel, 150
MCCLOUD, Alexander, 156;
Elizabeth, 156; John, 94;
Peggy, 94
MCCLOUGHIN, Alexander, 144;
Boyd, 144; Daniel, 144; Mary,
144; Neal, 144
MCCLOY, Neal, 22
MCCLUNG, Charles, 145, 146,
159; Elizabeth, 145, 159;
Hugh, 145, 146, 159; Jane,
145, 159; Martha, 145, 146;
Matthew, 145, 146
MCCLURE, Agness, 6; David, 43;
Elizabeth, 6, 43, 150;
Grizel, 6; James, 146, 150;
Jean, 146; John, 6, 141, 146,
150, 185, 188; Margaret, 141;
Moses, 6; Rendal, 141;
Robert, 6, 143, 150; Sarah,
143, 146; Thomas, 6, 143,
146; William, 141, 146, 150,
169
MCCOMMON, Isaac, 242
MCCOMPSEY, Mary, 218
MCCONEL, John, 3
MCCONNAL, Daniel, 144; David,
144; Elizabeth, 144; Hugh,
144; Martha, 144; Mary, 144;
Samuel, 144
MCCONNEL, John, 231; Martha,
249; Nancy, 231; Rebecca,
249; Violet, 249
MCCONNELS, Daniel, 10; Martha,
10

MCCOOL, Elizabeth, 78
MCCORD, Isabella, 224
MCCORKLE, Bentin, 169;
Catharine, 169; Sarah, 226
MCCORNNEL, Daniel, 169; John,
169
MCCOSLAND, Thomas, 190
MCCRABB, David, 16; Henry, 16;
Judith, 16
MCCRACKEN, John, 174
MCCREADY, Agness, 160; Annias,
160; Archibald, 160;
Elizabeth, 160; James, 160;
Margaret, 160; Martha, 160;
Mary, 160; Sarah, 160
MCCREARY, Elizabeth, 160;
James, 160; John, 160;
Joseph, 33, 160; Margaret,
160; Mary, 160; Rebecca, 160;
William, 160
MCCRERY, Joseph, 178
MCCULLEY, Archibald, 147;
Francis, 147; James, 147;
Thomas, 147
MCCULLOUGH, Ann, 162; Bella,
150; Betsey, 150; Catharine,
147, 162; Eleanor, 150, 162;
Elizabeth, 147, 162; George,
150; Hugh, 2, 147, 162;
Isaac, 147, 162; Isabella,
150; James, 147, 162; Jane,
150; John, 147, 162, 182;
Margaret, 147, 150, 162;
Mary, 147, 150, 162; Robert,
150, 239; Sampson, 150;
Sarah, 239; William, 150
MCCULLY, Elizabeth, 145; Fanny,
145; James, 145; Margaret,
145; Thomas, 145; William,
145
MCCURDY, Adam, 143; Archibald,
143; Hannah, 143, 163; Mary,
33, 37; Robert, 33, 72;
Watson, 185; William, 33
MCDERMIT, Archibald, 139;
Daniel, 139; David, 139;
John, 139; Joseph, 139; Mary,
139; Nancy, 139
MCDILL, Catharine, 152;
Elizabeth, 143; George, 143,
152; Hugh, 152; Isaac, 143;
Jacob, 152; James, 143, 152;
Jane, 152; Margaret, 152;
Mary, 143; Nancy, 143
MCDOWEL, John, 176

MCELROY, Elizabeth, 147;
George, 147; John, 147;
Margaret, 147; Samuel, 147,
193, 246
MCENALLY, Bernard, 147;
Elizabeth, 147
MCENELLY, Elizabeth, 155
MCFARLAND, James, 141; Jean,
141; John, 245; Margaret,
151; Samuel, 141
MCFARLIN, James, 155; Jean,
155; Margaret, 155; Samuel,
155
MCFUSON, Alexander, 134
MCGEE, Mary, 211
MCGIRR, James, 146; Margaret,
146; Nathaniel, 146
MCGLAUGHLEN, John, 236
MCGRANN, Hugh, 62
MCGROURTY, Catharine, 149;
Charles, 149; Frances, 149;
John, 149; Mary, 149
MCILVAIN, Elizabeth, 151, 153;
George, 151; Jean, 151;
Jennet, 95; Mary, 151;
Rebecca, 151; Robert, 151,
160, 171
MCINTIRE, Dinah, 162
MCKEAN, Elizabeth, 139; Hugh,
139; James, 139; Mary, 139;
Robert, 139; William, 139
MCKEE, Thomas, 173
MCKENNEY, David, 151; Esther,
151; Mary, 151; Samuel, 151
MCKENNY, George, 22
MCKESSECK, John, 153
MACKEY, James, 76; Sarah, 160;
Thomas, 160
MCKINEY, Joseph, 174
MCKINNEY, Agness, 139; Daniel,
149; Elizabeth, 139; James,
139; Jane, 149; John, 149;
Rosanna, 139; Samuel, 139
MCKNAUGHTON, Thomas, 128
MCKOWN, Elizabeth, 142;
Isabella, 142; Jane, 161;
Jean, 142; John, 161; Malcom,
142; Margaret, 142; Mary,
142, 161; Moses, 142; Samuel,
161; William, 142, 161
MACKY, John, 12; Martha, 12
MCLAUGHLIN, George, 110, 157;
Isabella, 141; James, 141,
153, 157; Jean, 153; John,
153; Margaret, 141; Mary,

Christopher, 169
OBER, Ann, 170; Barbara, 17;
  Benjamin, 32; Catharine, 170;
  171; Christian, 17, 123, 171;
  David, 132; Gungel, 32;
  Henry, 206; Jacob, 170; Mary,
  132; Michael, 170, 171
OBERHOLTZER, Anne, 169;
  Barbara, 169; Christian, 169;
  John, 82; Molly, 169
OBERLANDER, Peter, 169
OBERLE, Jacob, 240
OBERLIN, Adam, 49, 169, 171;
  Anna, 101, 169, 171;
  Catharine, 169; Christian,
  171; Christina, 169;
  Christina Barbara, 169;
  Elizabeth, 169; George, 171;
  Jacob, 101, 169, 171; John,
  171; Margaret, 169; Michael,
  169, 171, 222; Rebecca, 169;
  Susanna, 171
OBERLY, Adam, 153, 162;
  Catharine, 153; Christiana,
  162
OBERNOLTZER, Martin, 53
OBERSTEG, Abraham, 168;
  Benjamin, 169; John, 169
OBITZ, Charles, 159; Margaret,
  159
OBLINGER, Christian, 170
OCKER, Ann, 2; Barbara, 2;
  Casper, 2; Esther, 2; Henry,
  2; Jacob, 2; Martha, 2;
  Peter, 2
ODENWALT, Catharine, 169;
  Christian, 169, 170;
  Christina, 169; Elizabeth,
  169, 170; George, 169; John,
  169; Maria, 169
OESTERLEIN, Daniel, 45, 46;
  Elizabeth, 45, 46
OFFNER, Barbara, 168;
  Catharine, 168; John, 168;
  Martin, 168; Mathias, 168
OKELY, Elizabeth, 170; John,
  170
OLD, James, 34
OLIFANT, Charles, 169; John,
  169
OLWEILER, Barbara, 171;
  Catharine, 171; Elizabeth,
  171; Frederick, 171; George,
  171; Jacob, 171; Leonard,
  171; Mary, 171; Philip, 171

OLWILLER, Anna, 170; Elizabeth,
  170; Jacob, 170; Philip, 170
OMBY, Christian, 18, 184
OMOBERSTEG, Abraham, 168
ONEAL, Charles, 3; Margaret, 3
ONEIL, Charles, 169; Elizabeth,
  169; Prudence, 169; William,
  169
OPERMAN, Ernst, 179
ORNBY, Christian, 18
ORR, Joshua, 171; Robert, 171;
  Thomas, 171
ORTH, Barbara, 170; Catharine,
  170; Daniel, 170; Elizabeth,
  170; Rosina, 170
ORTMAN, John, 234
OSTER, Catharine, 170;
  Christian, 170; Henry, 170,
  217; John, 170; Louisa, 170,
  217; Magdalena, 170; Susanna,
  170
OTTO, Catharine, 170; John,
  198; Magdalena, 198
OVER, Christian, 73, 112;
  Jacob, 243; Mary, 243
OVERHOLSER, Ann, 243; Samuel,
  243
OVERHOLTZER, Ann, 170;
  Catharine, 170; Jacob, 170;
  John, 220; Mary, 170
OVERHOLZER, Elizabeth, 168;
  Joseph, 168; Martin, 168;
  Samuel, 168
OVERKVISH, Baltzer, 169;
  Barbara, 169; Jacob, 169;
  Michael, 169
OWEN, Ann, 169; Anna, 170; B.,
  149; Benjamin, 169, 170;
  Elizabeth, 169, 170;
  Jonathan, 169, 170; Lydia,
  170
OWENS, Ann, 171; Archibald,
  170; Elizabeth, 171; Jane,
  171; Margaret, 171; Thomas,
  171
OX, Christopher, 183
OYSTER, Christian, 168;
  Margaret, 168

-P-
PACKART, Jacob, 8; Mary, 8
PADEN, Hugh, 174
PAGAN, Agness, 173; Andrew,
  173; Archibald, 173; James,
  173

312   INDEX

PALM, Jacob, 100; Mary, 100
PALSPACKER, Peter, 172
PARK, Mary, 44; Robert, 174;
  William, 249
PARKER, Alexander, 173;
  Elizabeth, 173; Esther, 173;
  John, 173; Margaret, 173;
  Mary, 173, 186; Nancy, 173;
  Richard, 173; Robert, 186;
  Susanna, 186
PARKESON, Agness, 172; Agness
  Maxwell, 172; John, 172;
  Joseph, 182; Margaret, 182;
  Mary, 172; Richard, 171;
  William, 172
PARKHOFFER, Balthaser, 172;
  Conrad, 172
PARR, Grace, 186; William, 186
PARRY, David, 171; Elizabeth,
  171; Guin, 171; Roger, 171;
  Thomas, 171; William, 171
PASMORE, Thomas, 48
PASSMORE, Ellis, 148
PASTOR, Jane, 113; Peter, 113
PATIMER, John, 196
PATRICK, Ebenezer, 178;
  Elizabeth, 178; Hugh, 178;
  James, 178; Jane, 178; Jean,
  178; John, 178; Martha, 178;
  Mary, 178; Robert, 178;
  Stephen, 178; William, 178
PATTEN, James, 174; John, 181;
  Martha, 174; Summer, 181;
  Thomas, 181
PATTERSON, Agness, 173;
  Alexander, 179; Ann, 181,
  182, 202; Anna, 172; Arthur,
  179, 181, 182, 184;
  Catharine, 65, 175, 182;
  Caytron, 172; Christian, 175;
  Daniel, 175, 200; Eleanor,
  173, 179, 182, 184;
  Elizabeth, 5, 171, 177, 179,
  181, 182, 184; Francis, 172;
  Geney, 185; George, 173;
  Hannah, 181, 182; Hugh, 177;
  Isabella, 177, 182; James, 4,
  38, 171, 173, 177, 181, 182,
  246, 249; Jane, 181, 182,
  184, 185; Janet, 178; Jayn,
  172; Jean, 171, 182; John,
  61, 65, 173, 178, 181, 182,
  185, 191; Margaret, 173, 181,
  185; Martha, 177, 181, 182;
  Mary, 106, 171, 172, 173,

  177, 181, 182, 185; Matthew,
  178; Nathan, 182; Peter, 181;
  Rebecca, 171, 178, 181, 182,
  184; Robert, 172, 181;
  Samuel, 172, 177, 178, 181,
  182, 184; Sarah, 171, 178,
  181; Susanna, 171, 175;
  Thomas, 171, 182; William, 5,
  172, 173, 177, 178, 179, 181,
  182, 184, 185
PATTON, Abraham, 180; Agness,
  186; Ann, 185; Cunningham,
  150, 185; David, 180;
  Elizabeth, 175, 177, 180;
  Isabella, 186; James, 172,
  186; Jane, 178, 180, 185;
  Janet, 177; Jean, 139, 177,
  180; John, 139, 175, 180,
  185; Joseph, 180; Margaret,
  175; Marion, 178; Martha,
  180; Mary, 172, 175, 185,
  186; Nathan, 177, 180;
  Rebecca, 177, 180; Robert,
  175, 178, 180; Sarah, 180;
  Thomas, 172, 177, 186;
  William, 177, 180, 185, 186
PAUELIN, Detrich, 175
PAUL, John, 84; Philipina, 84
PAULUS, Elizabeth, 184; Henry,
  127
PAXTON, Agness, 174; Andrew,
  174; Esther, 174; Grissel,
  176; Jean, 174; John, 140,
  176; Lattis, 174; Margaret,
  174; Mary, 174; Robert, 174;
  Samuel, 174
PAYNE, Jasper, 178; Nathaniel,
  178; Phebe, 178
PEAK, Samuel, 174
PEAYDON, Hugh, 10
PECK, Christian, 41, 122;
  Peter, 185; Samuel, 176
PEDEN, Elizabeth, 183; Grace,
  183; Grizel, 202; Hugh, 11,
  177, 183; Isabella, 177;
  Jean, 183; John, 177, 183,
  252; Margaret, 183; Martha,
  177, 183; Mary, 183; Nancy,
  183; Samuel, 183; Sarah, 183
PEEBEL, Daniel, 177
PEEPELS, James, 174; John, 174
PEGAN, Andrew, 24, 181; Ann,
  181; James, 181; Jean, 181,
  239; John, 181, 239;
  Margaret, 181; Mary, 181;

SIMONE, Eve, 204; John Jacob, 204; Reyal, 204
SIMONY, Eva, 219; Rachel, 219
SIMPSON, George, 132
SINGER, David, 212, 237; Elizabeth, 212; John, 150; Margaret, 212; Martha, 212; Mary, 150, 194; Philip, 212
SINGHAAS, Casper, 224; Catharine, 224; Elizabeth, 224; Esther, 224; Eve, 224
SITES, Andrew, 200; Barbara, 207; Catharine, 207; Christine, 207; Elizabeth, 207; Eva, 207; Henry, 207; Jacob, 207; John, 207; Peter, 207
SIVELY, Elizabeth, 8; John, 8
SLABACH, Elizabeth, 68; Henry, 68
SLAGLE, Elizabeth, 250; Michael, 250
SLAYMAKER, Alexander, 210; Amos, 106, 119; Anne, 210; Catharine, 210; Daniel, 215; Elizabeth, 210, 218; Geils, 215; Henry, 155; Jean, 210; John, 151, 185, 210, 211, 215, 218; Margaret, 210; Mary, 210, 218; Mathias, 210, 215, 218; Rachel, 218; Rebecca, 218; William, 210, 211, 218
SLEBACK, Rosina, 55
SLEMMONS, James, 206; John, 206; Margaret, 206; Robert, 206; Sarah, 206; Thomas, 206; William, 206
SLIGHTER, Catharine, 169; Daniel, 169
SLOUGH, Christian, 234; Elizabeth, 234; Isaac, 234
SLOWENS, Harriet, 220; Sarah, 220
SMALL, Catharine, 80
SMEDLEY, Eli, 227; Joel, 227; Joseph, 227; Lewis, 227; Lydia, 227; Rebecca, 227; Sarah, 227; Thomas, 227
SMITH, Abraham, 206, 232; Alexander, 232; Anna, 232; Anna Maria, 221; Barbara, 208, 214; Catharine, 221; Charles, 257; Christian, 83, 118, 152, 194, 221, 227;

Christopher, 221; Daniel, 14, 220, 229; Dinah, 50; Edward, 50, 220; Elizabeth, 83, 208, 215, 216, 218, 220, 227, 232; Ephraim, 228; Frederick, 216, 218, 254; George, 208, 218, 220, 232; Hannah, 230; Henry, 89, 232; Isaac, 119; Jacob, 91, 93, 215, 218, 220, 227; Jasper Yeates, 257; John, 36, 51, 163, 180, 208, 214, 215, 218, 220, 229, 230, 232; Joseph, 227; Juliana, 208; Lewis, 232; Lydia, 53, 220; Magdaelena, 227; Magdalena, 91, 93; Margaret, 53, 216, 220; Martin, 208; Mary, 7, 89, 115, 218, 220, 232, 234; Mathias, 207, 208; Michael, 218; Nathaniel, 228; Peter, 7, 61, 215; Philip, 230; Rebecca, 53, 220, 232; Richard, 165; Rosina, 218; Salome, 232; Samuel, 172, 209, 227, 228; Sarah, 53, 220; Susanna, 27, 208, 232; Theobald, 218; William, 43, 50, 52, 203, 220, 230, 245
SMOKER, Barbara, 232; Christina, 232; Elizabeth, 232; Harriet, 232; Isaac, 232; John, 232; Maria, 232; Samuel, 232
SMUCK, Catharine, 211; Elizabeth, 211; Jacob, 211; Magdalena, 211; Solomon, 211
SMUCKER, John, 117
SNAVELY, Andrew, 217; Magdalena, 217
SNEBER, Anna, 209; Catharine, 209; Eliza, 209; George, 209; Mary, 209
SNEBLY, John, 74
SNEDER, Christian, 207; Elizabeth, 207; Jacob, 207; Margaret, 207; Michael, 207; Philip, 207
SNEIDER, Ann, 209; Barbara, 209; Catharine, 209, 213; Christian, 209; Christina, 213; Dorothea, 213; Eleanor, 213; Elizabeth, 209, 213; Freney, 209; Henry, 209; Jacob, 209; John, 182, 209; Joseph, 209; Margaret, 182;

326

INDEX

Mary, 209, 213; Peter, 209,
213; Philip, 213; Rebecca,
213; Sophia, 213; Susanna,
213
SNEVELY, Casper, 177
SNIDER, Christian, 77
SNODGRASS, Alexander, 2, 206,
241; James, 206, 207; Jane,
207; Janet, 206; Jean, 187;
John, 206; Joseph, 206;
Margaret, 206; Martha, 207;
Mary, 206, 207; Robert, 187;
Samuel, 2; Sarah, 207;
William, 206, 207
SNYDER, Christina, 232;
Elizabeth, 132; Emick, 232;
Fanny, 26; George, 25; Henry,
226; Jacob, 121, 167; John,
26, 122, 232; Lorentz, 220;
Peter, 132; Philip, 31;
Polly, 232; Sally, 232
SOEHNER, Catharine, 216;
Elizabeth, 216; Frederick,
216; Godlieb, 216; Jacob,
216; John, 216; Maria, 216
SOHL, Catharine, 218; Henry,
218
SOLLENBERGER, Abraham, 223;
Barbara, 223; John, 159, 223;
Mary, 159
SOUDER, Barbara, 218;
Elizabeth, 193; Esther, 218;
Eve, 218; Jacob, 193;
Rudolph, 218
SOUSMAN, Henry, 35
SOUTER, John, 170
SOWDER, Anna, 203; Benjamin,
203; David, 203; Elizabeth,
203; Esther, 203; Jacob, 203;
John, 203; Joshua, 203; Mary,
203; Susanna, 203
SOWER, Anna, 214; Barbara, 214;
Catharine, 101; Christopher,
214; Henry, 101, 214; Jonas,
214; Juliana, 214; Margaret,
214; Maria Dorothea, 214;
Michael, 214; Philip, 214
SOWERBEER, Catharine, 85; John,
85
SOWTER, Ann, 210; Anna, 210;
John, 210
SPADE, Anna, 232; Anna Maria,
232; Catharine, 232;
Christian, 232; Elizabeth,
232; George, 231, 232; John,

232; Susanna, 232
SPANGLER, Catharine, 233; John,
26, 233; Nancy, 26; Susanna,
233
SPEAR, Catharine, 214;
Elizabeth, 214; Hugh, 214;
Isabella, 214; John, 214;
Mary, 214; Nancy, 226;
Robert, 178, 214; William,
214
SPECK, Barbara, 228; Bernard,
228; Christopher, 228; John,
228; Lewis Sharlotte; Sophia,
228, 229; Magdalena, 228;
Mary, 228
SPEER, Anna, 79; Catharine, 79;
Elizabeth, 79; George, 79;
Juliana, 79; Margaret, 79;
Maria, 79
SPENTZ, Anna, 203; John, 203
SPICKELER, Christian, 141
SPICKLER, Anna, 211, 226;
Barbara, 211, 226; Catharine,
211, 226; Elizabeth, 211,
226; John, 114, 211, 226;
Martin, 211; Mary, 211, 226;
Susanna, 211, 226
SPILES, Elizabeth, 34; Herman,
34
SPITEL, George, 122; Magdalena,
122
SPONHOUR, Anna, 221; Jacob,
221; John, 221
SPRIGEL, George, 213; Jacob,
213; Joseph, 213; Mary, 213;
Michael, 213
SPRINGER, Ann, 32, 105, 258;
John, 105; Mathias, 32, 258
STAHL, Jacob, 6, 178
STAHLE, Jacob, 226
STAHLEY, Abraham, 223; Ann,
223; Benjamin, 223;
Catharine, 223; Christian,
223; Elizabeth, 223; Jacob,
223; John, 223
STAKE, Catharine, 229; George
R., 229; Margaret, 133
STALL, Jacob, 157
STAM, David, 153; Susanna, 153
STAMBACH, Henry, 209; Jacob,
209
STAMBACHER, Mary, 163; Michael,
163
STARN, Elizabeth, 252; Jacob,
252

144
STREIN, Jacob, 67, 238
STREITE, Christian, 251
STRENGE, Christian, 28
STRIBGE, Jacob, 167
STRICKLER, Abraham, 61, 218;
    Ann, 211; Barbara, 206, 211,
    218; Benjamin, 228;
    Catharine, 206, 226; Daniel,
    206; David, 228; Elizabeth,
    206, 218, 226, 228; Emile,
    226; Frances, 211; George,
    206; Henry, 50, 183, 211,
    216, 218, 226, 228; Jacob,
    137, 192, 206, 226, 227, 228;
    John, 158, 218, 228; Joseph,
    226, 228; Ludwig, 206;
    Magdalena, 137, 206, 211;
    Maria, 211, 218; Mary, 206,
    226; Nancy, 226; Ottilia, 50;
    Rosina, 206; Samuel, 228;
    Sarah, 226; Susanna, 226;
    Ulrich, 218; Veronica, 206
STROHM, Henry, 158; Mary, 158
STROMINGER, Rachel, 238
STRRLS, William, 155
STRUNK, Catharine, 208;
    Elizabeth, 208; Jacob, 208;
    Rachel, 232; Rebecca, 209;
    Sally, 209; Susanna, 208;
    Weimar, 209; Wymar, 208
STUB, Abraham, 189; John, 189
STUBBS, Betsy, 223; Daniel,
    223; Hannah, 223; Idah, 223;
    Isaac, 223; Joseph, 223;
    Mary, 223; Orpha, 223; Ruth,
    223; Sarah, 223; Thomas, 223;
    Vincent, 223
STUCKEY, Anna, 202; Anna
    Catharine, 202; Elizabeth,
    202; John, 202; Mary, 202
STUMP, Elias, 207; George, 207;
    Jacob, 207; John, 207
STUTENSROAD, Henry, 224; John,
    224; Susanna, 224
SUGAR, Elizabeth, 55; Peter, 55
SUMEY, Barbara, 206; Christian,
    206; Daniel, 206; Henry, 206;
    John, 206; Mary, 206; Peter,
    206; Samuel, 206
SUMMERMAN, Christian, 259;
    Elizabeth, 259
SUMMERS, Christian, 203;
    Fronica, 203; Joseph, 203;
    Mary, 203

SUMMY, Anna, 221, 227; Anne,
    227; Barbara, 131, 221;
    Christian, 227; David, 227;
    Elizabeth, 227; Henry, 227;
    Jacob, 221, 227; John, 227;
    Margaret, 221; Maria, 227;
    Peter, 131, 198, 215, 227,
    230
SUMY, Jacob, 73; Margaret, 73
SURRY, Peter, 120
SWAGART, Abraham, 22; Ann, 22;
    John, 22; Sybilla, 22
SWAR, Anna, 165; John, 22, 102,
    165
SWARE, Anna, 164; John, 164
SWARTZ, Abraham, 210; Anna,
    246; Conrad, 157; Feronica,
    168; John, 168, 210, 246;
    Mary, 210
SWEANY, Ambrose, 206; Miles,
    206
SWEESHER, christine, 207;
    Henry, 207
SWEIGART, Barbara, 219, 223;
    Catharine, 219, 221;
    Christina, 219; Daniel, 221;
    Elizabeth, 219, 221, 230;
    Felix, 223; George, 221, 223;
    Hannah, 223; Henry, 223;
    Jacob, 218, 221; John, 223;
    Juliana, 219; Margaret, 223;
    Maria, 223; Mary, 219; Peter,
    219; Philip, 219; Salome,
    221, 230; Samuel, 221, 230;
    Sebastian, 223; Susanna, 221,
    230
SWEITZER, Catharine, 214; Eve,
    214; Gertraut, 203; Henry,
    214; John, 203; Margaret, 214
SWEM, Catharine, 106; Stacy,
    106
SWENCK, Christiana, 8; John, 8
SWENTZEL, Henry, 99, 151, 257
SWER, John, 150
SWIFT, Mary, 224; Samuel, 224
SWIGERT, Elizabeth, 186; Sep,
    186
SWINGER, John, 194; Susanna,
    194
SWISHER, Barbara, 229;
    Elizabeth, 229; Henry, 229;
    John, 229; Mary, 229; Philip,
    229
SWOBE, Barbara, 223; Catharine,
    223; Daniel, 76; Elizabeth,

76, 223; Frederick, 31;
George, 223; Henry, 223;
John, 223; Mary, 31, 223
SWOPE, Barbara, 253; Catharine,
225; Elizabeth, 225; Emanuel,
225; Frederick, 225; George,
225; Henry, 253; Jacob, 225;
Mathias, 225; Sabina, 225
SYBERT, David, 220; Henry, 220;
John, 42, 124, 220; Peter,
183; Sarah, 183; Susanna, 220

-T-
TALBOTT, Eliza, 234; Sarah, 234
TANNEBERG, Anna, 235; David,
235; Elizabeth, 235; Maria,
235
TANNEBERGER, David, 71
TANNENBERG, David, 143
TANNENBERY, Anna, 45; David,
45; Maria, 45; Rosian, 45
TANNER, Susanna, 33; Ulrick, 33
TATE, Adam, 2; Benjamin, 2;
John, 2
TAYLOR, Enoch, 236; Esther,
161; Isaac, 51, 236; Jacob,
236; James, 236; Jane, 236;
Jean, 3; John, 161; Joseph,
236; Phebe, 236; Robert, 172;
Samuel, 236; Sarah, 236;
William, 3, 236, 237
TEMPLE, Elizbeth, 234; Jannet,
234; John, 234; Margaret,
234; Mary, 234; William, 234
TEMPLETON, Andrew, 235; Betsey,
235; James, 235; John, 235;
Mary, 235; Rosina, 235;
Sarah, 235
TEPLEY, Elizabeth, 236
TEPLY, Elizabeth, 235; John,
235
THARON, John, 189; Mary, 189
THOM, Elizabeth, 184
THOMAN, Ann, 234; Elizabeth,
234; John, 234; Susanna, 234
THOMAS, Adam, 56; Anna, 56;
Christian, 162; Dick, 141;
Feronica, 256; George, 236;
Godfried, 235; John, 235,
256; Juliana, 236; Maria,
235; Martin, 70; Mary, 141,
162, 236; Mary Salome, 235;
Philip, 236; Rosina, 235
THOMBURY, Joseph, 46
THOMPSON, Agness, 235;

Elizabeth, 235; George, 235;
Hugh, 235; James, 235; John,
181, 235; Margaret, 235;
Mary, 181, 235; Sarah, 235
THREAEMER, Wendel, 54
THRILL, Catharine, 158; Jacob,
158
THUMA, Ann, 237; Barbara, 237;
Catharine, 237; Elizabeth,
237; Feronica, 237; George,
237; John, 237; Maria, 237;
Peter, 237; Sarah, 237
THUMHARDT, Anna, 237; Godfried,
237; John P., 237
TIEMER, Henry, 218
TOCHTERMAN, Christina, 116;
Frederick, 116
TODD, James, 249; John, 55;
Mary, 55
TOEHTERMAN, Christina, 112;
Frederick, 112
TOM, Elizabeth, 182
TOMPSON, Agness, 235; Andrew,
234; Eleanor, 234; Elizabeth,
235; Ellen, 236; George, 153,
235; Hugh, 235; James, 12,
234; Jane, 236; John, 235;
Lydia, 12; Margaret, 234;
Mary, 234, 235; Miller, 236;
Nathan, 234, 236; Rachel,
236; Robert, 234; Sarah, 234,
235; William, 234
TOMSON, Margaret, 145
TRAGER, Ann, 237; Anna, 48;
Catharine, 48, 237;
Elizabeth, 48, 237; Jacob,
48, 237; Maria, 48, 237
TREAGER, Godfried, 237
TREGO, Mary, 108; Peter, 108
TREISH, Adam, 49, 234, 237;
Barbara, 234; Catharine, 234;
Elizabeth, 234; Henry, 49;
Leonard, 234; Magdalena, 49,
237; Margaret, 234; Michael,
234
TRIMBLE, Rebecca, 236; Samuel,
236; William, 236
TRITCH, Adam, 123; Catharine,
236; Charles, 236; Eve, 236;
John, 236; Justina, 236;
Magdalena, 236; Margaret,
123; Philip, 236; William,
236
TROUT, Abraham, 235; David,
197, 235; George, 235;

Hannah, 235; Isaac, 235;
Jacob, 235; Mary, 197, 235;
Paul, 235
TROUTMAN, George, 234
TRUMP, Andrew, 235; Barbara,
235; John, 235; Margaret,
235; Mary, 235; Samuel, 235;
William, 235
TSCHUDY, Mathias, 231
TSHUDY, Martin, 21; Mathias,
88, 199
TSUDY, Mathew, 3
TULCE, Esther, 32; John, 32,
258; Mary, 258
TURBETT, Dolly, 235; James,
178; John, 235; Samuel, 235;
Thomas, 235
TURMAN, Elizabeth, 48; James,
48; Rebecca, 48
TURNER, Thomas, 141
TWEED, Agness, 236; Ann, 236;
Anna, 236, 237; Archibald,
178, 236; Catharine, 236;
Elizabeth, 236, 237; Grisel,
236; James, 236, 237; Janet,
178; John, 236, 237; Joseph,
236; Margaret, 236; Mary,
237; Robert, 236, 237;
William, 236

-U-
UPPERMAN, John, 69; Mary, 69
URBAN, Dorothea, 237;
Elizabeth, 237; George, 237;
Jacob, 237; John, 237;
Joseph, 237; Lewis, 237;
Ludwick, 237; Philip, 237
URICH, Elizabeth, 123; Joseph,
123

-V-
VANALMER, Christiana, 11;
Conrad, 11
VANCE, John, 150; Joseph, 30
VANEDA, Bechtolt, 117
VARNS, Elizabeth, 105; Jacob,
105
VENEGER, Anne Maria, 238
VERNER, Benjamin, 236
VINEGAR, Anna Maria, 237, 245;
Christian, 237, 245; David,
237, 245; Elizabeth, 237,
245; George, 237, 245; Jacob,
237; John, 237, 245; Susanna,
237

VOGAN, James, 187; Margaret,
187, 238, 251; Thomas, 238,
251
VOGHT, Christian, 67, 238
VONDERAU, Adam, 171
VONEADA, Jacob, 61
VONIDA, Jacob, 2
VONIEDA, Philip, 23; Susanna,
23
VONKENNEN, Balser, 237;
Barbara, 237; Catharine, 237,
238; Hannah, 237; Jacob, 238;
Margaret, 237
VONNIDA, Philip, 99
VONNIEDA, Philip, 201
VONPHUL, Catharine, 76;
William, 76

-W-
WACHTER, Catharine, 247;
Elizabeth, 247; Frederick,
247; George, 247; John, 247
WACKERMAN, Catharine, 98;
George, 98
WADE, Andrew, 254; Catharine,
254; Charles, 254; Daniel,
254; Elizabeth, 254; Ignatus,
254; Jacob, 254; John, 254;
Mary, 254
WAECHTER, Elizabeth, 251; John,
251
WAGGONER, Barbara, 239;
Bernard, 215; Frederick, 215;
George, 239; Henry, 239
WAGNER, Ann, 192; Catharine,
254; Daniel, 192; Elizabeth,
254; John, 254; Maria, 254;
Mary, 254; Samuel, 254
WAGONER, Ann, 249; Anna, 47;
Barbara, 254; Catharine, 254,
256; Elizabeth, 249, 254;
George, 254, 256; Isaac, 208,
254; Jacob, 249, 254; John,
47, 254; Martin, 254; Mary,
249, 254; Sarah, 256;
Susanna, 249, 254
WAIHLER, Elizabeth, 253; John,
253, 254
WALDSHMITH, John, 201
WALKER, Andrew, 244, 246, 253;
Ann, 152, 244; Asahel, 51;
Asahil, 18; Ashael, 236;
Ashel, 148, 152; Hannah, 244,
246; Isaac, 236, 246; James,
245, 253; John, 244, 245,

WEIDEL, Adam, 243; Ann, 243;
Elizabeth, 243; Frederick,
243; John, 243; Magdalena,
243; Margaret, 243; Sophia,
243
WEIDER, Catharine, 76; George,
76
WEIDLE, John, 124
WEIDLER, Ann, 250, 255;
Barbara, 253; Catharine, 248,
255; Daniel, 250; David, 248,
255; Elizabeth, 248, 250,
253, 255; George, 248, 255;
Jacob, 248, 250, 255; John,
89, 248, 250, 253, 255;
Magdalena, 248, 255; Michael,
153, 248, 250, 255; Polly,
248, 255; Samuel, 248, 255;
Susanna, 89, 248, 255;
William, 248, 255
WEIDMAN, Anna, 111, 242; Anna
Maria, 242; Barbara, 106;
Catharine, 240, 242;
Christian, 111; Christopher,
242; Elizabeth, 34; George,
45, 93, 106, 224; Jacob, 34;
John, 240, 242; Mary, 240;
Peter, 160
WEILAND, Anne, 243; Christian,
243; Christina, 243; John,
14, 243; Magdalena, 14;
Susanna, 243
WEILANDT, Barbara, 227; Jacob,
227
WEIMAN, Agness, 239; George,
239; Jacob, 239; Maria, 239
WEIMAR, Catharine, 254;
Christopher, 254
WEINHOLT, Anna, 241; Apolonia,
241; Barbara, 241; Elizabeth,
241; Margaret, 241; Michael,
241; Nicholas, 240; Peter,
241; Philip, 241
WEINLAND, Ann, 240; Anna, 252;
Barbara, 252; Catharine, 240,
252; Christian, 240;
Elizabeth, 240; Esther, 252;
Jacob, 240, 252; John, 240,
252; Maria, 252; Susanna, 252
WEINMAN, George, 243
WEIS, Juliana, 219; Peter, 219
WEISERT, Barbara, 141;
Christopher, 141
WEISS, Catharine, 245;
Christian, 205, 245;

Elizabeth, 245; George, 245;
Jacob, 245; Justina, 245;
Margaret, 245; Mary, 245;
Susanna, 43
WEIST, Ann, 223; Catharine, 33,
35, 75; Christian, 33, 35,
75; Peter, 223
WEITH, Catharine, 208; Henry,
208
WEITZEL, George, 244; Jacob,
244; Margaret, 256
WELCH, Elizabeth, 193; Matthew,
193
WELSH, Jacob, 247; James, 245;
John, 58; Magdalena, 247;
Nicholas, 247; Philip, 247
WENDITZ, Daniel, 85; Susanna,
85
WENEGER, Anne Maria, 238;
David, 238
WENGER, Abraham, 51, 246, 255;
Adam, 168, 246; Ann, 205,
238, 239, 244, 245; Ann
Maria, 251; Anna, 51, 162,
238; Barbara, 239, 245, 246;
Cathrine, 239; Christian,
205, 238, 240, 242, 245, 246,
255; David, 251; Elizabeth,
239, 240, 245; Eve, 240, 245,
246; Feronica, 245; Henry,
238, 240, 246, 253; Jacob,
176, 239, 242; John, 15, 205,
239, 240, 245; Joseph, 98,
100, 239, 240, 242, 245;
Magdalena, 240, 255; Mary,
73, 239, 240, 245, 246;
Michael, 73, 240, 242, 245;
Salome, 239, 246; Samuel,
255; Stephen, 238; Susanan,
239; Susanna, 162
WENTZ, Catharine, 108; Thomas,
108
WERDENBERGER, Catharine, 195;
Samuel, 195
WERFEL, Abraham, 246, 248;
Adam, 248; Ann, 248; Barbara,
248; Catharine, 248;
Christian, 248; George, 247,
248; Henry, 246, 248; Jacob,
248; John, 248; Mary, 246;
Peter, 246, 248
WERMLY, Elizabeth, 125, 161;
George, 125; Jacob, 161
WERNER, Anna, 238; Anna Mary,
238; Barbara, 240; Casper,